So You Want to Be a

Financial Planner

Your Guide to a New Career

Sixth Edition

Nancy Langdon Jones, CFP®

So You Want to Be a Financial Planner
Your Guide to a New Career

First Edition September 2001
Second Edition December 2002
Third Edition September 2005
Fourth Edition September 2007
Fifth Edition September 2009
Sixth Edition September 2011

Nancy Langdon Jones, CFP®
www.nancysbooks.com
nancy@nancysbooks.com

AdvisorPress
www.advisorpress.com
1153 Bordeaux Drive, Suite 109
Sunnyvale, CA 94089
info@advisorpress.com
(408) 400-0400

Cover design by Peter W. Johnson, Jr.

ISBN 978-1-60353-015-6
$55

Printed in the United States of America.

Dedicated to the future of the Financial Planning profession
and to those who will help shape it.

IV

CONTENTS

CHAPTER ONE   1

Why?

A brief overview of the industry and thought-provoking questions potential financial planners need to ask themselves before embarking upon a career in the financial services industry.

CHAPTER TWO   13

Back to School

The importance of the CFP® credential; finding the right school; how to study; what to expect; sample questions from the comprehensive test; where to go for help; and the importance of finding a mentor.

CHAPTER THREE   49

Who's the Boss?

From Wirehouses to Sole Proprietorships, Banks, Broker/Dealers and Insurance Companies: What to ask, what to avoid, and what it takes to be on your own. Who can help and how to get paid.

CHAPTER FOUR   103

The Dreaded Regulatory Stuff

Keep out of trouble with the many and various powers that be by correctly setting up the practice, keeping proper records, and playing by the rules right from the beginning. Legal, compliance and ethics authorities provide straightforward pointers on how to run a responsible business.

Setting Up Shop

The software, the hardware, the network and other resources; tips on putting a professional financial planning office together; and a shopping list with start-up items. Advice from the best on what's needed to get started. Dealing with clients and staff, vendors and brokers, media and mentors.

Marketing 101

Tips from those who have been there and done that: The marketing tools that got them started and what they wish they had done differently. They know what works and share their expertise, so new planners can jump-start their careers.

From Plotter to Planner in Less Than Five Years

Blow-by-blow narratives from planners who have been in the industry five years or less, and how they made the transition. First-hand accounts detailing obstacles and triumphs encountered as new practices were dreamed about, created and now flourish in today's exciting financial planning community.

Get a Life!

Financial Planners tend to be type "A" personalities (aka workaholics). There are many diverse activities planners can participate in during the normal course of business, but it's crucial to keep balance. This chapter will explore ways to keep that balance, in spite of 60-hour workweeks.

APPENDICES

ACKNOWLEDGMENTS

There is no way this book could have been written without the help of an incredible number of generous, supportive individuals. There is likewise no way I could possibly thank all those involved! There are some, however, without whose affectionate nitpicking and nagging I could never have succeeded.

Bob Veres, my mentor and Dutch uncle. Thank you for sticking with me.

Tim Bennett and **Robin Vaccai-Yess,** editors extraordinaire, whose shrewd sense of humor and clever quips kept me from committing hara-kiri, in spite of ruthless admonitions and scrupulous content revisions. Thank you for keeping me on track.

Peter W. Johnson, Jr. and **Mattias Bergman**, distributor and co-publisher, always there with a graphic…or a safety net. Thanks to you and AdvisorPress, I have not only survived, but thrive on Amazon! Thank you for that soothing voice that was always there for me.

I am grateful also for:

My clients, who have welcomed me into their lives and shared their dreams with me.

The Nazrudin Project, kindred spirits all, but especially the NazLA group, Brent, Eileen, Eric, Gordon, Jane, Jim, Joel, Ray and Ronnie, who continue to challenge and forge the holistic, psychological aspects of this profession within an empathetic environment.

Ronnie, my wonderful paraplanner, who diligently dealt with the back-office, providing the vital time and resource link between client and book, smoothing the future path for both.

Jim Emmerson, a career-changer and colleague, who has given so much of his time as a skilled webmaster for both nljones.com and nancysbooks.com.

Debbie Gallant, Mike Heryford, Lieutenant, U.S. Navy Supply Corps, **Saundra Davis,** and **Carleton W. Moten**, for their eagle eyes and relentless proofreading.

Claude, my wonderful husband of 30 years, who lovingly fed me and carried me off to bed when he knew I'd had enough…and begrudged not the time I stole from us.

You, the future financial planners, who courageously posted questions and revealed dreams on the Financial Planning Interactive discussion boards.

My **friends** and **colleagues,** who generously shared stories, knowledge and information and unselfishly gave of their time and wisdom, so that the profession might grow stronger.

…and **Beth**.

FOREWORD

Chances are, if you've come across this book, you're interested in becoming a part of the financial planning profession. But before you jump in, you're asking yourself some very good, very basic, very important questions.

How hard will it be to become a planning professional? What hurdles and hoops will I have to get past?

If I get past them, what will I spend my days doing, and what difference will I be able to make in peoples' lives?

Can I make a living at financial planning?

Is this something I'll enjoy doing for the rest of my life?

Before you get to Nancy's answers to these questions and more, let me give you a quick "big picture" summary of what you're getting into, what planners do, where they typically come from, and what they think of their lives and careers.

Financial planning started as a revolution against the Old Way of doing things. The Old Way was to sell people things (investments, life insurance, sometimes coins and diamonds) whether the customer needed them or not. A small handful of salespeople decided that, instead of working in the best interests of this or that large investment firm, they'd start working for their clients.

This guerrilla movement spread, slowly and quietly at first, until finally it matured into a new profession, called financial planning.

Yes, there are still stockbrokers and life insurance agents who care more about selling you something than about improving your life, and there probably always will be. But if you want to become a financial planner today, the professional culture demands that your first goal is to make people better investors, and improve their lives.

This, I think, is a big reason why financial planning was recently selected as the best and most fulfilling profession in the United States. Another reason is that finally, after many years of struggling to find its place in the world economy, financial planning is now a relatively prosperous career. You can make good money at it, because what people want more than anything else from a financial professional is objective advice, from somebody who sincerely wants them to prosper from it.

Today, there are many different types of planner, just as there are many different specialties in medicine, law and accounting. And, since the profession is still relatively new, it is constantly reinventing its business models and structures. You can find excellent practitioners who are compensated by commissions through affiliation with a broker-dealer, and excellent planners who work only for fees paid directly by their clients, or who are paid directly out of their client portfolios. I think that within 10 years, the great majority of planners will have given up their commission revenue--in some cases, with the encouragement of their broker-dealers.

What does a planning office look like? Typically, it will include at least one "principal"--the owner or founder of the firm, who deals directly with its clients. One of the recent trends in the planning profession is for two or more independent offices to merge, and suddenly where there was one senior planner, now there are three or four.

The senior planner's work is often supported by a less experienced professional who does much of the analytical work on each client's financial situation, putting into the computer the client's income and net worth, insurance coverage, financial goals, current investments and a host of other things that relate to our financial lives. This "casewriting professional" will perform all the basic analyses, using spreadsheets or professional software. The issues are at the same time straightforward and complex. Can this person retire in 12 years based on the size and composition of the investment portfolio, and based on how much is being saved and invested each year? Is this person paying too much in taxes? Is there a will, an estate plan, powers of attorneys, life, health, disability, auto and property-casualty insurance?

In many cases, these casewriters are "planners in training," and often are "partners in training" as well. They're working on their CERTIFIED FINANCIAL PLANNER™ (CFP®) designation, and one day expect to have clients of their own--at which point they will hire their own casewriter, who helps and supports their work with clients.

The typical office also includes people who schedule appointments, send out correspondence and answer the phone, and sometimes others who work with the trading desk of the clearing firm or who tend the computer interfaces.

What does the planner do? The planner offers several important services:

1) S/he helps clients organize their financial lives. This, in many cases, is a huge undertaking. People typically buy investments on a whim, they have no idea what they need to save and invest to meet their retirement and other goals, their insurance coverage is an overlapping hodgepodge and the whole nether world of wills and powers of attorney is an ugly mystery better put off until death or (preferably) sometime thereafter. (If you aspire to do this for people, you will need to become educated in the raw basics of financial planning).

2) The planner helps people change their behavior. Every investor tends to panic when the market goes down, and there is a strong tendency to buy during euphoric highs. Many people don't save enough to fund their future goals; others, who survived the depths of the Depression, have more than they'll ever need and cannot manage to spend money for their own enjoyment. They need advice and counsel from somebody who they respect, and will not change their behavior unless the advisor can earn that respect. (This may be the defining "talent" of a planning professional; when casewriters are watched for partner potential, the first thing you look for is the ability to handle a client meeting and get clients moving in more efficient, personally beneficial directions).

3) Increasingly, financial planners help people define their deepest and most personal goals, and serve as a general contractor to help them build a better and more fulfilling life. This is where the planning profession is going; it is the logical endpoint of the journey that began when a handful of rebels decided to stop selling and start serving their clients. (As you gain life experience, and as you spend time with successful people who are able to afford to hire a planner, you learn how to provide this most valuable service for others).

All of the planning firms that I know started small. Originally, most planners were career-changers; insurance agents, stockbrokers or accountants who wanted to broaden their service offer.

Alternatively, people moved into the field with little or no financial training. The founder of the company has an interest in investments, takes night classes while maintaining his/her day job. Then, still working a day job, the planner began offering financial advice, for not much money, to friends, relatives and acquaintances. Over time, they referred friends, and the advisor began raising fees just enough to make ends meet. At that point, s/he would decide to offer financial planning full-time, sometimes in a home office, sometimes in rented facilities.

The client list would grow slowly until suddenly, one day, it seemed like there was more business coming in the door than could be handled. Then the advisor would face the usual issues of managing business growth: hiring people, making the usual mistakes and counting the usual small successes of any small business. Chances are, if you talk to even the most successful advisors today, they still feel as if they're running a struggling small business instead of the dominant planning firm in their market.

Today, people are getting into the business through a different route, gaining a college or certificate education in planning, and then joining one of these established firms as the person who handles trades or a casewriter for one of the senior planners. Eventually, this person will take on clients of his own, and works toward the day when he becomes a partner or buys out the firm from a retiring founder.

Planners who have done this for years tell me that there isn't another profession on the planet that lets you share more personally in the personal growth and success of other people. In this respect, it is tremendously rewarding and fulfilling.

But it also requires a great deal of attention to detail, and a willingness to study and learn the nuances of investments and portfolio development, tax and estate planning, how to structure charitable contributions and evaluate insurance contracts and a million other details that most people find tedious and (as a consequence) are willing to pay handsomely if somebody would just take them off their backs.

In addition, it requires the ability to communicate effectively with people, to let them know what you know, and to show them that you care about them and their lives, families and future. It requires listening skills, and a certain dose of psychology. You deal with successful people from all walks of life.

Finally, financial planners in the future will be increasingly expected to become exemplars of the successful, fulfilling life they preach. That means taking the time to understand what you, yourself, want out of life, and pursuing your own goals with the same passion that you expect from your best clients. Planners all over the country are pioneering business arrangements that allow them to cross-country ski in the evenings from their back porch, or take yearly vacation trips, sometimes with two or three of their favorite clients, or cut back on their lifestyle expenditures so that they can afford to reduce their work hours and have more time for relationships, art and music or smelling the flowers that most of us hardly notice in our hectic push to get ahead of the rat race.

If this interests you, if you have these capabilities within you, then the profession needs you. The truth is, there just are not enough financial advisors in this world to handle the need for their services. I once divided the number of households by the number of financial planners in each state in the country, and found that there are many thousands of unserved households for each planning office in virtually every part of this country. I don't know of any successful practitioner who can handle more than 200 clients at once, so the market is going to be bigger than the profession for years to come.

In fact, one area of quiet concern in the profession is that middle-income people are not being served by the planning profession today, because most advisors can hardly keep up with the wealthy clients who knock on their doors. Many firms that I'm in contact with have all but closed their doors to new business.

This is, in other words, a wide-open field.

Elsewhere in this book, you'll read that I was "kind enough" to encourage Nancy Langdon Jones to write the book you are now reading. The truth is, I welcome this book purely out of self-interest. Once people in the early stages of entering the planning profession become aware of my newsletter and web service, they would come to me with basic questions. Each year, I get many hundreds of requests from people who want to know how, step-by-step, they can become a financial planning professional. Often, I would send them away with some encouragement and general advice--and feel like I hadn't given them nearly what they asked for.

On the financial planning discussion boards, I've seen Nancy answer many of these same requests with a deft touch, drawing from her own experience and the experience of many others she has talked with over the years. But, again, in a single post, off the top of your head, you can only offer so much advice. What people really needed was a "how to" manual.

Now--finally--we have it. Finally, when people call with those difficult questions, I have a place I can send them, a resource I can recommend without qualification.

If I haven't discouraged you from pursuing a career in financial planning, then let me get out of the way and let Nancy answer your important questions in more detail. If you're attracted to this profession, chances are you have a wonderful life mission to fulfill, and this is a great place to get started. In my view, there is nothing more precious in this world than a financial planner in training, who will someday change peoples' lives for the better.

Best of luck in all you undertake.

Robert N. Veres
Publisher, Inside Information
http://www.bobveres.com

INTRODUCTION

This book was written to be read on a computer with access to the Internet. There are over a hundred links for websites you can visit to acquire additional information. My decision to publish in electronic format, in addition to traditional print, was two-fold:

First, we live in an era where technology is changing the way we work, play, and think on a daily basis. During the year it took me to write this book, the evolution in the financial planning profession astounded me! In Appendix B, I recommend four very good books to help you "get started." Two of them were published in 2000, and another in 2001. All were outdated before they hit the streets. By ePublishing, new editions of *So You Want to Be a Financial Planner* can be available within days of major industry events.

And second, it is important to me that *So You Want to Be a Financial Planner* be interactive. I want to hear about your successes and about your frustrations. I hope you'll share your experiences with education, Broker/Dealers, software, business plans, and anything else that's on your mind. I anticipate a bi-annual update, where I will incorporate stories of new planners, new resources, and new trends. It is only with your participation that *So You Want to Be a Financial Planner* can become the definitive tool to developing a successful career in financial planning.

Please join me at the Financial Planning Interactive website http://www.financial-planning.com. Click on "Discussions"

Bookmark these sites and let me, and others, know what's on your mind!

IMPORTANT NOTE:

Purchase of this book in print format entitles the purchaser to a free download so that the book may be read on a PC with Internet connection. To obtain the free download, please send an e-mail explaining where you obtained the print version (i.e. Amazon, Trader's Library, etc.) to nancy@nancysbooks.com and request your free copy of the current PDF file. Please be certain you have at least ten MB of storage on your e-mail server before requesting the PDF file.

Chapter One

Why?

Once upon a time, I was giving an after-dinner speech to a group of Nurse Practitioners, on the importance of understanding the family's finances. When it was over, one woman sat in the back of the room until it cleared, and then came up and told me she appreciated what I had said.

"My husband has been after me for years to take a more active role in our money," she began, "but I'm simply not interested. He enjoys doing the investments and does a good job. What I hate is his insistence that I sit down with him every month for a few minutes while he explains the brokerage statements and goes over our income and bills. The worst time is when I have to go to the tax accountant once a year and listen while they tell me where the numbers on the tax form come from before I have to sign the darned return!

"I'm going home now to tell him that the next time he wants to explain it to me, I really will pay attention," she continued. "Now I know it's because he loves me that he wants me to understand what we're doing."

It felt good to know that even one person had heard what I had to say that night. It was a couple of years later, however, that the full impact hit me. I had forgotten about the incident until the Nurse Practitioner from the after-dinner speech telephoned to tell me her husband had been killed in an accident six months earlier.

"Since his death, I've received dozens of calls from financial sales people wanting to 'take care of me,'" she explained, "just like you said I might. But I know right where everything is. I manage the bills, watch the stocks, and call the accountant every now and then. I haven't made any big changes. Now that the shock is easing, I'm ready to talk with you about making plans for the rest of my life."

The night I spoke to the Nurse Practitioners, I made a difference. That is why I am a financial planner.

The 2001 edition of *Jobs Rated Almanac*[1] put Financial Planning at the top of its list for the following reasons:

> 1. Make lots of money: Of course, if you sell lots of stuff. You can do that in any industry, if you're a good salesperson!

---

[1] In the 2010 edition of *CarrerCast's Jobs Rated* (the most recent list at the time of publishing) Financial Planning had dropped to number 17. The rankings are based on the cumulative scores that each of the 200 jobs rated earned in the five core job factors: Work Environment, Income, Hiring Outlook, Physical Demands and Stress.

2. Set your own hours: Uh huh. No problem, if you don't mind 60-80 hour workweeks.

3. Low stress: Oh, sure. Dealing with other people's money and lives has always been low stress, particularly in today's economic climate.

Financial Planning is not a way to get rich quick, unless your definition of riches is the reward deemed from the knowledge you have made a difference for the better, in the life of your client.

Years after I had started to practice as a financial planner, a friend invited me to a meeting of the Nazrudin[2] Project, an unstructured, leaderless think tank of sorts, in its formative years at the time. I sat back and observed while several people I recognized as leaders in the profession discussed how they truly loved what they did. They found such joy in their vocation that they would gladly do it for nothing, save the fact they had to put food on their own table. I had felt that way for years, yet would never admit it for fear of appearing silly, or worse, unprofessional. But here were well-known practitioners with exemplary practices, feeling just as I felt.

In those few hours, listening to the echoes around me, I realized for the first time that financial planning is a very specific career choice completely misunderstood by nearly everyone—including many of those who call themselves financial planners.

I am convinced the financial planning profession is not only in its infancy, but that the world *ain't seen nuthin' yet!* [3] It is also my conviction, and the belief of literally hundreds of my colleagues, that financial planners are increasingly engaged not just for investment and tax advice, but for helping clients achieve a comfortable current and future lifestyle.

On the bus to the airport from an FPA Retreat, I talked with Roy Diliberto, CFP®, CLU, ChFC, and then-Chairman of the FPA Board of Directors Executive Committee. He made a most profound observation about the profession:

"Financial Planning," Roy said, "is **looking at the future and bringing it back into the present while you can still do something about it.**"

Whoa. That can't be right! A former FPA Chair defining the profession in such esoteric, holistic language?

"We're so young, we don't have models yet," he continued. "I'm frustrated over it! The profession was born out of the insurance industry. We tried to build our practices by going

---

[2] Nazrudin is an experience, not a definition. Membership fee for Nazrudin is $50.00. If you are interested in joining, contact Roberta Lee-Driscoll at r.leedriscoll@gmail.com and ask for information. Be sure to include your name, mailing address, telephone number, fax number and e-mail address. Once your payment is received, you will receive further instructions on accessing the group's conversations on Yahoo.

[3] Al Jolson, "The Jazz Singer", 1927.

out and selling like the insurance companies, but it didn't work. People coming into the profession just have to become part of the infrastructure, gain experience, and work their way up."

"The compleat financial planner," according to David Brand[4], who participated in a discussion on the Nazrudin website, "understands who the client is, what s/he values, and respects where s/he is in life's journey. Sometimes, gently expanding an interest or awareness in a client's life is all that can and should be done. Financial planners have a unique opportunity to apply these 'life-enhancing' skills in their practice. They are requisite skills for any professional who wishes to excel in their craft."

I open my complimentary meetings by asking the prospect before me, "Why are you here?" If the response is something like, "We're looking for a better return on our investments," I cringe. Then I tell them to go talk to a stockbroker—or get another stockbroker if they don't think the current one is making enough money for them. It disturbs me when people are unclear on the concept; yet, even I have an awful time explaining exactly what a financial planner does. We do so many things, but I want to make this perfectly clear:

FINANCIAL PLANNING IS NOT ABOUT MONEY!

FINANCIAL PLANNING IS ABOUT LIFE...

ABOUT DREAMS...and how to achieve them.

Sure, investments, taxes, budgets, money stuff is involved. However, the operative word here is **life**, as in, "What do you want to do with it?"

One of the briefest encounters I have ever had with a potential client was also one I found most rewarding. Several years ago, I talked with a corporate executive who had been offered a "golden parachute" if he took early retirement. Over the phone, he told me in no uncertain terms that he was accepting the deal. His accountant and attorney had both said it was an outstanding offer. Everything fit precisely into his budget, and he was only calling because someone told him to "run it by a financial planner." Nevertheless, he informed me there was nothing I could say to change his mind. I told him my fee and arranged the appointment.

He and his wife arrived hauling a file box filled with pension information. I greeted them and walked them back to my conference room, asking if they'd like coffee. They said they would. I left to get it, shaking my head, wondering why I had agreed to meet with these people who had already made up their minds. I felt not only redundant, but also a little irritated that it was late and I wasn't enjoying dinner with my husband.

When I returned with the coffee, just to break the ice I asked, "Well...what will you be doing when you retire?" We all just sat there. The wife took a sip of her coffee. I smiled

---

[4] David Brand has over 30 years experience as executive manager of non-profit professional associations and was at one time executive director of the Financial Planning Association. David holds a Law Degree, as well as a Masters Degree in Public Administration.

and shuffled papers. The big box sat unopened on the floor. Minutes passed after which the husband reached into his back pocket and wrote out a check for my fee.

"I'm not going to retire," he said as he slid the check across the table to me. "I have nothing to do in retirement." His wife sighed with relief. It turned out their entire life revolved around his clients. He golfed with them, networked with them, supported them, and entertained them. I had asked the right question.

The husband had expertly evaluated all the money stuff. But he hadn't considered the life stuff! At first, I felt guilty for taking an hour's pay for only ten minutes of interface. When I reflected on this encounter in the scheme of things, however, it became incredibly clear to me. My client had paid me for invaluable advice. He thought he was coming to me about the money. He already knew about the money. His CPA had calculated the taxes. His attorney had considered the impact on his estate. His pension administrator had evaluated the cash flow implications. But nobody had put the picture together. No one had asked the client what he wanted to do with his life.

Before getting too far into this chapter, it's best to define what we're talking about here: **Financial Planning**. After all, this is a book about how to become a *Financial Planner* to presumably do *Financial Planning*. Simple enough, right? Wrong. Sit down while I explain the difficulty I had in finding a definition to put with either of these terms.

The CFP Board of Standards[5] spells out the six steps a financial planner needs to follow in order to complete a financial planning engagement. It looks like this:

The Financial Planning Process

- Establish and define the client-planner relationship.
- Gather client data, including goals.
- Analyze and evaluate the client's financial status.
- Develop and present financial planning recommendations and/or alternatives.
- Implement the financial planning recommendations.
- Monitor the financial planning recommendations.

Notice that this is a *process*, not a definition. Financial planners know what it is that they do, but I challenge anyone to come up with a universal definition of exactly what *Financial Planning* is. Save your energy. There isn't any such thing. Yet.

One "definition" of *Financial Planner* I found came from the InvestorWords[6] website, and looks like this:

---

[5] http://www.cfp.net
[6] http://www.investorwords.com/

"Financial Planner: An investment professional who helps individuals set and achieve their long-term financial goals, through investments, tax planning, asset allocation, risk management, retirement planning, and estate planning."

Tip of the iceberg. Well, maybe back in the olden days, more than thirty years ago, when *Financial Planning* was just beginning to emerge from its insurance-wrapped cocoon might financial planning have been so narrowly defined. Today, you will find, if you have read Bob Veres[7] comments in the Foreword, that it has grown to mean much more than a rudimentary "Financial Planner = Investment Professional".

Bob adds, "…improve their lives." **Improve their lives!** What a concept!

This is a "how-to" book for individuals considering a career as a financial planner, and if you are one of those individuals, then you'd better know something right from the get-go:

People entering the financial planning profession today will have to define it.

There's help. Bob has been sort of canonized as the financial planner's visionary. He possesses this knack (some would term it *peculiar*) of sensing where things are heading. I've been watching his uncanny prophecies come to fruition for almost three decades now. It's been long enough, in any case, to get my full attention. If you are just entering this profession, you had better sit up and take notice, too!

Once at the end of a speech to financial advisors, Bob told a story about an obviously successful retired person on the golf course with his buddies. You know the one…just like in the TV commercials for the major brokerages. In the commercials, someone looks at the satisfied retiree and asks, "Who's your broker?" In Bob's futuristic version, people will ask, "Who's your financial planner?"

Bob Barry, CFP®, FPA President at the time, summed it up in his speech at an annual FPA Conference:

"I cannot tell you how certain I am that the only way that we can make any true progress in defining a profession that will endure, is to define who we are. And I can tell you that if I ruled the world, by some date in the not so distant future, if you were holding yourself out to the public as providing financial planning, you'd be a CERTIFIED FINANCIAL PLANNER™ practitioner. I'd also hope that you wouldn't think of calling yourself a financial planner unless you were a CFP® practitioner. And, it's my wish that across this country, financial services firms that offer financial planning would know that they have to hire CFP® professionals to provide it, so that consumers would be clear, once and for all, that if they want financial planning they should go to a CFP® practitioner."

Names and ideas and models and scenarios have been tossed around in discussion groups with current practitioners all over the country, but they boil down to one thing: going forward, true financial planning professionals must take a holistic approach to helping their clients plan for the future. A background in psychology, an empathetic personality, and

---

[7] http://www.bobveres.com

plenty of diverse life experience are just as important in this profession as is academic coursework in the financial planning process.

The Nazrudin Project has been instrumental in perpetuating this new landscape on the financial planning horizon, and in making it available to consumers. Innovative work is being done by some of the finest financial planners in the nation toward developing an infrastructure that will educate the public to the availability of this new breed of financial planner. You had better prepare for it if you expect to be a part of this exciting, dynamic, pioneering profession that is just now surfacing.

Eric Bruck, CFP®, with the independent firm of Silver Oak Wealth Advisors, LLC in Los Angeles, California, reminded me of a Nazrudin chat awhile ago that used the metaphor of a jigsaw puzzle to illustrate a holistic approach to the financial planning process. The question posed was, "What's the most important *piece* to start with when putting the puzzle together?" ome thought it was the corner piece, or finding the edge pieces. Others thought sorting the pieces by color was the key. The logical piece to start with, of course, is the picture on the box top.

Without looking at the completed picture, it's much more difficult to assemble the many tiny pieces in the box. The financial planner of the future must first have the skill-set to guide the client's focus to the picture on the box. This has nothing to do with which mutual funds to own or what type of insurance to purchase. It has to do with first defining a vision for living life to its fullest. Without the picture that identifies those present and future dreams, there is no viable place to begin a plan. How much money a client has, or the percentage a client is making on his portfolio, has no relevance without the picture on the box. The planner must put the paintbrush in the client's hand and lend guidance and encouragement as the picture develops.

Taking this one step further, Eric suggests that "traditional" financial planners have put the cart before the horse. If the solutions are in the cart, then the cart belongs **behind** the horse. After all, how are solutions possible until you know where the horse is headed?

He continues to challenge the planner to discern the client's expectations in at least four distinct areas before even beginning to think what might be appropriate items to fit in the cart. Eric proposes the following as necessary ingredients of a fulfilled life:

- Health/Energy
- Sense of Security with the World
- Good Quality Relationships
- Contribution to the Community

And let's not forget a possible fifth ingredient: simply, Fun! There is no substitute for having the capacity now and then to just enjoy the moment. Once the client has come to terms with these components, then, and only then, does Eric feel it is time to begin filling the cart, but only at a pace with which the client is comfortable.

While researching websites and links for this book, I came across an article written by a CPA I had never met. Astounded by how perfectly the article summed up what I had been trying to explain from conception in this chapter, I picked up the phone and called Frank Sisco[8], CPA, PFS, a Personal Financial Specialist[9] and financial planner in New Rochelle, New York.

"Frank," I asked, "May I include your article in the appendix for Chapter 1 of my book for people considering financial planning as a career?"

His generous response led to an animated coast-to-coast conversation that lasted nearly an hour. In his article on "Sensitive Financial Services"[10], Frank has beautifully articulated what I see as the financial planning profession of the future. Certainly, there will be clients who need the direction and guidance of financial planners for short-term or temporary projects. But I truly believe the financial planning professional of the future will deal with unique clients on a long-term basis, just like the ones Frank illustrates in his article. It takes a special person to tune-in to the true needs and dreams of clients.

Take time now to read Frank's article in Appendix A. If you can't envision yourself doing what he describes for a sizeable portion of your clientele, then I suggest you reconsider financial planning as a career. The definition of *Financial Planning* may not yet be written in stone, but Frank's scenario is not far off the mark.

How Much Money Do Financial Planners make?

I don't know.

I'll admit right up front that I have a jaded eye when it comes to surveys, so it won't come as a surprise when I tell you I partly blame the Financial Planning Association's Annual Financial Performance & Compensation Study of Financial Planning Practitioners[11] for the common misconception that financial planners make a lot of money.

Let me begin by telling you that a good friend and colleague took me under his wing one afternoon and spent an hour explaining exactly why the study is valid and accurate. My friend made an excellent presentation that I understood thoroughly. Maybe I'm too dense, but I just didn't buy it.

---

[8] Learn more about Frank Sisco by giving him a call in New Rochelle, New York, at 914.740.4422, or e-mail him at ideasmoney@aol.com.
[9] The Personal Financial Specialist (PFS) is the financial planning specialty accreditation held exclusively by certified public accountants (CPAs) who are members of the American Institute of CPAs (AICPA). A CPA must demonstrate experience and expertise in a wide range of personal financial matters before being awarded the PFS.
[10] See Appendix A
[11] Results of the study have been removed from the FPA website.

Here's why: According to the CFP Board's 2001 Annual Report[12], there were 36,307 CERTIFIED FINANCIAL PLANNER™ certificants in the country in 2000. I searched through the Study and found only that the questionnaire had been sent to "a diverse group of...participants, ranging from small sole practitioners to large ensemble firms...with revenues over $10,000,000."

Since there are a whole lot more financial planners who are not CFP® certificants that are members of the FPA (who commissioned the Study) I can only assume that the universe of "diverse...participants" from which to choose was much greater than 36,307. I received the questionnaire. I don't have it any more, but believe me, it was really long. I spent a couple of hours getting through the first few pages, and then the questions got too tough for me. After consulting with Ronnie, my paraplanner, who also does our company's books, we answered a few more questions. Then some esoteric accounting terms that I couldn't even define came up and I threw the rest away.

The Study results include the 703 participants who responded to the survey. Seven hundred and three! I don't know about statistical analysis, but that doesn't sound like very many out of at least 36,307 identifiable financial planning practitioners. My contention is that those filling out the forms were mainly high producers selling commissionable products at large brokerages who are doing very little actual *financial planning*.

My friend told me he completed the questionnaire and sent it in. Why wouldn't he? He grooves on this stuff! Once I began writing this book, I also began inquiring as to who sent back the questionnaire. My research was anything but scientific, but of the several hundred people I asked, perhaps 15% had received the survey. Absolutely no one that I asked—with the exception of my friend—had taken the time and effort to fill it out and return it.

My hypothesis is that the Study is enormously skewed toward the large brokerages, where staff can fill in the questionnaire, utilizing published statistics from corporate tax returns and 1099s that the "participants" received showing commissions earned. Some of this shows up in the statistics, which report that the average sole practitioner makes less than the planner does in an "ensemble" practice.

Well, duh! Even I have heard of economies of scale. What was new to me is the term "survivorship bias." Nowhere in the Study could I find anything about practitioners who had left the industry, yet I am aware that many who enter the profession cannot make it for a variety of reasons—generally due to misconceptions about income. They don't make enough money to support themselves, having entered the industry because they read the Study, which showed the "average" income was lucrative and discovering just the opposite!

I'll bet none of those "under $5,000" planners participated in the Study. They were out looking for a job![13]

[12] The CFP Board's Annual Reports are archived on their website: http://www.cfp.net/Certificants/boardreport.asp
[13] Other places to find information on a career in financial planning is the Bureau of Labor Statistics http://stats.bls.gov/ and, for a more realistic picture, AdvisorBenchmarking.com http://www.advisorbenchmarking.com . Also, take the survey at http://www.fabestpractices.com/.

It wasn't until June of 2005 that Marilyn vos Savant's column in *Parade Magazine*[14] made clear to me what I had felt all along. The question concerned a survey sent to the membership of a union about which presidential candidate to endorse. Marilyn explained that a scientific poll required a random sampling. Replies from the union were voluntary and did not, in fact, represent the membership. The information from all those who chose to respond to the FPA Study was included in the report. How many of us, for a myriad of reasons, failed to "volunteer" information?

If you want to know how much money you can make as a financial planner, find a financial planner in your area whose practice you admire, take the planner to lunch, and ask! Don't stop there. Ask him what he did to get where he is. Ask him about the cost in time, dollars, and family. Ask him if it was worth it. And then take a different financial planner who is doing what you want to be doing and invite her to lunch. Ask the same questions.

Another site for information, especially for younger people, is http://www.startingout.com. Enter your state and check under Banking, Finance & Investment under the Career Finder tab. Scroll down for Financial Planner.

The Decision Process

What does it take to get started? One of the most respected and successful names in the profession is the late Frank Gleberman, CLU, CFP®. When I asked him for ideas on getting started, he came up with a profound and comprehensive treatise. Due to its length, I have included his entire paper in the Appendix under the title "Your Entry Level into the Financial Planning Profession". I hope you'll read it right now. It will provide a good overview and give you plenty to contemplate as you explore the rest of this book.

I'm frequently asked by college grads if they are too young to enter the profession and by career-changers if they are too old. "Only if you think you are," is my general response. Young people today are launching entrepreneurial careers with bells and whistles only members of their peer group understand. Career-changers can bring new perspective from decades of life experience. There is a place in financial planning for anyone with a passion.

Lest there is a concern young planners will have a difficult time entering the profession, let me help resolve that fear by suggesting the marketplace is ready and waiting. Michael Kitces, CFP* put it quite eloquently in an April 2005 post to the *Journal of Financial Planning Voice*[15]

---

[14] *Parade Magazine*, June 19, 2005.
[15] Reprinted with permission by the Financial Planning Association, *Journal of Financial Planning*, April 2005, Michael Kitces "The Millenials are Coming". The *Journal of Financial Planning* is the official publication of the Financial Planning Association. The *Voice* is an Internet Café discussion area for Journal readers to further explore articles. For more information on the Financial Planning Association, please visit www.fpanet.org or call 800.322.4237.

The Millenials are Coming

By Michael Kitces, CFP®[16]

The Millenials, also known as 'Generation Y' or 'Echo-Boomers', are coming. This generation of current youngsters, born from roughly 1981 through 2001, is just seeing its first and oldest members graduate from college and enter the working world. Already, though, the impact from this 70-million-member generation (that's right, as big as the baby boomers!) is being felt.

Have you noticed the craze for American Idol? That's the Millenials watching their peers on television. Astounded by the explosion of iPods everyplace in a mere two years? That's the impact of successful marketing to Millenials in school (and this is just the 'partial' impact from the Millenials old enough to own iPods!)

Just as the baby boomers defined jobs, the marketplace, and the services of successful businesses as they grew up, so will the Millenials as they enter the workforce. This tidal wave of new job entrants, flooding into the financial planning profession as the baby boomers begin to retire, will challenge the entire profession to re-define itself for the Next Generation. In the coming decade, new business models will be developed to address the needs of twenty-something and thirty-something Millenials as they establish careers and families. New products and services will be developed to fit their niches and needs—because the demand will be tremendous.

Unfortunately, the profession has fallen behind in setting clear expectations about how to develop a career in financial planning. Rising Millenials hope to achieve everything immediately, whereas veterans remember the slow and arduous journey of defining oneself as a financial planner, and the tremendous growing pains as the profession first established itself.

In the end, the two must compromise and meet in the middle—Millenials need to adjust their expectations down a bit to reflect the reality of developing a career, and veteran pioneers must adjust their expectations up a bit in acknowledgement that the current profession's career tracks can and should be faster and smoother than those who first pioneered the blazing trek through the wilderness.

For businesses and firms that seek continuity beyond the founding owner(s), developing methods and tracks to integrate Millenials to positions of leadership will be a key fundamental factor of success—the financial planning market, its services and products, and its business models will inevitably change in the future through the demands of the broader Millenial American public, and businesses with future Millenial leaders (who understand the market of their peers) will succeed just as baby boomers did with their own market.

---

[16] Michael Kitces, MSFS, CFP®, CLU, ChFC, RHU, REBC, CASL is Director of Financial Planning at Pinnacle Advisory Group and Co-Founder (with Aaron Coates) of NexGen.

And for the next twenty years, the real winners will be the firms that determine how to market and develop both the baby boomer AND the Millenials that are coming, and how to manage the transition of wealth between the two.

Make no mistake.

This is a book for people who think they want to become financial planners. It's not for those who want to be stockbrokers. It won't tell you how to invest your retirement funds. This book has nothing to do with selling investments or insurance. And it won't hand a new career to you on a silver platter.

What this book will do is tell you what's out there, show you where to find the fundamental resources to prepare yourself, and give you a supporting hand. If that's not enough, then perhaps you're looking at the wrong profession.

Conclusion

When my daughter Beth was doing graduate studies toward her Physician AssistantCertificate, she worked at Children's Hospital in Los Angeles. Once in awhile I'd visit her for lunch and she'd take me on a tour of the wing where she worked. It saddened me to see so many sick children, but watching their faces light up when they saw Beth was such a delight. She would pat someone on the back, give a hug to another, tickle a rib or two, and get down on one knee to listen to a soft whisper, as the children clamored around for attention. Next would come introductions to her Mommy amid much giggling as Beth asked a bandaged-headed boy what the Sultan had done with Billy and applauded Susie's success of three whole steps, even with the heavy brace.

Weeks later, Beth would come home and I'd ask, "How is little Tommy?" She would tell me that he had died a few days ago, and then describe, with such pride, how a new child had overcome a difficult obstacle. Beth has a gift. She can bring joy and laughter to these terminally ill children and somehow survive the everyday tragedies to remain upbeat and loving for the next ones.

"I'm so glad we have people like you in the world, Beth," I told her once. "I could never do what you do!"

"Mom," she replied. "You've been doing what I do ever since I can remember. It's just that I do it with medicine and you do it with money. Most of all, we do it because we care about the people we do it with."

Before embarking on any new career, take time to do some soul-searching. If you're going to be good at what you do, you'll have to know a lot more than you will find on the pages of a textbook. Yes, you need to learn the fundamentals, to pass the tests, to understand how the system works. But it's what bubbles up from deep down inside that will make the difference. Without passion for your chosen profession, you will miss out on the joy of it. Think long and hard before deciding whether you honestly have that consuming desire to be a financial planner.

If you do, then go on to the next page and begin your journey.

Chapter Two

Back to School

"The FPA reaffirms that all who hold themselves out as financial planners should be CFP® certificants and rededicates itself to promoting the CFP® certification marks as the cornerstone of the financial planning profession."

Pretty clear edict. The Financial Planning Association, the result of a merger between the industry association, International Association for Financial Planning (IAFP), and the professional association, Institute of Certified Financial Planners (ICFP), passed this resolution in July 2000. Translation? If you really want to be a financial planner, you'll need your CFP® certification.

Things have changed considerably since, at the age of 44, I enrolled in the College for Financial Planning's course and simultaneously entered the University of Southern California extension Financial Planning Program. My UCLA kids cringe every time they see the USC diploma on my wall, but I think it looks cool.

I'm one of those students who need to ask questions of a real, live instructor, and enjoys the intercourse from a classroom experience. There were 35 who showed up to begin the CFP-I class at the Hilton Hotel in Pasadena in 1983. Fifteen of us completed the course two years later. To this day, many of those remain close colleagues.

Thinking back, the way we did it made a lot of sense. During the risk management course, we all went through an outside insurance program and sat for the Life & Disability and Variable Contract license exam. While we studied for the tax part of the CFP® certification program, we enrolled in the H&R Block tax course in our neighborhood and became registered tax preparers. We took a five-day crash course together and passed the Series 7 securities exam while studying Investments in the CFP® certification program.

At that time, there was not yet a two-day certification exam and my years as a Realtor® qualified me for the work experience requirement once I passed the sixth course. Mid-way through the CFP® certification program, I became a Registered Representative for a Broker/Dealer, and began my career as a financial planner.

Today the same four "E" requirements exist for those wanting to obtain the CERTIFIED FINANCIAL PLANNER™ certification. They are:[17]

---

[17] Beginning in 2007, candidates for certification must have a bachelor's degree, in any discipline, in order to obtain CFP® certification. The college degree requirement is a condition of initial certification; it is not a requirement to be eligible to take the CFP® Certification Examination and does not have to occur before sitting for the exam or fulfilling the work experience. The bachelor's degree requirement was waived for those individuals who met all certification requirements prior to 2007. http://www.cfp.net/become/certification.asp

1. **Education**

   You will need to be knowledgeable in the following six areas of financial planning:

   > Insurance planning
   > Investment planning
   > Tax planning
   > Retirement planning
   > Employee benefits
   > Estate planning

2. **Examination**

   You will need to pass the CFP® Certification Examination.

3. **Experience**

   You will need three years of relevant experience in personal financial planning.[18]

4. **Ethics**

   You will need to sign statements adhering to the CFP Board:

   > Code of Ethics and Professional Responsibility
   > Financial Planning Practice Standards
   > Disciplinary Rules and Procedures

Selecting a School and Course of Study[19]

Choices abound! In 2011, there were over 150 CFP Board-Registered programs at both colleges and universities throughout the United States and online programs accessible worldwide. Whatever you do, don't just jump into the first program you find. This is an important step in your career, and you want to give yourself the best possible education. Unfortunately, some classes are simply set up to help you pass the exam, not to teach you financial planning skills.

If you are going to earn your CFP® certification, here's how to get started:

1. **Download or send for the *Guide to CFP® Certification*[20].**

2. **What is your purpose for acquiring the certification?**

This may seem like an odd question, but it requires a little soul-searching. Some people "collect" letters to put after their name. Others figure it's probably something they should do, but they want to get it over with the cheapest, quickest way available.

For those serious about a career in financial planning, obtaining the certification can be the best possible way to train. Place emphases on schools that reach out beyond the six required areas and offer classes in both financial planning practicum and on developing and managing a practice.

---

[18] View the CFP Board's Definition of Work Experience at http://www.cfp.net/become/work.asp.
[19] Education Programs http://www.cfp.net/become/programs.asp
[20] Request the *Guide to CFP® Certification* http://www.cfp.net/become/request.asp

Frequently, there are posts on the discussion boards from people entering the industry who want to know whether they will get the best financial planning training from Ameriprise or Merrill Lynch, or perhaps with an independent firm. You may learn outstanding marketing, sales, or service techniques with any one of the hundreds of Broker/Dealers and financial planning companies across the country, but you will not learn how to prepare a comprehensive financial plan for a client. The best way to learn that is by going through the educational process with a CFP Board-Registered program.

Unfortunately, the schools, faculty, teaching methods, and presentation vary greatly. I was fascinated as I listened to students discuss their experiences during a session at a national FPA event. Many were disillusioned and even angry at the quality of classes or support they had received from the institution they chose. Others praised their instructors to the hilt and felt the program they selected had prepared them well for entry into the profession. Clearly, it pays to shop around. It's a classic case of *buyer beware*! The CFP Board has posted a list of questions in the Guide[21] you should ask before plunking down tuition fees.

3. How do you learn?

Some have the discipline to set a self-study schedule and stick to it on their own. Others need intense classroom interaction in a structured environment. I needed as much help as I could get, and signed up for both a self-study course and classroom instruction. At the time, my tuition at USC included a one-day crash course prior to each live test. Literally hundreds of students would gather on the USC campus to go over case studies, calculations, and generally get our act together. But back in the '80s, most of us didn't even own a computer! Today, the basic choices remain self-study and live, on-campus classes with some online reinforcement.

The College for Financial Planning[22] in Denver started it all back in 1969. The American College[23] in Bryn Mawr came early to the game. I feel Jerry Mason, Ph.D, CFP®, CLU, ChFC set the benchmark for degree programs during his tenure at Texas Tech University[24]. But the logistics of earning a BA while attending on-campus classes in Lubbock, Texas, may not be practical for mid-life career-changers. Kansas State University[25] began a hybrid program in September 2001.

Texas Tech and Kansas State are also a part of GPIDEA[26], the Great Plains Interactive Distance Education Alliance, a consortium of Human Sciences Colleges at eleven universities. Students may pursue a degree offered by a single institution or multiple institutions. Each university brings a unique strength to the multi-institution academic programs. In a multi-institution program, a student is admitted at one institution and enrolls in courses at multiple institutions.

---

[21] http://www.cfp.net/become/programs.asp
[22] http://www.cffp.edu/index.aspx
[23] http://www.theamericancollege.edu/
[24] http://www.depts.ttu.edu/pfp/
[25] http://www.ipfp.k-state.edu/
[26] http://www.gpidea.org

4. What's your time frame?

Unless you've been collecting financial experience in a personal financial planning setting approved by the CFP Board, you won't be able to place the CFP® certification marks after your name for at least three years. I recommend you get started as soon as possible, but there's a lot to be said for working as a financial planner before starting the certification program. For instance, if financial planning professionals surround you, you have a ready-made advice and cheerleading group to help you through the tough parts.

If you have a well-paying day job, think about taking the classes during your off time. Most courses (with the exception of degree programs) are designed for working professionals and anticipate a two-year completion date. Look at your calendar and your transition plan and see how the course fits in. Socking away something from a job with steady income while studying could be a huge help during the first few lean years in practice.

If you're rarin' to go, others have proven it's possible to zip through the program and sit for the certification exam in record time. Take Michael Kapustin, CFP®, RFC, ChFC with Society Hill Financial Planning in Voorhees, New Jersey:

"It is possible to take the necessary courses and take (and pass) the test within six months. I know this because I did it several years ago. It takes a lot of discipline, a lot of time, and an understanding family (in my case, a wife). In my opinion, it also takes a familiarity with most of the subject matter as the building blocks for the vast amount of learning that you will need to do. You don't need to be an expert. You won't be one after the test either! If you are not learning it, don't rush it. Some of the material is difficult, most is not. It is just a lot of information on a lot of different topics. This is a great time to learn. Make sure you learn the material for you and not just the test!

"To move along as quickly as you want, self-study may be the only option. I took the self-study courses from the American College. I was satisfied with the material and feel it did its part in helping to prepare me for the test. Take a prep course before the comprehensive exam. Dearborn's was outstanding for me." Six months??? Wow.

Tim Murray, CFP®[27] passed the Certification Exam in November, 2001, exactly one year after enrolling in Florida State University's distance learning program. He also took and passed the Series 7, 66, and Virginia Life and Health exam in the same year. "Just to give a heads-up on what it costs to take the certification exam (in 2001)," offered Tim, "I spent $600 for the exam, $550 for study materials, and $50 for a hotel room between testing sessions. It was a $1200 event that I did not want to repeat!" Everything costs significantly more today.

---

[27] Tim Murray can be reached at TimMurray@MurrayFinancial.com

5. What will it cost you?

Of course there is more to consider than just the cost of the course. Some packages come with materials included and some with free re-takes of review classes if you don't pass the certification exam the first time. Do your own financial planning. Compare costs. Will you have additional travel or shipping expenses? What about support? Break down the fee and add on the extras.

Don't forget the cost of taking "crash" courses just before the CFP® Certification Exam and travel and lodging for the test site. The last thing you want to be is under pressure from freeway traffic on your way to the certification exam. Plan to indulge in some quiet time to clear your mind and be well rested and alert for the test. Besides, if you're late you lose. I mean, you are not allowed into the test, must wait until the next exam date to retake it, and shell out another exam fee!

Depending on the course of study you select, anticipate a rock-bottom budget (in 2011) of $6000 to get through the qualifying coursework, materials, reviews and the exam itself. If you need to re-take the exam or underlying courses, or enter into a degree program to prepare for certification, the costs could rapidly multiply.

6. How will you pay for the courses and CFP® Certification?

This question requires even more forward thinking about what you eventually plan to do as a financial planner. Many fine Broker/Dealers will pay, or reimburse you, for the cost of your CFP® certification. Some of them offer mentors or in-house classes of their own. If you are planning on affiliating with a Broker/Dealer, this is certainly a question you will want to ask them. Discounts are available from some schools for FPA members[28]. Many institutions offer a pay-as-you-go plan, and some require non-refundable tuition up front.

If you require special financing, see if it is available from the school you select. Don't forget to see if you qualify for the Lifetime Learning Credit when you're filing your income tax return. Remember that a penalty-free withdrawal from your IRA[29] may be a source of funds to help pay higher education expenses.

7. Research schools.

A complete list of CFP Board-Registered programs can be found in the *Guide to CFP® Certification*[30]. Once you've determined the sort of program best suited to your needs, make a short list of potential schools to contact. Phone or send for catalogs, or download appropriate material from the institutions' websites. Prepare a notebook or spreadsheet with questions and a place to enter responses from each school, including the date and person you spoke with, and then begin comparing programs. Include the following in your questions:

---

[28] If you are enrolled in a CFP Board-Registered Program, you can join the FPA at student rates.
[29] http://www.irs.gov/publications/p970/ch09.html
[30] http://www.cfp.net/become/request.asp

A. Verify information in the catalog is the most current.
B. What, exactly, is included in the cost? Tuition, books, support, etc.?
C. Ask about fees and payment options.
D. What is the anticipated weekly study time needed?
E. What faculty support is available; when and how is it delivered?
F. What is the pass rate for students who take the certification exam?
G. How long before you should be ready to sit for the certification exam?
H. Is there a crash course before the certification exam? Is it included?
I. May you contact former students for references?
J. Are career placement or intern programs available?

Tim Bennett, a graduate of NYU, suggests looking for schools in which CERTIFIED FINANCIAL PLANNER™ professionals teach most of the courses. "One of the problems that I had at NYU was that 70% of the professors were not CFP® practitioners, had never taken the CFP® Certification Exam, and had never done a financial plan. This was a shock to me, because the NYU brochure specifically states that the faculty members have *a practitioner's view of financial planning.*"

Tim Murray, CFP® selected the Florida State University program for the following reasons:

A. FSU has a good name (in general).
B. I didn't have to pay for the whole program at once.
C. Each of the courses had a very comprehensive "take home" midterm and final. Since I'd have to take the CFP® exam for any of this to be worthwhile, why go through the stress of six cramming sessions for each course. I saved my energy for studying for the Series 7, 66, insurance, and CFP® exams.
D. The scheduling of their classes suited me well.

Jeremy Hudson was a pre-med student at Texas Tech in Lubbock when he leaned about the financial planning program, located in the School of Human Sciences. He switched majors in his junior year. Texas Tech's financial planning program requires an internship to graduate, so it took him five years and a summer session to graduate. Would he do it all again? Yes, he insists, though admitted he'd rather have skipped the pre-med stuff and gotten right into financial planning from the beginning. He was excited about the program when we spoke during lunch at an FPA Retreat in Galveston Island, Texas, in the spring of 2007.

"Many of the professors have financial planning experience," he explained, "with a very challenging curriculum. Texas Tech's program is very comprehensive, hitting all areas of financial planning. I felt prepared to sit for the comprehensive exam." It would be eighteen months after graduation before he took the comprehensive exam, however, since he wanted to gain experience beforehand.

Equally impressed with his internship, a required 300 hours (three months) in order to graduate, Jeremy had nothing but good things to say about the firm he worked with in New Jersey. His employer wanted students to get involved, so he worked in all aspects of the firm and with the clients during his internship. The internship was so successful that after graduation, the firm in New Jersey hired him full time. In the meantime, the same firm has hired six additional financial planning students from Texas Tech's program.

Texas Tech Masters Program

By Zach Reyes & Nelson Rodriguez

The Personal Financial Planning program at Texas Tech University is considered to be the preeminent program in the nation. The opportunities available to students at Texas Tech are unrivaled. Many of these opportunities stem from the fact that the program was essentially the first of its kind and was one of the first accredited by the CFP Board of Standards.

Texas Tech is the only university that offers undergraduate, graduate, doctoral, certificate, and multiple dual-degree programs in Personal Financial Planning. The courses are taught by an exceptional faculty, many of whom are current or former practitioners. The unique opportunity to garner valuable knowledge from industry leaders, most notably Harold Evensky and Deena Katz of Evensky & Katz Wealth Management, is truly a blessing. Because of the diverse faculty, the Personal Financial Planning program at Texas Tech University is able to offer courses not found at other programs. These courses include, but are not limited to, the following: behavioral finance, business practices, communication and counseling, product evaluation, charitable giving, professional field experience, and professional technology. The field experience course allows students to attend professional conferences where we network with practitioners and gain industry insight and advice. The professional technology course provides the unique opportunity to become proficient in a number of financial planning software platforms used by firms nationwide; therefore, students get valuable practice with the software before entering the workforce. The professional technology course is taken in conjunction with a capstone course that integrates the knowledge gained from all other courses in the program and requires students to create a comprehensive financial plan. The entire curriculum is designed to give students the best hands-on experience in preparing for a career as a financial planner and offers many volunteer opportunities to help individuals with their personal finances while studying in the program.

In addition to these benefits, typically reserved for the largest of universities, students at Texas Tech still have the rare opportunity to develop personal relationships with the faculty due to the low student to faculty ratios in the undergraduate and graduate programs, 10:1 and 8:1, respectively. This provides the program with a family atmosphere, made evident from the first step into the classroom. Because of the program's intimacy, students feel comfortable enough to ask for help or advice from the professors and are fortunate to be able to have discussions with faculty who can provide different perspectives, thereby helping them discover options they may not have yet considered.

As a result of these tremendous opportunities, students come out of the program miles ahead of the competition and are sought out by financial planning firms across the nation. This is demonstrated by the exceptional 94% job placement over the past five years. The faculty, staff, curriculum, and support from students and professors make the Personal Financial Planning program at Texas Tech University truly extraordinary. The program at Texas Tech University is second to none for anyone considering a career in financial planning.

Boston University Online Program for Financial Planners

By Gavin M. Ganzkow

gganzkow@mindspring.com
(407)682-1814

I came to financial planning by a somewhat circuitous route. I'm an attorney, and for over a decade I served as the corporate counsel for an organization in the personal finance and financial education field. While working on legal matters great and small for this organization, I developed an appreciation for the value of financial planning and decided to learn more about it.

When I began looking into education programs, I knew what I wanted. First, since I was working while I was studying, I wanted a program that would allow me the flexibility of moving at my own pace. I focused on self-study programs which would not be tied to a class schedule. Second, I wanted a solid grounding in core subjects for the CFP® exam. Third, I place a premium on education and I wanted a program associated with a well-known educational institution, reputable in the field. These criteria led me to select the Boston University Online Program for Financial Planners[31].

I found the 18-month window for completion of the program manageable. It took me approximately 13 months to finish, and I believe this is average. I spent about 15 hours per week working through the courses. I began my studies in mid-2007 and finished in September, 2008.

I did miss the give-and-take of the classroom experience with the online self-study approach. The kind of person who learns well in a classroom setting, like me, may find the focus that a life instructor can provide lacking. Fortunately, tutors are available via e-mail who will answer questions about course material, and the answers to my e-mails were prompt and responsive. At the time I took the Boston University program, both the listed tutors were CFP® certificants.

I was very satisfied with the program substance, as it covered all the necessary bases for the CFP® exam, and then some. There were places in the course modules where I thought the text presentation could use some editing for clarity and organization, but generally the presentation was thorough. The on-line material was supplemented by a textbook purchased for each course, so the reading requirements were substantial.

Be prepared to answer lots of multiple choice questions in this program! Each course module ended with a quiz (a total of 88 quizzes in all.) I found some of the comprehensive course exams which concluded each course, particularly those in tax planning and investments, to be quite challenging.

---

[31] http://www.bu.edu/online/online_programs/

The bottom line is that I am glad I took the program, and I would take it again. Beyond the personal satisfaction I got from completing it, the Boston University Online Program for Financial Planners has sharpened my appreciation for the possibilities in the financial planning field. I can recommend the program based on this experience.

Another Boston University Online student had a similar experience. Dustin Rector, CFP® told me:

"I began the Boston University online program in January of 2007. I completed the program in May of 2008. I would typically complete 2 to 3 modules per week and then take some time off in between each course. The total allowed time for completion of all 6 courses is 18 months.

"As far as the online aspect is concerned, it has its pros and cons. I enjoyed the flexibility of the online aspect as I have a full-time job, a wife, and two small children. I was able to balance work, family, and study time pretty well. However, the discipline was not always there to stay on schedule. For instance, instead of giving myself a 'little' time off between courses, I would take over a month. Upon starting a new course I felt hurried, as I needed to 'catch up' and get back on track. In the end I was able to complete the course in 16 months as noted earlier. I found it difficult to be motivated to complete the suggested textbook reading.

"The course itself is very informative. The administrative staff at Boston University was superb to deal with and was customer friendly. I only contacted them a couple times early on and was satisfied with their service each time. As I progressed through a review course provider in preparation for the certification exam, I felt that the education that Boston University provided was more than adequate and was extremely thorough.

"Overall, the value and quality of the Boston University online program is hard to beat. I would recommend the course to anyone."

California Lutheran University's
California Institute of Finance[32]
Online MBA in Financial Planning/CFP Certificate Program

By Adam Broughton

The Financial Planner finds himself in a challenging professional environment today. The industry is still relatively young and, therefore, the boundaries of who is "in" and who is "out" are not yet entirely clear. Under these circumstance outsiders might easily confuse a Financial Planner for a distant cousin such as an insurance salesman, a stockbroker, a

---

[32] http://www.callutheran.edu/schools/business/graduate/cif/

consultant, or even the occasional portfolio manager. Even worse, without a clear professional distinction, the insurance salesman, stockbroker or portfolio manager might confuse himself for a Financial Planner!

The Certified Financial Planner designation (CFP®) stands out from this backdrop as the preeminent mark of professionalism by which to judge the "Ins" from the "Outs". For those who are committed to pursuing excellence in their craft, completion of the CFP® criteria is practically non-optional. Particularly in this field of study, bridging academic theory and practical application is key, since the Financial Planner acts as a gateway to concepts that are largely beyond the realm of understanding for the everyday consumer. The Financial Planner has to deal with the emotions of real people and move them from a place of fear and confusion to a place of confidence and sure footing.

California Lutheran University's Online MBA in Financial Planning program stands at the top of the list in its ability to present each curriculum topic in light of its function as a tool for the Financial Planner in his or her career. The program consists of sixteen courses (eight CFP modules and eight MBA courses) and tuition costs in 2011 are placed at $695/unit (approx. $2085/course). Although the costs might be considered high solely for a CFP® program, the coupling with an MBA program justifies the added expense. Since the cost of an MBA program today can range from $40,000 to $80,000 *per year*, the costs of Cal Lutheran's courses are relatively reasonable.

The primary challenge faced by online learners is the loss of community with other students and the lack of real time interaction with professors. Cal Lutheran has taken this challenge as an opportunity to design an online learning experience focused on maintaining that sense of community and which is conducive to ongoing conversation with instructors. Their efforts have not gone to waste! Upon logging in, students are directed to a landing page which contains content relative to the general finance industry as well as content connecting the student to the Cal Lutheran campus with event updates, registration information, the student bookstore and the library.

The landing page also contains links to the online classroom. Each course "classroom" contains a discussion board, chat room, assignment overview, and the syllabus along with several other standard items. One of the highlights of each course is the weekly class discussion in the chat room. The instructor logs in to present the weekly lesson lecture (live) and they are able to control the PowerPoint for the lecture just as if they were in a physical classroom with the students. The chat room itself gives students the ability to speak with one another using a standard computer microphone. Additionally, students have the option of calling a phone number to listen and participate in the discussion if they are not able to access a computer. The chat room also allows students to type responses, raise their hand to be called on, communicate with just a single person instead of the whole class and upload their own files for presentation if required. It is a very dynamic learning environment overall.

Usually, each course also requires at least one group project in which students coordinate on a case study, develop their own PowerPoint presentation and take control of the chat session for the week. These group projects connect directly to real world experience in that they teach students the skill of working with small groups in a virtual environment spread across multiple locations. This scenario is becoming more common in the digital age with multinational corporations and these group projects, although often challenging, are very valuable. In addition, with the growing use of WebEx style client meetings, knowing how to clearly communicate in a web-environment is becoming more necessary.

The weekly lessons consist of 1 - 2 chapters of reading in the textbook as well as several outside readings from financial publications. In addition, each course requires assignments to be posted to the discussion board for instructor review and a weekly exam on the material. Exams are typically open book, untimed and consist of 20 – 40 multiple-choice questions. In each CFP® module, the testing techniques and question styles are designed to mimic parts of the CFP® exam. This focus is very valuable preparing students' mindsets for eventually taking the exam.

As a note on the MBA courses, this program differs from a plain-vanilla MBA in that is an MBA *in Financial Planning*. In other words, the CFP® modules, are not the only place mention is made of the financial services industry. The reason this is such an important distinction is because each concept and principle covered in the MBA courses is presented as it applies to owning and managing a company in the financial services industry. Whether it is an analytical subject like accounting, or something more creative, like marketing, the professors are intentional about presenting the course material in meaningful ways for the Financial Planner/Business Owner.

The academic year is laid out in five terms and each course is eight weeks long, giving the program its "accelerated degree" status. Students should expect to spend 10 – 12 hours minimum each week per course. A workable schedule for a busy professional is usually one course per term. However, there are always those self-loathing individuals who insist on working full time and filling the rest of their waking hours with two or more courses per term. These people apparently are more conscious of their finite humanity than the rest of us and therefore work at a constant, breakneck pace. However, to protect the mental health of their students, Cal Lutheran recommends taking a maximum of two courses per term when working full time.

Overall, the Cal Lutheran Online MBA/CFP program gives working professionals a high degree of flexibility in completing a rigorous course of study. Their excellence shines through in the course content, the caliber of their instructors, and the obvious effort that has gone into fostering an online learning experience that maintains the community and communication of a traditional on-campus MBA program. More importantly, graduates of the program are equipped to make a lasting difference in the lives of clients and stand out as true professionals. As mentioned above, this industry is still developing and it needs Financial Planners who bear the CFP® mark with integrity, are professionally trained and can set the standard so that no outsider will have questions about who is "In" and who is "Out".

Northwestern University[33]

By Alan R. Menase

It all started in the library. It was a cold, damp day the type of day you get used to quickly in Chicago. As I briskly walked into the public library to attend a seminar on investing, little did I know that particular evening would change the course in my life forever.

The speaker at the library was a Certified Financial Planner by the name of Warren Arnold. He spoke about the basic asset classes and asset allocation. He went on about the different types of stocks and bonds and the common investment mistakes that investors make. I was drawn into this lecture, as I always have loved reading and learning about personal finance and investment management.

A week later I proceeded to contact him to learn more about what he does and his experiences as a Certified Financial Planner. I loved the idea of helping people plan on how to allocate their finances and resources to achieve certain goals that they set out to accomplish. I continued to do more research into the field and I was very delighted to come across the previous edition of Nancy's book. It was simply the most informative and resourceful book that I came across. It was exactly what I needed to help propel me into my new career choice. I was going to study to become a Certified Financial Planner, with a focus on working in the fee only side of financial planning. I wanted a chance to work closely with clients without pushing proprietary products that a brokerage firm would pay me to recommend.

In December of 2010, I enrolled in the CFP program at Northwestern University. I am currently taking Retirement Planning and Employee Benefits. The classes are small and the teachers do a good job of bringing their real world experience into the classroom. There is always time to interact with your peers and to ask questions to your teachers.

Around the same time that I started taking classes, I joined NAPFA as a student affiliate member. This has enabled me to attend local study group meetings at a discounted rate, which has served as a tremendous experience for me. I love being in such an open environment in which practicing financial planners happily share their experiences with the rest of the group. Moreover, the study groups have provided an opportunity to get an education about what is happening in the field, beyond what the classroom experience could provide for me. Speakers have come to these meetings to discuss a variety of different subjects from business succession planning to long-term care. I was also fortunate to have the chance to attend NAPFA's Basic Training during their national conference in May of 2010. I learned about how different planners got their start in the profession, discovered how to effectively market one's business and even received tips about the best CRM and planning software to use. I can't think of another profession in which I have met so many

---

[33] http://www.scs.northwestern.edu/pdp/npdp/fin-plan/

people that are so giving of their time and that truly want to provide aspiring planners the tools to succeed in the work that they strive to do.

Currently, I was elected to serve as Committee Secretary of a new subgroup of NAPFA called Genesis. Founder and President, Dave Grant wants to help form a group among his peers to help lead the next generation of planners interested in practicing in the fee only side of the profession. I am very excited about the opportunity to meet people among my age group and to help assist him in this worthy endeavor.

I am scheduled to complete the CFP program in September of 2011. By the end of the year I hope to find my first job in a fee only financial planning firm. I want to take the CFP exam in March or June of 2012. I have had a great experience thus far. I still have a lot to learn and I can only hope that the best is yet to come.

8. Compare schools and programs and make a decision.

Do some serious homework here. Wherever possible, follow up on the information you have. Ask questions on the discussion boards or at industry meetings. Talk to people who have recently attended the schools you're interested in. If anything is in doubt, telephone the school again and get updated information.

"I would place the biggest emphasis on talking to former students," recommends Tim Bennett. "While the school can give you most of the information you need as far as the facts go, they will obviously tell you that they have an excellent program. "Don't expect their brochure to tell you the truth," he continues. "To illustrate my point, in NYU's brochure, they say that the three main things that the students are taught are to:

A. Assess a client's needs and goals
B. Structure an effective financial plan
C. Evaluate actual plan performance

We did only a little of the first and absolutely none of the other two."

9. Enroll.

10. Set yourself a study schedule and stick to it!

It won't be easy, but it most definitely will be worth it in the long run. Once you're in the system, you'll start meeting more people, knowing the "in" group, and who to ask for help when you need it. Not only will the support from your chosen institution be there, but you'll be surprised to find, in most cases, the authors of your text books and the financial planners whose works are cited, are available and willing to talk with you.

Jeffrey Lambert, CFP® Director, Personal Financial Planning Certificate Program University of California, Davis Extension, suggests "putting together a study group for support, or at least connecting with others who are studying. College contacts, FPA, potential employers, or online discussion boards could be used to organize. It pays to be a good networker!"

As a member of the Financial Planning Association, you have access to discounts on educational programs offered through Kaplan College[34] and The College for Financial Planning[35].

Preparing for the CFP® Certification Examination

Beginning with the March 2012 exam, the education requirement for CFP® certification will include completion of a financial plan development course registered with the CFP Board. Questions on the two day exam will be derived from a new book of "Job Task Domains" with included principal topics. Check the CFP Board website for the list. It will be invaluable when studying for the exam.

The Financial Planning Association offers discounts on the Dalton review program.[36]

Every five years or so there are questions released for download from the CFP Board website[37]. A list of certification exam review course providers who have met certain criteria is also on the Board's website[38].

"After finishing the CFP® certification program, I bought all of the BISYS Educational Services (formerly Dalton, now a division of Kaplan, Inc.) books to review. They are excellent and worth every penny. I passed the exam the first time. Go to http://www.kfeducation.com/. Plan on spending at least 150 to 300 hours reviewing for the exam," says Tim. "If you've taken classes over a normal two year period, you'll need to review closer to 300 hours, since the material studied early on won't be as fresh in your mind."

Another review course that has received consistently high marks is an on-site, 32-40 hour class taught by, Kenneth Zahn, CFP® or one of his excellent associates. According to his website, Ken has been teaching the CFP® Certification Exam review course since 1995. Complete information regarding cost and scheduling can be found at http://www.kenzahn.com. Ken provides a complete pre-study book. The pre-study is application- and case-based rather than academic. His condensed classroom book is designed to focus the student on the key areas of the exam. The two books have about 2000 questions and numerous cases.

---

[34] http://www.fpanet.org/professionals/Membership/DiscountInsurancePrograms/KaplanCollege/
[35] http://www.fpanet.org/professionals/Membership/DiscountInsurancePrograms/TheCollegeforFinancialPlanning/
[36] http://www.fpanet.org/professionals/Membership/DiscountInsurancePrograms/TheDaltonReview
[37] http://www.cfp.net/become/examquestions.asp Caution! These questions should be considered for form only. DO NOT rely on the answers, as they may be hopelessly outdated due to changes in tax law or general policy.
[38] http://www.cfp.net/become/programs.asp

Some Comments on the CFP® Certification Exam and Exam Preparation

By Gavin M. Ganzkow
gganzkow@mindspring.com
(407)682-1814

Background: I completed the Boston University Online Program for Financial Planners in September, 2008 and obtained my Certificate in Financial Planning. I went directly from completing the education course to preparing for the CFP® certification exam. I chose Ken Zahn's Comprehensive Live Review for this purpose, and sat for the March, 2009 CFP® exam, which I passed. Following are some comments on the exam preparation process and the exam.

Moving directly to CFP® certification exam preparation after completing the education course was helpful in itself, as much of the material from the education course was still fresh in my mind.

I have two other general recommendations to make about exam preparation. First, as others have suggested, an exam review course is a practical necessity. An effective course should help clarify the material and focus your study efforts on what is important for the exam. I chose Ken Zahn's Comprehensive Live Review for this purpose and was pleased with the choice.

Second, engage in study activities which promote continual, active learning of the material. Challenge yourself with practice questions, exams and case studies to find out how well you really know the material. The exam tests your ability to synthesize material you have learned and use planning concepts and knowledge in ways a real-world planner would. Try to master this material beyond the memorization of facts, numbers and rules.

As for the exam itself, I can offer a few observations. Prior to taking it in March 2009, I heard that the exam is more "conceptual" than it used to be, moving away from calculation problems and a quantitative approach. I can't comment on any trend in the exam, but I think it is important to know the formulas, bring your financial calculator and be prepared to use it! In my experience, you will need it.

Even if you are satisfied that you have done a thorough job of preparing for this exam, expect some difficult, challenging questions during the ten hours. Do not let these questions throw you off stride – do your best and move on. You do not need a perfect score to pass the exam.

I am a licensed attorney and occasionally I am asked to compare the CFP® certification exam with a bar exam. This is a bit like trying to compare apples with oranges, but there are some similarities.

Like a bar exam, the CFP® exam is in part a reading comprehension test. Read the questions and answer choices carefully. And like a bar exam, the ten-hour CFP® exam is a mental marathon. You are likely to feel tired and drained when it's done. Though it may seem elementary to say it, a good night's sleep both before and between the exam days is important so that you stay as mentally alert as possible.

Do not underestimate this exam. The cut-off score to pass varies from one test administration to another, but I understand it is generally in the 70% range or perhaps a little lower. For the March, 2009 exam the pass rate was 52.3%. Consider these two percentages for a moment and this may give you a sense of the challenge that the CFP® certification exam can be.

***

In 2005 I attended a three-hour CEU session Ken taught during an FPA Retreat, where I met him for the first time. It was a Case Study, and probably the most fun I've ever had earning credits. About half the standing-room-only crowd had taken a previous class from Ken and couldn't wait to repeat the experience. I mean, he's that good! No one falls asleep or sneaks out of participating in the case study.

Mike Curtiss passed the comprehensive exam on his first attempt. "I took the Ken Zahn review course and attribute much of my success to that course. Additionally, I studied a great deal between the review course and the test date. I qualified for the exam by having a Certified Employee Benefit Specialist (CEBS) designation, in addition to passing two financial planning courses offered by the Wharton School. I may be one of the first to qualify this way since the CEBS avenue was only recently made available by the CFP Board."[39]

Another successful first-time comprehensive exam candidate is Daniel Leahy, who lives near Sacramento, California:

"I completed the certificate program in personal financial planning at UC Davis Extension in June of '03. I ordered the Dalton/Bisys/Kaplan CFP® exam preparation materials in August '03 and studied intently until I took and passed the test in November '03. I studied for many hours (at least the recommended 300 hours). Most of my study time was spent taking the online practice tests over and over and over. In addition to that, I did a lot of review with the flash cards and worked through all of the case studies. I spent very little time looking at the very thick overall review book. I prefer the more concise format of the practice questions and flash cards. I knew the case studies were critical, too, because those

---

[39] Individuals who hold the CEBS credential may complete two additional courses (Personal Financial Planning I and Personal Financial Planning II) from the Wharton School and the International Foundation for Employee Benefit Plans (IFEBP) to satisfy CFP Board's education requirement. These individuals will not need to complete a transcript review application or submit a transcript review fee. Instead, they should use the CFP® Certification Examination application form and attach a copy of the CEBS designation and either a transcript or score report showing completion of the Personal Financial Planning I and II courses.
http://www.cfp.net/become/education.asp#top

questions account for about 25% of the overall score on the CFP® Exam. Because I spent so much time doing self-study, I decided to save the $1000 cost for the Dalton/Bisys live review course, which proved to be a wise decision. So my advice to someone taking the test now would be:

1) Answer the practice questions until you're blue in the face.
2) Go through the entire set of flash cards several times over.
3) Be reasonably comfortable answering the case study questions.

"Another method I used was to focus on only one of the six major topics at a time. I would not move on to the next topic until I was consistently answering the practice questions in the 80%-plus range. This took about two weeks per topic, and then I repeated the process on a shorter time scale as the test date approached. Of all the other test takers I spoke to that day, I was the only one who felt confident that I had passed when it was all said and done.

"I also took the series 65 exam shortly after that, which was a breeze in comparison, and I used the Dearborn track series to prepare. The only additional study that was necessary was in the regulatory and compliance areas."

Take preparation for the CFP® certification examination very seriously. This is one test you do not want to take a second time! The pass rate for the November 2010 exam was 56.5% (the average historical pass rate since the exam's 1995 introduction is 61%.) The CFP Board has been reporting the pass rate since 1995, when the transition to the two-day certification exam was complete. Pass Rate of CFP® Certification Examination for Retakes is considerably lower, averaging 42% over the same period.

Caution! The CFP Board is very protective of their data bank of questions, and the ones released are often obsolete. The best use of these questions is to get a feel for style and composition. Do not accept the answers provided as accurate! As Jeff Lambert puts it, "This is not a load & dump exam! It is designed to test your ability to apply the material in practice."

In responding to a post on the FPi discussion boards asking for the best ways to get ready for the two-day, ten-hour certification exam, Nigel B. Taylor, CFP® suggested the following:

1. Obtain a couple of the previous examinations and review the questions carefully. Formulate your own answer, and then make a comparative review of acceptable answers that are often provided. Remember, not every "correct" answer reflects real life. Many acceptable answers on the comprehensive examination are the answers the CFP Board in Denver and the examiners want to see.

2. In deciding upon the best method of study, classroom education or self-study, you need to be honest with yourself. Some factors for consideration are:
   A. Finding sufficient time in your busy schedule to set aside without distractions.

B. Finding sufficient energy to study and absorb the materials in more than your short-term memory.

C. Having access to a professional support structure (mentor, etc.) to assist you if the course demands exceed your ability to comprehend particular concepts. If you cannot set aside time to really study without having to send your spouse to the movies, if you have children at home who demand attention, or if you are not currently in the business and have no mentor or support structure to assist you, I would recommend you take a classroom course.

3. Take a review class before the comprehensive exam—knowing the topic isn't always enough. Furthermore, you will be equally tested on the "first" thing you ever learned, as well as the "last and most recent" thing you learned, so it's good to train for the examination, just as many candidates train for the CPA exam and the bar. As the passing ratios show, many are unprepared for the sheer volume of knowledge they will need to impart over the two days.

When you're actually sitting for the two day comprehensive exam, consider this advice from Jon Lacy, CFP® with Lane Dickson & Lacy, LLC and a member of the UC Davis sponsored CFP® Certification Exam Review Course team.

"The CFP® Certification Exam is almost as much about Time Management as knowing the subject matter," suggests Jon. "You'll want to decide on a testing system that works for you." Here's a list of Jon's recommendations:

1. Answer all the questions you absolutely know immediately.
2. Circle the answer (in the test book) for questions you're a little unsure of (marked for review).
3. Draw a box around the question number when you have no clue (marked for review).
4. Read the mini-case questions first before reading the case (helps you know what to look for).
5. The first pass through: never spend more than 2-3 minutes trying to figure out the question. Mark it for review and move on.
6. If you don't know (on second review of the question) Guess and Go. Don't leave any question unanswered.
7. Watch for answers elsewhere. Sometimes a question will be answered in another question much later.
8. Don't let any question get you upset. Kicking yourself because you can't remember a fact or can't calculate a listed answer will only interfere with your ability to focus on the next question. Keep your composure.

Working With a Mentor

Before embarking upon a whole new career, I strongly urge you to line up a mentor to see you through the process. As you enroll in classes, interview with potential employers, study for exams, and shop for software, there will be times when you'll feel like quitting. There will be better times when you need someone to celebrate with—someone who understands exactly what you're going through. A shoulder to cry on, a reminder of your goal, and a heartfelt "way to go!" can bring triumph out of discouragement.

You may even need a "team" of mentors, or mentors for different facets of the journey. A spouse may be an ideal mentor, or someone who turned you on to financial planning in the first place. Maybe it's a business associate who knows you well, or a trusted friend. During my career, I cannot begin to count the number of times I have called upon someone, for whom I held respect and admiration, to ask for advice. Yet I don't remember a single incident where I was rejected. Sometimes the contact has been invaluable.

A number of years ago, I was at a crossroads in my career. Totally stuck. A friend suggested I talk to other financial planners who had practices that looked attractive to me, and see how they got where they were. There were some excellent planners within a reasonable distance from my office. I had heard some of them speak at national conferences and had actually been introduced to a couple of them at local industry functions. But I was certain they wouldn't remember me.

Deciding which of the half dozen planners to call was a problem. There were things about all the practices that appealed to me. I wrote out a short script, promising to stick it out until someone agreed to talk with me, and then dialed the first number. I was surprised to be put through immediately. Identifying myself as a financial planner, I explained that I had heard/met them at the such and such meeting, and hoped they might help me.

"Sure! Let's have lunch one day next week." Not certain I heard correctly, I repeated myself, and was met with, "Why don't you make up a list of what you want to know, and we'll meet at noon." We set the date, and encouraged, I called the next planner on my list. He, too, suggested a meeting, and asked if I was calling anyone else. I told him about my list, and that I was meeting the first planner for lunch. His response? He asked to join us for lunch. I stopped making calls and started my list of questions.

That luncheon turned my practice around. Not only were the two planners eager to tell me about their practices and help me employ some of their strategies, but they were interested in what I was doing in my office. Within six months, we were joined by the others on my list and set up a practice management study group that met quarterly for years.

During the initial months, I honestly felt I was the recipient of the greatest benefit. Before long, it became clear that these "mentors" of mine were deriving just as much good as I was from the collective brainstorming. Had I not made that phone call, asking for help, I've no doubt my practice would still be languishing out there somewhere.

The same holds true while you're working your way through the CFP® certification program. Contacts and friendships you solidify now, will serve you well as your financial planning career progresses.

Finding A Mentor

My naiveté during those early years continues to amuse me. Now, when I need mentoring, I go grab a mentor! I take it very seriously. A mentor should be specific to the subject requiring help. To paraphrase an old adage: if you want to know how to build a watch, you'll do better with a mentor who's a watchmaker than with a mentor who only knows how to tell time. That's why I've developed a list of what I'm looking for in a mentor, and don't just indiscriminately go on and on about my problem to any ear willing to listen. A mentoring relationship is not a one-way proposition.

The mentor must be:	The mentored must be:
Willing to teach	Willing to learn
Knowledgeable in the subject	Needing guidance in the subject
Able to articulate	Able to understand
A resource	A receptacle
Willing to spend time	Willing to take time
Caring	Appreciative
Approachable	Courageous
A problem solver	Able to apply solutions
Trustworthy	Deserving of trust
Passionate	Committed

When I'm seeking a mentor, I adhere to the following checklist:

- ❑ Define, specifically, the topic requiring a mentor
  - o Purpose
  - o Time frame
  - o Desired result
  - o Initial questions
  - o Outline or flowchart of anticipated project/goal

- ❑ Determine where/how mentors on this topic will most likely be found
  - o Industry
  - o Geographic area
  - o Preferred method for initial contact
    - ❑ Mail
    - ❑ Phone
    - ❑ E-mail
  - o Contact information

- ❑ Research potential mentors
    - o Current contacts
    - o Resources of current contacts
    - o Current organizational contacts
    - o Speakers
    - o Writers
    - o Internet
    - o Phone book

- ❑ Develop short list of mentors who appear to be compatible
    - o Name
    - o Contact information
    - o Reference source
    - o Results of contact

- ❑ Contact information and results
    - o Contact potential mentor
    - o Notes of initial contact conversation
    - o Entry into database (for current or future topics)
    - o Decision: affirm or reject agreement for current project

- ❑ Organize place and time to enter into agreement

When the Financial Planning Interactive discussion boards first appeared, I went there in need of support as my solo practice evolved. It was wonderful how forthcoming other planners were with ideas and recommendations. Sometimes I would dare to correspond directly with a poster to thank them for an answer and/or request additional information. Eventually, as I gained experience and expertise in my field, the roles began to reverse.

One day I realized many of the same questions were being posted again and again by people new to the boards. I knew a great deal about getting started in financial planning, and it became obvious to me that I should collect the answers into a book. But I'm a financial planner, not an author. What did I know about bringing a book to life? Nothing. Time to grab a mentor!

After whipping out my checklists, it was a short path to Bob Veres. In the financial planning profession, he is considered by many to be a visionary. He writes for many related publications and seems to have his finger on cutting edge trends. He obviously knows how to write, gets published all over the place, is respected in the business, and appears to know everyone!

Oh, sure. Like I could just pick up the phone and give him a call. He probably doesn't have anything better to do than talk to me! So I chickened out and e-mailed him. That way he could respond in his own time—if he wanted to respond at all. There was no way for him to know that he had already been my mentor for years. I was flabbergasted when he responded in hours. Not only did he respond, but actually encouraged me; told me my book was long overdue, and asked for a copy of my premise. Before long, names of possible publishers showed up in my inbox.

He volunteered (I didn't even have to ask!) to edit the first chapter I wrote and returned it to me with invaluable notations. He suggested I talk with this guy and that gal and include a chapter on thus and so. When I was bogged down and discouraged because I didn't have a committed publisher after a few months, he gave me a swift kick and told me to keep writing. Soon after, I discovered the world of ePublishing, and it was obvious that my book must be an eBook! Changes are rampant in the financial planning profession, and if I were to publish the traditional way, my book would be outdated before it ever hit the street!

Suddenly I had a publisher, a format, a date, and access to Amazon! And contact with my mentor was more vital than ever! The hardest part is not abusing the relationship. Out of fear, I want to turn to Bob at every juncture. But I've been pretty careful to bother him with only what's really important. There is nothing in this for him except my appreciation. Yet, he makes me feel accountable in some way and that gets me through the next page…the next chapter. When there is a real problem, I know he will be there to guide me. It's not easy to contact someone you hold in high esteem and just come right out and ask them to help you work through a problem.

A frequent poster on the Financial Planning Interactive discussion boards is Kay Conheady, a fourteen-year veteran of the Information Technology industry, who decided to be a financial planner in her next life. She held on to her four-day-a-week day job to pay the bills while she worked through the CFP® certification material from the College for Financial Planning. The neat thing about Kay is the way she jumps onto the website and posts whatever is on her mind at the time. She's not frivolous. Her questions are thought-provoking and well articulated.

It's the answers Kay receives that never fail to amaze me. She gets information and resource material from respondents with different areas of expertise. When she opened the door to her practice, she was already working with a terrific network of financial planning expertise. Kay already knows who to call upon when she needs help, be it in insurance, marketing, or finding the best college funding plan. She reminded me, tongue-in-cheek, that she also learned whom **not** to call.

"One of the other very important things I'm learning by posting and following the FPi Getting Started forum (and others) is what the *hot buttons* and controversies are out there and how to present myself when I broach touchy subjects," explained Kay. "For me, it is much easier, psychologically speaking, to bare my inexperienced soul online rather than face-to-face!"

The Residency Program

Alfred E. Hockwalt, then Director of Career Development for the Financial Planning Association invited me to the UCLA Lake Arrowhead Conference Center in October 2000 to observe first hand the much-touted FPA Residency Program[40].

---

[40] http://www.fpanet.org/EventsConferences/ResidencyProgram/

What an eye-opener! I walked into the main lodge to see what appeared to be a darned good stage production involving a couple in their fifties arguing over some retirement issues while their financial planner tried getting to the heart of the matter. The audience consisted of eighteen rapt attendees and half-a-dozen industry folk, most of whom I recognized. Occasionally, giggles or applause would burst from the group, and note taking on laptops and yellow pads was fast and furious.

The "actors" turned out to be Linda Barlow, CFP® and Dave Bergmann, CFP®, EA, CLU, ChFC, part of the extraordinary faculty transformed into case study characters. When the brief presentation ended, I followed Linda and a third of the audience out across the snow to a cozy cabin where the group nibbled on snacks and hashed over the impact of new information gleaned from the skit.

During lunch with Al, I was impressed with the enthusiasm and the diversity in age, experience, and occupational background in the room. Nearly everyone had recently passed the certification exam, and was in various stages of setting up a practice or looking for a position in the profession.

Tim Bennett, who passed the CFP® certification exam fourteen months after enrolling in the CFP® certification program at NYU, was one of the residents at the session I attended. Here is what Tim had to say about his week in California:

The FPA Residency Program

By Tim Bennett

I have always thought that the CFP® certification program taught at most colleges lacked a final class that covered two very important topics: how to do comprehensive financial plans and how to earn a living as a financial planner. So, imagine my surprise when I received a brochure about the FPA Residency Program that promised to teach that and more. It sounded too good to be true so I contacted several former residents (as the participants are called) to find out what they had to say. Every single one had glowing praise for the program. Veronica Hart insisted, "It was the best money I've ever spent on my career." Jeff Cedarholm added, "By learning tried and true methods from experienced mentors, my trial and error time has been cut down by years." And Deena Katz, one of the most respected financial planners in the country, told me that she has paid for all of her financial planners to attend. In fact, she was so pleased with what they learned there that she would probably send any new planners that she hires to the Residency Program as well.

After receiving so many wonderful recommendations, the only question I still had was which of the three Residency Programs to attend. My options were Bryn Mawr, PA, in the spring, Denver, CO, in the summer and Lake Arrowhead, CA, in the fall. Laura Tarbox, the chair of Lake Arrowhead's program, persuaded me to attend the program in California by insisting that the beautiful location in the San Bernardino Mountains was well worth the trip. Of course, it didn't hurt that Tarbox had been recently named by *Worth* magazine as one of the

300 best financial advisors in the country, and I wanted to find out how she became so successful.

It was with great anticipation that I arrived at the FPA Residency Program in Lake Arrowhead, CA. Tarbox was right. It certainly was a lovely location. We stayed at the UCLA Conference Center, a place so popular that it is booked up a year in advance. I'd heard that the Denver program had rather plain accommodations, so I was surprised by how nice our rooms and the meeting areas were. I was also looking forward to taking a dip in Lake Arrowhead. Unfortunately, because of the Residency Program's long hours, I never did make it to the lake.

The Residency Program is a very intensive week-long boot camp that teaches new planners how to take the technical knowledge they learned in the classroom and use it in real life situations. The main emphasis is on three case studies, based on a couple at three different stages of their life. The couple is played by two of the mentors who try to make it very challenging and interesting at the same time. Since the case studies we used at Lake Arrowhead included, among other things, a Russian ballet dancer stepfather, an alcoholic son, and a toilet seat manufacturing company, we didn't know whether to laugh or cry. We ended up doing a little of both. We received less and less assistance from the mentors as the week progressed. We did the third case study almost entirely on our own. The progress we made in one week was amazing. On the first case study, we made the mistake of focusing too much on number crunching. By the third case study, we concentrated less on the financial planning minutiae and more on the clients' feelings, goals, and objectives. "The purpose of the FPA Residency Program is to teach you how to think and feel like a CFP® practitioner," explained Ben Coombs, one of the mentors.

In between case studies, the mentors taught general sessions on gathering client data, explaining difficult financial topics in a way that clients can understand, and managing client expectations. In the evening, we broke up into smaller groups for rap sessions. Each group chose which topic they would like to discuss in greater detail. Some of the topics were fee-only vs. commission; starting your own financial planning business; the pros and cons of various financial planning software; and marketing. The final evening included one-on-one sessions where each resident got to pick the brains of three mentors of their choice. Much to the amusement of the mentors, I had brought a long list of questions with me to the Residency Program specifically for the one-on-one sessions. After they stopped laughing, however, the mentors gladly answered my questions.

The Residency Program taught me many important things. Here are just a few. I learned to listen carefully to clients, not only to what they said, but also to what they really meant. I also learned that clients want you to use words they can understand. I was eager to impress clients with my knowledge of Q-TIPs, standard deviation, and deferred contingent sales loads. Since I was confusing clients more than helping them, I figured out how to translate financial jargon into plain English. By the end of the week, I had also gained a great deal of confidence. I figured that if I could survive this boot camp, then most real clients would seem easy in comparison.

The program was a success due to the hard work and dedication of the mentors. Each one was an experienced CFP® certificant. Laura Tarbox, the chair of the Lake Arrowhead

Residency Program, is so successful that she can afford to regularly turn away prospective clients with $500,000 to invest. Helping her lead the program was Ben Coombs, one of the original CFP® professional's from the class of 1973. Coombs was instrumental in starting the FPA Residency Program (then known as the ICFP Residency Program) in 1985 when he was president of the Institute of Certified Financial Planners. After a ten-year hiatus due to lack of funds, the program was revived in 1998 with Coombs' help and sponsorship by TIAA-CREF. The other mentors were two successful sole practitioners, Linda Barlow and David Bergmann, and Jeff Lambert, a national board member of the FPA. Since the mentors all had different backgrounds and specialties, they were able to give us a wide variety of viewpoints.

The cost of the 2011 Residency Program was $2900 for FPA members; and $2600 for early registrants. The cost includes tuition, room and board. While I initially thought it was expensive, I quickly realized that 60 hours of instruction from financial planners who usually charge an average of $200 to $250 per hour was a bargain.

The program counts as three months of financial planning experience towards the CFP® certification. One creative resident thought that he could attend all three Residency Programs and receive nine months experience. Unfortunately, it doesn't work like that. Three months experience is the most you can get. In order to attend, you must complete the CFP® certification program required to sit for the CFP® certification exam. If you have a designation such as a CPA or ChFC that exempts you from taking the CFP® certification program, you are required to pass the CFP® certification exam. My fellow residents were a very diverse group. I thought that most of them would be in their twenties, but their ages ranged from 25 to 55. They included attorneys, accountants, a teacher, and even a doctor who wanted to work in the ER at night and do financial planning during the day. (He didn't mention when he planned to sleep). There were also several experienced investment advisors and insurance agents interested in making the transition to comprehensive financial planning. No matter what their background, however, they all had one thing in common: they were very enthusiastic about becoming financial planners.

The benefits of the Residency Program didn't stop when it was over. Since then, I have gone over my notes from the program several times, each time learning something new. I have also kept in touch with a few of the other residents so that we can bounce ideas off each other.

It's too early to tell how successful the residents of the recent programs will be, but Charles Foster, a resident at the first program in 1985, has been named by *Worth* magazine as one of the best financial advisors in the country every year since 1996. In fact, he thinks so highly of the Residency Program that he has been a mentor at the Denver program for the last three years.

Since the Residency Program originated in Denver, it is the best known of the three locations and sometimes sells out several months in advance. Because the other two programs started more recently, they often have openings available at the last minute. However, the accommodations and food in Lake Arrowhead and Bryn Mawr are superior to Denver, so it's just a matter of time before the word gets around and they sell out too. The material taught is identical in all three locations.

The FPA Residency Program surpassed all my expectations. I learned more about "real world" financial planning in one week at the Residency Program than I did in two years studying for the CFP® certification exam. At the beginning of the program, Ben Coombs promised, "The mentors are going to give you some street smarts." They certainly did. If you're serious about becoming a successful financial planner, I strongly recommend that you find the time and money to get there.

***

A few weeks after my visit to Lake Arrowhead, Linda Barlow shared some of the evaluation comments with me. On a scale of 1 – 5, the only number I saw was 5. Considering my brief encounter with the group, I'd have to concur. If you want to get a jump-start on your career, get thee to a Residency Program!

For current information on the FPA Residency Program, visit the website at http://www.fpanet.org/EventsConferences/ResidencyProgram/. Check back often, since the website is constantly updated.

Looking for an entry level position as a financial planner[41]

Speaking of jump-starting your career, here's where the serious problem lies, and it has little to do with the need for new blood in the financial planning profession. Independent financial planners simply don't feel they can afford to hire help and do not realize the benefits a talented intern can bring.

My own experience, sad to say, was typical, from what my colleagues have told me. Mine was a small, comprehensive, fee-only financial planning practice. For years my clients came solely from referrals, and I did no marketing. I employed a paraplanner who did data-entry, kept the books and ran my home office, and a clerk who came in once a week to file and get out mailings. I managed just under $25 million in assets for my financial planning clients, saw most of them every quarter, and was comfortable with net income. I was not seeking growth.

I felt I was becoming complacent, and needed someone young and aggressive to bring in a new perspective—someone to replace me, as comprehensive planner, and to eventually manage the office in the absence of the out-of-state owner to whom I would sell my practice.

With the help of a business coach, I envisioned this person. I did not spell it out, due to sticky employment issues, but what I had in mind was pretty specific: female, 30-40 years old, CFP® certification, living in close proximity, and willing to work out of my home office. I did no formal advertising but talked to students at conferences (Texas Tech, Virginia, etc.),

---

[41] **FPA Practice Management Center** http://www.fpanet.org/PracticeManagement/. **See Starting Your Practice.**

local networking groups, clients, instructors of CFP® certification programs in the vicinity, and professors at local colleges and universities (there are half a dozen excellent campuses in my area).

Over a two-year period, I interviewed over twenty individuals fitting the description I'd projected. While I met many very nice people, nothing clicked. Either I couldn't see the person working within the market I knew was there, or I couldn't see myself working in the cramped quarters of my home with the person. I made one offer, to a woman who taught economics courses at a local university and had the CFP® certification. She refused the salary I offered. While she had taken the CFP® certification program several years prior, she had never practiced as a financial planner, had minimal computer skills, and no practical experience in a business setting. But I admit, I wasn't aggressively pursuing an employee and could have been more diligent. I put the hiring process on the back burner.

Then, out of the blue one day, I got a call from a student who asked for an appointment to discuss a job. I was preoccupied at the time, set the appointment date, and thought nothing more of it until the young man showed up. I ushered him into my conference room and asked, "Why are you here?" It still amuses me that his response was, "I'm graduating in a couple of months and haven't found a job yet, so my counselor told me to come and talk to you." (One of the professors I had talked with had passed my information on to a finance major.)

The next question I asked him was whether he knew what a financial planner was: his refreshingly candid response, "No." His BA was in business with a minor in finance. I told him to go find out what a financial planner was, and if it interested him, to give me a call the following week. Interview over. He even forgot to leave a resume.

Eight o'clock Monday morning, the phone rang. He asked for another appointment. He came in with practically a term paper written on financial planning, his resume, a list of what he particularly liked about the profession, and a slew of questions about my specific practice. I hired him on the spot, pending salary negotiations, and invited him to lunch with my attorney to draw up an employment agreement. He both graduated from college and celebrated his 21st birthday the week subsequent to my hiring him; he began courses toward the CFP® certification almost immediately.

There was nothing about him that fit the profile I was seeking (nor was he looking for a career in financial services), but we convinced each other. He lived in another county, there was the gender issue, age, and on and on. But it seemed to work, and here's why:

1. Maturity. Though he was only 21 at the time of hire, he possessed a serious, straightforward attitude never acquired by many. I can picture this young man earning the trust and confidence of my clients, and their children.

2. Realistic Outlook. He understood how to separate the "business" of planning (after all, he was a business major!) from the profession itself. He told me he anticipated it would take about five years before he would experience the income and client levels he expected to achieve. He managed to get his degree in three-and-a-half years. We're allowing two years for the CFP® certification program.

3. Initiative. He made a presentation to me, rather than waiting to see what I had to offer. It may sound backward, but, doggone, it's hard to resist being courted! My company had a tremendous amount to offer, but I didn't have to say a thing. He took it upon himself to research my company and me, find out where we stood in the industry, know it was a profession he wanted to be in, consider his fit in my office, and go after the job. So often, students make the mistake of reading the glossy company recruitment brochure and wait for the company to make them an offer.

4. Work Ethic. First appointment, he showed up in a suit and tie, shook hands firmly, and answered questions honestly and directly. I was in slacks and a casual blouse, but he never saw that as a cue to dress down. Next appointment the suit and tie were still there. He asked about dress before coming to work the first day, was never a minute late to work, and when there, the work got done.

5. Foresight. I know he was disappointed with my salary offer. Yet, he looked past the initial period at future rewards and took the time he needed to evaluate and compare options before accepting the position. More important, he discussed his concerns with me so we could start out on the same page, with a goal of working through each chapter together. Salary increases were negotiated at the completion of each CFP® certification course.

6. Eagerness. In the same way he researched the profession, he plowed into everything asked of him with interest and enthusiasm. This is not to say he blundered ahead hit and miss. He presented drafts, made recommendations, accepted criticism willingly, and kept at a task through completion.

A plus I hadn't considered is that my office was computer literate and technology oriented, yet a big block of our time and budget was spent bringing in a computer guy every time there was a glitch. We certainly couldn't afford a full-time computer expert like larger companies and, luckily for me, computer skills were second nature to my new employee, just as they are to most college students who have graduated over the past few years.

My employee was able to show me how he could generate an increase in his income simply by saving me valuable time and money by not having to bring in outside help every time the computer locked up. Once he became familiar with the proprietary programs we used, he could fix things faster than the computer guy, because he knew our unique needs! He kept our website current, and talked tech geek with support when a glitch in our download needed reformatting—or whatever.

NexGen

It was wrought from the irritation young planners with exceptional skills felt when delegated cold calling and clerical tasks while trying to complete the experience requirement which would allow them use of the CFP® marks they had earned. A growing number of students began connecting at FPA meetings and conferences and realized they had common concerns and frustrations. Aaron Coates, CFP® and Michael Kitces, CFP® stepped up to the plate and NexGen was born. At long last, an ivory tower for those entering the profession.

With wonderful foresight, the creators of NexGen based it on three simple principles:

1. Support, advise, and encourage one another in our professional advancement.
2. Promote, foster, and direct programs that aid in passing the baton.
3. Explore issues common to younger planners, and seek means of accentuating the positives and finding resolutions for the negatives.

Wow! This is it! There are conditions, rules, age restrictions and agreements to sign, but there is also a generous affiliate membership for those wishing to join who can't meet all the membership requirements. More details can be found in Appendix F.

Financial Planning Essentials[42]

Without question, one of the best places to encounter resources if you're looking for work as a financial planner is the "Financial Planning Essentials" track during FPA's Annual Conference.

Scott M. Kahan, CFP® is part of the Strategic Team for Career Development for the FPA. He also heads up his own fee-only financial planning firm, Financial Asset Management Corporation, with offices in New York and Florida. He taught at New York University until 1997, is currently on the Kaplan College Advisory Board, and, in his spare time, teaches at Baruch College in their financial planning program.

"Everyone wants to be fee-only, working for an independent firm and making big bucks," Scott told me. "It's like everyone wanting a safe, liquid, high-yielding investment. People want one thing, but reality is something else. The best thing to do is to start out with a good firm, learn the basics, but keep on the lookout for the company you want to end up with. When it's time to make a move, you don't want to burn any bridges!" Scott thinks the FP Essentials can help new planners sort through employment opportunities.

Unlike the Residency Program, which focuses on plan preparation and building client relationships, FP Essentials is all about marketing and building a business. The two go hand-in-hand and are geared for those just starting or with less than two years in the industry.

Internships[43]

Obvious in every other profession but financial planning, working as an intern with an established firm is the best way to discover what it is you want and don't want to do with

---

[42] Check the FPA Annual Conference website for dates. http://www.fpaannualconvention.org/
[43] FPA Career Center: http://careers.fpanet.org/

your career. Until a few years ago, financial planning was so new there were few masters under whom to study. That landscape has changed dramatically with the advent of degree programs in financial planning from highly regarded colleges and universities, public recognition of the CERTIFIED FINANCIAL PLANNER™ designation, and baby boomers seeking help with retirement options.

If I had my 'druthers, Jerry Mason, PhD., ChFC, CFP® would be King of Financial Planners, and his cardinal law would be that all firms must sponsor interns. His 1993 paper on Financial Counselors has never been more pertinent[44]

In the January/February 2000 issue of *Financial Advisory Practice*, Dr. Mason authored an article on internships that should be mandatory reading for every financial planning firm and student. At Texas Tech University, where he co-founded the Center for Financial Responsibility, a minimum of 200 hours of participation in an internship program is required of all Family Financial Planning majors.

Texas Tech has an aggressive internship program, leading to a high percentage of placements at graduation. It's no wonder, when you see what these students have accomplished. Résumés for those seeking internships and entry-level positions can be found on their website.[45] The Family Financial Planning Program at Kansas State University[46] and the Financial Planning Program at Virginia Tech[47] also help students enrolled in their programs obtain employment through online posting of résumés.

In Dr. Mason's opinion, an internship is a logical step between acquiring basic education and applying it in a fulfilling career. Unrealistic expectations on both sides are the main reason the new hire/company relationship doesn't work out in an estimated fifty percent of cases. He compares the internship to a courtship that, with honest communication, may lead to a commitment.

The biggest hurdle, Dr. Mason believes, is the interviewing process. Independent firms often don't know what they're looking for, and that can turn a prospective intern off. Turnover is high, with many young people staying only six to nine months.

Dr. Mason blames the employers, who, he claims, "do stupid things. They don't ask students to produce coursework, such as term papers, financial plans, brochures and workbooks. Another thing they don't do is check references," he continues. "Talk to professors and teachers. Find out if the student comes to class on time. Is the student's attitude positive? Grades aren't usually that important."

Perhaps independent firms will learn one day soon. But, in the meantime, the onus seems to be on the intern or person seeking a position. The jobs are there, but until more hiring firms get up to speed, pay attention to Dr. Mason's unconventional, but vital advice:

---

[44] http://hec.osu.edu/people/shanna/mason.htm
[45] http://www.depts.ttu.edu/pfp/job_bank.php
[46] http://www.ipfp.k-state.edu/
[47] http://www.finance.pamplin.vt.edu/

"Never look for a job. Look for a company with which you may want to be affiliated and interview them. Be prepared. Be professional. Take business cards, plans you've done, résumés, and tell the company what you can do for them. Look at the best four or five offers you receive and compare firms. Once you accept the position, understand that the education continues. Get all the education and training you can. Read every day." Pearls of wisdom from Dr. Mason. Heed them.

Money hasn't yet been mentioned here, and there's good reason for that. It's a taboo subject. Ridiculous, isn't it, that everyone pussyfoots around the compensation issue when the subject is financial planning? It only gets worse later on, when the talk turns to commissions vs. fees.

But here we're talking about interns. My advice to you is to not let the money issue slide. Obviously, you're not going to make a lot of money during an internship, but your employer certainly expects you to be providing a benefit to the company, and you should expect more than a few credit hours in compensation.

Ask for no less than minimum wage, or negotiate a fee based upon an assigned project. If you are unable to provide value equal to at least your cost, then perhaps it is too early to seek an internship. Ask around.

If you are planning on interning just to sit back and watch how things are done, taking up time to have things explained, then you shouldn't be paid anything. If you come with an outline of how you could improve the firm's website, or a proposal for a new marketing plan, or a design for increasing back-office efficiency, then you can negotiate accordingly.

Saundra Davis, MSFP received university credit for her internship and felt the experience well worth it:[48]

Internships

By Saundra Davis, MSFP Golden Gate University

I began searching for internships in my very first semester in the financial planning program at Golden Gate University[49]. I was a mid-life career-changer and I realized that I would have to rapidly gain experience as I worked on the financial planning certificate and master's degree. It seemed that an internship would allow me to obtain academic credit and experience in my fast-paced pursuit of this new career. There was a host of information

---

[48] Saundra completed the CFP® certification coursework with Golden Gate. She worked as a consultant (associate planner) for three veteran planners, providing financial software data entry and case writing services before starting her own fee-only practice in 2006. "Most importantly," says Saundra, "I am very active with two local non-profit agencies (SF EARN and Tax-Aid) in providing financial planning services to the working poor in San Francisco." She can be reached at saundra.davis@sagefinancialsolutions.org.

[49] http://www.ggu.edu/academic_programs/financial_planning

about internships: the FPA National website; my local FPA Chapter had internship postings; and the college career center provided internship listings. After two weeks of searching and two interviews, I realized that the best fit for me would be an internship with a sole practitioner who could benefit from my small business development expertise.

Utilizing all of the resources available at my college, the CFP® Board website and the local FPA (San Francisco) Chapter website, I set out to find a "perfect fit," a sole practitioner who wanted some support in developing financial plans, and who would appreciate some support for administrative task and operational decisions. It was only after three interviews that I came to realize the elusive nature of the "perfect fit." It seemed that many of the sole practitioners had concerns about the amount of time that training a "newbie" would take from their already maxed-out daily schedules, not to mention the uncertainty of sharing the most intimate aspects of a small business to someone you barely know and who may at some point become a competitor. Despite these obstacles, I found the veteran planners to be supportive, informative and gracious in helping me find my place, even if it wasn't with them.

At an event hosted by my school, I met my match. The planner had more than twenty years in the industry and had started her own practice within the last five years. Her work ethic and investment philosophy was consistent with mine and I could see at the outset that she was willing to mentor me in this new profession. One catch—she didn't have an intern position…so, we created one. Together, we assessed her needs and what I needed to learn, and we developed an internship. We agreed that it would be a credit-only internship (3 units for my college), and I would have to pay my own academic expenses. We clearly delineated the number of hours, the work schedule, the responsibilities, and the limitations of the internship.

My academic advisor required a weekly update on what I was learning as it relates to the degree program and a final paper on a specific topic. This requirement forced me to be completely aware of every aspect of the work I was doing, as I needed to describe how the daily activities compared to what I had learned during my coursework. I learned to consider all of the aspects of financial planning for each task, for example, what were the tax implications of opening a particular account for a client? When conducting research, I was sure to look at all available resources before presenting my opinions to my mentor/boss. This exercise forced me to rely on all of the resources I had come to know as part of my academic program. It was clear that my "newbie" enthusiasm was welcomed and encouraged as my mentor/boss provided me with ever-increasing responsibilities and more challenging tasks.

At the end of the twelve week internship, we determined that we wanted to continue to work together, and we set out to create a position that would meet both of our needs. As for the internship, I would have never expected to be a 40-plus-year-old "intern," but it was truly the best experience for me as a career-changer. I learned about the financial planning profession, the obstacles of operating a financial planning practice (auuggh—software), and I became comfortable with not being "the expert," probably the most challenging aspect of being a career-changer.

Some companies are noted for their superior internship programs. Ameriprise (formerly American Express Financial Advisors)[50] and Northwestern Mutual[51] come to mind. Compensation packages for internships are already in place for these behemoth organizations. If you're talking with an independent firm, particularly one that is just awakening to the fact an intern could be of value, you may need to help them structure an appropriate salary.

J. Jeffrey Lambert, CFP®, Director, Personal Financial Planning Certificate Program University of California, Davis Extension, shared with me that the most difficult question he gets from students is one that does not have a neat and tidy answer. Students want to know where they can get a job, what they will do in that position, and how much they will make.

He tells students to:

1. Find out who you are and develop a personal vision and philosophy.
2. Read, listen and learn what others are doing.
3. Network and find a position that permits you to be on a career path that will allow you to fulfill your dreams and reach the heights of your potential.
4. Be patient as you continue to grow and develop the right opportunity for you.

Nevertheless, he is uncomfortable with his answers. Career path development has just recently become a priority for the professional associations. At this point, the financial planning career paths that are well developed are still sales oriented.

Jeff is not alone in his concern. In the last couple of years, FPA has put significant work into developing resources to serve new entrants into the profession. He exclaims, "I am excited for those entering the profession now. With FPA's help, both on a national and local level, it is possible to get much support for the development of your career. It may take initiative, creativity, soul searching and networking, but the resources are there."

One planner trying to create an intern/mentor program is Eileen Freiburger, CFP®, founder of ESF Financial Planning Group[52] in Manhattan Beach, California. Eileen's practice is based on a fee-only, hourly-as-needed model.

Before opening her own RIA, Eileen had been a manager in brokerage companies, Broker/Dealers and banks. Early on, she realized as a sole practitioner, she was missing the training, mentoring and coaching elements she enjoyed as a manager. So, Eileen created a model that enables individuals enrolled in Board-approved CFP® programs to begin assisting her on a project basis with her current cases. She exposes these individuals to her working model and gives them the opportunity to assist with data entry, Web-based software, projects, and general paraplanning work. While the pay is minimal, Eileen's business plan includes giving the candidate the opportunity to "jump start" his or her own practice and learning curve. In addition, she has actively been seeking CFP®s to join her. As you may eventually find in an hourly model, it's difficult to market, give seminars, network, meet with

---

[50] http://www.ameriprise.com/amp/global/careers/careers.asp
[51] http://www.nmfn.com/tn/global--nmfn_home_pg#
[52] www.esfplanning.com **Contact Eileen at** eileen@esfplanning.com

clients, and actually do planning work! Eileen's invited others to come under her umbrella and have a sliding percentage of the cases she handles. For the interns, she wants to give them a taste of what her model offers. She hopes to eventually see more people open their own independent hourly offices, or if a candidate doesn't want to have the financial obligations or market their own company, she has invited some to join her firm. She has high hopes of establishing several branches of ESF Financial Planning Group throughout Southern California. Several interns have left Eileen's practice to accept full-time positions with other firms.

"When someone's had a chance to learn about the industry and see the true day-to-day operations, it usually means they'll be more focused and better committed to the industry as a whole," she said. "I'm a very capable trainer and believe these individuals were probably in a better position to negotiate their initial salaries and incentives based on having a leg-up on understanding the industry, and having true hands-on experience with real training in financial planning software and cases applicable to the financial planning industry."

NAPFA

Future planners who really want to pursue a career devoid of product sales should acquaint themselves with the National Association of Personal Financial Advisors[53]. I asked Warren Mackensen, CFP[®][54] if there were any opportunities for entry-level planners within NAPFA.

"NAPFA has had a mentoring program in existence for some time for new planners who join the organization. A beginning planner is teamed up with a more seasoned planner. NAPFA also conducts a "Basic Training" two-day track at each of its four regional conferences in the fall, which would serve beginning planners well. Beyond that, there are local Study Groups that meet throughout the United States. The Study Groups, many of which meet monthly, are a great resource for beginning planners.

"We were all new planners at one time," jokes Warren. "At each conference, NAPFA ensures that there are sessions for all levels of ability and interest. We strongly foster education at all levels and never forget about the beginning planners. There is a special student rate for people enrolled in a CFP[®] certification program, and NAPFA offers a few scholarships at each conference to help defray students' expenses.

"Many NAPFA members hire interns. Of course, this is highly variable depending upon many factors," explained Warren, "But members have the capability of posting résumés on the NAPFA website."

Check out **NAPFA Genesis**. NAPFA members under the age of 33 are welcome. Their Mission Statement and Purpose are as follows:

---

[53] http://www.napfa.org
[54] Warren Mackensen created the ProTracker System[TM] Practice Management Software (now called Protracker Advantage) for his fee-only practice. http://www.protracker.com/

Mission Statement

NAPFA Genesis seeks to further the fee only financial planning profession for young professionals (under age 33) by being a peer support group for members as they progress through the profession from being a student to an associate to becoming a fee only financial planner. The group shares experiences, expectations, and a place to go through social networks, discussion forums, and conference activities.

Purpose

We seek to create a group for planners up to age 33. NAPFA currently has 133 non-student members in this cohort. Genesis is to be a support system for students who transition from their education, into their first role at a fee-only planning firm, and into their subsequent planning position. Older planners have wisdom but young planners need a peer group in which to ask questions and receive advice in a comfortable and non-intimidating environment. The initial focus will be to provide a user group through the NAPFA website and other social media opportunities. Other short term goals are to provide networking opportunities at various NAPFA conferences and educational content geared toward young planner issues.

Many planners discover the fee-only concept after trial-and-error in the commission-structured world. A future roll of Genesis is to reach out to the student body of various accredited under-graduate and graduate financial planning programs to further educate them on the fee-only concept. NAPFA currently has 45 student members up to age 33. It is expected that by reaching out to various educational programs, we will be able to increase this number of student members, and subsequently the number of NAPFA registered financial advisors and corporate professionals.

If you know of any students or planners that fit the above requirements, feel free to let them know to email NAPFA Genesis at napfagenesis@gmail.com

SUMMARY

1. Enroll in a CFP Board-certified program to learn financial planning principles.

2. Get a mentor.

3. Prepare for the CFP® certification exam and earn the certification.

4. Attend a Residency Program.

5. Discover options and opportunities at a NexGen conference or by attending the Financial Planning Essentials Track at a national or regional FPA or NAPFA conference.

6. Apply for an internship.

7. Begin your new career as a financial planner.

Sounds simple enough. However, the system has serious logistical problems. There is not yet an obvious path leading from Point A to Point B. To me, it all seems backward. The profession is losing an enormous number of highly qualified potential financial planners who are gobbled up in a sales-driven culture foreign to their original intent. Consumers, who need the help of serious financial planning professionals in ever-increasing numbers are the ultimate victims of this travesty.

Other vocations have predetermined career paths, and until the financial planning profession has such, it will never achieve the distinction it deserves.

Jim Barnash, past President of the FPA, wrote what I consider to be a defining article, which first appeared in the August 2005 issue of *Investment Advisor*. He concludes, "FPA has restructured and restaffed to transform our work in career and professional development. But this is a job that will require all who participate in the industry to do their part. I include independent practitioners, major financial services firms, the academic community, the CFP Board, and other membership associations. There will be plenty of opportunities ahead for all who desire to contribute to, shape, and practice in the profession of financial planning."

The CFP Board is working to "help people benefit from competent, professional and ethical financial planning."[55] Dr. Mason was instrumental in creating the Center for Financial Responsibility at Texas Tech. The Financial Planning Association has made great inroads with the Residency and FP Essentials Programs and is developing a National Internship Program. Colleges and universities across the country, and companies like Ameriprise, have responded by providing competitions, scholarships and funding for promising students. NAPFA Genesis and NexGen cater to those entering the profession.

But like the "herding cats" analogy, there is little coordination. Professionals, companies, students and consumers alike stand to benefit from a cohesive effort to bring this industry together. As the financial planning profession matures, the steps to take will become more obvious. Until then, ask questions, check references, find a mentor, put money in the bank, and jump on in!

---

[55] http://www.cfp.net/aboutus/mission.asp

Chapter Three

Who's the Boss?

Whether in a solo shop, fee-only practice, or selling commissioned products for a major Broker/Dealer, financial planners are in business. As you go through the process of deciding where to begin your financial planning career, do not lose sight of the fact that **you** are the boss and, ultimately, **you** are responsible for the success of your business.

The *E-Myth Revisited*[56] is my favorite business book. In it, author Michael Gerber talks about every business owner having three "people" inside: the Entrepreneur, the Technician, and the Manager. The Entrepreneur is the visionary who sees Utopia in all its wonder. The Technician is the worker, focusing on production. The Manager is constantly organizing, keeping things in order. Each of these "people" wants to be the boss.

All three bosses feel they are working for the benefit of the company, yet conflict arises because there isn't one "boss" in charge. No two are willing to relinquish control to the third. While the Entrepreneur is looking toward the future, the Technician is busy doing what needs to be done today, and the Manager just wants everyone to stay in the system where everything is accounted for.

As you approach the time to make a decision regarding those with whom you will be working in your new career, you have a myriad of things to consider. I suggest you start by being selfish. Think about who you are and what you want. You're the boss! In what setting will you thrive?

Leslie Strebel is a business coach to financial advisors, and former senior Certified E-Myth Consultant and fee-based financial planner. She is part-owner of Ultimate Results[57], the coaching arm part of the Strebel Planning Group in Ithica, New York. "Most business owners strive for an efficiently run business that is growing in value while providing excellent service to clients in a pleasant environment with happy employees," she told me. "And plenty of time for the owner to enjoy a balanced life outside of work, of course!

"Yet most small business owners I talk with are only benefiting from very few of these visions," she continued. "They experience long hours, worry about profits, and have little

---

[56] *The E-Myth Revisited: Why Most Small Businesses Don't Work and What to Do About It* by Michael E. Gerber, Harperbusiness, 1995.
[57] http://www.strebelcpa.com/services/businessdevelopment.htm . Leslie can be reached at Leslie@strebelcpa.com.

time for kids. One day, they find they are doing everything, and feel trapped, wondering where the vision has gone!"

I asked Leslie what could be done about this dilemma, and the answer, of course, was to not let it happen in the first place. Someone just entering a new profession is in the perfect position for prevention.

"Determine your Primary Aim," she explained, "before doing anything else. Don't think about other people, or even about your business. Don't confuse your Primary Aim with goals for income, fame, or other tangible things. Just think about you. Think about your core values, beliefs and desires—what you truly want out of life.

"It's an intense process and difficult for many of us, because we're used to caring about others and doing things for them before ourselves. Once you know the attributes of your Primary Aim, formulate it into a short phrase," she said. "Helping you discover what's really important to you is one of the ways E-Myth coaches guide you toward building a successful business. The Primary Aim is just the first step of many in building a business that works, and serves as the foundation upon which everything else is done."

The most focused summary I have heard concerning what to look for as you consider how to begin your career as a financial planner came from Jonathan Guyton, CFP® in an address to attendees at a reception in Boston during the first annual Success Forum, October 2000. He was gracious enough to allow me to reprint it here.

Words of Advice to the Next Generation of Financial Planners

By Jonathan Guyton, CFP®
FPA Career Development Chair

I.   The landscape for careers in financial planning has changed dramatically in the past ten years. As you survey it for your career opportunities:

> ➤ Never forget why you chose to be a financial planner.
> ➤ Associate yourself with a firm that looks like one you would want to refer your mother to.

II.   Financial planners used to have customers who sought information and products. Now, clients seek knowledge and wisdom to help them make a lifetime of sound, fulfilling decisions—an advisory relationship where the financial planning process, coupled with technical knowledge and people skills, provides the tools to help people improve their quality of life.

III.   For those looking to become practitioners, there seem to be two main points of entry to the profession at this time: Revenue Generator and Client Caretaker.

IV.   If you seek to become a Revenue Generator:
> ➤ Look for a firm that demonstrates a commitment to the CFP® mark.

➢ What are their requirements for new advisors to earn the CFP® mark?

➢ What are their expectations of their existing representatives to earn the CFP® mark? What percentages have the CFP® mark now? What percentages are enrolled in the CFP® program?

➢ Do they reimburse CFP® for program and exam fees? If so, after how much production?

➢ How do they demonstrate their commitment to the financial planning process?
   * Number of client relationships per advisor
   * PR message that promotes financial planning to current and future clients
   * Software and data collection tools that facilitate comprehensive planning
   * Percentage of advisors that are FPA members

V.   If you seek to become a Client Caretaker:

➢ You will likely be joining a firm that began with one or two founding principals and has grown to the point where the principals can no longer handle all the clients. Find out what their vision is for the next three to five years. How important will your role be?

➢ What is their philosophy about how value is delivered to clients? Do they utilize the "star system" (where value is provided through a sole advisor) or a team approach (where value provided by several professionals "institutionalizes" the client relationship)? How many clients does each "lead advisor" serve?

➢ How will they demonstrate their willingness to involve you in client meetings? When will this occur? What will your role be when it does? How will they ultimately provide an opportunity to establish relationships with clients that you will one day serve as "lead advisor"?

➢ What are the current owners' hopes/plans to sell the business some day? How do they believe that having you join the firm will increase its value?

➢ Is adequate staff already in place for client service and administrative tasks?

➢ What are the opportunities/expectations for you to be involved in future marketing efforts?

When I first decided to write this book, it was with the notion that after reading *So You Want to Be a Financial Planner*, anyone who wanted to would end up either working for an independent financial planning firm or starting one of their own. After countless hours of research, listening to story after story, attending conferences, and reading myself cross-eyed, I have concluded that I was wrong. Well, maybe not totally wrong, but probably premature.

There does not exist today an obvious and clearly defined route from any other career to that of a financial planner.[58] Huge strides are being made as the Financial Planning Association develops the Residency and FP Essentials Programs, NAPFA reaches out with

---

[58] An exception might be the accountant who earns a designation in financial planning and adds product sales or financial planning to the tax practice.

mentoring opportunities and the schools and universities offering the CFP® curriculum encourage planning firms to accept interns. Nevertheless, there is no clear-cut path.

Building Blocks to a Financial Planning Career

By Michael R. Fuhr

Independent financial planning firms are growing and there are a lot of opportunities for someone entering the financial planning field. The best option is to work for an experienced planner rather than trying to do it yourself from the start. While financial planning courses such as the Certified Financial Planner™ courses provide a broad range of valuable knowledge, there is much more to learn. Experienced planners have advice on how to start a financial planning career; there are many opportunities for learning through mentorship programs and financial planning meetings and conferences.

My advice is the following: **Define** what you want to do as a financial planner; **Find** the right job that fits what you want to do; **Learn** as much as possible, on and off the job; and finally **Re-Define** what you want to do.

Define what you want to do. What do you like about financial planning? Dislike? What type of clients would you like to work with? What size firm would you like to work at? Do you like interacting with people or do you enjoy research? Do you feel you have the ability to recruit clients? These are a few of the important questions that you should answer.

You should also create a rough plan for your future in this business. Think of your three year, five year, and ten year goals. I say rough because the more experience you gain, the more your beliefs, interests, and goals will change.

Find employment at a quality firm that fits with what you defined. "Quality" can mean different things. For example, it can be determined by the knowledge, expertise, and reputation of the potential employer. This is something you are going to have to determine for yourself before, during, and after the interview. What characteristics are you looking for in an employer and a firm? You may find that on paper, a particular firm may not be the type you are looking for, but in person, there are positive qualities and characteristics. The opposite can also happen. In the end, it pays to be open minded and do not pass up a good opportunity.

One size does not fit all. Do you think you would like to work at a small independent firm, where you will be doing a little bit of everything, or a larger independent firm where you may work in a specific area? Each firm is completely different, no matter what type of clients they serve or how many people work at the firm. This gives you more opportunities to find the right job that fits you.

It is important to interview your prospective employer. Some important topics to cover are their investment philosophy; their background – how did they become a financial planner, what motivates them; if they serve a type of client; the software they use; do they offer financial planning or do they only advise on investments; do they offer insurance products or advise on them. By asking these and other questions, you will get a good feel for the employer and firm and ultimately determine if this potential job will be a good fit for you.

Learning at your new job is key. There is a huge learning curve at the beginning, and this is the best time and your best opportunity to absorb as much information as possible. It is the main way you will be able to determine what aspects of financial planning that interest you most. Off the job learning is valuable as well. Spend some time on certain subjects that you either want or need to know more about. Don't rush this stage, as the more time you put into learning, the stronger and broader your foundation of knowledge is, and this will ultimately benefit not only you, but your firm and employer, and their clients.

Re-define what you want to do and your goals. In the beginning, this can change frequently, but the more experience you gain, you will have more solid and realistic goals. The financial planning business is constantly changing; you have keep up and continue to learn. Otherwise, you will be lost in the masses and not be able to attract and retain quality clients; and in the end, client satisfaction is the most important goal.

***

The primary reasons a financial planner new to the profession might want to begin with a Broker/Dealer or insurance company are name recognition, marketing support, and immediate draw. The primary factor that determines future success, however, is the financial planner's fit in the specific office of the selected Broker/Dealer or agency. If you are not comfortable in your environs and enjoy being with those around you day after day, the stress will clobber you before you have a chance to find out if you could otherwise make it.

If you'd like some help, consider FocusPoint Solutions[59] (for fee-based practice) and Turning Point, Inc.'s GoingIndependent.com[60] (for independent Broker/Dealer affiliation).   They will work with you to help formulate a business plan, set up operations, or introduce you to a suitable turnkey program or firm commensurate with your profile. Shop around! Do your own due diligence on these firms and make sure they will meet your needs for an affordable cost before doing business with them.

New Planner Recruiting, LLC

Caleb Brown, MBA, CFP* and Michael Kitces, MSFS, MTAX, CFP®, CLU, ChFC, RHU, REBC, CASL, CWPPTM are a couple of guys you really want to know!   They started a company called New Planner Recruiting, LLC[61] specifically to put students and career changers in touch with firms looking for entry-level planners.

---

[59] http://www.focuspointsolutions.com
[60] http://www.goingindependent.com
[61] http://www.newplannerrecruiting.com/

A graduate of Texas Tech, Caleb found himself being asked time and again if he could find new hires for established firms since "You know all the students." Seeing an opportunity, admitting how difficult the struggle was for him to land his first job, and realizing his passion to help others, he began to consider options.

In 2009, Caleb met Michael, who was working with the same concerns and solutions, having experienced a similar effort to getting started, and the partnership of New Planner Recruiting, LLC was born.

New Planner Recruiting works with 22 year old graduates and 55 year old engineers alike. Anyone who is seeking an entry-level job in financial planning is welcome to contact them. New Planner Recruiting, LLC's fees are paid by the firms recruiting new hires.

Finding the Right Fit

By Frank M. Gleberman, CLU, CFP® [62]
(1938-2005)

There are a lot of two-way streets today, just as there have always been. Those two-way streets (spell 'em o-p-e-n a-n-d h-o-n-e-s-t r-e-l-a-t-i-o-n-s-h-i-p-s) are between practitioner and company, practitioner and client, practitioner and fellow practitioners, company and practitioner's client, etc.

There is no disagreement on the part of yours truly that:

1. What we envision in the beginning is sometimes not the real world down the road.
2. What some insurance or brokerage companies are today may not be what they will become in a few years.
3. WE change and sometimes find another venue will fit our needs better.
4. Some practitioners are far better off answering only to themselves and not an insurance company or brokerage.
5. It is difficult (but not impossible) to obtain training personalized to ourselves rather than personalized to some insurance or brokerage company training executive.
6. Even in the best of worlds, we do not always make the best lifelong choices . . . in marriage, in selecting friends, in selecting investments, or in choosing the best company with which to develop our future practices.

But I certainly WILL reiterate that you should take the time to interview a sufficient number of companies to obtain a very broad view of the profession. Different sizes, different

---

[62] Frank Gleberman, CLU, CFP® enjoyed a long and distinguished career as a financial planner. He was a principle with The Century Benefits Group, Registered Representative of Jefferson Pilot Securities Corporation, and a Registered Investment Advisor with Economic Designs Corporation in Marina Del Rey, California, prior to his death in 2005. See Appendix F for more by Frank.

philosophies and other differences . . . just be sure to not limit your interviews to only one company in each category.

If possible, be sure to look for established financial planners who are looking for an intern or junior partner. I believe you will feel much better about yourself if YOU feel your choice is the RIGHT one. Lord knows, establishing a practice has enough challenges that you don't want to base your early years on a false premise.

Be open and honest with the companies with which you interview. My take is that there are practitioners with most of them who mirror your objectives and with whom you can identify. If you can't find any of those folks in a particular company, then I believe I'd scratch THAT company off my dance card. No matter how good their training, it evidently hasn't been the RIGHT training. If that company won't let you interview practitioners, RUN, don't walk, for the exit door from that interview. They're evidently hiding something.

When you DO find practitioners with whom you strongly identify, that also tells you something. And don't forget to ask them, as has been brought up on this string, "IF there was no penalty or loss in your compensation (commissions, etc.), would you leave this company?" And, "Why?" Those are honest questions that deserve honest answers. Right?

Above all, be true and honest with others. In that way, you're true and honest with yourself. Both ways, you are building a discipline that will also help you be true and honest with your clients.

BROKER/DEALERS[63]

Here's where I should put the A-list of super-special Broker/Dealers in the industry so you will know exactly whose door to knock on to get the *best deal* if you want to be a financial planner. *Best deal* being:

> *Outstanding payout*
> *Incredible technology*
> *Amazing training*
> *Fantastic brand name*
> *Remarkable etceteras*

Uh huh. Have you read the recruiting packages from these firms? Shoot, every last one of them has the most wonderful environment you could ever ask for, including all the bells and whistles, and your life with them will be perfect once you get through the interview maze and your name is on the dotted line.

Well, I had two major problems coming up with any list at all. First, the only people who would talk to me were the recruiters, reiterating the company line. They refused to allow me

---

[63] Most major financial planning publications put together an annual list of Broker/Dealers.

to quote their actual names, in case anything reeked of "not quite as advertised in the brochure." Second, talking to reps from various Broker/Dealers was fun, but I couldn't get their comments past their compliance people, in case readers misconstrued whatever it was they were really trying to say, or show, or not tell.

It doesn't matter what anyone said—or didn't. I've had enough experience, talked to enough people, read enough rhetoric on the discussion boards, and possess enough gut reaction to name some names in spite of it all.

Be aware, every company has a faction that is out to defame them. Every Broker/Dealer of any size has a website set up by disgruntled clients or ex-producers to vent their anger and share their misery. Read it for what it's worth, do your research, and evaluate accordingly.

Ameriprise[64]

Yep. The big guns. Three things about them put them on my short list:

1. They throw money at the Financial Planning Association
2. They wholeheartedly support intern programs
3. They encourage education toward designations like CFP® and ChFC

The fact is, an inordinate amount of beginning financial planners start out with Ameriprise. What surprised me is the number of planners that stay and build a career with them. I've not done a scientific study by any means, but my guess is the number is somewhere between 10 and 20%, and Ameriprise is diligently coming up with ways to increase that, like rolling out their "Platforms" program.

"Now we provide a career choice," an associate vice president with Ameriprise told me. "We use the acronym 'WDYWFY' when talking to recruits. WDYWFY means 'What do you want for yourself?' It's the same question we ask clients!

"We encourage advisors to create plans for themselves as well as their clients," he explained. "When acquiring new advisors, we ask, 'What do you want out of your career?' We offer them a career with a floor, but no ceiling—a solid platform upon which to build an independent practice backed by a great brand and a compliment of services, including transition advice for planners wanting to expand their practices or to retire."

"In another year or so, I'll switch to Platform Two," Alex Bishop, a planner in Charlotte, North Carolina, told me. "I'll pay a monthly fee for the franchise agreement and proprietary software, but have my own practice, called something like 'Bishop & Associates, a division of Ameriprise'."

Alex tried to start his own firm once before but found the biggest obstacle was lack of name recognition. "I'm confident I can go off on my own now," he said. "I've received a fine

---

[64] http://www.ameriprise.com/amp/global/careers/careers.asp On August 1, 2005, American Express Financial Advisors became Ameriprise.

education here, and I'm building a good fee-based business working as an employee on draw-plus commissions."

Jeff Murphy, CUE Financial Group, started his planning career with AMEX (now Ameriprise) after a six-year stint in the military and still keeps up on things there, though he's worked elsewhere for years. "I worked there for about twenty-two months," he recalled, "which included the lengthy and extensive training program."

"I'd live at home if you can for the first year or two for a couple of reasons," he advises. "One, you may need to keep your expenses down, and two, even if you get off to a great start and make a ton of money, you won't have time to do anything except go home and sleep anyway for the first eighteen months! They haven't changed THAT much.

"The first six months, I worked six days a week, at least 55-60 hours per week. For the first seven weeks, I was concentrating on studying for the Series' 7 & 63 and the insurance license, and memorizing the initial meeting presentation—twelve pages, typed, single-spaced, word for word! Saturday was phone calls from 9 A.M. 'til noon; Monday evening was phone calls from 6:30 'til 8:30; and Friday evening we called from 5:30 'til 7:30. Four days per week, there were 'classes' for half of each day on sales techniques or product information. The rest of the time was more phone calling or (hopefully) meeting with prospects.

"I forget the exact timeline, but the first six months or so, I got a ridiculously low salary, like $800 a month. Then I was on commission after that, but they gave a 'draw' of maybe $2,000 per month for twelve months. The worst part was that out of my paycheck (after the first six months), they deducted a ton of expenses: rent for the office, charge for the receptionist and administrative help, phone and long distance, postage on mailings, my computer lease if I didn't buy it (had to be through them), printer, EVERYTHING! On top of all of that, I had to spend about $1200 out of my own pocket on day one before starting any training. That was for the Series' 7 & 63 and insurance license study materials, taking the exams, licensing costs, etc. Sounds bad, doesn't it?

"On the flip side, it was great training. Shortly after I left AMEX, I read an article somewhere that was about 'The Top 20 Companies to Work For...and Then Leave', meaning to take your new skills and go elsewhere. American Express Financial Advisors was on the list.

"I still keep in touch with a guy I started with back in 1993, and he's still there and quite happy. Like everything, it is what you make it. Same with the leads. They are what you make them. You will certainly develop a thick skin calling those leads, but you can make some good money, too. If I was 22-ish, single with no commitments and could live at home, I'd still do it again."

Raymond James Financial Services, Inc.[65]

Claude and I vacationed in Ashland, Oregon one year, and I couldn't help myself from stopping by the local Raymond James office on Main Street. When I walked out an hour later, I was almost ready to apply for a franchise.

These guys really have it together. Robby Harfst and Jeffrey Monosoff, CFP®, are the sort of financial planners I'd feel comfortable sending my sister to. They told me of a recent client who wanted to know if she could afford to accept her company's early retirement offer. "It was a close call," Rob explained, "but we sorted through the complicated paperwork, ran Monte Carlo, and discussed the situation in light of her expectations."

When I asked if they did a complete plan for her, Rob laughed and said, "The cookie-cutter plans of the past are over. Our job is to listen and solve the problem currently facing the client."

They're able to do their job well because of the flexibility Raymond James offers. "Most offices are small, with only one to four reps, and are often family nucleuses with a husband and wife or father and son, plus a few registered assistants," Jeff told me. "Raymond James offers services for many different entities. There is a fee-only division, a group that works with institutions, such as banks, and then there is a boutique group of planners like we are. We do what fits best with the client's particular situation and use the most appropriate compensation method for the job."

"Every Raymond James office is unique," added Rob, who has owned his office since 1988. "There is no commonality. One reason for that is the complete absence of edicts from the home office on how to conduct business. There is no pressure to sell product or charge a certain way.

Raymond James is definitely worth a look, if your goal is to ultimately open an independent office under a Broker/Dealer's umbrella.

Waddell & Reed [66]

In 1983, I started with this firm. They were a bunch of "good ol' boys", but somehow I seem to have a soft spot for them. They're on my list for one reason: They are financial planners.

Really. It's difficult to find a Broker/Dealer who puts financial planning first, but I think Waddell & Reed does. The problem is that they have proprietary products. The W&R Funds are okay, but I really hate the idea of being tied in any way to a prescribed line of products.

Waddell & Reed promises a combination of "education, tools, materials, processes and programs you need to get started right away," according to the online brochure.

---

[65] http://www.rjfs.com/
[66] http://www.waddell.com/

"I was too chicken to start as an independent," says Gayle Johnson, a financial planner in Grand Rapids, Michigan. "Changing careers after nearly sixteen years in the non-profit sector was a big step. I took six months off to research firms in my area, study for licensing, and interview potential Broker/Dealers."

Finally settling on Waddell & Reed because of their emphasis on financial planning and client relationships, Gayle applauds the great training and support she received. "They practice what they preach," she admits. "I had a good experience with them."

Gayle spent a lot of time thinking about what she was leaving behind when she decided, after two and a half years, to seek out an independent firm. I asked her how difficult it was to leave Waddell & Reed.

"They had no non-compete clause in the agreement I signed," she explained, "but all of the mutual fund products I sold were proprietary and couldn't be moved. At the time, all of the insurance products with Waddell & Reed were proprietary as well[67]. Waddell & Reed is an excellent company to represent and my reasons for leaving were not at all due to any lack of satisfaction with my Broker/Dealer. I was motivated by my total dissatisfaction with the "politics" at my local office."

"I'm much happier at **FNIC**[68]," she told me. "I was able to transfer many accounts at NAV. Now I'm compensated by a combination of fee-based planning, commissions on mutual funds and insurance, and am growing my number of wrap accounts. I wanted to be independent from the beginning."

Royal Alliance[69] (A SunAmerica Company)

The goal of this company is "To be the industry's premier Broker/Dealer for independent financial professionals." I like the independent part. In discussions I've had with reps, it sounds like they mean it. Royal Alliance makes my list because of three things:

1. They have brand recognition (SunAmerica)
2. They don't push proprietary products
3. They foster independence

Gary Charlebois owns Pension Portfolios in La Verne, California, a traditional commission-based business selling investment products through Royal Alliance Associates, Inc. I talked with John Colston, an independent contractor with Pension Portfolios, who told me, "Royal

---

[67] Some Broker/Dealers manage their own (proprietary) family of mutual funds and reps are often encouraged to sell those funds to their clients first. When a rep changes Broker/Dealers, money invested in proprietary products would need to be sold if the client were to move accounts to the rep's new firm. This may incur undesirable income tax impact for the client, leaving the client with no choice but to remain with the original Broker/Dealer.

[68] Financial Network Investment Corporation: http://www.fnic.com (an ING company)

[69] http://www.royalalliance.com/

Alliance is committed to maintaining a platform for independents. There are a few proprietary products through the parent company, but absolutely no push to sell or do anything, except follow compliance guidelines.

"Compliance is really the main issue," John insisted. "The New York corporate office conducts compliance audits, and the Managing Executive[70] reports to a Regional Manager in their territory who, in turn, reports to the corporate office. Reporting requirements have tightened up; all applications and trades are submitted online utilizing Vision 2020, Royal Alliance's proprietary Internet-based system. Royal oversees the use of "A", "B" and "C" share mutual funds and other products, such as variable annuities. Compliance is a major topic of discussion at our annual meetings, more than in the past."

When I asked John if Pension Portfolios had considered switching Broker/Dealers, he replied, "No. Royal Alliance offers every type of program anyone could want. Each office can design their own way of doing business as long as they are compliant. We are happy with our commission/fee structure. We have no motivation to change. The same issues probably exist at other independent Broker/Dealers."

Brian Fenn[71], CFP®, CLU, ChFC, who left Royal Alliance to form his own fee-only practice in Charlotte, North Carolina, might disagree. "I was a different breed," he claims. "I was working with Royal Alliance, but compliance became a problem. They wanted me to state on my ADV that I had a 'conflict of interest' because I had a relationship with them. I certainly didn't consider my relationship with them a conflict of interest! But when a 'fee-only' client questioned the compulsory 'securities through Royal Alliance' I had to place on my business card, I began to wonder, why do I need a Broker/Dealer? They weren't set up to handle a practice like mine."

When I asked Brian if he could think of a better way to start out than with a Broker/Dealer, he agreed that, "Until the industry does a better job of working new advisors through the system, beginning with a Broker/Dealer makes sense. "Keep the vision of where you really want to be while getting the skills," he advises. "Work and network, and you'll get there eventually.

"There's a huge need for hourly practices," Brian feels. "I'm thinking of starting a separate division in my corporation just to provide hourly services." This brings us to the next type of working arrangement you might consider:

Others

It would be an impossible task to find information on all the available Broker/Dealers in the country and list the pros and cons of working with them. That's a job for you to do, in any

---

[70] "Managing Executive is Royal Alliance jargon for the Registered Principal who has On-Site Jurisdiction (OSJ). Gary Charlebois is the OSJ. He is required to hold a Series 24 Registered Principal's license.

[71] Brian Fenn owns Carolina Capital Consulting, Inc., a fee-only RIA specializing in doctors and dentists. http://www.3ccc.com

case. Only you will know why you entered this profession, where you feel comfortable working, and what you love doing.

Solicitation from Primerica, WFG/WMA, and agents with other multi-level marketing companies are often the first contact individuals have with "financial planning". I'll go out on a limb here and comment that agents with these companies generally keep to themselves and refrain from participation in the FPA or the rest of the financial planning community in general. Controversy surrounds their business practices.

To help you compare Broker/Dealers, Financial Planning Interactive[72] offers comprehensive analysis on over 62 firms. Rank and sort firms by payouts, revenues and services, or select up to four firms for in-depth comparisons. Most industry magazines also have an annual issue comparing Broker/Dealers

Turnkey Operations

The Garrett Planning Network, Inc.[73]

"When I read about Sheryl Garrett's training program in *Investment Advisor Magazine*[74], I signed up right away and got in on her second training session. It's exactly how I wanted to practice," said Veronica Hart, CFP®, a planner in College Station, Texas. "My business plan flowed straight from Sheryl's model."

As part of their plan to integrate more financial planning into their culture, Merrill Lynch created the position of "Planning Associate" for Veronica. "I went to Merrill with the intent of doing financial planning, and that's what I did," she claims. "They are really trying, and they do encourage reps to get their CFP® certification, but they have a very big boat to turn around," she said. When Veronica became pregnant with her second child and the doctor told her she had to reduce the stress she was under, she took the opportunity to leave. "Merrill has plenty of resources to devote to training, compliance, etc. If I ever made an error, Merrill Lynch made it right. Period. But I wanted to do financial planning, and I could see the Merrill managers weren't excited about it." She left after more than five years.

"This was a difficult financial change for me, but I was prepared, because I'd been thinking about it for years. I wanted to focus more on relationships and less on transactions and production," she said. "The difference is like night and day. There is no comparison! My time is flexible. Sheryl has provided me with all the tools she uses, which has saved me hundreds of hours. The model works really well for most Americans. It's how they're used to paying for services. They understand, accept and appreciate an hourly rate."

Dan O'Leary, CFP®, has been a commissioned financial planner to the middle class for over twenty years. He credits Sheryl's Network with turning his business around. "When I

---

[72] http://www.financial-planning.com/bd_scorecard/
[73] http://www.garrettplanningnetwork.com/
[74] http://www.advisorone.com/investment-advisor

started," he says, "my marketing plan was 'anyone with any money who could fog a mirror' was a potential client. Today, that approach is a recipe for disaster!"

He feels that the market for fee-only or fee-based services to middle income clients is enormous. Dan urges you to "Find out for yourself. Open the yellow pages and call every listing under 'Financial Planning'. Pose a question, such as, 'I just became eligible for my company 401(k) and would like help selecting investment options. What do you charge for this service?' I'll bet less than ten percent will be willing to help, and they don't advertise that service. Sheryl offers a 'soup to nuts' business system," Dan continues. "You don't have to reinvent the wheel. You can come home after the training and be on-track."

The Garrett Planning Network, Inc.

By Angie Herbers [75]

The Garrett Planning Network, Inc., founded by Sheryl Garrett, CFP®, in July 2000, is a group of like-minded financial planning professionals who are dedicated to offering Fee-Only Hourly services to people from all walks of life and income levels. Our services are geared toward Middle Americans, do-it-yourselfers, and consumers desiring periodic advice. Membership in The Garrett Planning Network offers financial planning professionals a complete turnkey business model, coupled with ongoing training and support designed to help them reach and serve a huge, untapped market. Members of the network receive a comprehensive set of practice management and marketing tools—proven strategies to manage a Fee-Only Hourly business.

I work alongside Sheryl Garrett to help financial planning professionals decide if Fee-Only Hourly financial planning is the right fit for them. We work directly with established practitioners who wish to either incorporate Fee-Only Hourly planning into their existing Fee-Only practices or transition their existing commission- or fee-based practices to successful Fee-Only Hourly practices. We also help new planners who wish to establish their own Fee-Only Hourly practices. The Garrett Planning Network's unique three-pronged system of turnkey materials, comprehensive training and ongoing support helps members not only streamline their start-up process but also maximize their success over time.

The Comprehensive Training Program offered is a three-day event conducted at our headquarters in Shawnee, KS. It is designed to help members get a successful start. Directed by Sheryl Garrett personally, this program walks members step-by-step through the workflow process. It clearly demonstrates our systems and efficiencies, and provides valuable coaching and information on "best practices" for a Fee-Only Hourly planner. We learn how to use the recommended software programs. We discuss practice management issues such as marketing, compliance, and how to efficiently track and bill our time. We

---

[75] Angie has left The Garrett Planning Network, Inc. to begin her own business of helping financial planning professionals hire, recruit and retain next generation talent. Read more about her in Chapter 7. www.FinancialAdvisorResource.com

observe mock client meetings and role-play how best to introduce ourselves in business settings. We learn how to secure client engagements, and discuss ways to present our financial plans and/or analysis to clients so that the client wants to refer friends and return for additional services. Our marketing consultant spends an entire afternoon with the group to answer questions on creating effective collateral materials, websites, marketing plans and more. We discuss how to work with the media and develop press partnerships.

The Garrett Planning Network's "Pathways to Success Retreat" is our annual meeting, aimed at bringing the entire membership together. We offer a variety of educational tracks addressing popular financial planning and practice management topics. This Members-Only retreat is included, tuition free, as a benefit of membership in The Garrett Planning Network, Inc. The retreat offers members the opportunity to grow their practices and gain valuable insights from keynote speakers and retreat sponsors. Most importantly, perhaps, the retreat gives members the opportunity to share ideas and resources in both formal and informal settings. We discuss what works in all areas of promoting and managing their practices. We are a motivated and generous group filled with highly accomplished professionals who enjoy sharing their insights with other like-minded practitioners.

Cambridge Financial Advisors, LLC[76]

Margaret Opsata, a freelance finance writer, interviewed Bert Whitehead, MBA, JD, founder of Cambridge Financial Advisors, LLC for *Financial Advisor Magazine* in 2000. Cambridge advisors are compensated by a retainer, which includes tax preparation and amending previous returns. I was intrigued by the operation, and was invited to meet Bert and spend a few days with him and several of his advisors.

One of the Cambridge advisors is Robert J. Schumann, MBA, CFP®, who compared the system with Sheryl's network:

"Last week I had a prospect who got my name and the name of a local member of the Garrett Planning Network (GPN) from the NAPFA website. The prospect followed NAPFA's advice and interviewed us both. The family was a typical middle-income household with gross income of around $65,000. Husband and wife were young school teachers (he full-time, she part-time) with a small child. Their household income was about $65,000. The Cambridge fee was around $5000. The GPN fee was $1500. After studying both offers, the family chose the Cambridge system. Why did they decide to spend $5000 instead of $1500? I believe they decided based on 'value' rather than 'price'.

"The Cambridge system is comprehensive, holistic, and focuses on taxes. I took three hours to study the family's tax returns from 1998-2000. The Cambridge retainer included amending previous tax returns for numerous errors. The total projected refund, including interest, on the three amended returns was over $3000: $5000 - 3000 = $2000 net fee.

"Now let's compare what else the family got for their $5000, in addition to more than $3000 in tax refunds. The Cambridge retainer included tax preparation, amended returns, tax

[76] http://www.cambridgeadvisors.com/

planning, portfolio review, asset allocation, cash flow analysis, budget, record keeping, insurance review, goal setting, estate planning, investment strategy, investment implementation, and year-end tax planning. Included in the price were simple wills, powers of attorney for health care, and living wills. The GPN retainer offered a limited eight hours of advice in three to four appointments. The Cambridge retainer was open-ended with unlimited appointments, telephone calls and follow-up questions.

"A limited retainer is not comprehensive, holistic financial planning. It's modular financial planning similar to that offered by insurance agents and brokers. In my opinion, Sheryl Garrett's greatest contribution is that she has made modular financial planning available to the masses on a fee-only, hourly basis. She has eliminated the conflict of interest created by a compensation system based on product sales/commissions.

"While fee-only, hourly financial planning is a great and much needed service, I believe my Middle America school teachers suggest that in the end, the market will choose the Cambridge system or variations of it, because it has five inherent advantages:

1) Includes tax preparation
2) Includes wills and advanced medical directives
3) It's comprehensive and holistic
4) It's an open retainer
5) Flat-fee retainer using value based pricing versus an hourly fee

"Taxes are the 'elephant in the kitchen' for most of Middle America. There is great value in getting the elephant out of the kitchen. The more complex the code becomes, the more that becomes true. We amend about 60% of all returns that come to us. For the 40% who don't need amended returns, we offer a limited retainer that is very similar to the standard GPN retainer.

"That's not to say the Cambridge system is perfect. The biggest threat to the Cambridge system is the proposal for a flat tax. The biggest weakness that I see in the Cambridge system is the time spent studying the old tax returns of the 40% who don't need amending. The second biggest weakness is the time and experience it takes to become proficient at reviewing tax returns.

"One could also argue that one system is not better than the other, because each meets the needs of different segments of Middle America. If we differentiate the market into price vs. value preferences and modular vs. comprehensive service needs, it would appear that both systems fit needs. I personally believe that the demand for fee-only financial planning is so great that advisors using either system will prosper. Meanwhile, by focusing on taxes, Cambridge has made comprehensive, fee-only financial planning affordable to most Middle Americans."

The Alliance of Cambridge Advisors

By Ed Fulbright, CPA, PFS

The Mission of the Alliance of Cambridge Advisors is to create, grow and support a thriving professional community of like-minded fee-only financial advisors who share and leverage their knowledge, resources, and experience, and who are recognized as being at the forefront of holistic financial planning for the benefit of their clients. We have all received training on the Cambridge System and are free to alter it to suit our individual practices.

The system focuses on the Tax Planning & Preparation, Estate Planning, Simple Will Preparation, Record Keeping/Cash Flow, Portfolio Analysis/Investment Strategy & Implementation, Retirement Planning, Insurance, Goal Setting/Life Planning, Marketing, Preliminary Appointment/Presentation Appointment, Limited Retainers, Administrative Issues and Supplemental Materials (ADV preparation, choosing a custodian, complementary programs like NAPFA's Basic Training and FOSTER, etc). It is not a planning by the pound system. It is a recommendation and implementation system at your client's speed. It is a very personal financial planning system.

Our clients are people who cannot afford to make mistakes. These clients include people who have up to $5 to $10 million in assets. Most planning systems focus on the rate of return of your portfolio. It is not an AUM (assets under management) fee system but a retainer fee based upon the client's net worth, income and complexity.

The Cambridge System focuses on helping clients relate to the ten most important factors to becoming and staying financially independent by knowing "How Much Is Enough":

1) How much money do you make? 2) How much do you save? 3) How much debt do you have? 4) Are you properly housed? 5) Is your house properly leveraged? 6) How stable is your primary relationship? 7) How much risk are you taking outside your portfolio? 8) How is your health? 9) How much tax do you pay? 10) Finally, what is the return on your investments?

During the first year, you are provided a coach/mentor to help you get around the barriers you discover.

I joined Cambridge Advisors five years ago for the following reasons:

It is a proven and validated system.

It includes areas of concern that you can control. You can influence rate of return through asset allocation, but you cannot control it in the short run. You can control how much they save and pay in taxes.

It saved me from paying the high price for unproven education, which could be higher than the first year fee. Mistakes or a lack of business has its cost, too.

A network of advisors with different areas of expertise to assist you with problems or questions.

It allows me to work with people of all income and net-worth levels.

I stay a Cambridge Advisor for the following reasons:

The great sharing of knowledge of other advisors, including software.

The referrals from other Cambridge Advisors more than paid for my initial fee and renewals.

It continues to save me money by helping me to avoid mistakes and find innovations that improve my business performance.

For more information about the Cambridge System, I would recommend that you visit www.cambridgeadvisors.com/advisors/home and/or purchase Bert Whitehead's Book *Facing Financial Dysfunction* from www.bertwhitehead.com. Bert is the founder of the Cambridge System. You are welcomed to e-mail me at edf@moneyful.com with your questions.

Efficient Market Advisors, LLC[77]

Herb W. Morgan is CEO of Efficient Market Advisors, LLC, an asset management firm in San Diego, California, that started operations in 2004. When I asked him to tell me about the company, he responded with the following:

"My company offers a Turnkey Third Party Asset Management Program (Efficient Market Portfolios) designed for advisors who fancy themselves more as Financial Planners than Money Managers.

"For a new advisor to get into the money management business, they need quite a few things:

1. The ability to manage money. I think that a little knowledge is dangerous here, and I think the vast majority of new advisors unintentionally give their clients a bad experience for the first few years.

2. Highly technical performance measurement and reporting software such as Advent. While this is expensive in $ terms to buy, the real 'cost' is in running it. Doing the daily downloads, reconciliation, actual portfolio management, etc. Next, the advisor must be able to produce and mail detailed and ACCURATE performance reports, above and beyond the brokerage account statements provided by a custodian.

---

[77] http://www.efficient-portfolios.com

3.	The ability to produce all the necessary fee billing statements and bill the accounts, deduct the fees and properly account for them.

"It's not that a talented individual couldn't do this; it's just that they can't do it profitably, in my opinion, until they get well north of $50mm under management. Also, the opportunity cost associated with all this operational work costs the new advisor time away from Business Development and, most importantly, from Financial Planning. (The business they are actually in!)

"So what do we do?

"Once an advisor (RIA) has signed a simple two-page agreement with us, they are given a username and password for our site. This allows them to go online and create an unlimited number of Investment Policy Statements for their clients. (I don't think anyone should ever allow a money manager to manage their money without one!)

"All potential clients take our risk-assessment profile. Our proprietary risk scoring mechanism assigns each client to one of fifteen model portfolios. Our minimum investment is $50,000.

"The way we actually manage money is by using a low-cost, tax-efficient ETF to represent each asset class. Client accounts are reviewed quarterly to determine if the account has moved a statistically significant amount away from its model. If it has, we rebalance it. If not, we just leave it alone. At the end of the year, all taxable accounts are reviewed for tax-loss harvesting (swap opportunities).

"Clients Receive:
Portfolio Management, Monitoring, and Rebalancing
24/7 online account access, including on-demand asset allocation, gain/loss,
	and performance reporting
Quarterly paper performance reports
Monthly paper brokerage statements

"Advisors Receive:
24/7 online ability to generate Investment Policy Statements for Clients
24/7 on-demand performance, asset allocation, tax reporting, and aggregate client
	AUM, activity reports, etc.
24/7 online client activity reporting

"We love working with new advisors! For many, this is a second business line as they come from accounting or insurance backgrounds."

DOING IT YOURSELF: FEE-ONLY ASSET MANAGEMENT

Sheryl Garret and Cambridge Advisors weren't around when I left FNIC to start out on my own, with a vision of charging flat fees or by the hour for projects. Aside from the fact that I nearly starved to death (but it was a different time, and consumers weren't yet ready for fee-only planners like they are today) there was another problem.

I began by offering financial planning for a flat project fee, or consulting at an hourly rate, but did not manage assets. Most people, no matter what the financial issues involved, need to invest. As part of the planning process, I would give general recommendations for their portfolios and send them off to find a broker. If pressed, I would recommend three or four I knew from my days in the registered rep world.

What I found was that I quickly got out of the loop where my client's investments were concerned. In spite of my brilliant work, the reps making the specific investment choices for my clients were playing havoc with my financial plans! Sometimes it would be a year before the client would return for a review, and the rep may have simply rebalanced the portfolio and not taken capital gains into consideration, throwing the tax planning off. Maybe the rep called the client to recommend a change and the client assumed since I had given them the name of the rep I knew about the change. Most of these were little things but things that had the potential for significant impact on long-range planning. I soon realized I needed to have more control over the day-to-day dealings in the portfolio.

It was years before things actually ended up as I originally visualized. It finally came together when I hired an economist to design the portfolios for our clients. We were still the bottom line. We gathered the information, did the financial planning, and told the economist what the objectives were. He designed the portfolio and explained to me why it was good for our client. We made the presentation. Once the client and our team agreed on the portfolio, the account was opened with Schwab, and our staff made the trades. Every day, the prices and holdings were downloaded into our portfolio management system, so when a client called or came in, we had up-to-date information about their investments, including current capital gain information.

We charged an annual retainer, which included financial planning, portfolio design, managed assets up to a specific dollar amount, and allowed the client unlimited phone calls and meetings. It was an ongoing process, and was never abused where our time was concerned. When something came up, the client called, instead of worrying that it'd cost too much. We referred insurance business but remained involved in the process, which was included as part of the retainer. We also offered an hourly rate for consulting, and for those just starting out, we had a special "simplified financial plan" which included a couple hours of our time and cost the client $500.

The way we worked gave the client a choice of payment options appropriate for their needs. We outsourced[78] what we didn't enjoy doing, and referred when additional expertise was required. Since most of our clients were on retainer, our income was fairly predictable.

---

[78] Two places to find ideas and information on outsourcing are: "Virtual Office Tools for a High-Margin Practice" by Joel Bruckenstein and David Drucker and http://www.focuspointsolutions.com

INSTITUTIONAL SERVICES

One of the biggest obstacles facing those wishing to include asset management services in their financial planning practice is finding an institution without a requirement for $25 million or more under management. Schwab, Ameritrade and Fidelity have all upped their minimum for new advisors. That does not mean you can't go to them with a good business plan and get them to relax their policy on a case-by-case basis. Be persistent if you want to work with them, but be aware that there are other options.

TradePMR[79]

There is no minimum account size for clearing through this discount broker. The company was started by a group of advisors unhappy with service they were getting from the big firms. They insist they will have no more than 25 new accounts per advisor, compared with 150 accounts per advisor at Schwab and Ameritrade.

They have an extensive fund list available with no transaction fee. Stock trades are generally less than half Schwab's fee. I talked with Michael Baldwin at the firm and learned they download to major management software. I was impressed with the friendly reception I received from my phone call and the frank answers to my questions.

Scottrade[80]

Another discount broker with no minimum account size is Scottrade. They are looking for advisors with experience a track record, and that's difficult when you're just starting out. But with a strong business plan it's worth a shot.

They pride themselves on their relationship management and communication skills. Their website provides excellent information on all aspects of starting and continuing a business successfully.

At least take a look at their website and see if you can't pick up some tips for your fledging business.

INSURANCE COMPANIES

Northwestern Mutual[81]

Jess M. Swick, CLU, ChFC, AEP[82], has been with the Northwestern Mutual Life Insurance Company for over thirty years, beginning his career while still in college, and has found the occupation to be intensely satisfying.

---

[79] http://www.tradepmr.com
[80] https://advisor.scottrade.com/
[81] http://www.nmfn.com/tn/careers--fr0--fr
[82] The AEP (Accredited Estate Planner) designation is awarded by the National Association of Estate Planners & Councils to professionals who meet stringent experience and education

"Northwestern provides significant resources for its Representatives," Jess told me over breakfast. "They provide incredible tools, software programs, and, of course, products to help people with important planning issues. When I am with a client, I do not think about income. I think about providing a quality service," he said. "If I help my clients get what they want, then I will be appropriately paid." Back to that in a moment.

Jess does personal and business planning and does a darned good job. He's proud to represent the Northwestern Mutual Financial Network, and was eager to show me the company's ten-page detailed data gathering form, which he goes through with every client. "With the fact finder, you gather vital information about the client that directly relates to their financial plans, goals and dreams. Insurance companies have become full service agencies to compete in today's environment," he explained. From the looks of the consumer material he displayed, they are doing a top-notch job of it. The company has invested a significant amount into software, training and other resources for their agents.

Jess loves working with people, and if he's not able to help a new contact, he believes it's either because the timing or the chemistry is not right. His philosophy is that if he meets with enough people, he will solve a lot of problems, which means he will provide a lot of products.

This brings us back to compensation. Jess tells his clients he gets paid in four ways:

1. The satisfaction of knowing he has helped.
2. He receives referrals, indicating they are pleased with his services.
3. Commissions from the sale of products.
4. Referring his clients to other professionals who help them with other services and needs.

Jess is one of those quiet "pillar of the community" types who are always ready with a helping hand. He has coached AYSO for twenty years, serves as President of the Board for OPARC, a non-profit organization dedicated to "enabling people with disabilities to reach their full potential," is on the board of the Claremont Community Foundation, is active in Kiwanis, is Moderator of his church, is on the board of directors for the Financial Representatives Association (7500 members) of the Northwestern Mutual Financial Network, and a 25-year member of the Million Dollar Round Table.[83]

I asked Jess about new people entering the financial services industry, and what sort of person might consider applying to Northwestern Mutual.

"Entrepreneurs make the best candidates. Those who are self-starters, who want to work for themselves and control their own destiny." he responded. "Northwestern has an exceptional training process, both locally and in Milwaukee. Our new applicants are carefully recruited,

---

qualifications, including two graduate-level courses administered by The American College. Learn more about it at http://www.naepc.org
[83]Million Dollar Round Table is an association of primarily insurance-based financial services sales professionals.

and about only 10 out of 100 are offered a contract." Jess continued, "However, turnover is very low. New representatives have to really hustle. The beauty is, you only need to work half days—any twelve hours. But it is worth it. Especially with Northwestern Mutual!"

Met Life

At the FPA Retreat in 2005, I talked with Martin Siesta, CFP®, who was just about to open the doors of his own company, Compass Wealth Management, LLC in New Jersey,[84] after eight years with Met Life. I asked him what it was like doing financial planning at an insurance company. Here's what he told me:

"Prior to working at MetLife, I was providing institutional portfolio management at a large bank. On Wall Street, I saw many people who made large sums of money and who saved very little. Most of them didn't like their job but continued to do it for the money. I saw that they were so unhappy with their jobs that they wound up spending most of their money on self-medicating through spending. My thought was that if I could help these people focus on what was truly important in their lives, it would be a good thing. Given their income, they should be able to pay for it.

"My first step was to find out who would do business and what type of business they would do. I began my own market analysis. I had also saved some money. Based on my analysis and my capital, I felt that I could survive three years and be able to grow my business with a focus on financial planning and long term relationships. I did not have my CFP® designation at that point and would have to get it. I also had no sales experience. I didn't realize it but, for most planners, this is an important skill. Even if you don't do 'product' and you are 'fee-only', you have to communicate the importance and value of planning. Equally importantly, you have to make sure that people implement the plan. How ethical is it to produce a book that is not used?

"Deciding where to work (and who would offer me a job) was the next step. I was not a CFP®. I had no network. FPA did not exist, and I was not aware of its predecessor organizations. I went through the classifieds. There were many firms advertising for financial advisors and unlimited income potential. If you have read them and gone to a few interviews, you know the disappointment that I felt.

"The wirehouses were stock brokers dressed in a new wardrobe. Not that this was bad; I was looking to learn and do financial planning. At one nationally known firm, they offered some compensation but charged you for everything from phones to clerical support. In meeting with them and going to a 'career day,' I felt that I was part of a group where they expected very few people to make it. I would also be required to do it their way. I felt (rightly or wrongly) that I had a viable business plan. I needed a mentor and an organization that could help me implement it. As I didn't have a CFP® designation, it didn't occur to me to apply at a fee-only firm.

---

[84] Martin Siesta can be reached at Compass Wealth Management, 973.763.0766.

"I interviewed at another major insurance company and got the feeling that they were more interested in who I could bring in as clients than any sort of career path. When I interviewed at Met, I got many of the same feelings. I took a screening test that basically said that I was too sensitive to be in the field. I showed the associate manager my business plan. He was very impressed and asked me to meet with the General Manager. It turned out that he was a CFP® designee and truly believed in the planning process. He pointed out that Met would pay for the CFP® training (provided I passed the courses). They had a planning platform, but he emphasized that there was selling involved. While you could charge for plans, primary compensation was from selling. While I had some misgivings about this, I came to realize that even fee-only folks were generally selling 'asset management services.'

"I have been with Met for eight years. What I have found is that, while the firm is important, who your mentor and/or manager is, makes a profound difference. If you don't have any sales experience, you will need it regardless of your compensation method or business model. Join an organization like FPA, so that you can learn to think outside the box. There have been times of extraordinary joy. I am a registered life planner at the Kinder Institute. At a national company sales conference, I gave a presentation on life planning. Over thirty people attended. They got it! There have been difficulties. There are co-workers that are not professional or ethical. There are times that products are not in the best interest of clients. You have to have your touchstones and your 'hearts core' values to help light the path. There are times where you and the company may be on different paths. You need to go back to the values. This journey is not for everyone."

John Hancock[85]

Charles G. McKenna spent twelve years with John Hancock—the last six in management.

"I was part of a small office that had less than thirty planners. Everyone was strongly encouraged to pursue industry designations. In fact, Hancock would reimburse you most of your expenses for the classes if you passed.

"Our regional VP was big on education and training, and he did not like managers splitting cases with reps. My manager never split a case with me and I never split a case with any of my staff unless the lead was totally generated by me. For example, if I had a client from my book of business give me a referral, I would ALWAYS bring a new candidate with me on the appointment. I would do all of the work and show the rep every step of the way what I was doing. I would then give the rep 25% of the case. I would never take a percentage of the reps business that was generated by their leads. Neither would any other manager that I had worked with while I was with the company.

"As a Sales Manager, my compensation was based on overrides of my reps. On first-year reps, I would earn 49% of their base commissions. If that new rep did not last a year, then I was "charged back" a percentage of his stipend salary or training allowance. After the first year, my compensation went to 28% override. After the third year, it was 15%, and after the fourth, it went to 7%, where it stayed.

---

[85] http://www.johnhancock.com/

"My GA would only allow me to bring on one new rep per quarter in each of the years I worked in management. He wanted me to make sure I spent enough time with the rep to teach them. Selling skills was a weekly class. Selling was not the answer but, rather, an emphasis on clearly presenting options to the prospect and helping them select which was most appropriate for them. We could choose from two systems: Financial Profiles or Expert by Sterling Wentworth. Both were great programs for comprehensive planning.

"We encouraged, and required, cold calling for the first quarter of a new rep's career. After that, we insisted that they look to alternative marketing methods.

"Out of the twenty-six people that I recruited, only three are still with Hancock. Another twenty are still in the industry. In my last three years of management, not one of my first year reps earned less than $75,000 FYC. The last two years, all of my first-year reps made over $100,000 in commissions and bonus. Those are very atypical numbers and were part of the reason that I climbed to be among the top ten managers in the company.

"Perhaps ours was a unique office, but I know that the offices near me had similar results. Perhaps it was our regional manager. He even encouraged us to give away our books to our reps.

"Hancock wasn't and isn't perfect; however, it was a great place to start and to learn. Make sure you have a very professional setting in the potential office and that the manager is respected. Ask to see the productions sheets for annual production clubs, and you will get an idea of what is going on there."

Well-qualified and interested people can have very different experiences with the same company, so I encourage you to speak with several individuals before making a decision.

What to ask insurance companies

Rev. Frank J. Szewczyk, MBA, M.Div., a former financial planner with a major insurance company, who currently has a "personal coaching practice helping people create a life worth living," suggests anyone considering an insurance company ask the potential manager these questions:

1) What is your personal ratio between hires and those who are still in the business? Companies have nationwide ratios but you want to know what YOUR manager's retention rate is for one, three, and five years.

2) What type of training will I receive—computer based, video, etc?

3) How long will the manager work with me? (Caution: most managers work with a new agent for a short period and move on to the next recruit.)

4) Will they assign you to a mentor? (This can be critical to your long-term success.)

5) Will they teach you how to prospect and use lead lists, seminars, and other methods besides friends and family?

6) Are they financial planners or financial sales organizations? A needs analysis is different from a full-blown financial plan. Try to determine if the goal of the representative is to sell a financial plan/needs analysis to sell more products or is the goal to give the client a plan for long-term success.

In terms of companies, most have some sort of training program, but, again, it depends on the local manager. For what it is worth, if you are housed out of the main office for the local organization versus a branch, you tend to have access to more training. Obtaining one's CFP® is the best technical training someone can receive.

A Different Approach, from a Related Industry

"My Man in Dallas/Ft. Worth" and I met online through the FPi discussion boards, and became instant friends. Kevin owned a Property & Casualty Agency, representing Nationwide Insurance & Financial. He offered P&C, Life (traditional and variable products), Health and Commercial Insurance. In addition, he had brokerage agreements to secure those insurance products not offered by Nationwide (LTC, Medicare Supplement, etc.) for his clients.

Definitely...*The Road Less Traveled*[86]

By Kevin Michael Lynch, MBA, CFP®, CLU, ChFC, RHU, REBC, CASL, CAP, RFC, CFS, CCS, LTCIS, CSA, CLTC, CFM, FPS

President, K. Lynch & Associates, Inc.
Dallas-Ft. Worth, TX
sav4later@aol.com

My entrance into financial planning has not been like so many of my brethren. I did not come to financial planning from insurance or investments, but, rather, I came to insurance and investments through studying to enter financial planning.

I achieved my college degrees through part-time studies over a fifteen-year period, culminating with my MBA in May 1985. Shortly after graduating at age 34, I discovered the concept of "financial planning" and The College for Financial Planning, Denver, CO. I began my CFP® studies in 1987 and finished them in September 1991.

---

[86] From *The Road Less Traveled: A New Psychology of Love, Traditional Values and Spiritual Growth* by M. Scott Peck, MD.

Beginning in 1991, through an "internship" with The Equitable Life Insurance Society, known today as AXA, I completed my Series 6 and 63 and became licensed for Life and Health as well. At the end of my internship 120 days later, I was not convinced that the general manager of the Houston, TX Equitable office was the person to properly train me for a career change, and I remained in my original career field, Auto Sales Finance. (AKA Ford Motor Credit, GMAC, etc.)

I did continue, however, working with a few friends and colleges over the next few years, providing financial services and basic financial planning under a registered DBA "Per$onal Financial Planning." In 1998, I was presented with an opportunity to make a career change and build a property & casualty insurance agency. My original business plan called for me to build a book of business with 2500 to 3000 policies in force, and then to devote myself to serving those clients as their financial planner. This would mean never having to make a cold call, as I would be calling on clients with whom I already had a relationship.

My carrier, Nationwide Insurance & Financial, had a great "Financed Community Agents" Program and I launched my agency in November 1998. Over the next 44 months, I built my agency to 2800 policies in force and completed additional studies in the field of insurance and financial services. These studies included completing the requirements for and earning the following industry designations:

Chartered Life Underwriter (CLU), Chartered Financial Consultant (ChFC), Registered Health Underwriter (RHU), Registered Employee Benefits Consultant (REBC), and, most recently, Certified Senior Advisor (CSA).

Would I recommend this entree into financial planning for you? Probably not, but it worked for me.

The down side of my plan to become a practicing CFP®: while I do have a book of business that contains about 1400 families, these clients know me first and foremost as their P&C Agent. Making the switch from providing a "commodity" type product to a service, such as financial planning, is not a natural progression for the majority of my current clients.

On the upside, however, what my P&C book of business does provide is a solid base of income from which I can now build a second profit center, under the umbrella of my current incorporated business, K. Lynch & Associates, Inc. With the income stream from my P&C agency, I have the base necessary to begin the process of incorporating Values-Based Financial Planning into my practice. My first prospects will be the 100 to 150 client families within my current book that have the means and the motives necessary to utilize my financial planning services.

From this initial group of clients, I plan to build a stream of referrals and within the next five years have a hundred clients providing a minimum annual fee-based income of $3500 to $5000 each...while retaining ownership, but delegating day to day operating control of my P&C business.

Will this plan work for you? I don't know, but it is the path I am now on and the path upon which I plan on reaching my personal and professional goals. Whatever path you choose, I wish you God Speed and Good Fortune.

What a Difference a Year Makes (2005 update)

In December 2003, my wife and I had a long talk about what I wanted to do with the rest of my life. Having successfully built the P&C Insurance Agency together, the one thing we were sure of was Property & Casualty Insurance was not "it."

As I indicated in my original contribution to Nancy's book, I built a P&C Agency for the sole purpose of having a fertile ground in which to plant seeds for future financial planning clients. My business plan for Nationwide Insurance & Financial plainly stated that I was building the P&C Agency to further my ability to become a fee-based financial planning professional. Initially, my desires along that path were encouraged, and I was assured that it would be possible to reach my goals within the Nationwide Family. Surprise! Once I was ready to branch out and focus on the Life and Financial side, I was told that it would not be possible after all. Why not? The reason (excuse) I was given was Nationwide was not prepared to "supervise" agents with a Series 7 and/or the operation of an RIA. Basically, they made it impossible to do fee-based planning within the Nationwide Insurance system…and as a captive agent, I was not free to set up shop outside the system and retain my agency.

After careful consideration and deliberation, I decided to sell the business on January 31, 2004, and "retire" from Nationwide. Fortunately for me, my age and years of ownership enabled me to qualify for an equity payment upon surrendering the agency to Nationwide Insurance. This gave me the security and confidence to make the move.

In late November, I had begun interviewing with all the prominent financial services companies in the greater Arlington-Ft. Worth, Texas, area, and I left no stone unturned. I interviewed with six major wirehouses and seven major insurance companies. Since I owned my agency and I could always retain ownership, I was basically interviewing them rather than the typical scenario of them interviewing me.

For those of you who have done the interview gauntlet, you know what I experienced. (If you never have, you wouldn't really understand.) When all was said and done, I had thirteen interviews and received eleven job offers. The company I was drawn to initially was A. G. Edwards. Their corporate philosophy was very much in tune with my own. Edwards is known for superior client service and for targeting the upper middle market. They also did not have a client minimum account size. Unfortunately, I failed to pass their employment-screening test, which supposedly foretells the likelihood of a prospective FA passing the NASD Series 7 exam. (FYI…The average passing score in 2003 was a 73. I scored an 86! So much for their screening exam and its reliability!)

The company I eventually selected, after twice "blowing the recruiter off" was Merrill Lynch. Based on their press and their reputation for great training, I felt Merrill Lynch would be an excellent springboard into the financial services arena. The one thing I knew for sure—no one would say, "Merrill who?" Having my last name wouldn't hurt either, as a conversation opener.

My original business plan clearly outlined my intent to focus on insurance-based products and services, and the hiring branch manager encouraged me strongly to pursue that avenue. He in fact commented, "We don't have anyone in our area who knows anything about the insurance side of the industry. You will do great!"

I started at Merrill on February 2, 2004, as a Financial Advisor in training with Merrill Lynch. For the first seventeen weeks, my job was to do nothing but study and pass the NASD Series 7, NASD Series 66 and the Texas State insurance exam. In addition, I was to prepare for my first two 'Assessments'. (Assessments are an internal series of "tests" that an FA must pass in order to be given a "production number" and, thereby, "go live.")

I sat for my NASD Exams and successfully completed them in early April and early May 2004. By June, I was bored out of my mind waiting for my peer group to catch up with me so we could all be scheduled for The Assessments. In the meantime, I used my time to study and prepare for Merrill's internal designation program, The Certified Financial Manager, CFM. This is a pretty decent program that consists of a Part A, heavy doses of the AAMS curriculum from the College for Financial Planning, mixed with Merrill proprietary products and services information, and a Part B, which consists of the Investment Module of the CFP® Designation Program. All Merrill FA's are required to complete this program within twelve months of getting their production number. As it turned out for me, since I already held the CFP® designation, I was exempt from Part B, and I had the program completed before I was even eligible to stand for Assessment. According to my mentor, he had never heard of an FA in Training completing the CFM before receiving a production number.

Also in May of 2004, I received an invitation to a reception for the new president of The American College, Dr. Larry Barton. The invitation was received because I was a graduate of the college, having earned a number of professional designations from them, and I was also a donor to the college, at a level considered worthy of inclusion in the group invited to the reception. Attending this reception would turn out to be a truly serendipitous event. More about that later.

Just a few words about the vaunted training at 'Mother Merrill'. Prior to 2000, Merrill Lynch had an exceptional training program. In addition to initial training within the branch system, new FAs went to Princeton, NJ for two weeks, after earning their Series 7 and Series 66. This training program fell victim to the cost reductions that occurred when the current CEO, Stan O'Neil, took control of the firm. Almost all of the training available at Merrill Lynch these days is provided on a computer system. Although the system is more than adequate, I do not know about you, but CBT is not my favorite method of learning.

From June throughout August, I also "hit the street." While I was not allowed to solicit business, since I did not have a production number, I was allowed to meet with prospective future clients and outline the products and services available through Merrill Lynch. While conducting fact finding interviews with approximately ninety prospective clients, I was filling my pipeline for the day when I would "go live" with my production number. It was during this period that I determined exactly why it is that the vast majority of Merrill FAs do next to no insurance business. I also discovered the concept of "splitting commission" on insurance business, within the company, had two chances of succeeding…slim and not at all!

The compensation systems for the insurance business and the world of wirehouses are not compatible. In the insurance world, the selling agent gets a commission on the sale of a policy and management receives a portion of the commission on the same sale. Using a Long Term Care Insurance Policy as an example, here is the problem:

- If an FA were to sell a GE Policy (or John Hancock) to a client, the street commission in the sale would normally be 60% of first year premium. The commission used by Merrill was 40%.

- The 40% is then placed on a "Grid." The Grid is the method used in the wire house world to pay commissions. The average new FA receives 40% on the Grid. So, by taking the 40% commission for the LTCi policy and subjecting it to the Grid, the selling FA/Agent now received only 40% of 40% of the commission.

- Assuming a standard risk 60-year-old client, a quality policy would have a price tag of approximately $2000. Any licensed Life & Health Agent with a standard sales contract with GE would earn at least 60% commission, or $1200 for the sale. The Merrill FA would receive only $320 for the same sale.

- If you were going to do as I planned to do, originally, and split commissions with a fellow FA for providing the client from his book of business to whom I would sell a policy, we would each earn $160 for our efforts.

Since the average full-time Long Term Care Insurance Agent makes about $65,000 to $80,000 a year, earning 60% commission, how many Merrill Lynch FAs to you think would spend a lot of time going through the sales process typical of a long-term-care insurance policy to earn $160? Go ahead. Guess!

Near the middle of August, it became clear to me that those in my "complex" who were succeeding, were doing so as members of a Team. In addition, there was a reason why these teams spent very little time on insurance products and services. Teams are highly touted at Merrill, and I decided it was time to find me a team.

Why a team? As a Financial Advisor at Merrill Lynch, you are expected to gather $7,000,000 in assets the first twelve months in production and a total of $15,000,000 by the end of your twenty-fourth month. Along the way, quarterly, you have "hurdles" to meet. If you miss a hurdle, you have until the next quarter to make it up. Miss two in a row and you will be asked to "seriously reconsider your career choice". The strength of being on a team is that the team will "assign" you the necessary assets at each of your hurdles to meet the requirement, as long as you are contributing to the team in the manner in which you have been charged.

In very short order, with the sponsorship of my sales manager/mentor, I was interviewed by a prominent team in the complex and offered a position with them. This team had a distinctive niche, concentrating wholly on High Net Worth Clients. Where the average FA at Merrill is chided for pursuing any client with an account potential less than $250,000, the team I joined was in the process of considering raising their minimum to $500,000.

Because of my extensive background in credit and lending, my team wanted me to focus on physicians and the lending and leasing products Merrill Lynch has specifically for this niche market. So, I was back into training, as my team wanted me to focus on physicians and the lending and leasing products Merrill Lynch has specifically for this niche market. After spending the next thirty days mapping out and planning a campaign to "reach out and touch" a group of physicians in the Ft. Worth, Texas, area, I was ready to launch my campaign. Remember, however, that I still had not gone though Assessment and I still did not have my production number.

One important note I would like to make about my Merrill experience concerns something I have stated repeatedly to posters on the Financial-Planning.com "Getting Started" board: It is never the company that will make you successful. It is always a person or persons who care about you and your success that will make it easier for you to succeed. This was true for me at Merrill, and it is true for everyone, everywhere, who succeeds.

My original manager at Merrill Lynch was focused on building his book and building his team. The "care and feeding" of the new FAs he was hiring was totally ignored by this individual. When I changed offices to the office where I was a part of a team, my senior partner was also the branch manager. This lady is one of the finest human beings and sharpest financial services professionals I have ever met in my life. She had the uncanny ability to wear multiple hats, simultaneously, and perform the duties and responsibilities of each without peer.

On a personal level, when it became obvious to her that I was not truly feeling like I was being properly trained and developed in my original office, she embraced my transfer to her office, whether I joined her team or not. Her concern was for the good of Merrill Lynch and my personal well being. She treated everyone in her office as though they were the most important employee in the branch. This is the kind of person you are looking for as a manager in the wirehouse world…or any other world within which you choose to develop your skills and talents.

One more comment about Merrill & their Teams mentality: It is obvious to anyone who carefully looks at Teams to understand why they are favored by Merrill and the other wirehouses. When a client is being served by a team of FAs, and one of them decides to move on to another wirehouse or, more than likely, to an independent arrangement, the client is less likely to go with the FA who is leaving. Since they are used to being served by The Team, and the Team is still at Merrill, they usually stay at Merrill (or whomever), too. And you thought it was so clients could be better served by a wider variety of talent. Right?

Remember the reception back in May for the President of The American College? While at the event, after having been introduced to Dr. Barton, I was in a circle of individuals who began discussing some future plans for the college. A portion of these plans included adding professional staff. I made a mental note of this and a few days later called a friend of mine at the college whom I had known for four years, because I had served as a volunteer fundraiser for the college. She gave me the president's number and I called him. After speaking with him for a few minutes, he asked me to forward a resume, and I did.

A few weeks passed and I received a phone call and a phone interview. It went well. A few weeks later, I received a second call and there were further discussions. These too went well, in my opinion. Then nothing, until early September.

September 1st or 2nd, I received a phone call from The American College, and the party calling me wanted to know if I remained interested in a position at The College. I stated I was and a phone interview was scheduled with President Barton. During this phone interview, it was determined that an in-person interview was in order, at the college, with a number of other management staff. It was set for September 9th. The rest, as they say, is history.

Effective October 1st, 2004, I was named Associate Vice President for Advancement at The American College. President Barton, a tremendously qualified and dynamic leader, calls me his "'poster boy for lifelong learning." My formal education includes three Associate of Applied Science degrees, a Bachelor of Science degree and an MBA. I currently hold six professional designations from The American College, including CLU, ChFC, RHU, REBC and, the newest program at The College, CASL. This past July 2005, I completed the Chartered Advisor in Philanthropy (CAP) program. I have also earned eight other professional designations including the CFP®, RFC, CSA, CSS, LTCIS, CFS, CLTC and the aforementioned CFM. At present, I am completing the LUTC program and the CLF program, both offered by The American College. One of my mottos has always been, "You can never know it all, but you can never know too much."

Why The College? Why leave Merrill Lynch and the potential income and prestige? Why "settle for" an academic institution and limited future earning?

To answer those questions, you need to know two things about me. First, I have had one consistent "secret desire" for my entire adult life: I want to be a college professor when I grow up. Second, I truly have a servant attitude. While I am as fond of the "big bucks" as the next guy, I believe you measure your life by what you give, not by what you get. The old Zig Ziglar truism really is: "You can have anything you want in life if you help enough other people get what they want."

I am not giving up on my desire to earn a terminal degree and teach at the collegiate level. As a matter of fact, being here in the academic environment, I am certain the desire will eventually become overwhelming, and I will therefore take the steps necessary to achieve my life-long goal.

To my way of thinking, if I were to become THE Financial Planner of all Financial Planners, realistically, I could impact the lives of 250 families, tops. By joining The American College and achieving the same level of excellence here as I would have demanded of myself at A. G. Edwards, Merrill Lynch, New York Life, or any other company with whom I would have affiliated, I have the potential to help produce thousands and thousands of ethical, well-educated planners. These planners can then each impact 250 families of their own. My contribution to the good of society will thereby be infinitely magnified.

Could I possibly contribute in a manner more worthwhile?

My original contribution to this book was a play on the words "The Road Less Traveled." I hope what I have added in this edition gives you greater understanding and insight into the profession and what twists and turns your journey may take for you, too.

The Only Constant ... is Change (2007 update)

Where do I begin with the latest chapter in my life, as it relates to the financial services industry? My last update was entitled, "What a difference a year makes..." This update has to be, "The Only Constant is Change."

When last we met, I had just embarked on a new career at The American College, as Associate Vice President for Advancement, an administrator, responsible for alumni fundraising efforts. After spending a year in Bryn Mawr, PA, I found myself with a home in Texas that simply would not sell and a wife of 31 years who was getting as frustrated as I was with living apart. So, in spite of working in a new career I was beginning to love, with regret, I accepted a small severance package from The American College and moved back home to Texas. Living in two states was expensive, and I was hemorrhaging cash.

Once I got back home, I was in the same position I found myself in, in the late fall of 2003...what was I going to do with the rest of my life? What subsection of the financial services industry would give me the career challenge I was seeking, while, at the same time, allow me to contribute, in a positive manner, to my fellow man.

As I looked again at all the opportunities in the financial planning world, I decided to give Smith Barney the opportunity to add me to their stable of highly educated, hard working financial advisors. My selection of Smith Barney, as opposed to rejoining Merrill Lynch, or any of the other regular suspects, was predicated upon my being told during the interviewing process that Smith Barney allowed, and even encouraged, fee-based financial planning. Imagine my dismay in learning, after two months of in-branch training, as I prepared to travel to Hartford, CT, for my formal training, that Smith Barney did not, in fact, allow fee-based financial planning...rather, they allowed wrap accounts. Not even close to the same thing now, is it? In all fairness to my branch manager, I do not feel he misrepresented the opportunity "with malice aforethought." The words "fee-based financial planning" simply have a different meaning in the world of wirehouses.

Either way, I found myself at a crossroads. However, since I had invested two months into getting myself "ready for the street" with Smith Barney, I decided to stick with it and go through their training and come back ready to start building a financial advisory career. After all, they were a top-tier company, and they did have name recognition and a very broad portfolio. So what if they didn't really allow financial planning done on a fee basis. I thought it was strange, however, that they had a mandatory training program for FAs wanting to engage in "Wealth Management" which had, as its first step, completion of Smith Barney's proprietary Financial Planning Specialist designation program. Yep, for those of you counting, I completed another designation program.

I spent three miserable weeks in Hartford, attending Smith Barney's formal training program, essentially receiving company propaganda and being trained to cold call. Not to take anything away from the positive aspects of the training, there were a few blocks of instruction that were actually beneficial, and the travel day to New York, to see the trading desks in action and to receive briefings from people who are quoted frequently in the Wall Street Journal, was worthwhile. Overall however, it was a terrible use of one's time, and almost 100% of it could have been better accomplished with Webinars.

I got back from my formal training the week before Christmas and beginning the first week in January, 2006, I hit the phones. It did not take me long to realize that my life's work was not going to be found cold calling affluent people, looking to capture their business from their current broker. To say I was disenchanted is an understatement. My intent to use direct mail, seminars, and personal networking was not met with enthusiasm by my Branch Management. Nor was the idea to be an insurance specialist within the branch system. We will not even discuss the challenges represented by trying to get approval from Compliance on the type of marketing I wanted to do. Suffice it to say, if you have a creative bone in your body, the wirehouse world will do all it can to crush it, and you.

Recognizing that I was not going to be able to do what I wanted to do in the world of wirehouses, I decided to cut my losses and return to an arena where I had realized success and try once more to revive my original business plan from my days of building my P&C Agency. I was going to build a book of 3000 policies in force and provide fee-based financial planning to my own book of business. This time, however, I was going to do it in conjunction with a large, independent credit union that would have a branch system and thousands of depositors. In addition, I would find one with a brokerage operation, where I could finally do fee-based financial planning.

In April of 2006, I joined a large Credit Union in the DFW area, with about 55,000 depositors. My task was to open an office in Tarrant County to reflect the success of the office in Dallas County, so I accepted the challenge and began. This particular credit union had a division with a Financial Advisor, managing about $35,000,000 in assets. He was doing a great job for the environment in which he operated. He was a Series 7, but he did primarily transactional business. He did not do any real advising, per se. The fit was there for me to grow into the position of being able to build an insurance book and then cross-sell financial services and planning to those clients.

Imagine my surprise when I found that this insurance operation, having existed within the credit union for over eight years, had no client management system. I found this out when I asked for a list of auto policy owners who didn't have other products with us. Much to my dismay, I was told we didn't have "those kinds of records." To make matters worse, the existing agent did little, if any, marketing, had no advertising collateral materials, and, because the insurance group contributed such a small amount to the bottom line, was not even considered to be a core business of the credit union.

The only good news was I was hired by the CFO and reported to her, directly. I brought my concerns to her and was immediately confronted with "budget this and budget that," but she was an intelligent lady and realized to reach the mutual goals we had to grow the business, some investment would be required.

Item one…Marketing. We hired an advertising company who assisted us in getting lobby materials and brochures highlighting the insurance group and their portfolio. Two months later, in late June, the materials were delivered.

Item two…my office, which was within glass walls, within the greater lobby area of the second largest branch, had lettering added to the glass so walk-in traffic knew we were there. That was accomplished within ten days, as I did it myself.

Item three…a search was launched to evaluate the existing client management systems available for P&C operations, and after a special presentation to the board to get approval to spend the money, we acquired the Hawksoft System. That was in July, three months after joining the organization.

Item four…an organized, planned marketing campaign, targeted specific groups to respond to specific products was designed and submitted for approval and implementation. This became the undoing of my association with the credit union, because the management of the credit union did not envision the insurance group becoming the contributor that other departments had developed into. They were still living in the days when just because you had someone sitting at a desk in the lobby selling something, that was all the marketing you needed to do. For any of you reading this who have ever worked in the bank channel for smaller banks, I am certain this sounds like "déjà vu, all over again!"

The bottom line was, I felt like the cartoon character with the little black cloud hanging over his head.

At this same time, my wife came to the realization that it was time to go back to work. She had been a "stay at home" wife since we sold our business in January of 2004. She went into the marketplace and was quickly offered the opportunity to join a P&C operation. It was then when she came to the point where she asked me one night, "If I am going to be working in insurance and you are going to be working in insurance, why don't we do it for ourselves again?" Because you don't know my bride of 33 years, you really don't understand the magnitude of this question, but suffice it to say, I agreed and we embarked on a new adventure, where we find ourselves today, building a new P&C shop, again, from scratch.

When Nancy asked me to update my story, I almost…almost…decided not to, because I felt my "adventures" over the past three years really wouldn't contribute to the efforts of this book. But as I thought about it, and after Nancy's encouragement, obviously I realized it would. The reason for agreeing to do so is because where I looked at a period of time and saw that nothing of value was really accomplished, that was not really the truth. The truth is, I took a chance and I explored the worlds of the wirehouse, twice; academia, as an administrator; and working within the banking/credit union world. I was able to learn that those were not really the roads for me, and how valuable is it really…to know where you don't belong?

I hope that my story helps you when you are having the same doubts about where you belong and what you should be doing in your financial services career…and your life.

As I build a new P&C agency here in Texas, I see a new adventure on my horizon, because my bride has asked me another question recently. Her latest inquiry was, "You know, Kevin, if we are ever going to live in eastern Tennessee, when are we going to do it?" (My bride and I have vacationed in eastern Tennessee twelve of the past thirteen years, and we have said for years, that's where we want to retire.)

But that will be a discussion for the next revision of Nancy's book. If it does come to pass, however, I bet you will see me, finally, doing full service, comprehensive financial planning!

Hey, a man can still dream can't he?

(2009 Update)

For the past 18 months I have been a Financial Associate and now a Financial Consultant with Thrivent Financial for Lutherans. Thrivent Financial is a fraternal benefits society serving almost 3 million members nationwide. Thrivent Financial for Lutherans came into being in 2002, when two fraternals merged, forming the largest fraternal benefit society in the US. Those fraternal companies were Aid Association for Lutherans and Lutheran Brotherhood. Today Thrivent Financial for Lutherans is a Fortune 500 Financial Services Company, managing almost 62 Billion Dollars in assets, and offering a full range of insurance and investment products and services to our members and prospects. While we are still focused on being the financial services company of choice for Lutherans, we can now serve the needs of all Americans.

Thrivent Financial allows advisors to assist people in combining their faith, family and finances using their personal values as their guideline or benchmark.

The biggest reason I decided to join Thrivent Financial was because of their being a faith based organization and their commitment to the Financial Planning Process. Thrivent Financial has taken the financial planning process we all know and love and added a few twists to make it their own. The Thrivent Financial Advisory Process consists of a series of meetings, which are provided at no cost to the member or prospect. The original introduction meeting or The Connect Meeting, is followed by a follow up meeting, called The Gather Data Meeting. The Gather Data meeting is followed by the closing meeting, called the Take Action Meeting. The entire financial planning process is intertwined within the TFAP (Thrivent Financial Advisory Process). The financial planning tool most commonly used to produce plans for middle Americans is Financial Profiles+, again customized for Thrivent Financial and called the "Primetime Plan." For more affluent members or those with more sophisticated needs, we also have access to NaviPlan, on a fee basis.

In addition to offering the basic plan, we also provide different programs, such as Asset Match®. Asset Match® allows a prospect to have their risk profile compared against their actual holdings. This service uses Ibbotson tools and provides a strong basis for properly evaluating their investments.

Thrivent Financial for Lutheran Financial Associates are not "stock brokers." We are financial service professionals who use a financial planning process based approach to assist members and prospects in developing a financial plan that will help them reach their financial goals. For those desiring to focus more on the investment side of the business, Thrivent Investment Management has a full range of services of asset management products, including non-discretionary as well as discretionary platforms. Financial Consultants and Senior Financial Consultants with Thrivent have access to our Thrivent Investment Management platform as well as a Brokerage operation, giving us access to a number of first tier companies through selling agreements.

While this might sound like an advertisement for Thrivent Financial, I said all that to say this...the most important reason I am associated with Thrivent is because of the good works we do as a company, through our commitment to giving back to our communities. Thrivent Financial for Lutherans, as a fraternal benefit society, is a not for profit organization. Those monies that would normally be paid to the IRS as taxes on profits are returned to our churches and communities through organizations like Habitat for Humanity and charitable works done in the community by members of Thrivent's Chapter system. If you have a charitable urge and you are a member of Thrivent, you will always have plenty of outlets for your "giving back" urges. In truth, as a Thrivent Financial Consultant, I can honestly say the more I do to help my members, the greater my financial rewards and the greater the good that can be done by Thrivent Financial for Lutherans.

As a Thrivent Financial for Lutherans FA, I do well by doing good. I can be proud of the fact that my company's senior officers weren't hauled before Congress to explain their part in the financial meltdown of 2008. Our bank, Thrivent Financial Bank, received no TARP money. Our insurance company Thrivent Financial for Lutherans still holds AM Best's highest ratings.

And in closing...Yes...of course I have completed additional professional designations since last we met. In 2008 I completed my last LUTC Coursework and received my LUTCF designation, from The American College. In 2008 I also completed the FIC (Fraternal Insurance Counsellor) designation and in early 2009 the FICF (Fraternal Insurance Counsellor Fellow) designation. These last two are designations particular to the world of Fraternal Benefit Societies.

So as you call see, my journey as a Certified Financial Planner^{TM} continues down that "Road Less Traveled." I am, however, getting closer to where I have always wanted to be in this career field. Every member I serve receives a financial plan before they receive a single recommendation regarding products or services for implementation. There is no prescription before diagnosis in my practice. Although I remain primarily commission based today, I can see the day when I will be more and more fee based.

For many years I have had a motto, "Plan for the Expected, Insure and Invest for the Unexpected."

(2011 Update)

The Journey Continues…

When I updated my contribution to this book, in July 2009, I had just returned from participating in the sales conference for which I had qualified for my first year's sales efforts, as a Financial Consultant for Thrivent Financial for Lutherans. It was held at the Gaylord Conference Center, on the Potomac, just outside of Washington DC. (A recommendation: wear very comfortable shoes and clothing when you tour Arlington National Cemetery and watch the Changing of the Guard at the Tomb of the Unknowns. If you are a military veteran, from any service, it is a once in a lifetime experience you want to give as a gift, to yourself.)

A few short months later, I found myself in the Board Room of The American College, in Bryn Mawr, PA. where I was presenting an original case study to the faculty. The purpose of the presentation was to demonstrate my abilities as a teacher/lecturer as well as my abilities to develop and present original work. Yes, dear reader, I was being interviewed for a faculty position at The American College. On November 1st I began my career as an academic, as an Assistant Professor of Insurance. My initial responsibilities were focused in the area of professional education called the LUTC/FSS Program. (LUTC stands for Life underwriters Training Council. FSS stands for Financial Services Specialist.) The LUTCF Designation and the FSS designation are entry level programs specifically designed to launch a new agent/advisors career, with solid sales and process knowledge. To me, these courses represent some of the most important courses a financial services professional will ever take. They can, and have, made the difference between a short and a long career in the business of financial services.

Since beginning my career here at the college, as a faculty member, I have contributed to the field of financial services by authoring/editing two text books. The first was *Techniques for Prospecting: Prospect or Perish*, (FA 200) published June, 2010 and the second is *Essentials of Disability Income Insurance*, (FA 211) published April, 2011. My third textbook, *Fundamentals of Insurance Planning*, (HS 311) is due out in October, 2011. The first two texts are used in the LUTC/FSS programs. The third text, Fundamentals of Insurance Planning, is a core course in the three primary designation programs of The American College; the CLU, (Chartered Life Underwriter) ChFC (Chartered Financial Consultant) and the CFP (Certified Financial Planner.) (Note: The CFP is not a designation conferred by the American College however, the college is one of the major providers of CFP education and the college enjoys a considerable amount of success in our CFP training efforts. As of the writing of this update, the last passing percentages on the National CFP Exam for those students who studied with the American College vs. the average number passing the exam was 14 percentage points higher.)

In addition to my academic achievements in the areas mentioned, as you might suspect, I have continued my professional as well as my personal education. Since 2009, I have completed the FSS designation and the CLF designation. (Chartered Leadership Fellow.) I also have completed 8 of 15 courses in my pursuit of the "terminal degree," for which I have longed my entire life. I am completing my Doctor of Business Administration degree at Wilmington University, in New Castle, DE. I expect to have all my course work completed at the end of Spring Semester, 2012. I will then complete my dissertation, with a targeted graduation date of summer, 2013. (As an aside, my screen name on my Yahoo E-Mail Account is dr2be2013@yahoo.com.)

For those who are interested, I am tentatively pursuing research on the educational and training needs of Financial Advisors, in preparation for advising "non-traditional clients and couples." Any of you who have been presented with the planning needs of a same sex couple or a non-married opposite sex couple will recognize that our traditional planning tools and techniques are of little value in serving these clients. (If you would like to participate in this research, you can reach me at dr2be2013@yahoo.com.)

By the way, for any of you with a life insurance background, you will appreciate the irony in the following. In late 2010, I was notified by NAIFA, the National Association of Insurance and Financial Advisors that I had been awarded the National Quality Award. This award is given to financial services professionals for the persistency of business they had sold in the prior 12-24 month periods. What does that mean? The business I sold has stayed on the books! What does that indicate? I sold the right product, for the right reasons, to the right people, at the right time. Needless to say, I was pleased to learn that, according to my institution, I am the only active professor to have ever been awarded a National Quality Award from NAIFA.

What else am I doing to contribute to my field and my fellow financial service professionals? I host a daily magazine styled program on The Wealth Channel, called "Wealth Today." (www.thewealthchannel.com). The short 5-8 minute program features information, updates and a short interview from a noted industry professional as well as a Sales Tip. It is a fun assignment and one which I enjoy doing, immensely. Visit me on the web and check out the archived materials.

In an earlier update I mentioned that I wasn't sure how my career machinations could be helpful to new planners or planners with a little more experience. I suggested then that perhaps it can serve as a demonstration that there are many ways to the top of the mountain, but you still have to make the climb, one step at a time. Now, I hope than you can see that it is never too late to pursue your life's dream. For me, that is/was a "terminal degree" and a career in academia. At age 59, I realized the first part of the goal...I became a College Professor, with now I have publications on my resume. The second and final part of my life's goal will be the achievement of my DBA degree, in summer, 2013. By then I will be 62. The fact is however, if I am still alive in 2013...I will be 62 either way. I prefer to be 62 years old with my DBA completed! How about you?

There is an old saying I have remembered ever since the first time I heard it, when I was in my twenties, *"If it is to be, it is up to me!"* What do **you** want to accomplish in this field? Where do **you** want to work? What kind of practice do **you** want to establish and build? How can **you** best contribute the gifts **you** have inside **you,** to this field and noble profession?

What ever it is you decide you want to do, remember another old saying I love, *"I WILL climb this mountain. You will see me at the top...or find me dead on the side of it."*

Take the material in this book and start by charting out **your** course, to the top of **your** mountain, whatever and wherever it is.

©Kevin M. Lynch

WIREHOUSES[97]

When I "talk" with beginning practitioners on the industry bulletin boards, one of the most frequent questions is: should I start out with a member firm or wirehouse? These are the companies that are most actively recruiting people into the financial services industry, and a big part of the initial discussion centers on their training programs. Isn't this a great way to get training in the business?

The answer, of course, is yes and no. Although several of the larger brokerage firms have stepped up their training in financial planning, the ex-brokers I've talked to generally think there was a lot more hype than substance to the training they received. Scott Dauenhauer[87], who worked with three different brokerage firms in his career before he launched his own independent firm, wrote an essay chronicling his experience. "The programs focus solely on sales and product training," he says. "I attended one such program, and 95% of the training focused on cold-calling sales and learning proprietary product. Brokerage firms want 'salespeople', not highly-skilled financial planners."

Many people getting into the business will find the sales (and especially the cold calling) process repugnant and degrading. Your real training comes if and when you manage to acquire a client through this process and you begin to gain some real-world experience in helping people organize their financial lives. If Scott and others can be believed (and I think they can), this is going to be largely a self-teaching experience.

You should also recognize that working for one of the larger firms will reduce the things you can recommend to a client or prospect. "A public company owes its first loyalty to the public shareholders," says Scott. "The people who own stock in a company must have their interests protected. A public brokerage firm's loyalty cannot be 100% to their customer."

In the real world, that means that you are expected to direct client assets in directions that are most beneficial to the company. In fact, your income will depend on it. "A broker is paid a percentage of the revenues that he/she brings to the firm—typically 25 to 40%," says Scott. It is not, however, that simple. Brokerage firms determine the payout percentage for each individual "product." They control product flow by paying higher amounts for product the firm wants to move (sell). Each firm works differently, but depending on the product a firm wants to emphasize, they will pay a broker a higher percentage of the revenue to induce him to sell what the company wants him to sell. For example, if the company wants a broker to sell a "wrap account," they may tell the broker that he will receive a higher percentage of

---

[87] The entire essay can be found on Scott Dauenhauer's website:
http://web.mac.com/scottyjd/iWeb/MeridianWealth/Publications.html

the fees they generate from that particular wrap account. If the broker wants the higher revenue, he/she will migrate toward selling that product.

Finally, says Scott, the broker many times is under tremendous pressure from management to sell the latest mutual fund offering from that brokerage. "Many branch managers," he says, "have compensation tied to the amount of proprietary products the branch sells. The manager's interest is in getting the highest bonus possible, so he, in turn, puts the pressure on the brokers to 'pound the phones,' and sell their 'latest offering'."

It goes unspoken that if a broker does not participate in selling the new offering, then things will not be easy for him/her. "I know of one broker who was told, 'I don't think this firm is the right place for you,' after the broker refused to sell the new fund offering," he says. "It turned out that he was the only one to not submit to the pressure. He eventually left that firm. I can't begin to tell you how many voice mails and e-mails I received from management to sell the 'new' offerings. I never succumbed if it was not in my client's best interest. Be aware that the pressure is on the broker to sell certain products or else he/she risks losing their job. The conflicts don't stop there; they go on, but I think you get the picture."

But wait a minute; why does the planner who works for a wirehouse get only 25 to 40% of the commissions he or she generates through the recommendation of investments? The answer takes you into a murky world that Scott calls "The Broker Food Chain"—which, he says, even the brokers don't usually fully understand.

Does all of this mean that you cannot work with a large public company and still do a good job for clients? Not necessarily; but it does mean that it can be harder. Be aware that the company expects to be reimbursed for its training efforts. If you become successful, and you decide to leave the firm, many companies will file legal claims that the clients you've been working with at the firm are the "property" of the firm. They will file a temporary restraining order (TRO) on you, barring you from talking to these clients after you've left.

It doesn't matter if you are looking at working for a large institutional brokerage, an independent Broker/Dealer, or a small independent planning firm. The point is, **read the employment agreement and ask questions!** Pay particular attention to what will happen to *your* clients if you leave the company.

In many cases—I would say most—these TROs (as they are commonly known in the business) are not upheld, and the courts recognize that clients and consumers have the right to select anybody they choose as an advisor. But the legal bills and temporary injunction against talking to clients when you leave can be a factor in your decision as to whether the wirehouse brokerage training is as great a deal as the recruiter might make it sound.

What follows is a candid essay discussing Pat Collins' transition from wirehouse rep to firm owner:

Greenspring Wealth Management[88]

By J. Patrick Collins Jr., CFP®
President

There are dozens of paths to choose when entering the financial planning industry. I must admit that I knew very little about any of those paths when I was offered a job at Merrill Lynch. Like any 24-year-old, I thought I could do anything, and when many of the managers told me that eight out of ten of my peers would be gone in two years, I paid little attention. Almost immediately I knew two things: first, I loved this profession and the impact we as planners can have on people's lives, and second, I wasn't going to retire at Merrill Lynch.

As I look back on the four years I spent at Merrill Lynch, it is easy to see how the corporate culture was developed and why they have been successful as a company; everything revolves around sales. Whether you were a rookie or veteran at the firm, you were always ranked versus your peers, whether comparing assets, production, or the newest sales contests. While this environment of pressure and competition was good for sales, I found it to be the opposite of everything I loved about the profession. In the end, financial planning is not about us and how much we can do in production, it's about our clients and how we can help them lead a better life. Almost four years from the day I began at Merrill Lynch, I left the firm and started my own fee-only firm.

I spent nearly two years thinking critically about how I wanted to work with clients. There was little to no information at the time on making a switch from a Broker/Dealer to a fee-only firm. Here are the steps I took before I actually made the transition:

1. Develop Core Values and Statement of Purpose: Many firms either never complete this step or do it once and never look at it again. The creation of these two principles should help you answer the question, "Why do you exist?" We created six core values which are non-negotiable for our firm: Passion, Integrity, Stewardship, Excellence, Objectivity and Community. Our statement of purpose is, "To serve others and have an impact in their lives." This is the most important step in the process, since it will drive every decision you make as a firm.

2. Long-term vision: Where do you see yourself and your firm ten to twenty years from now? Just as in financial planning, you must first know the goal before you can begin the planning process. Many brokers that break away from their firms choose to open a small independent practice serving a core group of clients and having ample amounts of free time, while others may prefer to devote every waking moment to building a large, highly profitable practice. You should begin and end this step with reviewing your core values and statement of purpose. For example, our firm's long-term vision is to become a middle-tier firm focusing on our surrounding area. Since our Purpose Statement is, "To serve others and have an impact in their lives," we believe our client base must remain fairly small in order to "serve" them well, but in

---

[88] http://www.greenspringwealth.com

order to have an "impact in their lives," we needed to be large enough as a firm to have sufficient resources to execute our vision.

3. Firm Structure: For the purpose of this discussion, I will narrow our choices to commission firms and fee-only firms. Planners that work for commissions typically get paid to sell financial products, while planners that work in a fee-only capacity are paid for their advice. There is much more to research about this step (licenses, registration requirements, compliance, etc.), but it is critical to determine how you want to work with clients and if that vision aligns with your core values and purpose statement. For example, we determined that our firm should be fee-only because Objectivity was one of our core values. Typically, if advisors are not paid to sell products, they tend to be more objective. When you have developed core values that you truly believe in, the decision becomes easy.

4. Client Retention: If you are breaking away from a major wirehouse, you no doubt have a client base that you will need to make a decision on how to handle. First, you should determine what your ideal client at your new firm should look like (size, personality, needs, etc.). There should be minimum standards, set and you should use those standards to determine which of your current clients fit the mold. Again, if you are having any trouble with this step, you should consult your core values and purpose statement. For example, because our purpose statement is "To serve others and have an impact in their lives," we decided to maintain a small client base in order to effectively implement this vision. Because of this small client base, we needed to work with higher-paying, wealthier clients, in order to remain profitable.

5. Legal Counsel: First, I am not an attorney, so none of this section contains any guidance that should be construed as legal advice. There are two reasons it is of utmost importance to hire a competent attorney: registration requirements for your new firm, and employment agreements with your prior employer. First, there are specific items that must be completed when registering your firm and developing compliance procedures (contracts, marketing material, licenses, etc.). A securities attorney or compliance consulting firm can help develop these documents and implement these procedures. Second, many wirehouses have their brokers sign non-solicitation agreements and an agreement to re-pay training costs. If you are planning on taking clients with you when you leave, there are three areas I have identified that must be planned for:

   a. Agreement to repay training costs: typically, if you leave within a certain amount of time from your date of hire, you are required to repay a portion of your training costs. While I was through this period, and therefore was not liable for these costs, others I know have told me firms often enforce this provision in your contract.
   b. Stealing of firm information: anything you take from your employer can be construed as stealing firm information. It is important that you speak with your attorney about how to go about documenting and obtaining any information on your current clients.

If you're considering transition, Turning Point, Inc.[89] has a website with plenty of resources to help you research and make some important decisions.

BANKS AND CREDIT UNIONS

Many banks and credit unions are affiliated with Broker/Dealers today and offer an increasing range of financial planning products and services. Payout tends to be on the low end, but the experience in a relatively safe environment can be valuable.

Robin Vaccai-Yess, CFP®, owner of her own practice,[90] suggests working in a bank environment or for a bank-owned Broker/Dealer has added difficulties. "There are very stringent regulations in place to ensure that the customer understands that the investment products being purchased through the Bank Rep are not FDIC-insured. Because of these additional disclosure requirements to customers/clients, many Registered Representatives find the additional paperwork a hassle. No one expects to walk into a big brokerage firm or wirehouse and find FDIC-insured products, although they are available today."

Leaving a lucrative career with Schwab to find something more satisfying, Jim Heitman, CFP® started his own hourly, independent practice a few years back, only to be lured away by a challenging opportunity to introduce a financial planning division at a major bank. Given his broad experience in the profession, I asked him to tell me what it's like working in a bank. Here are his informed impressions:

---

[89] http://www.goingindependent.com/registeredreps/
[90] http://robinyess.com Read Robin's getting started story in Chapter 7.

"Banks have had in-house financial advisors for some time, but planning is just beginning to make its way into the bank brokerage platform. There are two ways planners are working in banks.

"The first is in a sales capacity, as an advisor. This is much like the traditional registered representative position, but you have a bank behind you. Though the banks tend to be more conservative than most brokerages, they have the advantage of great placement in the community, and the presence of banking services gives you the ability to be more involved in your client's financial life. If you have a heart for planning, ask about the firm's current planning services, what the future plans are, and how large a part of the business will be planning. These positions have all the pros and cons of a traditional sales position.

"Alternatively, some banks are creating planning departments that will provide planning directly to bank clients, or through an existing advisor network. This is more of a pure planning position, and these positions are harder to find. Some advantages to these positions are a steady paycheck and focused planning work. Though you will not have the earnings potential available in a sales position, salaries can be competitive, depending on how serious the firm is about growing financial planning.

"One negative to working in the bank environment is regulatory compliance. The banks are governed by several regulatory bodies and tend towards conservatism in internal regulations. This can make compliance cumbersome as compared to other types of firms. If you are coming from a wirehouse or independent firm, the level of regulation will surprise you, but once you learn your company's approach you will adjust. If you are just starting out, you will not notice a difference!

"Planning is new to most bank and bank brokerage organizations. Until the industry settles on a sustainable model, you will see a wide variation in how different companies provide planning, and constant (and rapid, and chaotic) change. If you want to be on the cutting edge of changing an industry, maybe even helping to guide the change, then check out planning in the bank environment. There will be bumps along the way, but that's what keeps it interesting."

WHAT TO ASK BEFORE YOU SIGN

Questions you'll want to ask of any company you interview:

1. How do you train new reps/employees? Will I have a mentor?
2. How many people have been with the company over two years?
3. What's the average production in the office?
4. How many hours a week will I be expected to work?
5. Will emphasis be on financial planning or gathering assets?
6. What products and services will I provide to clients?
7. How much support staff will I have?
8. Will I have quotas to meet? Proprietary products to sell?
9. How is compensation earned? Salary? Draw? Commissions?
10. What expenses will I encounter?

11. Are there any Medical/Dental/Life Insurance benefits? What's the cost?
12. Is a pension plan available?
13. What about tuition reimbursement for CFP®, ChFC, etc.?
14. What happens if I want to leave? What REALLY happens?

Jon Lacy, CFP® reminded me to point out that whomever you go to work for, there will be tradeoffs. "There is no free lunch," he intones. "If a firm is going to help pay for your licensing, pay for your office/phone/etc, and pay you a starting salary—there is going to be a cost. You will be expected to 'produce'—make money and do it fast. There will be pressure for you to sell products. Ultimately," he says, "you decide how you will work with clients (fees vs. commission, selling vs. planning, etc.)."

In addition to his activities with the full service (both fees and commissions) financial planning firm, Lane, Dickson & Lacy, LLC, in Diamond Springs, California, Jon teaches Investment Planning as part of the CFP® Board-registered curriculum at UC Davis. He teaches with the UC Davis sponsored CFP® Certification Exam Review Course team, serves on the Board of Directors for a non-profit organization, and is on the local School Board.

His advice to newcomers entering the profession: "Once you're licensed, affiliated (B/D or RIA) and designated (CFP® or other) GET ACTIVE (in your community). There is a tremendous need for professionals to serve. Working in a Corporate Customer Service Environment for over six years prior to entering Financial Planning, I learned a very simple truth: People don't care how much you know until they know how much you care."

Non-Compete Clauses

Just after publishing in September 2001, I received an e-mail from a reader who was disappointed that I hadn't devoted much space to non-compete clauses. I agree it's important, and would like to re-print, anonymously, his experience:

"I really had not heard of non-compete clauses until I read AEFA's several-hundred page franchise agreement and came to that section. It certainly isn't talked about, and, to me, is a critical aspect of a job decision. I guess they didn't want me to know about it...I've been sponsored by AEFA for all my exams and was about to sign their agreement. The non-compete clause was like hitting a brick wall for me.

"Their non-compete clause states that there can be no financial contact (signing up a new account, selling insurance, or any financial advice) for a period of one year after termination. After six years, the non-compete expires. AEFA has a P1 track in which you are an employee and a P2 track in which you come in as an independent contractor. I fully understand having the clause for P1 advisors, where all expenses are paid. Because of the rigid schedule AEFA has for new planners (60 hours per week, including EVERY Saturday morning; I have three young children and an aging mother), I was going in as a P2 to plan my own business (and time) and was paying for EVERYTHING, including the right to use "the name." It just didn't make sense that I should be paying for all that and they keep my clients if I leave. It's simply out of balance in my mind.

"After consulting with some other FP friends of mine, they unanimously stated that they would not sign that deal. I didn't."

FEES vs. COMMISSIONS

Eventually you'll need to deal with the issue of compensation, so you might just as well start forming some opinions now. Warning: Some real rabble-rousers out there are waiting to jump into the fee fray at the drop of a hat. My advice? Don't take the bait. Look at the argument from as many angles as possible, figure out what you will be most comfortable with, and then get to work helping clients with their financial planning.

Tad Borak, J.D.[91], one of the moderators on FPi, reworked one of his posts dealing with the debate. His lucid explanation should help you figure out where to begin:

Commissions & Fees
By Tad Borak, J.D.

I think it's important to keep in mind that the term "commission" isn't unique to financial services; it's an old term defined in the law. The definition varies by context, but generally it means compensation paid by a product or service provider to a broker/agent for facilitating a sale (often the compensation is a percentage of the transaction value). So whether something constitutes a commission is a question of legal terminology, as defined in places like the California Labor Code.

Part of the problem might be that the issue is too close to home, so the distinctions are blurred. A 1% AUM fee and level-load product paying 1% per year both appear to contain elements of the "commission." But just because a fee and commission are financially similar doesn't mean the terms are equivalent, and equating them misses the essence of the conflict. Instead of looking at financial products, I like the car analogy, because it's so clear what constitutes a "commission" at the dealership.

If you buy a car from a dealership, the dealer pays the salesperson for making the sale. No sale, no compensation. Some models (Durango) pay better than others (Neon), so you may be steered towards one end of the lot. You won't hear much discussion from the salesperson about going someplace else and buying a competing car, of course, nor about how you might be able to get a few more years out of whatever you drove up in. And you know that when you walk in the door.

That's a commission, because there's a broker/agent facilitating a transaction and being paid for doing so by the product provider. The buyer doesn't pay the salesperson, at least not directly. And the salesperson isn't being paid for designing or manufacturing the car, just for selling it, and for providing whatever information (and persuasion) is needed to facilitate the

---

[91] Tad's bio can be seen on the FPi moderator site at http://www.financial-planning.com/global/discussions-hosts.html

sale.

Six months later, you bring the car to the garage because it doesn't start. Maybe it needs a new starter, or maybe a starter and a battery, or maybe a starter, battery and engine-control module. As items are added, the garage's labor charges go up, because it takes more time to diagnose and repair the problem. And if you bought the Durango, your bill may be higher for a similar repair, because it's a more complicated vehicle than the Neon.

Would you then infer that the garage works on commission? Probably not, that's not what's going on. They're charging a book rate for performing different tasks based on complexity and time required. There may be some proportionality between the labor charges and the number/cost of parts replaced, but fundamentally, I don't think anyone would say that they pay commissions to have their car serviced. You could make the argument, but it would be kind of silly wouldn't it?

We can imagine a garage that did actually work on commission. You would pay only for the replacement parts, and the garage would receive a percentage cut from that. There would be no charges if nothing was replaced, even if they spent hours on your car. That type of garage would have an incentive to replace parts—as many, and as expensive, as possible!

OK, so back to financial services...did you facilitate a sale and get paid for doing so by the product/service provider (directly or via your B/D)? Then it's a commission. And it introduces two potential conflicts of interest that are inherent to commissions: the need for a transaction to occur for you to be compensated, and the discrepancies in compensation among different products. For the most part, these conflicts are why anyone gives a whit about the differences between fees and commissions, even when the two appear financially identical.

Contrast the "fee." With both hourly and AUM fees, the advisor is paid the same whether or not a transaction occurs. These fees have nothing to do with the sale of products; rather, they are the way that a client compensates the advisor for whatever services have been provided. And the compensation is the same irrespective of which products/investments the advisor recommends. So this may raise other potential conflicts of interest (e.g., AUM fees arguably encourage asset-gathering), but it avoids the two I mentioned above.

If we wanted to push the analogy further, we could compare the cost of one of those "bumper to bumper" add-on warranties to paying an AUM fee, and hourly labor charges to hourly planning fees. With the former, you pay a certain cost for the warranty per year, and any repairs are covered at no additional cost; with the latter you pay only when something breaks. Ongoing "maintenance" of a financial plan and associated investment portfolio aren't all that different, at least in some advisory practices. But that's stretching the analogy a little thin!

I was a fee-only financial planner and registered investment advisor. I received no commissions whatsoever for anything. Once upon a time, I held all the necessary securities and insurances licenses, but they have all lapsed or become inactive. For me, it was a decision that evolved from the simple fact that I wanted to do financial planning and didn't want to sell anything except myself. I have to admit, the idea of getting up every morning knowing that I had to find another client in order to implement a transaction didn't set well with my personal mindset.

John Lewis, CFP® feels much the same way, but understands how difficult it is to go it alone:

"Most new reps can't afford to take the fee-based route from the beginning due to the lower, initial pay-outs. So, many go the transactions route and collect commissions off the sale of Class A or Class B mutual funds, for example. If you have to make your quota, the manager isn't interested in how well you are doing meeting your Year-One projections in a Five-Year plan. How are you doing today, this week, this month, this quarter?

"Assume you're a star and you have accumulated $10 mil in mutual funds assets. In the second year, your trails are $25,000 based on the $10 mil the previous year (and no growth). If you keep a third of your GDC, you're staring at about $8 to $9K. Guess what? You have to shake the trees again to find more prospects, in order to get back to where you were. You're stuck in your own version of 'Groundhog Day.'

"I'm a fee-based independent rep. I left the insurance world after two years to make a go of it on my own. It stinks sometimes, but I'm gonna survive. I'd recommend forgoing the commissions route on investments, build a stream of income, charge a fee for the creation of a financial plan, sell some insurance products because your clients will need them, and develop a well-rounded financial planning practice. After all, we tell our clients to diversify; shouldn't we, too?"

Some of the neatest people I know are commissioned salespeople in the financial services industry. Many of them are highly regarded CERTIFIED FINANCIAL PLANNER™ practitioners with respected Broker/Dealers, giving their clients wonderful, unbiased advice, and no doubt making three or four times my annual income. I'm more comfortable charging a fee for taking a holistic view of my client's needs, which includes non-financial concerns, and sending them off to an expert in those areas that need more attention than I'm qualified to provide.

If you're coming from a successful background in sales, and the thrill of the close is near and dear to your heart, then that is exactly what you should be doing! You have an incredible talent that shouldn't be wasted! It simply boils down to integrity. I'm referring to that gut feeling that tells you what it is you are doing is honestly the best possible solution that you believe is available to your client at this moment in time. You won't be able to do that unless you have the education and experience as a financial planner, and you have enough accurate information from your client to know the product you're selling is appropriate to the situation.

Compensation is relevant. Just don't let it interfere with how you can best serve your client.

IT DOESN'T ALWAYS WORK

My enthusiasm and just plain love for this profession has made it difficult to keep personal bias out of this publication as much as possible. If you are to accurately evaluate your own potential in this industry, it is only fair you have exposure to both sides. So it is with deep gratitude that I include the following courageous and unedited memoirs from a colleague:

My Journey Through a Financial Planning Career

By Edward Mora, CFP®, MBA

It's not always easy to look back at a crucial career choice and admit that it wasn't successful. My experience in the financial planning industry spanned from 1993 to 2000 and was marked with deep lows and exhilarating highs, many extraordinary relationships (some I would rather forget), and many lessons learned. After much soul searching, I ultimately left the industry I devoted seven years of my life to. I wish to share my experiences in the hope that they will shed light on the reality of building a successful career as a financial planner.

Over the course of my financial planning career, I attempted probably every angle possible for a financial planner—running my own practice, working on commissions for a large insurance company and a boutique financial planning firm, and being a salaried planner and manager for a boutique planning firm. Along the way, I earned an MBA, became a CERTIFIED FINANCIAL PLANNER™ (CFP®) and Chartered Financial Consultant (ChFC), and obtained a Series 6, 7, 63, 65, and insurance license. In addition, I was the author of a bi-weekly financial advice column in a local paper and very active in the local chapter of the Financial Planning Association. I truly was committed to the profession and expanding my knowledge base.

When I joined the industry, working on commissions for a large brokerage or insurance company was the only option to get experience. There simply was not (and still isn't) a defined career path for those who would like to pursue financial planning on a salaried basis. Earning a living off commissions was extremely difficult and required a lot of faith to continue. I joined a large insurance company straight out of college, and in my first year, I made a grand total of approximately $10,000; not enough to live on and consequently I went into debt. I remember thinking at the time that I had wasted a whole year in "sales" and it wouldn't look good on resume. Since I had put in the effort to get my Series 7 and insurance license, I figured I'd give it another six months.

Well, six months later I decided to become a salaried planner for a small firm in Century City. This was actually an enjoyable experience, from the aspect that I could accrue the benefits of helping individuals plan for their future, but not have to worry about paying my rent. I worked there for a roughly a year and half, earning around forty thousand a year. I ultimately left the firm, not for dislike of my job, but because my boss was very difficult to work for and the environment was just too hostile for my liking. This, however, led me to my brief stint as an independent planner.

At the time I was leaving this job, my mother informed me that her company was offering early retirement to thousands of its employees. I thought it was an opportunity I couldn't pass up, so I quickly registered with a small Broker/Dealer and was on my way. I put on a couple of seminars, acted like I had experience galore (though I was only 25!—there is another lesson here: 'perception' is everything), and closed a bunch of rollovers. I think I made around sixty thousand dollars from front and back-end loaded mutual funds in those two frenetic months. But it was at this point, where I think I realized that making the "big dollars" in financial planning wasn't going to happen for me.

Knowing that I made this money through an "easy" connection, I tried to get referrals to extend this winning streak. As with my early days, here is where I just wasn't very adept. In addition, I knew if I wanted to really make this a successful business I would have to reinvest much of those earnings. To a 25-year-old with that much in the bank, the idea of being able to actually have a decent investment portfolio and being able to afford some small luxuries was simply too much to pass up. Bottom line, I chickened out and wasn't willing to take the risk of continuing on my initial success. However, my gut instinct and inability to bring in additional prospects let me deal easily with this fact. I took off for Argentina for three weeks to figure out what my next step was.

I decided that a salaried planning position was the route for me and joined another independent planning firm, helping them to establish their investment management department. During the next three-and-half–years, I really stepped up in the education department, achieving the ChFC designation, then challenging and passing the CFP® exam. I was on a roll, so I decided to get a business degree from Loyola Marymount University in Los Angeles and eventually graduated summa cum laude with an MBA in Financial Decision Systems in 2000. Throughout my time at this firm, I helped to acquire and manage $75 million in investments and build a thriving financial planning and executive compensation practice. Commensurately, I rose from a technical analyst to Vice President of Investments in that short time.

Admittedly, I was enjoying good success at the firm but the reality was, as is the case in most relatively small planning shops, the pay was simply not that inspiring. When I left, I was making about sixty thousand a year (that included my quarterly bonuses) even though I managed the most profitable part of the business. When planning my career with the president of the firm, I inquired about what it would take me to earn $100K, and the answer was basically: "You'd better become a producer to make that kind of money."

Well, one thing that getting my MBA during the peak of the Internet revolution taught me was that there was plenty of money to be made with good industry experience and a business degree. So I positioned myself as such and secured a job with a Big 5 firm as an e-business consultant focusing on the financial services industry. I am still helping clients, but not on the "front line"; rather, my clients are American Express, Zurich Financial, and Morgan Stanley. And the difference in pay? Well, my salary almost tripled, so I can't complain there.

In summary, financial planning was a very interesting though unprofitable career for me; however, it can be very profitable career for some. Here are some things I learned during my journey:

Ed's Parables:

- **If you're not very good at the prospecting/selling part of the business, you will never make a lot of money** (there is, of course, many definitions for "a lot" of money). Put another way, do you want to cold call every day to make fifty thousand a year?

- **If you choose to work for a large brokerage or insurance firm, expect pressure and quotas to sell proprietary products.** There is very little financial planning done at these firms—mostly investment planning.

- **Getting a CFP®, ChFC, or other credentials will not guarantee you more clients.** However, the education you will receive is well worth the effort. In my opinion, the CFP® is by far the best and most respected designation.

- **The most knowledgeable planners I worked with were at independent firms and fee-based.**

- **Despite what the Jobs Almanac says, financial planners have a lot of stress and not a lot of free time!**

I was fortunate enough to run into Ed a few years after he'd sent me this and asked him how things were going at the accounting firm. Though I was as familiar as the next person with recent headlines, Ed's response still surprised me. When I told him I thought "the rest of the story" might be of interest to readers, he graciously agreed.

Coming Full Circle
(2005 Update)

By Edward Mora, CFP®, MBA

When Nancy asked me to give an update to my original essay, I, of course, agreed immediately. Upon re-reading that essay on my trials and tribulations in the financial planning industry, I felt a tinge of both satisfaction and sadness: Satisfaction in knowing that I had accumulated a great level of knowledge and experience, but sadness that I wasn't ultimately successful in establishing myself in the industry. Re-examining my reasoning for leaving the industry, I still feel it was the right choice at that time.

I had left off with my career transition to a Big 4 management consultant. Those were heady times in the consulting industry and I certainly benefited from the favorable hiring environment. But, alas, as the market crashed and the recession ensued, consulting firms shed thousands of jobs. I was caught up in a round of layoffs, so after two years at the firm, I was once again looking for employment.

Fortunately, I landed a job quickly as a Vice President in the investment management subsidiary of a large regional bank. While having a CFP®, ChFC, and planning background was important, the real reason I was hired was because of my MBA and consulting experience. In other words, structured thinking and project management skills are very valuable commodities. My role consists of strategic planning, product development, project management, and new business development support.

As I learned my way through the bank, I noticed that no financial planning services were offered. Given my background, I obviously felt that holistic planning was absolutely critical to serve clients effectively. Only recently have I had time to do something about this. I've embarked on a campaign to convince the bank to change its approach to the marketplace by embracing holistic planning as its primary service methodology.

Bringing about this type of change within a large organization has certainly been a challenge, but thus far the buy-in has been excellent. It's been wonderful to once again be immersed in the planning world, this time in bringing about the ideals that were instilled in me through my prior experiences and obtaining the CFP® designation.

It was those experiences, from all different aspects of the planning world, which shaped my belief in financial planning. So my life has indeed come full circle—while I may not have succeeded in having my own planning business, I find great satisfaction in knowing that I'm now doing everything I can to make competent and comprehensive financial planning available to many more people than I could have ever reached.

SUMMARY

Morris Armstrong, CFP®, CDP[92], was a career-changer who became a financial planner after twenty-three years as a banker. "I managed portfolios of currencies, deposits and bonds. Millions of dollars were transacted on my word alone, a far cry from the Broker/Dealer environment," he told me. "It was exciting, stressful, fast-paced, stressful, afforded plenty of opportunity to travel, stressful, and paid well," he joked. "In a retrospective moment, playing the *coulda-woulda-shoulda game*, I can sure see things I would have done differently." Today, Morris is owner of Armstrong Financial Strategies[93], a fee-only Registered Investment Advisor in New Milford, CT.

Morris came up with ten things that he's learned over the years—some of them the hard way:

Lesson #1: Thoroughly research the industry and companies.

Lesson #2: Read very carefully all of the paperwork; seek written clarification.

---

[92] Certified Divorce Financial Analysts (CDFAs) are financial specialists who have successfully completed an intensive training program from The Institute for Certified Divorce Financial Analysts. (https://www.institutedfa.com/) They are trained in the complex financial issues of divorce.
[93] http://www.armstrong-financial.com

Lesson #3: Don't plan on much assistance; you are on your own.

Lesson #4: You do not have to accept every person as a client.

Lesson #5: Never forget that you are selling your services and yourself.

Lesson #6: Develop and follow a business and marketing plan.

Lesson #7: Learn to wisely prioritize and allocate time to all facets of life.

Lesson #8: Thank people who do something nice for you.

Lesson #9: Take the time to learn the software; know how the information flows.

Lesson #10: Become active in your community financial planning organizations.

Looking over Morris' list, I would have to agree. Taking his lead, I recommend the following:

ACTION LIST

- Seek career counseling and/or read Gerber's book.

- Get a handle on your "Primary Aim."

- Write a vision or mission statement.

- Research companies with a philosophy embracing your vision.

- Interview everyone and learn everything you can about the company before making a decision.

Chapter Four

The Dreaded Regulatory Stuff

Anyone can call himself or herself a financial planner, right? Yep. But consumers are getting pretty savvy, and they no longer accept just "anyone" as their financial planner. As recently as the early nineties, it was rare that a potential client asked me about my credentials or background. Today, I'm surprised when a prospective client doesn't come in loaded with a list of questions that put me in the hot seat! Then they often whip out the answers from the last planner they visited and compare notes before hiring an advisor. In fact, it's not unusual to have them come in with a computer printout about me, generated from the Financial Planning Association website.[94]

You don't want clients who hold back information and run off at the drop of the market any more than your client would want a planner who didn't keep informed and in compliance. To get started right, you'll need to make some serious decisions.

Plan for Yourself First

Begin by envisioning what you'll be doing in five years, and then backtrack to determine how you will get there.

- Learn what worked for others.

- Attend Financial Planning Association chapter meetings[95] and conferences[96].

- Read trade journals and visit financial planning websites.

- Interview Broker/Dealers and independent practitioners, particularly those doing what you want to do.

- Participate in discussion groups and ask questions.

- Take your time, keep an open mind and stay flexible.

With few exceptions, you need to register in some capacity with a governmental regulator in financial services in order to be paid as a financial planner[97]. Once you decide where you want to begin, the path to register is relatively easy to navigate. Your first decision is whether

---

[94] http://www.fpanet.org/plannersearch/search.cfm?WT.svl=2
[95] http://www.fpanet.org/Connect/Chapters/ConnecttoaChapter/
[96] http://www.fpanet.org/EventsConferences/Conferences/
[97] Seek competent advice pertinent to your state to be certain you follow proper procedure and obtain appropriate licensing and registration. This is especially true if you intend to sell or advise on insurance issues.

you will start your own independent practice or work for someone else. It boils down to three possibilities.

Three Ways to Become Registered:

1. Registered Representative (RR)

When you work for a Broker/Dealer, your supervisor, manager, or employer will tell you what licenses, exams and registrations you need to sell the products and services they offer. The company might provide classes to help you pass the first time. They will instruct you on what forms, agreements and records to keep, and what payout, commissions or salary you'll receive.

You will be a Registered Representative under your Broker/Dealer's NASD registration. Should you ever change your Broker/Dealer, you will need to transfer your registration to your new Broker/Dealer.

2. Investment Advisor Representative (IAR)

If you join an independent firm, you will register as an Investment Advisor Representative (IAR) of the independent advisory firm. Again, your supervisor will tell you how and where to register.

I think the best way for someone new to the financial planning industry to begin, is by interning with a good independent firm. The problem is that independent firms haven't generally awakened to the fact that interns can benefit them every bit as much as they can help the intern! Once you find a firm you like that is willing to take you on as an intern, go for it! You may eventually end up a partner. You might be able to negotiate the expenses of getting licensed and registered as part of your employment agreement.

3. Registered Investment Advisor (RIA)

The scary way is to jump right in and do it by yourself! The main advantage to becoming a Registered Investment Advisor on your own is also the main disadvantage. Whether you do it right or wrong, you're the bottom line.

The rest of this chapter will assume the reader is considering an independent practice, and will be responsible for making all of the decisions.

Things You'll Need to Know Before You Register:

1. Business Form

If you start out on your own, your first concern will be your business form. Will you be a sole proprietor, corporation, Limited Liability Company, partnership, or something else?

There are books written on the pros and cons of business forms, and I urge you to do plenty of research and get information from your accountant and legal advisor before making a final decision.[98]

2. Fee Schedule

How you charge for your services is integral to your ADV filing and your agreements, so it must be determined early on. Always think "disclosure." Your ADV must always contain current and accurate information. Amending your ADV later to include a different payment method isn't a problem.

3. Custody and/or Discretion

You don't want either. Don't even think about it! Custody means you have your client's money or securities in your possession. Discretion means someone else may have custody, but you can get it if you want. Both are rampant with conflicts of interest and additional compliance procedures. The more control you have over your client's money, the more regulatory hoops you need to jump through. Just don't go there.

4. Client Contract or Agreement

Before transacting business, you and your client must understand exactly what is expected from each of you. Unfortunately most contracts, out of necessity, require esoteric and often cumbersome language to protect the interests of both parties.

For fifteen years, I tried to perfect an agreement that wouldn't make me feel like apologizing every time I handed it to a client. I gave up. I still apologize, and then make my client read through it thoroughly with me before they sign. In the end, I know we're both more comfortable knowing we understand the specific terms of the engagement.

Don't ever simply copy another planner's contract and use it as your own. Make certain it is a true representation of how you personally do business, not what you think looks good! Your ADV will mirror your contract, so the two had better agree.

Your contract will need at least the following elements:

A. Parties:
   Your name or company and the name of your client. This may seem straightforward, but there are a number of considerations to be made. If your client is married, is the spouse a de facto client? Are life partners considered a single client? Identification of your client may affect other parts of your agreement.

---

[98] BFi has a basic comparison chart to help recall the differences in the most common entities. http://www.bizfilings.com/learning/comparison.htm

B. Services:

An explanation of what you will do for the client, and how your services will be delivered. I have different contracts depending upon the engagement. One agreement covers continuing financial planning and asset management provided under my retainer, and another deals with hourly consultations and short-term projects. I've seen effective contracts that list items to be checked off if they are to be part of the engagement. Unless you are an attorney or accountant, this may be a good place to document that you will not be providing legal or tax advice. If you don't analyze property and casualty insurance, so state. Be as specific as possible.

C. Authorizations and Implementation Procedures:

Things you can do, like trade in your client's account, deduct fees from your client's account, and the steps that must be followed to enact transactions.

D. Responsibilities:

Things you expect from your client, such as copies of financial documents, income tax information, completion of questionnaires, attendance at consultations, cooperation from your client's other advisors, etc.

E. Confidentiality:

Your privacy policy statement, and any exceptions, in writing. Should your client wish to allow you to share information directly with his or her other advisors, define the nature of the information and documentation necessary to do so for each specific instance.

F. Term:

How long the contract will last and how to cancel it if your client changes his or her mind after the contract is signed. Spell out whether the contract is for a specific project with a set deadline, or will continue until written notification from one of the parties within a specified period.

G. Compensation:

How you will get paid. This section needs to be very specific. Consider such issues as minimum account size and billing in advance or in arrears. (Billing in arrears or as work progresses is best from a logistical standpoint. If you bill clients in advance, that amount should appear on your balance sheet as unearned income until earned.) State whether pro rata billing will be from the time the contract is signed, the money deposited, or an agreed upon date. Define the date and/or period of asset valuation if pertinent. Identify what will be specifically excluded from the compensation arrangement, such as brokerage, legal, or accounting fees charged by a third party.

H. Basis of Advice:

Where you get your information. Generally, your recommendations will be based on analysis, education, documents, and other sources that are available to the public. You do NOT make recommendations based on insider information.

I. Conflict of Interest Disclosure:
    Other interests you may have that could affect the service you provide, such as involvement in another business venture, affiliation with a particular securities or insurance firm, etc. Include a listing of the states with which you are registered.

J. Miscellaneous Provisions:
    Arbitration or mediation clauses, notification of changes in ownership, how consent should be obtained in case of assignment, receipt of ADV by the client, effective date of the contract, etc.

K. Acknowledgement:
    Signatures of the Parties, testifying that they have read and understand the contract and agree with the terms. Also include the date the contract was signed.

Once you have finished writing your contract or client agreement, and believe it contains all the necessary information, I strongly urge you to have an attorney knowledgeable about securities contracts take a look at it. At the very least, troubleshoot with a mock client. Go over each section and play "What if...." Be brutal.

Pretend it's five years from now and your "client" is unhappy with your service, investment performance, manner of compensation, etc. How will your contract help avoid lawsuits, yet be fair to both you and your client?

Set up a scenario where it's five years from now and your client, Mr. & Mrs. X, are ecstatic at the advice, performance and service you have rendered. But Mr. X calls to whisper in your ear that he is leaving Mrs. X, wants you to sell everything, and send the proceeds to his Swiss bank account. What can/should you do, according to your contract?

Use your imagination. Pick up the business section of a major metropolitan newspaper on any given day and put yourself in the shoes of the financial planner being sued, arrested, accused or convicted. Also, pick up a copy of Katherine Vessenes' book, *Protecting Your Practice* [99]. Then take another long, hard look at your contract. Don't miss the opportunity to attend one of Katherine's presentations at a meeting or conference. She makes protecting your practice and other legal and ethical considerations a whole lot of fun!

Some of the compliance services, such as Beverly Hills Regulatory Consultants Group LLC, The Consortium, and National Regulatory Services, offer mock regulatory exams, which walk you through an audit and leave you prepared for the real thing.

---

[99] *Protecting Your Practice* by Katherine Vessenes. Bloomberg Professional Library. 1997. Ms. Vessenes also has a disk available as an add-on purchase, which contains sample documents and contracts.

According to Tim Murray, CFP® [100], who left an independent Broker/Dealer to set up his own RIA a few years ago, if you take the time to do it correctly from the beginning, the rest is easy.

"What are the true 'compliance costs' for a small solo shop like mine?" Tim reported. "Very minimal. I recently had my first audit by the Commonwealth of Virginia, and it went really well. Just some very minor tweaks to what I was doing. I spend very little time and/or money on compliance because I do things the right way and have very little to worry about. People who are not ethical, and, for that matter moral with their business, are not attracted to the RIA model because you actually have to be on the client's side of the table when providing advice. What a concept!"

Getting Registered:

If you begin your own practice, you will become a Registered Investment Advisor (RIA) and have your own ADV.[101]

If you receive compensation (commissions, fees, wages, prizes, etc.) for financial services, you must register with the Securities & Exchange Commission or the state in which you do business. The magic number is $25 million under management, with a little wiggle room between $25 million and $30 million. When you have authority to exercise any sort of control over client assets in excess of $30 million, you must be registered with the SEC.

If you're just starting out, you won't be managing $25 million, so you will need to register with your state. Go to http://www.nasaa.org →Industry & Regulatory Resources tab at the top of the page, then Investment Advisers (left side drop-down menu). Read the FAQs first, then everything else on that page. Check out every single link, because the information is vital! Make note of the contact information for the Regulator in your state. Find out what they require in order for you to do business.[102] Become intimately familiar with the forms you will need to file. Get comfortable with the site because you'll spend a lot of time here while getting started.

The Series Exams and What to Expect:

Study materials and coursework choices abound on the Internet. Caveat Emptor!

---

[100] http://www.murrayfinancial.com/

[101] I have no idea what ADV stands for. It's probably an acronym for "Advisor Registration", but in any case, in most states, you need to be registered. Your ADV is the document evidencing your registration.

[102] **Note:** Most states have a de minimus exemption that allows you to work with a few clients (generally five) in that state without registering, as long as you don't have an office in that state. If your first clients are friends and relatives in other states, this may be particularly important!

Series 7: General Securities Representative

Every full-service Broker/Dealer will require this exam. In fact, you cannot take the Series 7 exam without a sponsor. Passing it will qualify you to register with the NASD as a General Securities Representative (Registered Representative) and sell stocks, bonds and mutual funds. You will be allowed six hours to take the 250-question test. A passing score is 70%.

The Series 7 is a difficult test. You are advised to plan at least a six-week study period to familiarize yourself with the material. I highly recommend a live, hands-on, five-day cram course immediately prior to taking the exam. Believe me, you don't want to have to take this test a second time. Do what you have to do to get through it, and get on with your life!

Caution! Sometimes the company you work for (typically an insurance company or bank) may sponsor you for only the Series 6 and explain that's all you need, since you will be selling only mutual funds and variable contracts under their jurisdiction, not individual securities. Don't buy that! If there is even the slightest possibility you may work one day with a full-service securities firm, you'll have to have the Series 7. Get it over with right from the start. Offer to pay the difference in costs between the Series 6 and 7 licenses if the firm tries to argue that the Series 7 is more costly than the Series 6.

Series 63: Uniform Securities Agent State Law

In addition to the Series 7, you must pass this exam in order to sell securities in a given **state**. The Series 63 isn't exactly fun, but compared to the 7, it should be a piece of cake! There's a lot of common sense involved in the questions, but it's best taken right on the heels of the Series 7.

You'll need to learn a lot of legal terms and consider ethical issues, so spring for a workbook or a course and take the time to study and pass the first time through. You will have an hour to answer 50 questions, and need a score of 70% to pass.

Series 65: Registered Investment Adviser Law Examination

Whether you're working for an independent advisor or striking out on your own, if you will be holding yourself out as a financial planner, this is the one you'll probably need. It's required in most states in order to become a Registered Investment Advisor (RIA) or Investment Advisor Representative (IAR). The exam contains 140 questions to answer within a three-hour period, but only 130 are graded. The remaining 10 questions, which appear randomly, are pre-test questions. A passing score is correctly answering 89 (68.5%) of the 130 questions. Some states may have a higher pass-percentage requirement.

A registered person associated with a Broker/Dealer will also require this license to sell wrap-type products and engage in fee-based asset management, along with their commissioned products.

Series 66: Uniform Combined Law Exam

This exam combines the Series 65 and 63 exams. The only reason you would take this exam rather than the Series 65 is if you are with a Broker/Dealer and also need the Series 63.

With permission from General Counsel at NASAA, here are some sample questions from the Series 65 and 66 exams, which were revised beginning in 2000 to include more financial planning issues. The questions also appear on the NASAA website.

SERIES 65 & 66: sample questions (the answer in bold)

1. Using multiple asset classes in an investment portfolio reduces which of the following?

   1. Liquidity risk
   2. Credit risk
   3. Interest rate risk
   4. **Market risk**

2. Under the Securities Act of 1933, which of the following is NOT a security?

   1. **Futures contracts**
   2. Corporate bonds
   3. Investment contracts
   4. Stock options

3. Under the Uniform Securities Act, "sales" include which of the following?

   I   Giving a security as a bonus for a securities purchase
   II Making a bona fide loan of stock
   III Entering into a contract to sell a security for value

   1. III only
   2. I and II only
   3. **I and III only**
   4. I, II, and III

4. Which of the following statements is true about required minimum distributions for traditional IRAs?

   1. They must begin when the individual retires.
   2. They must be completed over a five-year period.
   3. They are mandatory as of April 1 following the calendar year in which the owner reaches age 59 1/2.
   4. **They are mandatory as of April 1 following the calendar year in which the owner reaches age 70 1/2.**

110

5. A husband and wife are 55 and 57 years old, respectively. The husband plans to retire at 62 and the wife at 65 and both are healthy. What is the most appropriate estimate of the time horizon for their retirement portfolio?

1. 5 years
2. 7 years
3. 8 years
4. **20+ years**

CERTIFIED FINANCIAL PLANNER™ practitioners, as well as Chartered Investment Counselors (CIC), Chartered Financial Consultants (ChFC), Personal Financial Specialists (PFS) and Chartered Financial Analysts (CFA) are exempt from taking the Series 65 in order to become RIA's or IAR's in most states.

Caution! Passing the CFP® certification exam does not automatically qualify you for the designation. You must also meet the three-year experience requirement before actually using the CFP® certification marks.

If your Broker/Dealer doesn't have a study track available to you, or if you plan to test on your own, there are some good courses available. Check your local schools and universities, or begin an online search[103]. Do your homework! To learn more about the Series 63 and 65 tests, see http://www.nasaa.org →Search →Exams.

Since its inception in 2000 until recently, I served on the North American Securities Administrators Association (NASAA) Exam Advisory Council. The Council was charged with modifying the content of the Series 65 exam to include investment vehicles, economics, ethics and legal guidelines within a financial planning environment. My participation includes writing and reviewing items for the Series 63 and 65 tests. When I accepted a position on the Council, I had no idea the incredible amount of concern that went into writing the questions. The test development organization is committed to preparing an examination that will test competence. A tremendous amount of time and expertise is devoted to weeding out "trick" or unclear questions. If you are serious about becoming a financial planner, then I'm convinced you should have the knowledge required to pass the exams.

Preparing and Filing Form ADV:

All Registered Investment Advisors must file ADV Part I and Part II online and Part II will be available to the public. It costs $150 for a one-time set up fee and $100 annually, plus the renewal fee charged by the state(s) in which you register. To learn more about the IARD system, see http://www.nasaa.org Industry and Regulatory Resources → CRD/IARD. Form ADV on the IARD system is the same for both the SEC and the states requiring

---

[103] http://www.nasaa.org → Search → Exams → Exam FAQ → Exams → Exam Study Material Vendors

Investment Advisors to register. You can see the form and instructions on the NASAA website.[104]

Caution! I cannot emphasize enough the importance of getting currently accurate information from the home state in which you intend to set up your office and practice! The rules for each individual state are constantly changing. At some point, everything will be done online. But we're not there yet!

Fortunately, help is available. There are compliance people, attorneys, other advisors, and state regulators who can help you process your ADV. When I first registered, I sent away for the form that arrived in a big package with incomprehensible instructions. I had to look up most of the words, but finally filled the thing out and sent it in, only to have the state send it back. The California Department of Corporations and I went back and forth so many times we practically had our own postal franchise before we were finished. To tell you the truth, I was never comfortable that I knew for certain just what I was admitting to by answering some of the questions the way I did.

A few years later, when I went into partnership with another advisor, we hired Nancy Lininger with The Consortium[105] to fill out the Partnership ADV. She grilled us for hours with tough questions about how we did things and set us straight on the best way to develop our business. The ADV was accepted as submitted the first time through.

When the partnership fizzled, I learned how to withdraw my ADV and took the chance of registering by myself again as a sole proprietor. This time, thanks to Nancy's meticulous explanations of each facet of the ADV, it was accepted immediately. I was working with National Regulatory Service (NRS)[106] by the time I incorporated, and it was easy to withdraw the sole proprietor RIA and re-register as a corporation on the Internet.

My corporation used EZ-2000™, NRS's registration forms software, which let us easily update our ADV whenever we filed an amendment. Instead of printing a bunch of copies (which are required to give to clients prior to working with them) that may become outdated with a change, we printed on demand. With NRS, all information is automatically transferred to the ADV forms. Another company with similar software is National Compliance Services, Inc. (NCS)[107]

Tips from Nancy Lininger of The Consortium:

I asked Nancy if she had any hot tips for new advisors filing their first ADV, and she jumped right in with what turned out to be three pages chuck-full of information. Listen up! What follows can save you a whole lot of time, grief, money, and a bottle of Tylenol. Here's a boiled-down version of what she told me:

> *1. If you "borrow" language you like from someone else's ADV, for crying out loud, make sure it*

---

[104] http://www.nasaa.org/industry___regulatory_resources/investment_advisers/758.cfm
[105] http://www.liftburden.com
[106] http://www.nrs-inc.com →Investment Adviser
[107] http://ncsonline.com/ →Investment Adviser

agrees with what you do! I have seen so many ADVs with inconsistencies. The wording might look good, but if it says, "bill in arrears" and you actually bill in advance, you're setting yourself up for real trouble when the auditor comes calling.

2. *In theory, advisors should understand all the rules before filling out their ADV. In practice, the form looks simple, but an inadvertent answer could end up giving you custody when that's not what you intended at all.*

3. *Begin with your marketing plan. Know what services you provide, and the fee you will charge. It's easier to transfer what you're doing to your ADV than to try and fit what your ADV says into your practice.*

4. *Know how you are compensated. You can call yourself "fee-only" if you have **no** Broker/Dealer affiliation. Some Broker/Dealers allow you to retain a separate RIA. If, in addition to your RIA, you are a Registered Representative of a Broker/Dealer, you are fee-based, fee-offset, or commissioned, but **not** fee-only.*

5. *Disclose ALL business activities where required. If you sell shoes one day a week, you are engaging in a "business activity" which must be disclosed.*

6. *Know whether you have discretion and/or custody. If you are a trustee for your client, have general power of attorney, or can deduct fees without complying with specific procedures, you may have custody and be subject to regulatory hoops you haven't acknowledged.*

7. *Have an agreement, in writing, disclosing all fees, conflicts of interest, scope of the engagement, and a clause that disallows you from assigning your client's account without written confirmation.*

8. *Once your ADV application has been submitted, WAIT until you get authorization before giving advice.*

9. *While awaiting authorization, set up files for proper record keeping under the SEC rules, prepare your Policy & Procedures Manual (a.k.a. written Supervisory Procedures, even if you are only supervising yourself), Privacy of Consumer Information documents, and research errors & omissions insurance. (Coverage is not mandatory.)*

10. *Keep your ADV current! File amendments when required (at any time during the year material changes occur). At a minimum, file annually to reflect the number of clients, dollars under management and percentage of time devoted to financial planning and other activities, and make your annual ADV offer to clients.*

ComplianceMax[108]

Bob Adams, CFP® had such high praise for ComplianceMax I just had to call and see what all the ruckus was about. I picked up the phone and pretended to be a new planner wanting

---

[108] ComplianceMax http://www.compliancemax.com/Portal/ NRS has purchased ComplianceMax but the product is still available.

to get registered. Told Jim Gibson, the sales manager I'd been to the website and probably wanted their ResourcesPLUS™. "Whoa!" He said. "Tell me about yourself. We're kinda' old fashioned here and want to get to know our customers before we recommend products." Well, that sold me.

I asked Jim to send me something about the process, and here's what I received:

ComplianceMax is a national regulatory compliance firm in business since 1999. We offer a full range of services for the new and established investment advisor, including consulting, audit and a complete Web-based technology platform specifically designed for the small- to mid-sized firm. With hundreds of clients all over the United States, we have the experience and expertise to help your firm implement a strong compliance program.

At ComplianceMax, we believe that a successful advisor's practice is built upon a solid foundation. That foundation begins with a strong commitment to a culture of compliance. Your commitment, coupled with a systematic compliance program, helps position your firm for long term growth and success.

The benefits of a strong compliance program are compelling. With a good compliance foundation, your business can be operational faster and scale seamlessly as your business grows. With confidence that your compliance program is strong, you can focus on running and growing your business.

We can assist you with SEC and State regulatory compliance so that you do not have to do it alone. ComplianceMax has helped firms of all shapes and sizes get on the road to compliance and stay there.

As a new Investment Advisor, registration is the first step in your compliance program, and ComplianceMax has been the trusted partner for hundreds of new entrants in the investment services industry. Whether you want to "do-it-yourself" and just need some consulting and assistance from our expert team or you want to let us take care of the entire project, our goal is to achieve accuracy, professionalism and timeliness in the registration process.

ComplianceMax offers a "flat fee" package for new investment advisors that includes:
- ADV Part I
- ADV Part 2 and applicable schedules
- Form U-4 for advisory associates
- Concurrence filings with associated BD
- Completion of IARD entitlement forms
- Completion of jurisdiction-specific documents
- Investment Advisory Agreements
- Consultation regarding post-filing regulatory requirements and filings
- Guidance regarding IARD account funding, current and future regulatory filing costs
- Special request response to regulators
- Complete Registration file, upon completion, including "Model Office" compliance file folder labels

Once you have completed the registration process, SEC regulations and many states require you to put in place an ongoing systematic compliance program. The new advisor can address this with Resources™, our step-by-step compliance framework designed to get your firm on the path to compliance and keep you there.

We actively monitor regulation, interpret SEC and State rules, and assist you with a regulatory implementation plan designed around a series of monthly Web-based compliance modules or workbooks. All that's required of you is a few hours per month and a strong commitment to developing a "culture of compliance."

Our Resources™ program is a complete compliance program designed specifically for the small- to mid-sized firm and includes all the tools you need including:

- Monthly compliance workbooks
- Online Policies & Procedures Manual
- Online Business Continuity Plan Manual
- Model Forms & Document Library
- *Observations*™--our quarterly newsletter
- Monthly Web seminars on selected compliance topics

The final step in developing and implementing a successful compliance program is having the ability to customize your plan to fit your firm. If you need personal assistance at any time, the ComplianceMax team of professional compliance consultants is available on an hourly basis or special-project basis.

ComplianceMax takes the guesswork out of compliance by offering simple, comprehensive and affordable regulatory solutions.

Tips from Patrick J. Burns, Jr., JD
Advanced Regulatory Compliance, Inc.[109]

I called Patrick to ask for some Regulatory Tips, and here is what he said:

1. *Be prepared for a state or SEC audit – plan for them to show up anytime, on any day. Undergo a "mock" audit if you are unsure how your firm would fare.*

2. *Attend industry events, conferences and the like to keep abreast of rapidly changing regulatory requirements.*

3. *Treat compliance as an important part of your business, and devote sufficient time and resources*

---

[109] Patrick is Chairman, President, CEO and co-founder of the Advanced Regulatory Compliance, Inc., whose services include assistance with investment advisor registration, the IARD system, investment policy statements, Form ADV, codes of ethics, and written supervisory procedures. http://www.advreg.com/

to it.

4. *Cover hot button regulatory issues within your written supervisory procedures. These issues include disaster recovery and business continuity, best execution, soft dollars, directed brokerage, etc.*

5. *Ensure your firm has a workable code of ethics to prevent regulatory issues or embarrassing incidents at your firm.*

6. *Test your compliance structure periodically to ensure it is designed to do what it's supposed to do – prevent problems.*

7. *Review your business relationships at least annually – have your business partners run into compliance problems over the past year? If so, what have they done to ensure they do not have additional issues, especially ones that ensnare your firm?*

Tips from Katherine Vessenes[110], JD, CFP®, *Protecting Your Practice*

Katherine on Notes:

"Get good processes and procedures in place from day one, so you can say, 'I **always** did *xxx*!' File notes are the number one most important thing! Have a good filing system, with original, contemporaneous information.'""'Ask every client: 'What are your specific goals? What expectations do you have of me as your advisor? What expectations do you have of your investment returns?' Make note of the responses. Give a copy of the notes to your client and ask them to initial if they are accurate. Do it right there while you're with the client! If the responses are out of line, make a note of it and have the client initial the note!"

"When you see a lot of clients, pretty soon they begin to run together. Make notes about how you feel about clients, about their goals and expectations. Keep them in a central database so your entire staff can see them when the file is opened."

Katherine on Compliance Manual:

"**Read it!** Know what's in your compliance manual. It takes about forty hours to complete a compliance manual. There's help available, but be careful! I've seen some nationally known firms with horrible contracts! Don't just copy stuff. Be sure your compliance manual contains specific information about **your** operations."

Katherine on E&O Insurance:

---

[110] Katherine Vessenes, JD, CFP® is the author of *Protecting Your Practice*, Bloomberg Press. http://www.vestmentadvisors.com/about/people/katherine/

"I'm amazed at how few fee-only planners have it! It's like saying, if you're wearing a seat belt, you won't have a car accident! It's stupid to think you can't get sued if you don't get commissions!"

The SEC has a letter that addresses common compliance issues discovered during audit at http://www.sec.gov/divisions/ocie/advltr.htm. It's well worth reviewing.

Beverly Hills Regulatory Consultants Group LLC, The Consortium, NRS, and NCS all offer compliance products, service, and software to make your life easier. Many independent firms are cropping up to help new advisors through the process. Look for them. First, talk to other advisors. Find out what/who they're using and how happy they are. If you don't have a Broker/Dealer with a compliance department at your disposal, you definitely need a source that will keep you updated. Beverly Hills Regulatory Consultants Group LLC and NRS let you download a PDF file with their newsletter. Check out the "free stuff" on the NCS site while you're at it.

Record-Keeping Requirements:

As an independent advisor, you're required to keep your Policies and Procedures Manual, Notice of Privacy Policies and Practices[111] (effective 7/1/2001), Client Contracts, Investment Policy Statements, Form ADV Part I and Part II, and certain other records available for audit at all times.

In 2000, an amendment to Rule 204-2, under the Investment Advisers Act of 1940, allowed investment advisers to *"create and maintain any required records using any form of electronic or micrographic media, as long as the adviser:*

1. *Arranges and indexes the records to permit easy location, access and retrieval of any specific record.*
2. *Provides promptly (no more than one business day after the request) any of the following that an SEC examiner requests:*
   a. *A legible, true and complete copy of the record in the medium or format in which it is stored;*
   b. *A legible, true and complete printout of the record; and*
   c. *Means to access, search, view, sort and print the records.*

When maintaining records electronically, the adviser would also be required to establish and implement policies and procedures to reasonably safeguard the records from loss, alteration, or destruction, to limit access to the records to properly authorize personnel and the Commission, and to reasonably ensure that any reproduction of an original record is complete, true and legible when retrieved."

---

[111] The FPA has guidelines and sample forms available free to members, and regulatory services have sample Policies and Procedures Manuals, Notice of Privacy Policies and Practices, Client Contracts, Investment Policy Statements, etc. for purchase.

NASAA has adopted the SEC Recordkeeping Requirements for Investment Advisers, under Rule 203(a)2[112], which, for most advisors, includes the following:

1. Receipts and Disbursements Journal
2. General Ledger
3. Memorandum of each order
4. Bank Records
5. All bills or statements, paid or unpaid
6. Financial statements
7. All written communications and Agreements (including electronic)
8. List of all discretionary accounts
9. Advertising and reasons for recommendations of specific securities
10. Personal transactions of Representatives and Principals
11. Client Records, including
    a. Powers Granted by Clients
    b. Disclosure Statements
    c. Solicitors' Disclosure Statements
    d. Performance Claims
    e. Customer Information Forms and Suitability Information
    f. Written Supervisory Procedures

The list gets longer if you have custody and/or manage assets, or if your state requires additional records be maintained. These records must be kept in an accessible place for five years from the end of the fiscal year during which the last entry was made. For the first two years, records must be onsite.

Prepare a filing system and diligently maintain these records from day one. In our office, we had a filing cabinet with files, each bearing the appropriate label. Our operations flow chart provided for copies of all relevant documents to be placed in the proper compliance file at the time of execution. Inside files for required records that do not pertain to our business, we placed a written statement that the record is not applicable to our company.

Errors & Omissions Insurance:

Do you need it? Probably. Back in the days of limited partnerships and heavily loaded mutual funds, few planners were insured, and there were fewer firms willing to insure them. In the twenty-first century, lawsuits over the LP debacle have subsided, and consumers have a vast variety of investment options with a myriad of cost structures available. Now that financial planning and asset management have come into their own, coverage and costs have become reasonable, and E&O insurance is affordable, even for the sole independent practitioner. You don't expect your home to burn to the ground, but you probably have homeowner's insurance. Your health may be terrific, but you still maintain health insurance. I know you're a great driver, but you need automobile insurance.

---

[112] http://www.nasaa.org/Industry___Regulatory_Resources/Investment_Advisers/456.cfm

I'll never forget a seminar I attended a number of years ago. The speaker was a well-regarded planner who had prepared a financial plan for her long time client. A life insurance policy was recommended, but the policy was never purchased and the planner hadn't followed up on that particular issue. Years later, the person for whom the policy was intended, died. The survivor sued the planner for not insisting that the insurance be purchased. In this case, the court ruled there was no negligence on the part of the planner. Yet the event took a year away from the planner's practice, cost over $50,000 in defense, and the emotional toll was devastating.

Your practice should be protected. Depending upon the nature of your practice, personal background, and credentials, there may be discounts available. Costs and coverage vary greatly, so shop around.

My Experience:

I talked with Tony Bougere, Sr. VP of Marketing, and asked him to tell me about The Markel Cambridge Alliance[113], and what I had to do if I wanted to apply for professional liability insurance with his firm.

"We specialize in service to our policyholders and help them prepare their practices for protection," he told me. I was surprised to learn how proactive Markel Cambridge is in encouraging their policyholders to contact them if they are concerned about a particular situation.

"We'll investigate to mitigate the circumstances if necessary, and recommend procedures to prevent an uncomfortable incident from getting blown out of proportion and becoming a claim." Tony went on to say it was not unusual for Markel Cambridge managers Nancy or Bud Bigelow, to recommend changes to client contracts or suggest methods of reducing risk exposure.

The process was painless. I applied online to receive an application packet, which included a list of questions I should ask before applying for professional liability insurance, a specimen policy, brochure, the application, and a checklist of submission requirements. I sent the completed application with Parts I and II of my Form ADV, samples of my client contracts and LPOAs, plus a copy of my current Certificate of Insurance (so I could arrange for prior acts coverage) to a broker in my state.[114]

Markel Cambridge specializes in small- to medium-size Registered Investment Advisor firms and welcomes applications from newly emerging practices.[115]

SUMMARY:

---

[113] http://www.markelcambridge.com, tboughere@cambridgealliance.com.
[114] Applications must be submitted through a licensed surplus lines insurance broker in the state where the insurance is to be placed.
[115] See sample E&) application in Appendix D

While the compliance and regulatory side of things may seem like a big headache, you'll have an even bigger headache if you don't do it right the first time. Chances are good that one day you'll be audited, or even sued. It'll be really nice if all your books and records are pristine from the start and you don't have the frustrating task of undoing all the problems.

Action Plan:

1. Decide on your game plan:
   A. Broker/Dealer
   B. Employee/Independent Contractor
   C. Your Own Business
      a. Develop Business Form
         1. Obtain physical location, business license, fictitious name, etc. as applicable
      b. Check NASAA for proper registration and examinations in your state
         1. Prepare for and pass required exam(s)
      c. Determine Compensation Structure
      d. Prepare Client Contract or Agreement(s)
      e. Set Up Record-Keeping Files
      f. Research E&O Insurance
      g. Submit Form ADV

Chapter Five

Setting Up Shop

I lean back in my office chair, prop my feet up on my desk, and sip iced tea. My eyes are closed, and a smile is on my face as I contemplate my dream of the perfect practice. I envision my office, my clients and colleagues, my daily routine, and the relaxed, yet dynamic, outlook of my future…

I open my eyes and look out the window, where I see green. There are lots of trees, and birds singing. A quiet, rural residential area with privacy. Easily accessible. I feel comfortable here in my chair, looking out the window, seeing what my clients will see, listening to the birds, relaxing. Yes. It's a nice environment in which to contemplate my clients' financial concerns and develop solutions. My dream places me on the walkway outside, and I step through the front door.

An inviting entry area, with current lifestyle magazines, and today's edition of the *Wall Street Journal*. My receptionist is engaged in welcome chitchat as coffee is served. Venturing down the hallway and into:

My private office. I see wood. A warm, serious place with a simple, spacious desk. An ultra-thin big screen monitor, showing beautiful worldwide landscapes, waiting only for my touch to become instantly alive with anything I wish to explore. A file. A research piece. Audio and/or visual contact with a colleague or client across the country. Historic records all efficiently archived and securely backed up. On one wall is a bookcase filled with slim, leather-bound client binders containing minimal necessary information, in preparation for the next appointment. Beside the binders are some of my favorite professional books. I wander into the next comfortable office and greet members of:

My competent team of advisory professionals, paraplanners, and clerical personnel, who are diligently contacting clients, preparing reports, and arranging engagements. Weekly staff meetings keep everyone informed. We all have Internet access to everything we need. Those advisors choosing to work in remote locations join the meetings through video conferencing. Everyone sets their own hours and decides on their work sites.

Our completely integrated software provides for a single entry to seamlessly flow from initial prospect contact to client, and on into comprehensive financial planning, asset allocation, portfolio management, and information dissemination back out to the client. Data is automatically downloaded and backed-up daily, and is constantly and securely available to advisors and clients through the Internet.

Peeking into the conference room, I find a spacious, oval table surrounded by comfortable chairs, each with a console to accommodate audio/visual equipment and computer connections. In one corner is a cozy arrangement of loveseats and coffee table for more intimate meetings. A credenza with refreshments and supplies fills space on one wall, and another serves as a control area containing a large screen, computer-activated presentation equipment, and reference library. This room is designed for quick rearrangement into a small theatre for educational sessions.

Across the hallway is the rest room, with fresh flowers and sparkling tile, good lighting, colorful tissues and clean cloth towels to refresh visitors as they come and go. I return to my private office and settle into my chair to contemplate:

A normal workweek. It's flexible. Four days a week, business takes priority. My day starts at the gym to work out four or five mornings each week, a couple of them with a personal trainer. I'm in the office by nine, checking e-mail and preparations for the day's events. My staff sees that my schedule is in front of me, and agendas and reports are ready for client meetings. Sigh. I knock myself upside the head and...

Come back to reality. I consider for a moment that actually, I wasn't so far from my dream after all! When I sold my practice in 2004, it was easy to transfer client files on CDs. I can't stress enough the value of having a paperless office. Audio/visual technology was available, but still too costly and not really necessary for my small office. The only thing still really missing is an affordable single-entry software program, but there are good options available, including outsourcing. [116]

My wonderful staff did keep me on track, and schedules were flexible. Mike, the portfolio designer who purchased my practice, resides in another state, yet through advanced communications systems, we were constantly in contact.

For a long time, I felt I couldn't afford another assistant, yet when the opportunity came along, I took the chance and hired an intern. Having interns in the firm brought a constant stream of new ideas and enthusiasm and lightened the work load. The mentoring relationships that developed were personally rewarding.

I look out the window, where I actually do see lots of trees, and hear birds sing. Life is good, and I love what I do!

That's what my office was like. It certainly didn't start out that way, but things were different in 1983, when I was a 40-something-year-old Realtor by day and a student pouring over financial planning textbooks by night. I started out with a Broker/Dealer, and for a time I had an office in their branch. To stay closer to my client base, I added an office in an executive suite and eventually moved out of the Broker/Dealer's office entirely. Soon after, I became an RIA, converted to a fee-only practice, and let my securities licenses lapse. When a new complex was built nearby, occupants of our suite were solicited for space in the new building. An attorney, a CPA and I, all tenants of the executive suite who enjoyed the networking companionship we had established, signed an agreement to rent space in the new complex. Our intention was to share the expense of hiring a secretary/receptionist and purchase office equipment, while keeping our practices separate.

---

[116] *Virtual-Office Tools for a High-Margin Practice* and *Virtual-Office News* by Joel Bruckenstein (http://www.joelbruckenstein.com/) **and David Drucker** (http://www.daviddrucker.com/)

I let my lease expire, put my desk, chairs, and filing cabinets in storage a month before our agreement was effective, and went on vacation. We were to move into the new offices in June. It was actually November before the new complex was approved for habitation, but by the end of July I needed a place to meet with clients and to work, so I moved my desk, temporarily, from storage into a bedroom vacated by one my kids. The CPA and attorney encountered similar problems and found office space elsewhere.

The move scared me. I felt it was unprofessional, and my clients would feel the same. I was afraid I would spend time playing with my dogs or doing the laundry instead of working. Oddly, just the opposite happened. I found myself working more than ever. Before, if I had a dinner meeting, I would leave the executive suite, attend the meeting and head home after to get a good night's sleep. Now, I would leave my home office for the meeting, return at eight, stop for a moment to check e-mail, get involved in an unfinished project and find myself falling into bed at midnight. I had no problem leaving the laundry alone, and with most clients, the dogs were assets!

Remarkably, another thing was happening. It was the attitude of my clients. Instead of dwelling on my appearing out of place or unprofessional, they seemed more relaxed, and tended to open up more. Once I became aware of that, I realized I had discovered the perfect place for my office. As the kids left for college and marriage, I commandeered the bedrooms for additional office space. I have never looked back! I had two separate offices, a conference room, storage room, reception area, and access to the rest room and kitchen. It worked out beautifully! When I needed a larger space for a seminar or reception, there were schools, conference facilities and hotels available to cater any function. Meantime, the overhead was great.

What do you see out *your* window?

"I chose a home office for convenience and overhead," claims Joseph Ponzio, a financial planner from Elmwood Park, Illinois, who chose to start out in a home office. "Do some people ultimately choose not to retain my services because of a home office? Sure. But those might not be my target clients anyway. Because of such low overhead, I can maintain a small number of clients and still make a great living. Ultimately, as I bring on other staff (I currently have one advisor with me) we may choose to set up an office." Before deciding on his home office, Joe asked himself the following questions:

    Can I concentrate on work at home?
    Can I walk away at the end of the day and have family time?
    What level of overhead do I want/can I afford?
    Will people view a home office as unprofessional (or smart)?
    How many? (enough to justify higher overhead?)
    Why? (are these the clients I want long-term if I want to work from home?)
    Will I invite clients to my home or visit them at theirs?
    How will they view either?
    Will this cost me a significant amount of business?
    What will I do when additional staff is needed?

Joe adds, "Don't forget to get a Post Office Box. I used to have mail come to the house, but I do not trust the Post Office to deliver the important stuff (nor my neighbors to not throw it out if it comes to them)!"

How Two Set Up Shop:

A thread on the FPi Getting Started/Career Development discussion board revealed the process used by two financial planners who struck out on their own in 2000. Their stories are re-told here with permission:

David J. Moran, CLU, ChFC, CSA
The RTA Group
Plymouth, Massachusetts

My background is insurance based. I grew up in the captive agency system working my way through the ranks as an agent, sales manager and home office trainer. In that time, I earned my CLU & ChFC, won all kinds of awards and felt pretty good...until. Until I decided that the best way for me to succeed in the future was to build my own business in the fee-based financial planning and investment management arena. In '98, when I left the insurance business, there were very few options to explore that would give me the total independence I desired.

I didn't just jump into the fee-based business with no clients and no assets. I dove in face first! To wit, two small children (ages 4 and 5 at the time). My wife and I have always felt that the most important thing we could do for our relationship and for our kids is for mom to be home with them, full time.

So, no clients, no income, just a business plan—and away we go!

After interviewing the Broker/Dealers and insurance companies (posing as financial planning firms), I set off to register in Massachusetts as an RIA. I had the requirements of series 7, and ChFC, as well as work experience. I hired National Compliance Services[117] to handle the ADV writing and filing. I highly recommend them to anyone thinking of registering as an RIA in their state—they have the contacts and experience to help you avoid the inevitable mistakes.

I spoke with Schwab, Waterhouse[118], Vanguard and Fidelity. I opted away from Fidelity, because it was my concern that I would be fighting an uphill battle to create my own "brand" with their name so prominent on all marketing materials. Vanguard wanted $1 million in Vanguard funds to start (yeah, right), and Schwab didn't take me too seriously. TD Waterhouse, on the other hand, made me feel like I could actually pull this off! They

---

[117] http://ncsonline.com/

[118] TD Waterhouse merged with Ameritrade in 2005 and kept the Ameritrade name. Their advisor site is http://www.tdainstitutional.com/ and they remain a popular custodian.

returned my calls, and although they wanted a substantial commitment after twelve months, I went with them. I am extremely delighted with their service, follow-up and technology. A shameless plug for TD Waterhouse Institutional Services at this point isn't out of line, is it?

I chose Centerpiece[119] as my portfolio management software for some of the same reasons I chose TDW. Their people made me feel like I could pull it off. I spoke with IA's who use the program (as well as others) and felt pulled between Advent and Centerpiece. The Centerpiece sales guy threw in some extras and sealed the deal.

As for planning software, I use LifeGoals LGX program. It's okay, I think. My problem is that being a sole proprietor, I make decisions and have to give them time to work without the advantage of bouncing ideas off other people in the office. (I do talk to myself a lot but find I don't like some of the answers!)

For funds and stocks, I use Principia[120] - and like Centerpiece, I'm sure that I am utilizing about 35 to 40% of the capabilities at this point. When deciding between marketing my practice and learning the ins ands outs of software, I always choose marketing.[121]

The reality is that I have begged, borrowed and borrowed some more to make this happen. My office is a "dedicated suite" in my home, aka the basement. When scheduling meetings, I give the prospect the option of meeting at my place or theirs. It runs 70/30 at theirs. I go out of my way to make it easy for people to do business with me.

One more recommendation for anyone crazy enough to do it this way: Read, read, read. Read everything you can on owning and running your own business. A book that helped me tremendously is *The E-Myth* by Michael Gerber[122]. The first edition was written in the 80's with a revised version put out more recently. I can only comment on the older one because that is the one I read! What it taught me is the importance of systems. Having systems in place for all the activities of the business lets you run the systems that run the business. Once you grasp that philosophy, it takes all the mystery out of it!

The real reason I've done it this way is so I can be there for my family. I get the kids on the bus in the morning and am there to get them off after school. I haven't missed a school play or a baseball game yet. They're only small once.

Little did I know the dramatic changes that would come a few years later:

---

[119] http://www.schwabperformancetechnologies.com/ Centerpiece is currently available only to new users who custody assets with Schwab. The only other major choice today is Advent.

[120] http://www.morningstar.com/products/clmppro.html

[121] Learn more about Dave's marketing campaign for RTA in Chapter 6: Marketing 101.

[122] The revised version is *The eMyth Revisited* by Michael E.Gerber, Harperbusiness, April 1995.

Dave Moran, CFP®
Sr. Vice Presisdent
Evensky & Katz
Coral Gables, Florida

So, here I am in Coral Gables, Florida. If anyone had asked me if I could see myself working (let alone living) in South Florida I would've thought they were nuts. I'm a Boston boy after all, and everything I know about Miami comes from Don Johnson. But, if anyone asked me, "How'd you like to take it up a notch and work with Harold Evensky and Deena Katz?" I would have given that some serious consideration…

When I started the RTA Group in 1998, the goal was to build an entity of value that I could either bring my children into when they were ready or sell for a nifty profit to an outside buyer. My sense is that most entrepreneurs have the same thought and rarely understand the magnitude of the sacrifices they will be making along the way. The reality (as demonstrated by recent industry papers) is that the landscape changes rapidly in the advisory profession, and unless a firm is well capitalized or the owner has the financial wherewithal to maintain a certain standard of living while taking almost nothing out of the business, then things will only get tougher.

I have always been very passionate about "Career Development" and creating a career path for professionals in our industry. To that end, when I was in Massachusetts I was the "Director of Career Development" for the FPA of Massachusetts. In that capacity I would occasionally receive calls from people asking, "How do I get into this business?" This question would keep me going back to the FPA website to see who is hiring and what they are looking for. That's when I saw Deena Katz was looking for an experienced advisor for her firm. I sent her an e-mail so I could get more details about the job in the event I could help her find the right match based on my contacts. Well, one thing led to another, and we got talking about the possibility of me interviewing for the job. All I can say is that I felt a professional connection with Deena Katz like I had not felt before and was extremely interested in learning more.

Well, that was just about two years ago. In the interim, I went through the process of preparing the kids to move away from the only home they knew and for my wife to leave the small town she was born and raised in. Part of the deal with Deena was that at my expense I would spend some time working and living in South Florida, and we would have a "trial" period. It might have been as late as the afternoon of the first day that I knew this place was for me. So, now the job of getting the rest of the family down here was left to my wife. We decided that the Thanksgiving break was the best time for the kids to start in a new school, and that would give me the time I needed to get my RTA clients used to the fact that although I would still be their advisor, it would be impossible just to drive down to my waterfront office unless they wanted to come to Florida.

So much good has happened in my life since then, and I can honestly say I've made the right move. I certainly don't miss shoveling snow, that's for sure!!

Scott Dauenhauer, CFP®
President
Meridian Wealth Management
www.meridianwealth.com

I opened my office at the end of 2000. I went through NCS and they were a big help. They helped me transfer my information to the IARD.

Schwab told me that they would let me in with no assets as long as I hit $3 million by the end of the first year. If I don't, then they will charge me about $600 a quarter. I don't know if they offer this to everybody, but they offered it to me. They have been very helpful and very responsive; I can always get somebody within a couple minutes, no hold time.

I bought Principia[123]. I also bought AASim[124] from financeware.com and am test-driving Naviplan[125]. I haven't really found a software program that does what it says. My primary software is Excel. I also purchased the Text Library System[126], which, for the price, is a great value. It helps you automate your practice and makes it so you are not re-inventing the wheel. It is a great tool for keeping in contact with your clients, prospects, and centers of influence.

I went another step, which added significant costs, but I believe will pay me back and then some in the end: I hired an advertising company to write and produce a personal brochure and postcard as well as stationary and logo that all matched. They did an incredible job. I use the postcards as my primary marketing piece (they are all four-color). This set me back about $12,000, including the printing (I printed a huge amount). I also started my own website and used AdvisorSquare. They do an o.k. job, but they charge too much on a monthly basis. I spent a lot of time on the content (probably too much), and I am constantly updating the site with articles that I write and articles written in the press that I feel are appropriate.

I use Advent[127] for my portfolio accounting. This was a big decision, since it cost me about $4500, plus a yearly licensing fee. The software has a huge learning curve that I am still on. The reason I chose them is because I think my practice is more focused on the middle class and I didn't want to have to pay a minimum fee for each client.

Instead of renting office space, I work out of my home. I was working out of our second bedroom, but my wife and I are having a baby and my office is being turned into a nursery. Now I am remodeling the garage to make room for my new office. When I meet with clients, I use an executive suite by the name of REGUS Business Centers. They rent me space by the hour to meet with clients and the place is primo. They model their business on Ritz-Carlton. They also answer my phones and give me a prestigious address. I pay $175 a

---

[123] http://www.morningstar.com/products/clmppro.html
[124] http://aasim.com/
[125] http://www.naviplan.com
[126] http://www.financialsoftware.com Text Library System is now Practice Builder.
[127] http://www.advent.com

month for that service, plus the hourly fees to rent the conference rooms. I haven't had any client complaints. They actually like the idea!

My wife is a teacher, and her income is definitely helping as I start this venture. I am actually marketing my services to public school teachers. There are no fee-only planners in my area marketing to them, only annuity reps. Needless to say, there is a lot of room for growth. We have over 19,000 teachers in Orange County. I am working my butt off and wearing more hats than I ever dreamed, but I love it.

MAKE A LIST AND CHECK IT AGAIN AND AGAIN

If you're starting out with a Broker/Dealer and plan to maintain space in your Broker/Dealer's office, or if you'll be joining an established practice, then your costs are pretty much pre-defined. You may be responsible for some sort of space rental agreement, might need your own computer, and may have to pay a fee to log onto proprietary software systems. But that expense should be minimal compared to the cost of opening your own office.

If you'll be on your own, I strongly urge you to do a little dreaming. Opening a home office was strictly a happy accident for me, but looking back, I sure wish I'd thought of it from the beginning. Give some thought to where you expect to be five years from now and begin with that in mind. It never hurts to be ahead of the curve when negotiating space and technology needs.

In Appendix E, you'll find a suggested list of things you may need before you open the doors on your own private practice. Much of the cost will be dependent upon the location and cultural setting at the time and place those doors open. My office was in Southern California, but in San Bernardino County. Things cost a lot less there than they did just a few miles south or west, in Orange or Los Angeles Counties. Of course, my homespun style and fee schedule reflected expectations from middle-income clients that may be quite different from the multi-millionaire professionals in Century City.

Juan Caballero has a practice in Puerto Rico. In 2003, he queried the FPi discussion boards about fees to take the various exams and associate with a Broker Dealer. Unfortunately, Juan only received one very comprehensive response. It's worth looking at the thread if only to consider potential costs you may have. Juan holds Series 6 and 63 securities licenses and is licensed to sell Life Insurance and Variable Products. His start-up expenses in 2003 were:

B/D "service" fee: $100 annually
NASD Registration: $185 annually
Securities Registration with State Department: $150 annually
Series 6 Exam: $60
Series 63 Exam: $65
Materials: $90
Fingerprint Cards (times three): $25 each
E&O Insurance: $1989 annually

Local Life Exam: $150
Local Variable Products Exam: $150
Insurance License Renovation Fee: $150 annually
Financial Software: $500 annually
Stationary: $150

These costs were considerably higher across the board by 2011 and don't include a number of items you may need to include. It's easy to overlook local government fees for licenses and exams. Overestimate and incorporate an emergency allowance when estimating your budget.

If you associate with a Broker/Dealer, they can help you determine necessary expenses, but if you're thinking of opening your own practice, look at the more comprehensive list in Appendix E.

SOFTWARE

One necessity we all have is software. I've often joked that my financial planning software was a yellow pad and pencil with a good eraser. But the fact is, you can't get much further than a ballpark guesstimate with a yellow pad. Those brief notes and rough estimates will eventually need to be input to specialized software that will spit out multi-color graphs and charts and precise calculations for clients.

My dream office included an integrated software program to include contact, asset, report, and education management. I'm convinced no such thing exists today in the financial planning world. We're told the profession is too new and too small to warrant such extravagance. I personally think that's a crock, but being a complete klutz with computer programming, let alone installation, I'm in no position to bargain.

I did have conversations with some pretty heavy hitters in the industry, and here are the candid results of those encounters. Stay awake! New stuff is coming down the pike every single day. Don't miss out on the product you need because you weren't paying attention! And don't, for crying out loud, be stuck with an obsolete product because you think you can't afford to change! In today's financial planning environment, you simply can't wait for the perfect solution. You must be prepared to upgrade or even switch entirely to a new format! Purchase financial planning software with the intention of replacing whatever you have within a few years. And keep your fingers crossed that before long, one of those techie geeks will finally make a name and fortune for him/herself with an integrated program. Please!

Until recently, John Olsen hosted the Software/Technology Boards for Financial Planning Interactive, which is where I was introduced to his comprehensive knowledge. Today, when I am considering a new software program, John is one of the first people I contact for information. If it's out there, John's taken it for a test drive.

FINANCIAL PLANNING SOFTWARE

By John L. Olsen, CLU, ChFC

The first difficulty many practitioners (especially new practitioners) encounter with "financial planning software" is that the term itself is as precise as "financial planning"—which is to say, so vague as to be virtually useless. What does it *mean*? The frustration wrought by this confusion is evident from the question often voiced by planners:

"What IS financial planning software anyway, and how can it help me in my practice, and how can I decide which program or programs to buy?" Let's attack this question by breaking it down to its three components.

1. What is "financial planning software"?

That term covers a lot of ground, but generally refers to computer programs, which help the user perform one or more of the following general tasks:

Retirement Income Planning. Here, the focus is on *projected income levels.* Programs in this category may use "deterministic" modeling (assuming that a chosen rate of return on assets—individually, or as a group—will be earned, each year, with no variation, for the entire period. Often, the user may input one [unvarying] rate for pre-retirement and a different [unvarying] rate for post retirement) or "stochastic" modeling, such as "Monte Carlo simulation" (where *variations* in the chosen rate are considered).

Estate Planning. Here, the focus is generally upon "net wealth transfer to heirs." Some EP packages do little or no *cash flow* analysis. Some make *required income* a *constraint*, funding any shortfalls in income by liquidating assets. Nevertheless, the focus is *usually* upon one or two Future Values (e.g.: Net to Heirs at first death and second death).

Investment Planning/Portfolio Management. Here, the focus is on *the type of assets owned and how they perform.* This category includes "straight analysis" programs, such as Morningstar's "Principia" and Wiesenberger's "Investment View"; and "asset allocation/portfolio optimization" packages, such as Frontier Analytics' "Allocation Master" and Advisoryworld's "Power Optimizer". Recently, some software vendors have combined portfolio optimization/asset allocation with Monte Carlo Simulation.

Client/Task/Asset Database Management. This category may be more in the nature of "housekeeping" than "planning". It includes *Client/Contact* management programs, such as "Act" and "GoldMine"; and *Client/Contact/Asset* packages, such as EZ-Data's "Client Data System", "dbCams", and "Centerpiece". These packages are more focused on record keeping than on projections.

Tax Planning. Most packages which are devoted *strictly* to tax planning are intended for the Accounting market, but nearly all programs in the other categories we're looking at take Income Tax into consideration. Some also consider Estate and Gift Tax.

Cash Flow/Debt Management & Planning. *Debt management* is one area in which the software manufacturing sector has fallen down on the job badly. A few programs permit some limited analysis of "debt what if's". *Cash flow*, on the other hand, is a large component of some FP software but a minor consideration in others.

"Capital Needs Analysis". "CNA" programs have been in use in the life insurance industry for decades. Typically, they seek to show a Net Present Value—the *total dollars needed today* to fund clients' goals for Survivor Income if Client/Spouse dies, Income if Client/Spouse becomes disabled, Retirement Income, and Education Funding.

"Comprehensive" Financial Planning packages. These programs attempt to do several—or even *all*—of the seven tasks listed above.

2. How can this software help me in my practice?

First and foremost, a software package is a *tool*, not a Magic Wand. What it *won't* do is enable you to perform planning and management tasks that you don't understand. For example, if you haven't any idea how to complete an Estate Tax Return, getting the 706 preparation program from Zane's or ProBATE Software is just asking for trouble.

Second, even if you feel comfortable in a given area of planning, you don't want to use a software package, which "does" such planning as a "Black Box", the output of which you can be assured is "right." *No* software package is certain to be free of "bugs" and "glitches," and *all* of them produce results based on *assumptions*—some of which may not be explained fully in the documentation (as if anyone ever reads documentation). Facts which lead to a couple of Operational Rules:

1. If you don't know the assumptions that underlie the results you're examining, you can't possibly know if those results make sense.

2. If you aren't sure of where a number came from, you can count on being asked.

That said (and if we haven't scared you off the idea of using *any* software), let's look at how using financial planning software, of one or more of the types described above, might be a *good* idea—how it can help you in your practice.

A *lot* of planning is mere arithmetic. Computers do arithmetic a lot faster and more accurately than humans do. Moreover, some of the math in financial planning is complicated enough that most of us simply *can't* do it "by hand."

"What if" is the very essence of financial planning, and "what if" scenarios are difficult, if not impossible, to do without computer help, especially if we're examining the impact of changes in *several* variables. The best FP software packages allow us to model the effect of a whole assortment of different assumptions and possible strategies.

Your Time Is Money. Not only can you, using appropriate financial planning software, do planning which you wouldn't even attempt without it, but you can do so relatively quickly. The value of your billable hour is enhanced.

Presentation Is Everything. A really good FP program can produce text and graphics that look simply *terrific!* Some even allow you to customize the text and format. For "in person" planning (where you are actually doing "what if's" right in front of the client), some packages allow you to see the result of a changed assumption or value immediately, right on screen. The *impact* on the client is often enormous.

Your Practice Is a Business. As planners, we often spend a distressingly large portion of our time simply running our practices. Billing, correspondence, compliance (every planner's favorite task), and the like take up otherwise-billable hours. To the extent that you can do these tasks *more quickly, accurately, and efficiently,* you "increase the hours in your day."

3. How can I decide which program or programs to buy?

While the process of selecting financial planning software is anything but easy (which is why planning firms and individuals hire the author to help them do that), asking yourself a few key questions—and spending some serious time and effort in addressing those questions—can make it more bearable

A. What do you want the thing to do? The decision process starts right here. Give a *lot* of thought to this question, because, if you don't have a pretty clear idea, you won't be able to make a good decision.

BE SPECIFIC! Include what you *want,* what you *need,* what you *don't want,* and what you *don't need.* Specify *why* you feel as you do.

WRITE IT DOWN!

B. Ask other practitioners how they would answer this question. Not only will you hear ideas you hadn't thought of, but when you put the responses you hear into the perspective of what you know about the nature of the respondent's practice, you'll get a better idea of the Nature of the Problem.

C. Reduce what you have to an itemized list of FACTORS. Make sure that there's as little overlap as possible. (Each factor should be both specific and unique.)

D. Make up a spreadsheet. The first column should list the programs you're considering, *beginning on the SECOND line.* Assign each FACTOR you have identified to a separate column (headed by the name of the FACTOR on the *first line).*

WEIGHT the FACTORS. Apply a Weighting Factor (e.g.: 2.0 = VERY important to you; 1.0 = "neutral" [neither VERY important nor VERY unimportant]; 0.0 = VERY unimportant to you) to each FACTOR you've identified. Enter this WEIGHTING

FACTOR *on the second line of the spreadsheet* (directly beneath the corresponding FACTOR heading).

MAKE A PHOTOCOPY OF THE SPREADSHEET you just made (or, if you're doing this on a computer spreadsheet, **COPY THE RANGE** to an area to the right of the existing spreadsheet).

Score each program for how well it handles the factor in question ("RAW SCORE") and enter the scores in the appropriate cells.

Multiply the RAW SCORES in each column by the WEIGHTING FACTOR for that column and enter the result in the corresponding cells of the second spreadsheet (or tell Excel to do it).

ADD UP THE WEIGHTED SCORES FOR EACH PROGRAM. The higher the number, the better the program *for your particular needs.*

This procedure won't *guarantee* that you'll end up with "the perfect software library", but you will have reduced the task to manageable proportions. At this point, you should have only a few packages to evaluate.

E. What constraints will you apply? This includes:

Hardware limitations. Will you use it on a Network? (Some packages won't run on one, or cost a lot more for a Network version.) Will you want to swap files between a desktop and a laptop? (Some packages make this easy; some don't.)

Who will use it? Consider the "learning curve." A *lot* of software is purchased and then shelved because it's simply too hard to learn for the folks who will have to use it.

Cost. Make sure you take into account the *ongoing maintenance fees.*

Compatibility with other software. Unfortunately, most financial planning software doesn't talk to other financial planning software. But some programs do and most will (eventually). *If you expect to be able to use a program with one or more other programs, make sure you ask the software manufacturer for SPECIFICS on this point.* (Vague promises of "cross-application compatibility" won't cut it!)

F. How will you and your staff learn the program? Most planners decide on "do it yourself", which is rather curious, given that we're in the business of helping clients to *avoid the pitfalls* of this strategy. Consider these factors:

Are you a "pro" at learning/teaching software? If not, then an *amateur* will be running your training program.

How much would hiring a "pro" cost, in billable hours?

Do you really want the aggravation?

If you decide to "do it yourself," make sure that you know what sort of training the software manufacturer provides (other than manuals, which aren't "training" at all).

If you decide not to try to *learn* the program or programs you purchase by yourself, you may want to consider whether you want to make the purchasing decision on that basis. A software consultant who is familiar with the strengths and weaknesses of *all* the programs out there (or many of them, at any rate), *and* who understands the financial planning business, may save you not only time and effort but money as well. After all, isn't that what *you* do for your clients?

©Copyright 2001 by John L. Olsen, CLU, ChFC
***

Some of the most common sense, easy to understand information I've ever read on financial planning software comes from Joel Bruckenstein, CFP®.[128] In June 2001, he published an article on MorningstarAdvisor.com that sets forth what to consider before shopping for products. The editors at MorningstarAdvisor.com have graciously granted permission to reprint the article here:

A Step-by-Step Guide to Finding the Program That's "Right" for You

By Joel P. Bruckenstein, CFP®

When evaluating financial-planning software, there is one universal truth: No one program is "right" for everybody. Arriving at the proper fit for your practice requires a commitment from you. The more you put into the process, the better your chance of success.

Financial planners are not a homogeneous group. We may all adhere to the six-step process, but the similarities end there. There are legitimate philosophical differences among intelligent people as to how a plan should be designed and implemented.

Some planners favor detailed multiyear cash-flow-driven plans, while others prefer a goals-based approach. Some planners want to supply the client with extensive written documentation, while others believe that "less is more." Some place a high premium on charts and graphs, while others prefer text and tables.

Our client bases also differ. Those catering to middle-class clients will have different needs than those who deal exclusively with wealthy clients. Small-business owners present different challenges and opportunities than do middle-level executives.

---

[128] Joel has co-authored *Virtual-Office Tools for a High-Margin Practice* with David Drucker, published in 2002, and available at most online bookstores. If you're setting up an office, you need this book. http://www.joelbruckenstein.com

Where to Begin

Before you begin your search, I suggest that you think long and hard about where your practice is today and where you want it to be in the future. What does your client base look like? Do you expect it to change? What types of services do you currently provide, and will you expand your offerings in the future?

Also, think about your approach to planning. Do you want to develop goal-based plans or cash-flow-based plans? Will you be presenting long, detailed, written financial plans or shorter written plans and action lists?

You should also think about whether or not you will be doing the data entry now and in the future. If you will be doing the data entry yourself, ease of entry may be less of an issue. If an assistant will handle the data entry, context-sensitive help and clearly laid out screens are a plus.

Capabilities You Need

Now, think about the capabilities that your program should possess. Whatever your approach to planning, your program should be capable of handling cash inflows and outflows, whether they are even or uneven. Typical cash inflows would include employment income, self-employment income, Social Security, pension income, and annuity income. Outflows would include fixed and variable living expenses, mortgages, taxes, and contributions to retirement plans.

The program should also allow you to invest excess cash flow in the investment of your choice and direct how short-term deficits will be covered. If assets are to be sold, which ones and in what order? If you intend to borrow, at what cost, and what are the tax implications?

In addition to the basics, think about what other functions are critical to your practice. Do you have clients with employee stock options? How about restricted stock? Investment real estate? Collectibles? Assets denominated in foreign currencies? Commodities? Certain types of assets require specific tax or accounting treatment. If your clients own such assets, you need a program that can deal with them. Just don't pay extra for capabilities that you don't need.

In the area of income tax, you probably want a program that can calculate both federal and state income taxes. If your clients typically own ISOs or other tax preference items, the ability to calculate and report AMT becomes essential.

If most of your clients are young and middle-class, they may not be interested in paying you for elaborate estate plans, so the ability to illustrate basic estate-planning concepts should suffice. Wealthier clients will obviously have additional needs. Can the software model the strategies that you typically recommend? Does it allow you to model multiple cash flows to or from an individual trust? Does it accurately compute estate taxes?

There may be other features that you desire, such as the ability to import or export to other programs, charting and graphing capabilities, etc.

Prepare to Compare

Once you have written down your wish list of capabilities, try creating a table or spreadsheet that will allow you to compare a number of programs. Then compile a list of candidates. You can start with a broad list (a number of publications produce a list of programs), or you can start with recommendations from reviewers, colleagues, and discussion groups. Check the MorningstarAdvisor.com[129] website for a list of my software reviews.

To learn more about the programs, contact the software companies by telephone or online. If certain features are essential to your practice, make sure those features are available, and ask specific questions about the strength of those features. Programs that don't meet your needs will be eliminated, leaving you with a short list.

Check Them Out

It's now time to request demos and look under the hood. Each company should supply you with a working program, not a scripted presentation.

Try installing the software. Does it load seamlessly on your computer? Do you get any error messages? Enter a case and play around. Hopefully, the program will not freeze up or cause other problems. As you work through the case, spot check some of the calculations, so you understand how the program operates. Print a number of reports. Can you control how reports are generated? Can you edit them? Are the calculations correct?

Request the telephone number for technical support and try calling them a few times. Make sure that you can reach them and that they can answer your questions. Find out if their hours of operation are convenient for you. Ask about support policies, frequency of upgrades, hours of operation, manuals, and training materials.

The Final Cut

By now, most contenders will have fallen by the wayside. At this point, one final step may be necessary to arrive at a decision—inquire about a live or online training session. Many of the better companies are beginning to offer this option.

I recently attended all-day training sessions conducted by Net Worth Strategies (for StockOpter) and EISI (Naviplan Extended). Both were excellent.
Experienced instructors walked the class through an actual case study, one designed to use numerous program features, allowing the attendee a hands-on opportunity to use the software as one would in the office.

The training sessions allow you to ask questions as they arise. They also give you the opportunity to observe how other attendees react to the program, which may reveal facts that you overlooked. An added benefit of attending training sessions is that they force you to focus your attention on evaluating a particular software package for the allotted time, something that is often difficult to do at the office.

---

[129] http://www.advisor.morningstar.com

When you're making the final decision, spend as little as necessary to purchase the capabilities you need, but don't make price alone the deciding factor. If two programs can do what you want, but one produces a plan in significantly less time, they are not equal. The one that saves you (or your staff) time is probably the best buy.

If all of the above sounds like a lot of work, it is. But if financial planning is your bread and butter, then it is time and money well spent.

WWW.VIRTUALSOLUTIONSCONSORTIUM.COM

For a wonderfully comprehensive list of virtual office tools and information, visit www.virtualsolutionsconsortium.com, a website devoted to giving you a "one-stop resource for virtual staff and service providers." The site is a veritable who's who of industry leaders, including many mentioned elsewhere in this book – all in one place. If you can't find what you're looking for at www.virtualsolutionsconsortium.com, it probably doesn't exist.

BOTTOM LINE ON TECHNOLOGY:

There is no bottom line.

Stay secure.
Backup often.
Budget generously.
Watch for new systems and products.
Check frequently for upgrades and patches.

RESOURCES:

Most financial services publications and websites have frequent articles on software and often run comparison surveys. Financial Planning usually includes an annual software survey: http://www.financial-planning.com → Advanced Search → Software Survey.

Joel Bruckenstein and David Drucker publish a monthly newsletter, *Virtual Office News* at http://www.virtualofficenews.com. Joel is also the technical writer for *Inside Information*, http://www.bobveres.com

Bob Veres' **Inside Information** at http://www.bobveres.com contains Recommended Software/Web Services, along with current product reviews. **Inside Information** is a subscription site. I think you're crazy if it isn't included on your *gotta' have it* list. Links to almost every other financial planning website you will ever need are here.

http://virtualsolutionsconsortium.com. Sign up for their newsletter!

NOTES ON SETTING UP SHOP

Chapter Six

Marketing 101

This will be a relatively short chapter for two reasons:

1. I don't know much about marketing.
2. There are entire libraries and degree programs on marketing.

Don't interpret that to mean this isn't one of the most **important** chapters in this book. It doesn't matter whether or not you want to sell anything, or think you have anything to sell. You do. Before anything else can happen, you have to sell yourself: to an employer, a client, a lender, a landlord, etc.

Unless you can sell yourself and earn the trust and confidence of whomever you are dealing with, you will not succeed in this or any other service-oriented business.

Some of what I know about marketing came from a missive appearing in my inbox a few years ago[130]:

Explanation of Marketing

Identify the common marketing technology or term for each of the following:

1. You see a handsome guy at a party. You go up to him and say, "I'm fantastic in bed."
   a. Direct Marketing

2. You're at a party with a bunch of friends and see a handsome guy. One of your friends goes up to him and, pointing at you, says, "She's fantastic in bed."
   a. Advertising

3. You see a handsome guy at a party. You go up to him and get his telephone number. The next day you call and say, "Hi, I'm fantastic in bed."
   a. Telemarketing

4. You're at a party and see a handsome guy. You get up and straighten your dress. You walk up to him and pour him a drink. You say, "May I?" and reach up to straighten his tie brushing lightly against his arm, and then say, "By the way, I'm fantastic in bed."
   a. Public Relations

5. You're at a party and see a handsome guy. He walks up to you and says, "I hear you're fantastic in bed."
   a. Brand Recognition

---

[130] Author unknown

6. You're at a party and see a handsome guy. You talk him into going home with your friend.
    a. Sales Representative

7. Your friend can't satisfy him so he calls you.
    a. Tech Support

8. You're on your way to a party when you realize that there could be handsome men in all these houses you're passing. So you climb onto the roof of one situated toward the center and shout at the top of your lungs, "I'm fantastic in bed!"
    a. Spam

It is vital that you have a Marketing Plan as part of your Business Plan. Nothing will get you off the ground running faster than a well thought out strategy for bringing clients in the door. Whether you have a major brokerage behind you or are a one-person shop, ultimately it's up to you to bring in your own clients.

Before you can design a marketing plan, you'll need to make some fundamental decisions about your practice. You'll need a company name, of course, and a solid idea of what it is you can/will do (mission statement). You should have a pretty good handle on what sort of clients you anticipate (middle-market, corporate, wealthy, retired) and the image you desire to project (casual, professional, academic, etc.) to clients and associates. Once you have a grasp on these things, it will be easier to proceed with marketing.

If you're starting from scratch, check out Marie Swift's Impact Communications, Inc.[131] She offers everything from an hourly consultation to a complete turnkey identity package at an affordable price. Go to the websites of Impact Communications clients to see examples of their work.

If you're interested in receiving occasional e-mail notices with a link to current marketing and practice information, take a look at the E-Tips archives. Under the Resources drop-down menu, click on E-Tips Success Strategies and enter your information for a free subscription.

Another good marketing resource, which includes access to personal and business coaches and tips on insurance-oriented material, is the site hosted by the National Association of Insurance and Financial Advisors[132] (NAIFA). Their "Gateway to the Internet" website, Financial Services Online,[133] offers a free e-mail subscription to *Financial e-News*, a bi-monthly publication worth perusing.

An absolute master at marketing is W. Aubrey Morrow, CFP®, President of Financial Designs, Ltd., a fee-based financial planning firm in San Diego, and host of "The Financial Advisors"[134], a weekly show on Money Talk Radio.

---

[131] Impact Communications: http://www.impactcommunications.org
[132] http://www.naifa.org/
[133] http://www.fsonline.com
[134] http://www.moneytalkradio.com/

Aubrey, one of the most energetic people I know, always seems to have a zillion ideas that appear to come right off the top of his head. So I asked him for some help. He created a scenario: "I'm ready for a career change. Hey, money buys happiness, and I like to be happy; it's therefore logical to work with money somehow. Since I would like the freedom and the unlimited income potential, I-want-to-be-a-financial-planner."

Thinking historically, Aubrey explained to me how stockbrokers and life insurance agents are trained:

"In the 'hiring process,' the interview leaves them with illusions of becoming a 'financial planner' with great financial wealth to follow. In reality, the generally 'very good' training period includes teaching to gather the facts on how people earn a living, how they spend, and what areas they commonly overlook. What is found, of course, is *inadequate* estate planning, poor risk management, wrong investment purchases, little retirement planning, excessive taxes, bad debt, etc.

"Before long, the honeymoon is over.

"During the stockbroker/insurance agent's training period, they are taught to maintain a list of 'whom do I know?'

"At the conclusion of the training period, it's now time to *MAKE CALLS*! Huh. 'Why don't people like me? Was it something I said?' During this period, most 'I want-to-be-a-financial planner's' self esteem is lower than whale shit on the bottom of the ocean (yes, you may quote me)." Aubrey doesn't mince words.

"Now comes the 'reality' of why so many people do not make it in this business: because they are not able to handle rejection—know anyone who likes to receive calls from someone trying to sell them something? It's natural to react negatively.

"For the 'determined' I'm-going-to-be-a-financial-planner, it's time to map out your prospecting options. Keep in mind, as Michael Jordan sez, 'Just Do It!' Success leads to more success."

MARKETING for the Determined
"I'm-Going-to-Be-a-Financial-Planner"

By Aubrey Morrow, CFP®

GETTING STARTED: First, evaluate your strengths and weaknesses. Ask a friend to confirm. Whatever you do, do it naturally; otherwise, you will come off as a salesperson sounding like a recording.

Then, in no particular order:

MAKE A LIST OF EVERYONE YOU KNOW: Create a letter or classy wedding-style card announcing your new profession. Describe briefly (in few words) how you help people "solve personal financial issues," etc. Enclose your business card. Don't mass mail to a zillion people. Mail selectively. On your list, categorize names which you feel are tops (like List 1, 2, 3). Mail, for example, 25 per week, and CALL them for an opportunity to visit.

GET REFERRALS: This is absolutely the best source of new clients. One way to do it is to provide your client a sample letter (which your other clients have used to introduce you to their friends). The letter can be on the client's letterhead with "copy" to you. Of course, you mail it when you want to meet new folks. (Note: don't date the letter in advance.) When you (the planner) mail the letter (from your client to their referral), you send a copy to your client so they will be aware of it being sent (especially, if the referral calls to ask about you).

You can also have a sample letter on your letterhead and simply mail your letter to the referral with copy to your client.

SEMINARS: These days there are an abundance of "instant seminar" materials—all pretty good. Companies like Emerald Publications[135] in Rancho Bernardo, California provide an extensive list of seminar materials for financial planners. The seminar topics vary from overall financial planning to specifics. This is an excellent way to break into the business!!! It's professional. Call for their catalogue. They also have two-day training for planners covering A-Z on "how to do it."

These "instant" workshops can be used in many ways:

1. Send flyers in local newspapers announcing your workshops.

2. Team up with another professional to conduct workshops (split the cost of marketing). You can do workshops on literally all the topics (tax planning, estate planning, retirement planning, long-term-health care, etc.). There are endless topics. To me, seminars are the Number Two best way I have met clients. Number One is referrals.

CREATE A FLYER: About your services and distribute it everywhere. Offer a free consultation on something, such as a review of their life insurance policy, income tax return, etc. This is relatively easy and, giving lots of 'em will get results. They're not always the best clients, but it's a start. Of course, once you have a happy client, you should get happy referrals (from your happy client).

SPEAK: At service clubs, community organizations, etc. Most cities have companies who produce lists of clubs and organizations in their city. In San Diego, we have the "Source Book", a three-ring binder listing all service organizations in the city by name and contact. A planner could use this list to advise them of the planner's availability to speak (using the Emerald and similar materials). BTW—this is a piece of cake…it's too easy! Service clubs are always looking for speakers, so it's a nice match. Of course, the speaker will make available handout information and an "Evaluation Form" for comments and future appointments.

---

[135] http://www.emeraldpublications.com/

NEWSLETTERS: Easy to do and makes you feel good about yourself. You can buy software and write your own (allowing you to say what you want) or subscribe to newsletters, which have your picture and contact information pre-printed. I use Emerald's newsletters. I buy three types: one for retirees, non-retirees and business owners. You can send them monthly, bi-monthly, quarterly, etc. Expect to pay in the neighborhood of fifty cents each (not including postage). It's a nice way to keep your mug in front of clients and prospects. You can always offer a six months free newsletter to prospects. It's also a good idea to make it available when you speak. Otherwise, most folks do not want you to contact them. If they want your newsletter, they will provide you their contact information.

TEACH: Adult education classes. Most colleges have evening adult education classes. You can create a course called "Fundamentals of Financial Planning". The course could be taught over a six-week period, once per week, for two hours per class. Guess how many modules Emerald's Complete Financial Planning Workshop has? You guessed it—six. Emerald also has workbooks available to go along with the program; great materials for "your" students. I did this and it works very well. And it's easy. For anyone who is interested, check with your local JC or college and get their catalog on adult classes.

COLD CALLING: Worse than a cold shower. The worst. However, that's how the brokerage firms and insurance companies train. After your classes, it's time to "dial for dollars" or an appointment, that is. What's even worse is the person who says "yes" to your pitch does not know how to say "no" to anyone. However, the brokerage and insurance companies are noticeably successful, so I cannot argue with success. It's strictly a numbers game to start.

DROP–BY'S: Yep. For those of us who cannot handle calling a zillion people with no face, some of us (like me) decided to drop by businesses. In the old days, we did not have all the sources available today, like instant lists in books, and now the Internet. I actually planned cold calling going business to business. My "research" at the library with Dunn & Bradstreet lists showed me "SIC" codes on businesses and businesses by address. There were lists available of all the businesses listed next door to each other. I listed names of the owners / president's and literally "dropped by" and asked for the contact person.

This works…if you have the guts. Also, when you do land a good business owner, the referral letter idea on his/her letterhead is "the best!"

ASK: Other planners how they market and how they got started.

Remember: Marketing is everything.

Robin Vaccai-Yess, CFP®, a planner in Highland, New York, opened her independent fee-only practice on January 1, 2001. Prior to that time, she spent over a year working on her business and marketing plan, which has proved to be a tremendous help in attracting clients to her brand new practice. Robin has some straightforward, step-by-step tips on how to get your business up and running:

Marketing Your Financial Planning Practice

By Robin Vaccai-Yess, CFP®

Just like investments are only a part of a financial plan, a marketing plan is only part of your business plan. Marketing is the means and methods that get your name out to the public; advertising is only a part of marketing. Initially, you should have a plan for at least the first year of operations on a month-by-month basis. With a new practice, your marketing is about building a presence, name recognition, and credibility through various methods.

1. **Have a logo, business cards, letterhead, and a brochure** designed and professionally printed. Steer clear of perforated, self-printed business cards. Image is important, and you don't want clients thinking you were up late the night before printing your business cards!

2. **Send a press release** to all newspapers (local dailies and weeklies) in your area announcing the opening of your new practice. If you've got a niche, stress it. Keep the press release short, double-space it, and make sure it's grammatically correct. A typo in a press release is like cutting your own throat.

3. **Get a website.** Have it professionally done and make it an extension of your advertising and print materials. Prospective clients should be able to go to your site for more information than what they see in your print ads or get from your brochure. Revisit your website regularly to update and improve it. You don't need a counter on a website, but make sure your Web hosting company provides a means for you to check traffic, so you can monitor your marketing efforts.

4. **Get your name in the paper.** Write letters to the editor and send out regular press releases that include a professional press photo (readers love to associate a face with the name they're reading about). If you do something new, like publish a newsletter for clients, join a board or professional organization, or volunteer, use it as a tool to communicate with the press.

5. **Advertise in your local or regional newspapers.**[136] Here's the key to successful advertising – size isn't everything, frequency is. Don't put in the biggest ad you can afford if you can only afford to run it for two months. It won't do it. While in real estate, it's location, location, location, in advertising, it's repeat, repeat, repeat. Of course, your message has to solve a problem for the consumer or invite them to call you, but it should be regular. Always use your Web address in your newspaper ads – remember #3 above: your website is there to give more information. Advertising doesn't have to be display ads; it can be a simple classified ad – as long as it's regular.

---

[136] After a year in practice, Robin claims she "would limit my use of print advertising. The methods that work best are writing articles, and teaching classes and workshops. New clients and/or referrals come from these, but print advertising's results are limited. Naturally, the advertising sales reps tell you about keeping your name out there, but a word-of-mouth business is a better one." Read more about Robin in Chapter Seven.

6. **Join the Chamber of Commerce** and go to meetings, luncheons, and fundraisers. Meet the business community and let them know what you do – networking is your best advertising.
7. **Volunteer** to join the library board, the arts council, or the school board. Get involved and get your name out there. It's the best way to meet people.
8. **Compile** a list of centers of influence and send them quarterly newsletters or problem-solving tools.
9. **Write articles** and send them to business editors. Business journals are often looking for usable articles. If you can write, do it. You'll get your name in the paper as a credible source, which is a lot more beneficial than any size ad you can pay for.

Even with an aggressive and comprehensive marketing strategy, it'll probably take two to three years to build a practice from scratch, but it'll be worth it.

USING A "SYSTEM"

Whether it's a manual from your nationally known Broker/Dealer who spends millions advertising on the Super Bowl, or a book you borrowed from the library, a great place to begin is with a wheel that's already been invented. Here are a couple of ideas to get you started.

Bill Bachrach

"My only regret is not doing this five or six years earlier," said Brian Fricke, CFP®, a financial planner in Florida and graduate of Bill Bachrach's[137] year-long Trusted Advisor Coach® program. Plunking down a hefty, non-refundable fee, plus hotel costs and airfare to San Diego four times in the year 2000, brought his financial planning practice to an entirely new level.

Brian credits his pursuit of *Values-Based Selling* principles for a dramatic increase not only in revenue but also in the character of his business. He says he "grew up in a commission-based world, with all the problems inherent in serving 500 clients." When he switched from commission to fee-based planning a few years ago, he applied the 80/20[138] rule to slash his client base. He loved Bachrach's book and devoured the accompanying tapes but blamed himself when the results weren't what the book promised. To determine what he was doing wrong, he signed up for the coaching program.

"It used to take at least a couple of meetings just to get a client to commit to working with us, and several more meetings to gather information, prepare and implement a plan. I learned interviewing techniques enabling me to establish a high-trust relationship during an

---

[137] Bill Bachrach's website is http://www.bachrachvbs.com/
[138] Pareto's Principle: "In any series of elements to be controlled, a selected small fraction in terms of number of elements almost always accounts for a large fraction in terms of effect."

initial meeting with a potential client. Today, inside an hour, a client will turn over all the necessary documentation, sign my agreement and pay my retainer. Alternatively, we can determine that a potential client is not a match for our firm. That alone was worth every penny."

"Bill has this 'being done' part of the program. I determined how many clients I needed to get where I wanted to be, and when I reach that number in a few months, I'll 'be done.' My practice will have just the right balance of clients and revenue for me, and I'll stop accepting new business. I'm telling my clients if they have friends or family looking for a financial planner, let them know, because the doors will be closing."

Shortly, another planner in Brian's office will be attending the three-day *Values-Based Selling*[TM] Academy training, a course he highly recommends for any financial planner, no matter their years in the industry.

Keith Laibson, a planner in Charlotte, North Carolina, learned about Bill Bachrach from a senior partner with his firm. Keith purchased Bachrach's book *Values-Based Selling* and was motivated later when he attended a conference where Bill spoke.

"I made a commitment to do the 'What is important about money to you?' question at the beginning of all my initial interviews. While it was difficult at first," Keith admits, "I got results and positive feedback from the clients. I use the roadmaps, which help me guide my client to what I am trying to accomplish. It attracts a certain client to our firm: the type we want to work with!"

Practice Builder

Ed Morrow's Practice Builder (formerly Text Library System)[139] has a drip-marketing module. He has literally thousands of continuously updated articles, with a schedule for sending them periodically to prospects. Once a prospect is in the system, the work is done for you. When you log onto the program, the prospects or clients who are supposed to receive a contact that day or week pop up as a reminder. All you need to do is click on the processing to have pre-selected information prepared for each individual contact.

BRANDING

A logo. An image. A mark. A slogan. Something that says ***YOU!*** whenever it's seen. At some point, you'll need whatever it takes to set yourself apart. Even if you represent a huge conglomerate, you are special.

Dave Moran, CLU, ChFC, CSA[140] left the captive insurance agency scene in 1998 and set out to make a name for himself as a fee-based planner. Literally. One of the first things he did was to design a logo and motto to stick on tee shirts and hats, which he gives to clients and

---

[139] http://www.financialsoftware.com
[140] In 2003, Dave closed RTA and moved his clients to a new firm. Read about the transition in Chapter 5: Who's the Boss?

influential people. "It's a real kick to see your own company logo and slogan on people," he says, "They love it!"

It was a deliberate move on Dave's part to name his company the RTA Group. "For anyone thinking of going independent, I'd suggest giving a lot of thought to the name of your business—don't just blindly call it 'John/Jane Smith Financial Planning, Inc.' If you want to build a business, then having your name attached may hurt when it comes time for you to pull back in later years.

"The idea is to build an image or a brand that people associate with you, not the other way around. For example, my company name is 'The RTA Group.' The obvious question is, 'What does RTA stand for?' That's exactly what I want people to do. Stop me. Ask that question and then listen. It's up to me to have an excellent, rehearsed response. I say, 'Risk Transfer Action Group: I show people how to transfer the risk of outliving their money—that's what financial planning is all about!' The logo is very nice, and my slogan is 'Your Wealth. Your Security.' It's on everything I do."

Peter Montoya[141] has built an entire industry around helping advisors promote themselves. He has written a book entitled *The Brand Called You* with co-author Tim Vandehey, available through all the usual places.

Andy Gluck's Advisor Products, Inc. offers "one stop for all an advisor's marketing needs" and incorporates branding, newsletters, brochures and website construction at http://www.advisorproducts.com.

INTERNET

The Internet is here to stay, and if you want to stay in business, you'd better be on it. You need a Web presence, preferably one from which prospects can learn about you and your business, and can contact you through an e-mail link. Having your own domain name is a big plus. Register a great company name for yourself at Network Solutions.[142]

When Andy Gluck, president of AdvisorSites, Inc.[143] virtually invited me to see the etchings and other things in his workshop, I had no idea what an exciting time I was in for!

I was in my office in California on the phone with Andy, who was out there in cyberspace somewhere, when he gave me a Web address to log onto. A few keystrokes and secret passwords later, I was behind the scenes at AdvisorSites, Inc., wandering up and down aisles of logos, photographs, artwork, and all manner of templates. He asked me to pick one, and had this been for real instead of research, I would have had a dicken's of a time making up my mind!

---

[141] http://www.petermontoya.com
[142] http://www.networksolutions.com
[143] http://www.advisorproducts.com

As it was, I selected a nice scene from the photographic area, and, at Andy's prodding, invented a company "name" and wrote a couple of quick comments loosely resembling a marketing campaign. Then I sat back stunned as my "company" jumped to life on the monitor before me. "I sorta' like orange," was my reply when Andy asked if I was satisfied with the letters and colors on the screen, and, suddenly, the words scrawled over the picture were in orange—a terrible color for words on a Web page, by the way!

Next, I was presented with a menu of stuff just like I've seen at the websites of some very impressive companies. Andy told me to check boxes if I wanted them on my Web page. I could have stock market data, links to client portfolios, newsletters (written by me or others—whatever I wanted), links to interesting sites, and a whole bouquet of innovative ideas from which to choose. Happily checking several boxes and clicking OK brought me to a fairly finished product that, in spite of the orange letters, looked really neat!

"This," said Andy, "Is what your clients and prospects would see if they clicked on your website. They could see the news of the day, find out what the market was doing, check their personal portfolio (if you wanted them to) and e-mail you, right from the site."

"Oh, sure," I replied. "Like I could afford this." I was amazed at what a low monthly fee (plus set up) could buy! When I mentioned I already had my own logo, Andy said it was no problem to incorporate it into my website. What's more, once my website was up and running, all I had to do was use my new password to get back into that fascinating workshop of Andy's, go to my own special room, and play around with my choices to my heart's content! First thing to go would be the orange letters.

There is no question that you need a website if you are in business today. If you have a Broker/Dealer, compliance dictates that you'll need to play by their rules and do what they tell you. AdvisorSites has created sites for reps at dozens of different Broker/Dealers. If you're independent and have no Broker/Dealer, Andy's company specializes in helping you create your own brand and can make your company look like a financial services giant.

Before leaving the Internet, don't forget to look into networking sites such as LinkedIn[144] and Plaxo[145]…and, of course, let your friends on Facebook know what you do!

NICHE MARKETING

In his controversial White Paper entitled "The Future of the Financial Advisory Business Part II: Strategies for Small Businesses," Mark Hurley[146] insists independent advisors will not survive without developing a successful niche business. The first step to creating such a business is to develop specialty services, by focusing on client problems shared by a select group of people.

---

[144] http://www.linkedin.com/
[145] http://www.plaxo.com/
[146] Mark P. Hurley is President and CEO of Undiscovered Managers Funds. His first Undiscovered Managers white paper was "The Future of the Financial Advisory Business and the Delivery of Advice to the Semi-Affluent Investor."

Dr. Lynda Falkenstein is the *Niche Doctor*. Her niche is helping others find their niche. Her book, *Nichecraft:*[147] *Using Your Specialness to Focus Your Business, Corner Your Market and Make Others Seek You Out*, is filled with worksheets and ideas to help you do just that. Dr. Falkenstein was the guest speaker January 18, 2001 on Financial Planning Interactive Live Forum[148]. Check the Chat Transcripts (left side drop-down menu).

When Andrew F. Hylton, LUTCF[149], ChFC signed on, American Express Financial Advisors had a winner. In 1994, in search of greener pastures, Andrew researched new opportunities. He was swept off his feet by what American Express offered, and the romance hasn't ended.

Andrew is black (African-American). He looked around his community in Southfield, Michigan, and saw too many African-Americans weren't utilizing the services of financial planners. "There are a lot of successful black people who only know about CD's and real estate," said Andrew. "As a whole, our community is not educated about what comprehensive financial planning is and what it can do, or the financial tools of the general securities market. People fear what they don't know." Today, thanks to Andrew and the niche he has developed, that is changing.

A planner in Southern California, Scott Dauenhauer, CFP®, was appalled at the choices available for his wife's 403(b) plan. Determined to do something about it, he became an expert in education benefits. Today he publishes a newsletter entitled *The Teacher's Advocate: Protecting Teacher's Financial Interests* and has found his niche.

Before he retired from his job as Sr. Vice President of Operations for a division of a large computer company, Stephen J. Fazio, CFP® sought out a financial planner to advise him on his pension portfolio. "I ended up with 30- and 40-year-olds telling me what to do with my money," Steve told me. "It didn't take long to realize that they were working to be where I already was and that I could do this for myself!"

Steve enrolled in a CFP® program, began attending FPA meetings, and signed up with Financial Network Investment Corporation. "Retirement is when you do what you want, when, where and with whom you want." His niche is dealing with clients that were just like he was, approaching or beginning retirement. He provides credibility that was lacking in the corporate environment when he needed a financial planner. "My God!" he exclaims, "I wish I'd found this thirty years ago!"

I have a suggested starting place if you're looking for a niche. There are some incredible resources available through the Society of Certified Senior Advisors[150], and the certification course is filled with important information. In 2000, I earned the CSA designation, and while that is not where the emphasis on my practice lays, the education I received has been

---

[147] http://www.falkenstein.com/store.htm
[148] http://www.financial-planning.com/
[149] Life Underwriter Training Council Fellow, The LUTC Fellow designation is conferred upon only those individuals who meet or exceed the qualification requirements determined by LUTC and The National Association of Insurance and Financial Advisors (NAIFA), joint sponsors of the designation. http://www.theamericancollege.edu/ search LUTC.
[150] http://www.society-csa.com/

invaluable. Consider structuring educational seminars on senior issues and taking your show on the road to senior citizen centers.

Something else to consider: Beneficiary Directory[TM][151] Mark Kaizerman, CFP®, has written a book by that name. We all tend to be disorganized and often have problems getting our hands on important documents in a hurry, especially under stressful situations. Mark's book, along with a workbook and forms, is the place to get all that stuff together. He takes it a step further by recommending the completed document designate a key person (read Financial Planner) to have access and permission to share information with specified individuals under certain conditions. Arranging seminars to emphasize the importance of gathering this data may be a good start to developing a list of prospects.

NETWORKING

The American Heritage Dictionary[152] defines the verb network: "to interact or engage in informal communication with others for mutual assistance or support."

What a wonderful concept, particularly for one just starting out! Think about the benefits you both might derive from a conversation with someone who understood your motivation, related to your marketing concept, and may share a mutual need.

Nearly 100% of this book came from, was driven by, or completed through contacts I have made during my career as a financial planner. What contacts I didn't have in place from networking were introduced to me from associations directly evolved from years of networking within and without the industry.

Long before I became a financial planner, I was a member of the American Business Women's Association[153]. I attended monthly local chapter meetings and was active on the board. The organization was supportive as I made the transition from real estate to financial planning. My first several clients were almost all referrals from members of ABWA. Yet, it was years before a single member of ABWA became a client. Much of the value I add to my practice is the huge referral source I can be for my clients. I frequently refer to ABWA members for services and information. Networking is not a tit-for-tat thing. It is the act of acquiring and nurturing valuable contacts and resources. As your network grows, so does your opportunity to know someone who is able to help, or who can put you in touch with someone who can help, or someone who needs your help, whatever the circumstance.

---

[151] http://www.beneficiarydirectory.com/
[152] The American Heritage® Dictionary of the English Language, Fourth Edition Copyright © 2000, by Houghton Mifflin Company. Published by Houghton Mifflin Company. All rights reserved.
[153] http://www.abwa.org

How Networking has Brought in Business

By Bob Adams, CFP®[154]

It is critical that as part of your marketing plan, you create a strategy on how you will get wide exposure to potential clients in your community. My experience, and also that of others I know, suggests that traditional advertising, such as yellow pages, isn't very effective. I think this is because we are in a "trust" business, and trust is built up by getting to know someone and becoming comfortable with them. Once I know people, I've had them tell me things that I imagine they haven't told many others. This level of trust is very necessary for the type of data gathering and on-going consulting we do as financial planners. People generally pick their financial planners on the basis of a referral or from someone they already know and trust.

I often see colleagues thrust cards at potential prospects after a brief introduction and I think to myself, that my colleague has most likely just wasted their time and energy. I've found it far more effective to introduce yourself in the briefest way without causing the person you've just met to put up their "shield," because they are expecting to be sold. By building trust and common experiences with that person over time, they will contact you if they want your services, or you'll be in a position to approach them at a later time. I've watched with some amusement some of my younger colleagues quickly and aggressively moving around a room shaking hands and passing out cards. You can see the body language of the person they are approaching as they take a step back. Networking can be very effective, but I recommend your goal is to establish frequent contacts over time as opposed to "hit and run" guerrilla marketing.

One of the first steps I took was to join my Chamber of Commerce. The Chamber provides very low-cost exposure within your community to a large number of the major business people and indirectly to their friends and family. The secret to using the Chamber effectively is that you need to become fully involved in as many of their activities as you can. Most Chambers hold "monthly mixers" affording you an opportunity to network among other Chamber members. The key is repetition. Go to every event and get to know people. Let them get to know you.

About a third of my clients have come from the Chamber or from Chamber referrals. One of the best activities many Chambers have is called their Connect Club. The Connect Club meets once a week and is made up of twenty-five business people with the restriction that they need to each come from a unique business (e.g. only one financial planner per group). The group refers business to each other and, in most cases, members of the group use each other's services when needed. Each member gets thirty minutes twice a year to present to the group. Meeting once a week gives everyone an opportunity to really get to know you. This group has been very helpful to supporting my new business, both in helping provide other trusted services I need and also in providing me clients from within the group as well

---

[154] Bob passed the March 2003 CFP® Certification exam and met the experience requirement allowing him to use the Marks in early 2006. Read more about him in Chapter 7.

as productive referrals. Joining and becoming an active part of your local Chamber of Commerce is an excellent use of your marketing time and budget.

Another very important and rewarding part of your "outreach" program can be donation of your time to civic and service organizations. I donate two hours of my service as an item that is bid on in silent auctions at various charitable events for educational support groups. This raises money for a good cause, and it has gotten me some very beneficial public relations exposure.

Whenever I give presentations to service groups I always raffle off a gift-certificate for two hours of my time, and this has resulted in several new on-going clients.

Networking doesn't have to mean you are present. It could be your business card or a client providing a referral.

Increasingly, clients searching for a financial planner will take the often-given advice of interviewing at least three planners. Remember that your job is to get on that list, and sometimes something as simple as a business card will get you on the list. I was fortunate enough to begin working with a client who saw my business card on the coffee room bulletin board of the Executive Meeting Center I use. I was fortunate enough to get into the interview process, and he and his wife subsequently choose me to work with them. My client acquisition cost was 6.25 cents.

Networking can also involve having your clients be an extension of you by providing referrals. It is important when you do reviews or have other client contact to let your existing clients know that you are actively seeking to expand your practice. I make a point of discussing with clients periodically the scope of services I provide and the type of clients that I am seeking. Leaving them a few business cards is a very inexpensive way for them to provide a friend or family member with a professional reminder of your contact information and services. I think potential clients are much more likely to contact you in the future if they have a card in hand as opposed to a scrap of paper with your name on it that can easily be lost.

Outbound marketing is fundamental to building a practice. Sometimes people incorrectly think of "marketing" as just an expense. While it is certainly an expense that needs to be effectively spent, it is also a necessity. Don't be afraid to try things and realize that not everything will work. Marketing is a combination of creativity, experimentation and copying the successful techniques of others. In order to connect with my local community, and also to get my name and services exposed to a large number of allied professionals in my community, I joined a number of groups, and I tried a number of ideas.

Ten outreach ideas I used:

1. Booth at a local Art and Wine Festival (not a good venue for meeting potential clients)

2. Joined local Chamber of Commerce and their networking/leads group

3. Joined large local community service group

4. Donated a financial plan to "silent auctions" for charitable fund raisers (high impact)

5. Delivered presentations to local service clubs (they are always looking for speakers)

6. Held individual lunches with local CPAs and attorneys to discuss opportunities where we could work together

7. Worked with local financial planners within FPA and the local community to develop a source of referrals (an unexpected bonus was referrals from local brokers who referred to me clients who wanted financial plans for which they weren't licensed to provide)

8. Participated in several "health and information fairs" at a local retirement community

9. Used Google's "sponsored ads" and craigslist.org to run free ads

10. Once I attained the CFP® marks, I began successfully using the enhanced listing service of PlannerSearch on the FPA website. This is only $99 a year, and it has resulted in a 70-fold return on investment. The secret is to follow-up daily or periodically via e-mail with those consumers searching for planners.

The lesson from PlannerSearch, the Chamber and other outbound techniques is all very similar. There are many potential clients out there looking for our help. Connecting with them requires persistence, repetition, patience and an outbound marketing plan.

Network to expand your horizons, and to improve your general knowledge-base so you can provide more benefit to existing clients. Be discriminatory. It is said that if you want to soar with eagles, you shouldn't hang around with turkeys. There are eagles in every profession and at every level of society. Find out where they congregate.

You may find yourself networking in different arenas. If you are "niche" marketing among professional bowlers, you'll want to join a bowling league, subscribe to bowling journals, attend bowling conventions, and know where to buy bowling shirts. Eventually you will develop a fine network where you will know someone who introduces you to someone that will add to all you already know about bowling. All those people will know you are a financial planner.

Before long, you will be an expert in all the things that professional bowlers need, where they go, what they spend their money on, how much they save, and who holds the accounts. Professional bowlers will recognize you as "one of them" and you will be their source for information on which bowling journals have the best information, where to buy the nicest bowling shirts, and, of course, obtaining excellent financial advice personally tailored for professional bowlers.

One of the organizations to which I belong is the National Association of Estate Planning Councils[155]. I was looking for a place to meet more attorneys, life underwriters, and CPAs who understood the intricacies of estate planning. After attending my first meeting, I knew I had found the right source. When I inquired about membership, I was told that the membership consisted of 30% each in the disciplines I sought and 10% of "others," which included trust officers, financial planners, foundation directors, etc. There was a waiting list for the "other" category.

"You need more financial planners," I explained, "to pull the teams together. Financial planners should be right up there with the attorneys, CPAs and life underwriters." I petitioned for membership. Ultimately, the Association has changed their bylaws, and today, financial planners are on equal footing in chapters across the country. Originally, I simply wanted to be around professionals who could enhance my estate planning capability. The attorneys, underwriters and accountants I network with have taken my business to another level. I like being around the eagles. My clients like it, too, and enjoy the benefit.

Wealth Advisors Network[156]

Don't forget to network within the profession. Janet Tyler Johnson, CFP® has created an amazing website to get you started. Her Wealth Advisors Network provides a free membership. According to her brochure, the site was "founded to create a place, one place, where advisors could go to find all of the resources dedicated to the Independent RIA." Janet invites you to "come be a part of a community whose mission is to help improve your business and your life."

Benefits of membership include a resource directory of companies that support the Independent RIA, articles written by some of the industry's movers and shakers, podcasts of interviews with industry experts, and email listserve for members to share best practices ideas and an 3-newsletter.

MEDIA

A few years ago, I set as my goal to become "known" to the media. I tried all sorts of things, but by far the easiest was simply signing up on the CFP Board Media Resource[157] list. This benefit is only open to CFP® practitioners, but it's certainly something to strive for.

When I first signed up, I was daunted by the list of over eighty categories. I checked general and relatively safe things, like "retirement" and "financial planning for middle-income families." Soon, I realized how stupid that was. Everyone else was checking those same things. I started doing "niche" stuff—checking categories that are more esoteric. For instance, when the rules changed and it looked like "529 Plans" would become an important part of college planning, I set out to make myself an expert on them.

---

[155] http://www.naepc.org
[156] http://www.jataj.com/wan-home.html
[157] http://www.cfp.net/media/contacts.asp

The first year I signed up, it wasn't very long before I began getting calls from places I'd never thought of, like "The Tennessean" with a specific question. I treated the reporter with respect and enthusiasm! Shoot! My name in a newspaper in Tennessee! Yippee!

Early on, I received a call from a freelance reporter on the East Coast. She happened to be doing a story on real property, and how it fit into an investment portfolio of mutual funds. Right up my alley! We hit it off personally and spent an enjoyable half hour discussing the topic over the phone. A few months later, we had a flurry of calls from people wanting to make an appointment for a free consultation. I had been quoted in Southwest Airline's *Spirit Magazine*. Southwest flies into Ontario, near my office, and people read that magazine!

I responded with a sincere thank you to the reporter, and we have kept in touch. She writes regularly for different publications and quotes me somewhere about once a year. There is absolutely no way on earth to buy this sort of relationship!

After a year or two, the calls started coming from more prominent consumer publications, such as the *Los Angeles Times*, *Money Magazine*, *Worth* and finally, the *Wall Street Journal*. Eventually, hardly a week went by that I didn't get at least two or three calls from the media.

Start with your local paper. Introduce yourself to the business editor. Suggest feature articles covering topics in which you have expertise. Remember, readers aren't experts, and they don't want esoteric stuff. They love lists, like "Ten Things to Do with Your Tax Refund" for an April edition, or "Six Steps to a Sexier (or Safer) Portfolio", depending on what the market's up to.

Learning to deal with the media is not difficult, but I've learned from seminars and experience some things that work.

1. Prepare a "media" kit for yourself. Have all the pertinent data pertaining to your name, company name, credentials, location, etc. handy.

2. When a reporter calls, ask what the story is about. If it's not a subject you can talk about, admit it right up front. Don't waste their time.

3. If you **can** talk about it, use real examples. Think of a client situation. Embellish if you need to get a point across but make it interesting. Consumers enjoy reading about realistic situations. Think of neat sound-bites or tag-lines for a variety of situations.[158]

4. Ask when the reporter's deadline is. If you can call them back, it will give you time to get your thoughts together and come up with something pithy to say.

5. Find out when the article will be published. Watch for it and send the reporter a brief note thanking them for mentioning you and commenting on something terrific that the reporter has said. Perhaps suggest a follow-up piece or another topic altogether.

---

[158] "…keep socking it away." Well, it was okay for the *Wall Street Journal*, when they asked what should be done with extra money once a debt was paid.

6. ALWAYS return a reporter's call! Even if it's just to tell them you can't talk with them this time because you're leaving for Tahiti in five minutes. Establish the contact and ask them to please call again.

7. Start your book of clippings! Don't forget to reference your quotes on your Web page and in your public relations folder in your office waiting room.

SEMINARS

There are some wonderful seminar presentations available commercially, but if you're starting on a shoestring, call the sales reps from some of the mutual fund companies you work with. Not only do they have great literature, but they are also trained to help you promote their funds. Many major mutual fund families will have reps that will actually prepare, and sometimes deliver, a seminar for you.

Mutual fund companies have developed some of the best consumer educational materials I've seen. Most of them have PowerPoint presentations available on a variety of generic topics. Some offer independent advisors CDs that include a complete seminar package, and often will attend your function and actually make the presentation for you.

I don't exactly use seminars any more as a marketing tool, but if the purpose is to bring in new clients, then the result is the same. One Saturday each quarter Mike Ling[159] continues to invite clients to a breakfast get-together at a nearby university. We try to vary the program utilizing educational and entertaining topics. Mike gives an economic overview, and takes a few minutes to introduce staff and mention new happenings in the office. Next comes a twenty- to thirty-minute presentation on a topic of general interest—everything from how long to keep old tax returns and other records to the hottest things to do during retirement or a look at vintage autos clients have restored.

The invitation goes out to every client and center of influence. Postage for the event is incidental, since Mike would be mailing some sort of contact information to that list every quarter anyway. The university, which lends credibility with an appropriate setting, serves a delicious hot buffet, accommodating forty to fifty people. The room is always animated, and the only problem is having to break in and quiet everyone when it's time to introduce the speakers. The cost is under $500 a quarter, and clients often bring highly-qualified guests who later call for an appointment.

There's not a marketing expert out there with half a brain that won't agree client retention is incredibly more valuable than finding new clients. Of course, there will be attrition, but if your objective as a financial planner is long-term relationships with existing clients, then you'd better spend time nurturing the clients you have!

---

[159] Mike Ling, with Berkeley, Inc. purchased my practice in 2004. Previously, he designed and managed the client portfolios for NLJones, Inc.

SUMMARY

Never underestimate the importance of marketing!
Include a marketing plan in your business plan.
Read everything you can on marketing in a service industry[160].
Think "outside the box" for marketing ideas.
Maximize your special talents in marketing efforts.
Nurture existing clients, for they are your greatest source for referrals.
Network with fellow professionals.

---

[160] Appendix B includes a book list with a section on marketing.

MARKETING IDEAS

Chapter Seven

From Plotter to Planner in Less Than Five Years

Back in the early eighties, I was a Realtor struggling with my conscience every time a young family with a baby would want to buy a house I felt they couldn't afford. Lenders would squeak their loan applications through with double-digit interest rates, and I worried the family would go bankrupt if they had another child or were laid off. On the other hand, if I didn't sell them the house, I couldn't afford to put food on my own table.

When the College for Financial Planning put on a presentation for the Board of Realtors, they got me all excited about the prospects of it being my **job** to tell people whether or not they could afford a house! I signed up on the spot. Half way through the course, I left real estate and began working as a financial planner.

I'll never forget being wined and dined by a large Broker/Dealer, who promised to send me to New York for training and painted a glamorous picture of my exciting future with the firm! Stars were in my eyes, but I hadn't even made it to my car when I realized that what he had actually promised was, "If it's Friday and you haven't made your quota, get out there and sell something to someone, whether they need it or not, or you're outta' here!"

It was quite a disappointment to learn that most financial planners really got paid by selling stuff. But hey, I got to do the financial planning part on the way to finding out how much money the client had.

Some of my study group went to work for a small, regional independent Broker/Dealer, and I followed suit. I sold mutual funds and limited partnerships to friends, family, and eventually, a growing clientele. After a few years, a large, national Broker/Dealer bought out the company I was working for. At the first annual seminar with the new firm, the Chief Compliance Officer gave a wonderful talk. Right up until the close, when he reminded us all to, "Get out there and sell...sell...sell!" I thought, NO! I want to plan, plan, plan!

I stuck it out for a few years but finally went to my manager, John Jackson, and explained that I really just wanted to write financial plans for a fee. He gave me a big hug, said he'd miss me, and wished me success. John's still on my list of all time neat people, and I'll always be grateful for the solid training I received under his tutelage.

The next few years were spent proving people wouldn't pay a financial planner just to write a plan. Why should they? Most Broker/Dealers would give consumers a "free" plan (so they could find out how much money the client had!). Things have changed.

Today, people entering the financial planning industry have some solid choices and options. Other chapters have dealt with compensation issues, and my personal experiences are terribly outdated, thank goodness! What follows are case histories of financial planners who "made it" during their first five years, with updates telling how their practices have evolved.

Mike Ling, CFP®
NAPFA-Registered Financial Advisor
Berkeley, Inc.
Boise, Idaho
Michael@berkeleyinc.com

Mike joined the Navy right out of high school, so was late getting started in college.

He had no clue "Financial Planning" existed as a profession when he graduated with a BA in economics from the University of California at Berkeley. He set off for Boise to make his mark in the world but was disgusted with the job market in the early 90s. Scrambling to make ends meet, and hoping to make contacts that would jump-start his career in economics, Mike took a job marketing for a Berkeley alumni but soon realized he wanted more control over his own destiny.

His drive and determination, coupled with a strong background in economics, secured him a position with American Express Financial Advisors, where he feels he received excellent training. But he felt from the beginning that he wanted to emphasize the financial planning for his clients, rather than use planning as a loss leader to sell products. In November of 1995, Mike left AMEX and all his clients to start a small fee-only practice of his own.

Did you have a business plan?

"No. I had an idea of what I wanted, but it wasn't written down. I just did anything I could to survive!"

What were the biggest obstacles you faced?

"Credibility."

What did you do right?

"I started to look for organizations where I could become known. First stop was the Cal Berkeley Alumni Association of Idaho. I developed contacts with Estate Planning Attorneys and CPAs. I took them to lunch and asked them to tell me what they do and how. I focused on them, and helped them to believe in what I do. There are no reciprocal arrangements. I need competent people to refer my clients to."

How did you get training? Did you have a mentor?

"I completed the coursework for my CFP® through Florida State's program on the Internet and received my CFP®. There was truly great training with AMEX, and I was assigned a mentor. But only three out of ten of the people who started with AMEX at the same time I did are still there."

160

How long did it take to start making money?

"It took three incredibly long years and a working spouse—who has since divorced me! Rent and software were the biggest expenses. I netted less than $6000 my first year. This is my fifth year in the business, and I expect to net nearly $100,000."

If you had it to do over again, what would you do differently?

"Not much. I would have been willing to work as a paraplanner in an independent office—but there's no such thing in Boise."

Where do you see yourself in five years?

"I'll be acquiring a practice in California within that time frame. The deal's already started. I expect my net income to be around $175,000. I'll have a personal assistant (my new spouse), a couple of paraplanners, and a receptionist in both Boise and California. I expect to max out at about seventy clients in Boise and twice that many in California, with a couple of Investment Advisor Representatives already being groomed to become partners.

"I plan to retire at 55—when I'll probably hire someone to do my investing, so I'm not emotionally involved."

What's the best advice you could give someone just starting out?

"I'm amazed at the number of advisors who really don't know what they're doing! You have to specialize, because you can't do everything. You must know comprehensive planning, but use expertise in other areas where you can't independently evaluate the situation. Build a good professional network! You must like doing things independently. Be confident and work with conviction."

2002 Update:

"The past year or so have been solid years for my firm and me. While business growth has been a goal, I've also wanted to better balance my personal and professional lives. I've spent more time with my new wife and we play golf regularly. I'm happy to report that my handicap has reached seven. And during the same time, my business has increased by 30%. During bear markets, clients appreciate the extra services provided, such as ongoing comprehensive financial planning and ongoing tax planning in their accounts. I have also been involved in establishing a new not-for-profit in Boise that provides training young adults in the food service industry as well as helping to feed the local underprivileged population. It reminds me of the Old Milwaukee beer commercial that concludes by stating, 'It doesn't get any better than this'."

2005 Update:

"In the past three years, I've acquired a business partner, and we have two employee advisors as well as an office administrator. We're approaching $80 million in assets managed and I would expect that to increase by about $10 to $20 million annually. This is my tenth year in the business, and I expect to net about $200,000. We are more concerned with addressing the needs of current clients than with growing our client base. We will eventually hire someone to help with the California clients, but at this time, those clients are not concerned with our long distance relationship, so we'll wait until we can identify the perfect person. And if we grow in either Boise or California, we would prefer to hire a female advisor who could remain an employee or eventually become a junior partner. I used to think that I would retire at age 55 but that's now looking as though it will be closer to 60.

"Last year I purchased the California clients[161], and I've been traveling about two times per quarter to meet with them. I also recently became a NAPFA member, and I am amazed at how organized, focused and helpful that they are. I've belonged to other organizations, and NAPFA is head and shoulders above the rest. If you're seriously considering working without selling products, contact NAPFA to determine if they would be a good fit."

2007 Update:

"Wow, it's interesting reading my previous comments. My business has developed significantly in the past two years. Last month we built and moved into a new office building. We occupy 1800 sq/ft and lease the remaining 900 sq/ft. We continue looking for a suitable advisor to be permanently located in California, but it's difficult finding someone with the necessary analytical and personal skills. Ideally, it would be an attorney or accountant with a background in estate planning. We also need to expand our administration staff in Boise, but our incorporation of Protracker software has increased our efficiency, so this will not be critical until later this year.

"We now serve 170 ongoing clients and manage approximately $130 million. Our company growth continues to come from referrals from clients and professionals (specifically CPAs). While I have received many inquiries from the NAPFA referral program, we have not had many contact us directly. Until we can increase the company's capacity and settle into the new location, we will limit active marketing.

"The NAPFA conferences I've attended during the last two years have been superb. Many members are innovative thinkers and leaders, and the organization has remained small enough to provide a congenial and intellectual atmosphere."

2009 Update:

"The past 18 months have been brutal. We were broadly diversified but this didn't prevent our accounts from declining about 25%. We lost very few clients, though. During this decline 7 clients have moved their account (from a client base of 190). This experience has further strengthened our resolve to continue researching investment assets to broaden portfolio diversification.

"During the past year we've also attempted to rely on Naviplan for our financial planning software. This year we finally threw up our hands in disgust. We evaluated a few of the other

---

[161] Mike purchased my practice effective 7/1/04.

162

major programs and settled with MoneyGuide Pro. We can't be happier with the software as well as the knowledge and attention we receive from the support staff."

2011 Update:

"My firm continues expanding. In the last 4 years we have added 30 clients and we manage about $150 million. In addition to using MoneyGuide Pro (this is the best, most efficient planning software available) we've been using Finametrica for determining client risk tolerance and have found that these two programs work well together. I spent nearly 2 years on the NAPFA Western Board. The more NAPFA advisors I know the more I realize how important NAPFA is. The membership is small enough (a fraction of the FPA) that you can easily contact other advisors for advice. And the general public is becoming better educated on the advantages and disadvantages of the various compensation models. I'm finally finding that most prospective clients have visited the NAPFA and my firm's website. My business partner is a board member with the Idaho Better Business Bureau (BBB). Between NAPFA and the BBB prospective clients usually conclude before the initial meeting that we are serious about being a knowledgeable professional and committed to client satisfaction."

Barry L. Kohler, JD, CFP®, CLU
BDMP Wealth Management
Portland, Maine
BKohler@bdmp.com

As clients in his law practice began to age, they became more concerned about how the pieces fit together, so Barry set out to find a client-focused financial planner to work with—especially someone who would take a really comprehensive view of his client's situation. What he found in his area were what he calls "one-trick ponies"—advisors who were really trying to sell insurance, mutual funds, or some other "product." He is outspoken in his opinion that, "in the late 90's, most so-called planners didn't have a clue about their clients' whole picture, and woe to the client who fell into the hands of those few who were 'highly competent and totally unscrupulous'."

Barry is no ordinary attorney. He actually wanted to **solve** family law problems instead of add to them. Tired of having to work in an adversarial setting and charge in six-minute increments, he went to a vocational counselor. Testing revealed a desire for a high degree of autonomy, coupled with an interest in people, and financial services popped up.

The founder of an independent planning practice (NorthStar Retirement Strategies)—himself an attorney and insurance company executive—approached Barry to help launch the financial planning firm. Barry left his law practice after twenty-two years to join NorthStar in 1997. In April 2000, he challenged the CFP® certification exam and became the financial planner he couldn't find.

Although both Barry and his partner Barbara Appleby are "recovering" attorneys, they are careful not to practice law and do not draft documents. They work with the client's legal counsel or refer them to competent counsel. "We get so many referrals from lawyers, we'd be foolish to compete with them!" he says.

Did you have a business plan?

"No. But the founder of NorthStar did. The plan was to seek mid-career attorneys and accountants—who came from a client service rather than a sales and marketing background—and train them as financial advisors. It seemed easier to do this than to take a sales and marketing person and make them into a client-focused advisor."

What were the biggest obstacles you faced?

"Wondering how to eat in the meantime! I watched others trying to transition with no outside income. A few 'ran out' of family and neighbors as clients and didn't know (and worse, did not want to learn) how to prospect. Others spent too much time on very detailed planning and were not able to make a living because they could not work in a cost-effective fashion.

"It's still hard to explain what it is we do. We try to help clients reconcile their values with their financial situation. People hunger for this service, but many don't know exactly what it is they hunger for."

What did you do right?

"From the beginning, I was committed to doing the right thing for each client, whether I made money or not."

How did you get training? Did you have a mentor?

"I had a *de facto* mentor (that is, *he* didn't know I thought of him as my mentor). He taught me that clients typically come with cares and concerns, and rather than tying to impress them with how much you know and how much skill you have in preparing comprehensive plans, what the clients want is a process that will end with their having 'peace of mind.' In other words, they just want to feel better."

How long did it take to start making money?

"As we discovered, the founder's plan had a major flaw. He thought bright, articulate people who care about doing the right thing for their clients would have prospective clients beating down the door. No matter how good the business plan and the practitioner, in my experience it still takes three to five years to build a practice.

"I was fortunate in that I had accounts receivable from my law practice, the founder gave me an advance against future income, and my spouse worked."

If you had it to do over again, what would you do differently?

"Nothing. Well…I might have negotiated a longer safety net; a more gradual transition. But I was tired of practicing law."

Where do you see yourself in five years?

"One of five or six professional planners in a firm. The original model for NorthStar was traditional: everybody does everything. We're now heading toward substantive specialization, with each planner having expertise in a particular area or areas. Our business is a relationship business. Almost any of the individual "parts" can be outsourced! It is the relationship and advice we offer that are the keys."

What's the best advice you could give someone just starting out?

"If all you want to do is make lots of money, then forget it! Win the lottery and engage in financial planning until it's all gone.

"Coming from another career is a terrific thing to do, but there are no shortcuts—we all have to pay our dues. I think the most effective planners are in their 40s and 50s, with life and family experience."

2002 Update:

"After our founder left the company in January of 2000, Barbara and I acquired the company. Almost from day one, we had offers coming in 'over the transom' to affiliate, to form a strategic alliance, to sell or be acquired, etc. Almost all were from product vendors seeking yet another distribution outlet.

"Then, in late 2000, we began discussions with the largest independent regional accounting firm in northern New England: Berry, Dunn, McNeil & Parker, with 100 CPA's and offices in Maine and New Hampshire. In April 2001, we sold our independent planning firm, and became an affiliated firm, now known as 'BDMP Wealth Management.'

"It has been an interesting time for a couple of former lawyers turned financial advisors to find themselves in the heart of a large accounting firm! The acquisition was not without tradeoffs. We now have help with infrastructure costs, which were keeping us from reaching the next level of planning sophistication, and we have introductions to business owners, professionals, and other high net worth clients. On the other hand, we are a part of a bureaucratic organization with all that implies.

"Our work with clients continues unaffected by our new affiliation: we continue to help them integrate the various aspects of life into a cohesive plan that reflects the values and goals of each client or client family. The accounting firm exerts no influence on how we do business (other than supporting our fundamental view to continue to do what is in the client's best interest, regardless of short term compensation issues). Next step of my personal plan: encourage the firm to open the long-talked-about Florida office so I can split my time between Maine and Florida, working with our 'snow bird' clients in the winter and our Maine clients in the summer!"

2005 Update:

"The process of integrating our financial planning practice into the accounting firm has proven to be much more difficult than either side anticipated—the cultural gaps are wider than we thought.

"While we have gotten meetings with clients with whom we might not have otherwise met, we are still not getting as many as we should be getting. The accounting firm is comfortable with the planning and investment sides of our practice, but the insurance side continues to lag. Even when they know the client needs insurance (e.g., business buy-sell situation), they still feel awkward referring to "their" own insurance people.

"Yet, we continue to grow. We recently have hired our third planner, Kristin Guibord, an MBA and 'investment geek' with about twelve years of experience in the industry. Kristin is ten years younger than my partner, who herself is ten years younger than I am. We are committed to building an entity that will survive the loss of any one of us, and which will continue to serve our clients and their families."

2007 Update:

"We continue to make gains: some of our best referrers have retired, but new partners in the accounting firm are proving themselves to be avid supporters of Wealth Management. The present plan is to shift our approach. Many CPA's see themselves as their client's 'most trusted advisor.' The advisors in the Wealth Management group positioned ourselves as desiring to serve in that same role for the client. The obvious (at least in hindsight) result was fewer referrals. We are now positioning ourselves as supporting the client's most trusted advisor (the CPA).

"In terms of working with clients, the specialization in our firm is further along as well. My personal practice now is much more heavily oriented towards planning (financial and estate or wealth transfer planning) and insurance. Kristin, whose passion is investing, is working with my clients on investment issues. Great for me; great for the clients!"

2009 Update:

"My practice—like that of most colleagues I meet at conferences—continues to evolve. The transition away from a focus on investments to a focus on planning and insurance was mostly complete when the economic and credit crisis began in October 2008. As a result, when Kristin and I met with clients, she and I tended to have different conversations with the same clients. Kristin's conversations focused more on the economy and the markets— and what changes to make to the portfolio, if any. She tried to keep clients focused on controlling what they could and making peace with what they could not control.

"My conversations with these same clients expanded that discussion—helping clients think through in more concrete and practical terms what a (hopefully, temporary) decline in their portfolios really meant. In part, this was an exploration of what lifestyle changes we recommended clients consider, and re-focusing clients on 'needs' vs. 'wants'.

166

"In terms of my personal practice, the theme has been 'collaboration'. One exciting new aspect of the evolution of my practice has been the opportunity to work collaboratively with other professional advisors on planning and implementation for high net worth clients ($20M+). Primarily this work has consisted of advanced wealth transfer strategies (lifetime and post-mortem), traditional entity strategies, and newer estate planning strategies. While these high net worth clients are not as plentiful in northern New England as in other parts of the country, I have been fortunate enough to work on a number of such cases—mostly in the role of leading the advisory team. This work has been exceptionally satisfying professionally.

"A second evolutionary trend in my practice, one which dovetails nicely with the advanced planning, has been the opportunity to work collaboratively with one of the principals in our affiliated accounting firm with business owners beginning to contemplate transition, succession, or exit planning from the business. For most business owners, the business is the largest single asset in their "portfolio." And there are specific strategies these owners can take to maximize the value they receive when they are no longer working as actively in the business . . . provided they implement changes well in advance of the transition! These strategies require a seasoned CPA with business savvy. But the inter-relationship between business planning and personal planning is obvious—and the best results for the client can only come from the business advisor and the personal planner working in concert.

"The third aspect of my present practice has been an interest in asset protection planning. Again, this is an area that should only be undertaken (at least in my view) collaboratively with a knowledgeable attorney and a knowledgeable tax advisor. This specialized area of planning also fits well with planning for high net worth clients and business owners. As a result, my practice feels well-positioned to grow synergistically over the next years as these three independent threads knit more closely together.

"In addition to these 'substantive' changes in my practice, I also try to model the behavior I recommend to clients. I often suggest clients think creatively about how they tick, when they are at their best, and how they prefer to work. The trick is to find the mix that meshes with life outside of the office.

"Thinking about myself in those terms, I realized the 9 - 5 work day was not the best schedule for me—that I could be more productive and happier working differently and utilizing available technology. So with the agreement of the team, I changed my schedule. I now arrive at my desk most days by 6:15 a.m. and (try to) leave between 2:00 - 3:00 p.m. Then I hit the gym for an hour or so. Once I get home, I will work remotely for another hour or so (or call clients or colleagues in time zones where it is earlier in their day!) This produces a much better work-life balance for me and allows me to show clients 'I walk the walk, not just talk the talk'!"

2011 Update:

"My principal responsibilities in our ensemble practice are (a) new business acquisition, (b) planning and advanced wealth transfer planning, and (c) insurance. I continue to have a supporting role in developing the business transition planning work along with one of the principals in the accounting firm with which we are affiliated.

"The economic turbulence (from the Recession), has made the last couple of years difficult for my personal practice in all three areas—as I know it has for many of my colleagues around the country. As a result, there are two issues with which I am currently struggling.

"In the new business role, my task is to bring new clients to the firm, or at least to 'open the door' and introduce prospective new clients to one of my partners in the Wealth Management group. I would likely be involved in the planning for the client, and any insurance issues to be addressed, but one of my partners would take on any investment management work that results from these clients. Although 2009 was a very successful year with regard to new client acquisition, 2010 was perhaps the worst.

"The advanced planning work I do is a source of great professional satisfaction. However, because northern New England is a relatively poor area, I now have serious doubts whether there is enough wealth (and wealthy families) here to make this a viable practice niche. "Moreover, even clients and families that are wealthy feel (like everyone else as a result of the Recession) less wealthy now than they did a couple of years ago.

"The (temporary) increase in the federal gift and estate tax 'applicable exclusion amount' (AEA) to $5M per person adds to my doubts about the viability of a high net worth planning practice in northern New England. One consequence of the increase in the AEA means there are even fewer clients who need/can benefit from advanced planning; i.e., there are fewer potential clients motivated to undertake such planning. This issue is not limited to northern New England, of course, as I am hearing it from estate and wealth transfer planners around the country.

"A second issue is this: my personal interest (and practice) has been devoted to planning and insurance. But neither of these areas generates meaningful recurring revenue. One of the main reasons I left the practice of law was because I did not like the economic model: having to recreate annual income anew each year. The "annuity revenue" model of financial services (e.g., 1% recurring revenue based on assets under management) was much more appealing.

"With the exception of the 'new business' which I generate, by focusing my personal practice on planning and insurance, I have recreated exactly the economic model I wanted to leave—the one that led me to change careers in the first place. While 2009 was, again, a great year for me insurance-wise (substantial policies required for a $50M planning client), 2010 was abysmal. Ditto for advanced planning cases.

"My partners are, on the whole, understanding of the ups and downs of the economics of a planning and insurance practice. In reviewing the numbers for last year, however, they rather forcefully pointed out how small my column was and how large theirs were (due, mainly, to the recurring revenue produced by assets under management).

"The issue presented for me is this: how do I receive 'credit' on an ongoing basis for business I help develop—especially after the first year—even when I am not personally involved in the ongoing asset management. Without accomplishing a structural change to achieve this, I am back to the economic model I left! Just like prior updates . . . Stay Tuned!"

Jason Gongaware
Chapel Hill Investment Analysts, Inc.
Greensburg, Pennsylvania
(7/9/72 – 10/1/09)

Making a comfortable income and at the top of his career as a highly regarded trauma nurse, Jason looked around one day. What he saw were people twenty and thirty years his senior who couldn't wait to leave. Though committed to his challenging work, he realized it was only a matter of time before he, too, would burn out.

That's when, in 1995, he walked away from his burgeoning career and enrolled in the University of Pittsburgh, intent on earning a degree focusing on economics, political science and history. "My wife, and everyone else, thought I had lost my mind," he laughs, "leaving such a high paying job that I truly loved."

He was married to a registered nurse, and their income was great until Jason started school. Frustrated when he couldn't find a financial planner to work with his family, he began to consider the industry for himself. The family scrimped and saved while Jason studied. A short-lived relationship with an insurance company disillusioned him for a brief period. Then, in 1998, he went to work for a company that is now Chapel Hill Investment Analysts, Inc. as a service assistant, preparing applications and making appointments.
In 1999, his wife quit working and the couple's first child was born. Today, Jason coordinates the investment policy committee for his firm, and it doesn't look like his wife will have to return to work any time soon.

Did you have a business plan?

"No. At first, I didn't realize I was going to be a financial planner. However, once I decided to work in this field I knew that integrity and education were the key to success, so I focused my energy on learning the business, providing objective advice, and becoming an advisor, not a salesperson."

What were the biggest obstacles you faced?

"It was hard to go from being a respected professional in nursing to being an entry-level assistant. Suddenly, I was the low man on the totem pole."

What did you do right?

"The effort I put forth let me build something partly my own. In the hospital, I was more of a cog in a wheel. Once I decided on financial planning, I went to FPA meetings, took short courses, everything I could to enmesh myself in the business. Now I have a flexible schedule. It's long hours, but I have control."

How did you get training? Did you have a mentor?

"There was a certain amount of training with the insurance company, but it focused on generating commissions. I wanted to be an advisor. I had a good background in economics, but after getting my degree, it was mostly self-taught. I'm a voracious reader! Also, the owner of the company I work for now has been instrumental in my education."

How long did it take to start making money?

"I was lucky in that I didn't have to generate income at first. For the first two-and-a-half years, I was salaried. Now I'm working for a percentage of the firm's profits, plus a salary, and I now earn more than I did as a nurse.

If you had it to do over again, what would you do differently?

"I would have skipped the cookie-cutter insurance company training program, and I might have gotten my CFP® while still a trauma nurse with a good income."

Where do you see yourself in five years?

"I expect to help my firm grow substantially while having a larger leadership role in the company. I'm currently enrolled in the CFA[162] program, and expect to have my MBA within six years"

What's the best advice you could give someone just starting out?

"Act as an advisor right from the beginning, not a salesperson. Focus on education, objectivity, and service."

2002 Update:

"The corporate structure at Chapel Hill Investments changed, and the company was split into smaller divisions but has maintained its focus on financial planning and asset management. I'm definitely on track to take a more active leadership role, and my title is now Vice President and Portfolio Manager for the Investment Analysts, Inc. division. I still expect to finish the CFA program within the next three years, and follow it with my MBA."

2005 Update:

"Now that it has been several years since I made my original comments, I am even more convinced that I have made the right decision in moving to an investment management position. Our firm has evolved and we continue to grow in a way that allows me to enjoy a good quality of life. While I work hard, I work with people I enjoy, doing a job that I love, and that gives me the flexibility to spend time with my family and on my outside interests. I continue to focus on the investment management aspect of our business. While I have not completed my CFA or MBA, I look forward to achieving these goals!"

---

[162] Chartered Financial Analyst: Designation given by the Association for Investment Management and Research (AIMR) to those who pass multiple exams in the areas of accounting, economics, money management, and security analysis.

2007 Update:

"Our company has continued to grow, and so have the challenges I face on a daily basis. However, since we first spoke in 2000, I have continued to enjoy my work more every day. Warren Buffett states that he feels like tap dancing to work every day, and I have the same feelings. I have not completed my CFA or MBA because of my focus on growing our business. While they (CFA/MBA) are still long-term goals, I do not think that they have hampered my progress.

"My role is focused on managing our portfolios. The president of the company focuses on asset gathering and financial planning, and I focus on investment management. This system works very well for us, since it is based on our strengths. Fortunately, I am able to work from a home office the majority of the time to allow for a great work/life balance. However, we are still facing many challenges, such as keeping up with technology, adding value in a continually commoditized industry, developing systems that can be scaled to even larger numbers of clients without adding undue staff or capital costs, and compliance."

2009 Update:

"The major change in my professional life since my 2007 update is the market upheaval of the last few years. Fortunately our portfolio management philosophy helped us to do relatively well despite the turmoil. This is rewarding to see that our hard work benefited our clients in a very measurable way. My professional role has increasingly focused on portfolio management to my great pleasure. I find my work to be stimulating and rewarding while also allowing me to enjoy an outstanding work/life balance. When I look back at my initial comments and then at the updates, I am struck by how I am as much excited today about the future as I have been in the past."

Tom Davison, MA, PhD, CFP®
Summit Financial Strategies, Inc.
www.summitfin.com
Columbus, Ohio

Utilizing his Doctorate in Cognitive Psychology, Tom spent twenty years as a technical manager for AT&T before accepting a buy-out offer in 1998. He was ready for a change, though the offer accelerated what he had in mind by six months.

Always interested in the numerical side of things, Tom's awareness of financial planning goes as far back as 1972, when he first started investing on his own, and he has researched the industry for years. To get an idea what the business was like, he read not only trade publications, but also technical journals.

Back in the '80s, he had a couple of different firms do a financial plan for him, to see how they approached it. In 1992, after reading John Sestina's book *Fee-only Financial Planning: How to Make it Work for You*[163], Tom did a financial plan for his parents.

While working full time at AT&T, Tom enrolled in the College for Financial Planning's CFP® Certification course and supplemented the home study materials with one day a week classroom study at a local university. At the same time, he wrote in-depth notes on a variety of planning topics. These came in handy in demonstrating to potential employers that he was serious and capable. One set of notes dealing with Net Unrealized Appreciation of Employer Stock in Qualified Plans has been published in CCH journals.

In 1998, Tom went to work for Summit Financial Strategies, Inc., and is still incredulous at "how much risk this little firm was willing to take by letting me work with them!"

Did you have a business plan?

"I felt a written business plan was more helpful to a sole practitioner. I always wanted to be in a firm—part of a team."

What were the biggest obstacles you faced?

"Culture shock! Things are done a lot differently at a firm with six people than they were at AT&T where there were hundreds of people to interact with everyday. Here, we have to take our coffee cups home to wash them! The hardest part for me was getting clear on which business model I'd be comfortable with. I know I'm not cut out to sell products. I'm way too analytical."

What did you do right?

"Preparation. Finding the right fit is much more important than the technical stuff. Making the switch wasn't easy, but I did it with confidence, because I knew what the field was like and my goal was clear. All that time and energy I spent going to FPA meetings, reading trade journals and talking to others in my classes helped me sort out the business model I wanted."

How did you get training? Did you have a mentor?

"One of the members of the firm took me on as a project."

How long did it take to start making money?

"I started out making one-sixth of what I was making with AT&T. Lucky for me, I'm not the primary breadwinner! My wife is an Information Technology Director. I'm not in this business for the money. More than anything else, I'm doing this for amusement. I like it!"

---

[163] J.K.Lasser publishes Mr. Sestina's book. Similar material is covered in Sestina's newest book, *Managing to Be Wealthy: Putting Your Financial Plan and Planner to Work for You*

If you had it to do over again, what would you do differently?

"Very little. Information about financial planning is hard to get. For instance, what is a financial plan? The answer's different depending on whom you're talking to."

Where do you see yourself in five years?

"In five years, I'll pretty much be doing what I'm doing now, but I'll be getting really good at it!"

What's the best advice you could give someone just starting out?

"Do everything you can do to find out what it would be like in the final position. Be an intern! Approach it like you would approach moving to another city."

2002 Update:

"Still doing what I was doing before. Haven't gotten really good at being a financial advisor yet, but keep getting better. I feel good about working with clients— that's so rewarding, and what this business is all about. The clients I probably work the best with tend to be corporate folks—that ties to my AT&T experience—and retirees. The team environment at our firm has been wonderful; personally, I can't imagine making as much progress if I were a solo practitioner. I'm blessed to have found such a supportive environment.

"I need variety and like to have a new 'extra' project every month or two. Volunteering for professional activities is welcomed, even from a newcomer—I've reviewed several things for the FPA, written articles for myStockOptions.com and the local press, got little pieces in trade journals, and participated in exam question reviews for the CFP® Board of Standards. I've done a lot in some particular areas, such as employer stock options, and have been appointed to the Advisory Board of myStockOptions.com. Each thing that comes up is a learning experience and forces me to continue to develop depth and breadth, as well as a broader set of contacts to turn to. All of these things circle back to the client work. I'd really encourage everybody, especially those of us new to the profession, to try out different ways of participating—it is hard to imagine that you can be helpful until you jump in and work through whatever comes up."

2005 Update:

"Progressing along professionally. The contacts I've made have helped get me into a variety of professional activities (e.g., running a NAPFA study group, making presentations on a few different topics at financial planning conventions, doing a session of the Securities Industry Association executive training program, writing more articles). You often don't know ahead of time what activities will have the most future value. Doing what you find interesting and personally rewarding, trying several different things with different people, and generally having fun tends to lead to good things, but the paths and people develop in unforeseeable ways. My professional activities tend to be technical in nature. The specific activities have been chosen so that I could learn from them and directly apply to client situations."

2007 Update:

"Now a partner in the firm I've been with, due to the generosity of the other partners. As members of a firm, we each contribute in different ways. Personally, that's a reason I joined a firm originally—I can't know or do everything and never wanted to. It is wonderful to have people around me daily who have skills and knowledge that compliment mine. For me, being a part of a larger group is both challenging and self-serving: I get to do more of the things I enjoy the most, and less of the undesirable aspects. At the same time, it is quite clear that our contacts outside the firm have been extremely valuable to us in many ways. Trying to find the right balance is always tricky—there is just so much going on in the financial planning world. Everybody's balance point and approach is different—striking one that works for you is a key."

2009 Update:

"The economic turmoil of the last year has made work more challenging. Times of rapid change are times of rapid learning. The opportunity/requirement to revisit core assumptions and business practices are priceless, and will improve our work for years to come. Our firm has been steadily growing by hiring the best of the interns who join us from local universities. Working with the five now on staff in a mentoring role, especially in these rich but tumultuous times, has been very rewarding.

"Just re-reading my series of entries in Nancy's book is enlightening. She's provided a format for career progression stories that individually may not be that instructive, but collectively a very rich picture for those first encountering the profession."

2011 Update:

"Continuing to enjoy the field, and the firm I'm in. Feel like I'm evolving to more emphasis on wisdom than milking the technical side ever more. Mentoring newer staff and influencing the firm's direction is taking up more energy. Getting more comfortable with marketing activities to add to the more internal and emphasis on fellow professionals. Always something new that's rewarding, providing variety and new challenges."

Rich Chambers, CFP®
Investor's Capital Management
Palo Alto, California
richc@feesonly.com

Though interested in personal finance and helping friends and family make investments for over thirty years, Rich spent his entire career in the technology industry. While working his way up the corporate ladder, he began putting money in real estate. Dealing with tenant problems soon dictated a switch to the stock market for his personal portfolio. Early success with his own investments brought co-workers seeking advice and the realization there were a great number of people who either didn't like to invest or weren't good at it. They needed help.

In 1992, as a software engineering manager at 3Com, Rich enrolled in the CFP® course at the College for Financial Planning, determined to take at least one course per year. In 1998, he began his own company, garnering a few investment clients.

When he passed the comprehensive exam in 1998, Rich left 3Com and spent time with a fee-only financial planning firm as an intern, in order to gain experience. There, over an eight-month period, he learned, "stuff not taught in books!" He also learned he couldn't survive on such a small, erratic income.

To supplement his income, he spent a year with a high tech start-up company and was finally ready to strike out on his own with Investor's Capital Management, the company he had started a few years earlier.

Did you have a business plan?

"Sort of—on the back of an envelope. It was more like knowing my goals: 1. Have my own business (just like my dad). 2. Help people with financial issues (because I'm good at it). The revenue goal was easy: I knew I could do better in the future on my own than employed as a software engineer."

What were the biggest obstacles you faced?

"I didn't have a sense of the reality of the business. Compliance, registration, the SEC...it's all scary! There's so much beyond the classroom: producing reports, the practical applications, finding resources, tools, etc."

What did you do right?
"Early on, I began holding workshops on employee stock options. In Silicon Valley, everyone has stock options. You can really hurt yourself with those things!

"I was smart to get my CFP® right off the bat, even though I didn't know what I was doing at the time. It was lucky for me that the CFP® is the designation that came out on top. There was so much to pick from at the time!"

How did you get training? Did you have a mentor?

"I was lucky to have landed an intern job where I could use my technology background to help bring income. Those eight months with a financial planning firm were very instructive. There are two friends I can always ask, who are great resources. Nothing formal, just strong professional relationships."

How long did it take to start making money?

"Well, I'm making much less than I did at 3Com, but I expect to break even this year, my third. Within eighteen months, I expect to see annual revenues of $150,000. My office is in my home. I hate paying rent, so when we look for a new home, I'll look for one with an office that has an outside entrance. Software, research, and conferences are my highest cost items."

If you had it to do over again, what would you do differently?

"I should have started sooner! I didn't because of the money; waited until I could afford it."

Where do you see yourself in five years?

"I'll have built up a good asset base and have one or two partners. We'll keep administrative staff to a minimum with technology, and will probably hire an intern to service the smaller clients. Smaller clients need so much help! I'll be spending the majority of my time with a small group of wealthy clients I really know and like."

What's the best advice you could give someone just starting out?

"Get your CFP® and join the FPA to enrich the whole experience. Get a job and start earning the experience requirement as soon as possible."

2002 Update:

"I expect to be profitable this year (finally). We did move to a larger home that has an external building I am using for my office—there's even room for an associate or two. I have an intern now—someone I met at a CFP® retirement class that I teach at UC Santa Cruz Extension.

"Working with Allied Professionals has been a big help in attracting new clients. My best contacts have been with a Wealth Management firm, a mortgage loan officer, and a CPA.

"More than I had expected, I am concentrating on middle-income clients. Partly because I joined the Garrett Planning Network, Inc. and liked the business model and partly because I really enjoy helping people more like me.

"Currently there are just over 100 clients and three-quarters of them are hourly consulting clients who are self-directed investors. Most of them subscribe to a monthly investment service that I offer to keep their portfolios up-to-date, and we meet twice per year. The other quarter of the clients choose to delegate the investment management to me. For all clients, I charge an hourly fee for financial planning.

"The typical new client wants to rationalize their investment portfolio and understand the how's and when's of retirement. I offer a Basic Financial Plan that covers both of those topics. Clients can add on financial planning modules as needed to the Basic Plan, e.g., income property analysis and estate planning."

2005 Update:

"2004 was a nicely profitable year! And 2005 looks like a 44% increase in net income over that. here are three of us now—Julie and Jennifer are both candidates for CFP® certification, meaning that they have passed the enormous two-day exam. They both have their own financial planning and investment management clients and are well on their way to building successful practices. We are working on a partnership arrangement.

"Our best referral resources are current clients, allied professionals, and NAPFA. Julie and Jennifer have been prospecting by holding seminars on College Planning.

"We have helped over 350 clients to a brighter financial future. About a third of those invest with us, either doing the work themselves with our oversight or by delegating the whole task to us. We have over $88 million at Schwab Institutional.

"Hourly project planning, retainer arrangements, and investment management are our core service offerings. We offer a unique "Tune-Up" plan for $2400 that provides an all-interactive experience for the client—in two separate meetings, we review all their financial records, organize them, and provide detailed recommendations on investing, retirement, and cash flow, and a quick review of stock purchase plans, stock options, insurance, taxes, and estate planning.

"I also manage investments for other financial planners that do not wish to. They retain the client relationship and delegate all the investment work to me.

"We are maxed out for space in our physical environment. We have chosen to have only professionals in the organization—no administrative assistance. This will be a challenge going forward, and we hope to make more use of outsourcing, since we can't add permanent personnel in our current location. Currently, we have one independent contractor doing various projects for us, and we will likely have a part-time intern for a few hours a week soon."

2007 Update:

"Big progress—the three of us formed a partnership last year. While we all practice in the same fashion, we do have our own specific clients, and we provide backup for each other when necessary. We have a buy/sell agreement for retirement and disability. My two wonderful partners are Julie Schatz, CFP®, and Jennifer Cray, CFP®.

"Our choice to have only planning professionals in the organization still holds, although we do make good use of part-time planning, research, an administrative assistance. Our physical space is limited, so any additions to professional staff must be in a second office. Perhaps that step will occur this year if we find just the right person as a potential fourth partner.

"Our revenues in 2005 were up 65%, and in 2006, up 32%. Last year, we were rated by *Financial Advisor* magazine (7/06) as the second-fastest growing RIA firm in the country in the $100M to $300M managed assets category. We have $168M with Schwab Institutional and a few other places (we love Schwab). We are primarily passive (index) investors making significant use of the Dimensional Fund Advisors family of mutual funds.

"Our largest expenses are E&O insurance, accounting, software, and programming for our customized rebalancing software.

"Our major referral sources are current clients and allied professionals. I have joined the Paladin Registry, which has been very instructive toward effective communication to prospects.

"We have helped 600 clients to a successful financial future. At this point, we are all feeling a bit maxed out, so we have, reluctantly, restricted the number and type of future clients that we serve. This is my last year as a Garrett Planning Network member, as I no longer qualify as an hourly, as-needed planner.

"Project planning, retainer arrangements, and investment management are our core offerings. My minimum planning fee is $3600, and $500,000 is the minimum for investment management. My comprehensive planning and investment management offering is a net worth-based retainer that further reduces conflicts of interest. Retainer clients receive extensive goal setting using the Kinder EVOKE™ method."

2009 Update:

"We have helped more than 750 clients to a successful financial future although some of them might wonder about that with the stock market down so much!

"Investment management, project planning, and retainer arrangements are still our core offerings. My minimum planning fee is $5,400 and the minimum assets for investment management is $500,000. The minimum retainer is $8,000 annually which includes investment management and planning and the fee is based on net worth.

"The biggest change is that we have two offices now. My two partners are in an office suite about one mile away and I remain in my home-based office right next to my home. A big challenge has been to access our portfolio and CRM systems remotely. We employed True North Networks to install and administer a remote server for us where Portfolio Center and Junxure are located. We use Net Documents for remote file access.

"Our office staff has grown significantly to four. They all work part-time, some from their home offices. One of our staffers is a Certified Financial Planner™ and she concentrates on investments and planning for clients. Another is taking the course work leading to the CFP® certification and she helps with office tasks and planning. Our stay-at-home mom staffer does Excel, Word automation and other programming tasks. Lastly our newest staff person is also a client and she concentrates on downloads, quarterly processing, and rebalancing.

"Our largest expenses are for the staff, office rent, accounting, and E&O insurance.

"We custody 99.8% of our client assets at Schwab and enjoy a close relationship with their team. Service is always great. We use Dimensional Fund Advisors as our primary mutual fund resource. Thanks to the great bear market, our assets are down about 25% at Schwab to $157 million from the fall of 2007 to March 2009. My net income is down a similar amount. But we are expecting a deluge of new clients once the bear takes cover! Our main referral sources remain our existing clients and allied professionals."

2011 Update:

"Time to cut back. In 2010 I searched for two other compatible planners looking to expand. One needed to offer managed accounts similar to mine and the other needed to offer a more do it yourself approach like I did. Both needed to be fee-only, be a CFP® or a CFP® candidate, and use a passive approach to investing utilizing Dimensional Fund Advisor's funds. With effort I did find the two and using the assistance of FP Transitions, we developed agreements that provided an excellent transition for my clients. So far, out of about 75 clients, only one has resigned.

"The transition to the new planners occurs in 2011 with my involvement. Retained by me are about 35 managed account and financial planning clients, leaving more time available for other pursuits. My intentions are to provide service to the remaining clients for as long as I am able.

"The other pursuits involve a rebalancing software business that needs marketing attention. I developed a rebalancing system years ago in order to save time and provide more timely and accurate rebalancing of client accounts. Commercial rebalancing systems were too expensive, too complicated, and took away my control of the trades. I've continued to develop the system over the years and want to offer it to other like-minded advisors that can help share the development cost.

"I plan to have time for mentoring of new advisors, as that has been a very rewarding experience for me over the years. I would concentrate mentoring on building a positive cash flow business model and providing efficient investment and planning services.

"Lastly I am volunteering at the local humane society helping with canine socialization and training. That's been an interest of mine since we have two Scottish terriers at home."

Cecil Provost
Waddell & Reed
Saratoga Springs, New York

In 1982, Cecil graduated from the State University of New York in Potsdam and went to work for Raytheon as a software engineer, moving on as a system specialist with Digital Equipment Corporation, only to follow his own entrepreneurial spirit and enter the residential real estate field in 1987.

Cecil was named "Rookie of the Year" by his local real estate board in 1988 and commenced purchasing investment property for his own portfolio. Thirteen years later, with a successful career as a Realtor, he became restless and looked forward to a new challenge. Financial Planning seemed logical, since he had always considered himself a Real Estate "Advisor," rather than a salesperson. He thought about business consulting, purchasing different franchises, and other businesses. But he kept returning to financial planning.

He talked to a number of large financial planning and insurance firms, researched job fairs, the Internet, Monster.com[164]…and, finally, decided on a major insurance company trying to reinvent themselves as a financial planning firm, where he received a salary and benefits. But five months after joining, Cecil became very disappointed in the training, micromanagement and captive agent atmosphere and left for the planning focus, more independent culture, and strong management support he found in the local office of Waddell & Reed. He has since obtained his CMFC designation and begun the CFP® course on his own.

Today, although he maintains his Realtor's license to service former real estate clients, he is focused on expanding his financial planning clientele with Waddell & Reed. Cecil and his wife, Sarah, a speech therapist in private practice, hope to start growing their family as well, within the next year.

Did you have a business plan?

"Absolutely: I'm an entrepreneur at heart but realize that success is dependent on having a solid plan. I knew how I would build my business, by working my extensive network of former clients and business associates, but first needed the education to service them. I just had to find the right system to support me in my education and growth in this business."

What were the biggest obstacles you faced?

"I'm a classic case of not knowing enough up front about how the business works to know what questions to even ask. I wish I knew 'then' what I know now. I'm still learning! I expect to thrive, not just survive, in anything I do. When I first entered the field, I didn't realize how much more education, mentoring and support I would need to really excel as a financial advisor." I knew how to prospect and service clients, and how to market myself, but in this field there's a huge learning curve of specialized knowledge—investments, insurance, compliance issues, etc. That was my biggest challenge, becoming competent in a very complex new field."

What did you do right?

"I got my Series 7 out of the way first, I tried to find a company focused on planning instead of sales, I developed a comprehensive business plan, and I marketed myself well.

"Well, having owned a business before, the idea of no overhead is one I'm getting used to pretty quickly!"

---

[164] http://www.Monster.com

How did you get training? Did you have a mentor?

"I already know how to manage clients and run a business. But I found quality education, training and mentoring with the manager at my Waddell & Reed office. I also took it on myself to enroll for the CMFC at the College for Financial Planning, completed that in my first three months at Waddell, and now am working on my CFP®."

How long did it take to start making money?

"I started off strong in my first couple of months, but once I became frustrated with my first company and decided to make a change, my productivity fell off until I made the move and got settled at Waddell & Reed. Now business is going great.

"Since I continue to operate my real estate business, this wasn't a factor for me, only an enhancement. I like someone else to have the overhead!"

If you had it to do over again, what would you do differently?

"First and foremost, I would begin the CFP® program while still working in my previous career. Get the basics so that you can hit the ground running in this field. As far as choosing a place to work, I should have done more thorough research. I was swayed by 'friendships' and didn't make good business decisions. Personal relationships clouded my judgment. I should have explored financial planning sites[165], vault.com[166], and Broker/Dealer sites."

Where do you see yourself in five years?

"I'll expect to stay with Waddell & Reed, but if something changes there I would consider setting up my own practice. I anticipate having at least 400 clients, with several paraplanner/assistants to do the background work. I'll be planning for the employees of organizations, such as medical groups and the Board of Realtors."

What's the best advice you could give someone just starting out?

"Start with what you know. For me, it was Realtors. My local Board of Realtors has 2000 members. I do workshops for them, offer planning services at a discount, act as a resource for them, and look for referrals.

"I believe that prospecting and personal marketing are two critical skills for success in this business.

"Find a manager with a good track record of developing first year associates and one with a well structured training program. You'll need good training."

---

[165] Financial Planning Interactive: http://www.financial-planning.com
[166] http://www.vault.com/

2002 Update:

"I set up an independent practice affiliated with Raymond James in February, with offices at a local bank. I love the unlimited variety of solutions that I can offer my clients, and it's nice to have some business come to me through the bank (fewer referrals than I expected, but generally good quality).

"Of course, I'm faced with the additional challenges that come with running your own practice. I've spent a lot of money this year on computer equipment and software, hired a fantastic licensed assistant twenty hours a week doing admin stuff and some plan prep, and may hire a second part-time clerical person after the new year to let Lin focus on paraplanning.

"I'm still working on my CFP®. The plan to take the test in November got pushed back because my wife and I had our first child in October. I'" now shooting for the March exam. I've been teaching quite a few seminars and am getting published with articles in some local publications. I love the career, feel like I've established a solid foundation, and expect to see my practice really take off in the next couple of years."

2005 Update:

"I'm still working as an FA, now through NEXT Financial. In February 2004, I accepted an opportunity to work for PageOne Financial (an RIA based near Albany NY), and they have a relationship with NEXT, so I moved my licenses there. I spent 2004 as Director of Business Development for PageOne, traveling around the country working with other FA's. But my wife and I had our second child in October, and I decided that I didn't want to be traveling so much, so I gave up the BD position with PageOne in January 2005 and went back to just being an FA and Realtor.

"I have a relatively small practice, maybe 200 clients, and that's comfortable for me. At this point, I'm taking new clients by referral only. I have a great assistant in the FA business and also have built a nice real estate firm with great staff, so things are busy but going well. I never did finish my CFP®, and at this point I don't have any time or immediate plans to do so (although I know it would help)."

2007 Update:

"I actually decided to leave the FP business last year and went back to focusing 100% of my energy on expanding my real estate company and related businesses (land development, mortgage company coming later this year). Although I built (and sold) a nice FP practice, I found that no matter how I tried, I could never get as excited or feel as rewarded by the results in financial planning as I do in real estate."

Robin Vaccai-Yess, CFP®
Highland, New York
www.robinyess.com

Robin was a stockbroker for five years before quitting to have a family and participate in a variety of odd jobs from her home over the next five years. She worked as a graphic designer, did marketing for other firms, worked on restaurant menus and ran a temporary agency. From 1996 until 1999, she was engaged in the College for Financial Planning's CFP® self-study program, simply because the industry excited her.

At 35, she went to work for a small financial planning company with a Broker/Dealer affiliation and left after a year-and-a-half to establish her own fee-only firm. She opened her doors on January 1, 2001, and feels like a kid in a candy store. "There's nobody around here like me! Every year I get older and my life gets better!"

Did you have a business plan?

"Yes! And I keep looking at it. It's twenty-three pages long and took me six months to plan. A business plan is extremely important! You must outline what you need to do and what it'll cost to get started!"

What were the biggest obstacles you faced?

"Worry! Fear that I was cutting off my income. I had sleepless nights a full month before and after opening my office!"

What did you do right?

"Because of my business plan, I knew I could do it! Part of the business plan was marketing. I bombarded the local press. There are no fee-only planners within an hour of my office, and that intrigued the press. They wrote about me. My involvement with the press led to a call asking if I would teach a financial planning class in the local school. I got paid, have a new credit on my resume, and I get to meet people! All this within weeks of opening my office!

"I joined the Chamber of Commerce and teach Personal Finance through Adult Education classes."

How did you get training? Did you have a mentor?

"No mentor. My training was disciplined self-study. I watched how things were done in the firm I was working for. I kept visualizing how I would do it differently. And I read!"

How long did it take to start making money?

"I paid all my bills in the third month from cash flow. I took out a home equity loan to get started, but I'm taking care of all my bills, including the loan payment, from what the business is bringing in already. Next thing is to start paying myself."

If you had it to do over again, what would you do differently?

"Set more cash aside instead of borrowing."

Where do you see yourself in five years?

"I'll be living comfortably in this small town, serving the middle-class, helping people who need it get unbiased advice. My clients want financial planning. I'll be managing assets on retainer. And I expect to be netting $100,000."

What's the best advice you could give someone just starting out?

"Write a business plan! Know your market and competition, and know how they are marketing. Read Harry Beckwith's *Selling the Invisible: A Field Guide to Modern Marketing*.[167]

"You have to be a 'Jack of all trades' when you work in financial planning. Having a bunch of credentials and spitting out numbers doesn't cut it. Be a good listener, and good with people. If people feel you're not listening and understanding them, all the facts in the world won't matter."

2002 Update:

"Yes, I am still in the business. At the end of my second year in fee-only practice, it is finally just getting to be a self-supporting practice. (The surge in cash flow I experienced in March 2001 turned out to be temporary!) If I had to do it all over again, I still would, but I'd be more realistic in how long it would take to turn positive cash flow and I wouldn't spend so much on advertising but would teach workshops and write articles—both of these have been the biggest source of new clients for me. My advice to anyone starting is to plan on at least two, if not three, years to really see steady cash flow.

"If I had to do it all over again, I...
- Wouldn't purchase ProTracker, because I've never really used it, and I ended up buying ACT! a month ago, which is more than useful for my type of practice, not to mention a hell of a lot cheaper.
- Didn't and still wouldn't purchase Centerpiece. I don't call asset management the main focus of my practice, so that would have been more money (and a lot) thrown in the toilet.
- Would establish a niche right away. My first is in divorce planning and now the second is working with non-traditional couples, which is less stressful and more rewarding!
- Would have more cash available up front and would plan on cash flow not being positive until into the second or third year. I was way too optimistic with that!"

---

[167] Harry Beckwith, *Selling the Invisible*, Warner Books, 1997.

2005 Update:

"Yes, I am still in the business, and reading my notes along the way is interesting! Soon enough, I'll be finishing my fifth year in private practice and get a steady stream of referrals. I still practice as a totally fee-only planner and charge flat retainers for investment management and hourly fees otherwise.

"I've made a major change recently, which is building a 12' x 20' addition onto my 12' x 12' home office, and since hindsight is 20/20, I should have done it from the get go. I have a separate entrance and separate bathroom, large conference area, and one large U-shaped desk area. My clients are enjoying the short drive out to my very private country property in the Mid-Hudson Valley.

"My best piece of advice remains—keep your overhead low and plan on not making any real money for at least three years. Market yourself because that's what you're selling, even if you're fee-only and aren't really selling anything. Forget about the print ads. Focus on what you think you should be doing in your practice and not what you read about in magazines and industry publications. I've learned that I'm not looking to grow a big firm, wear dry-cleaned suits, or be a staff-manager. I want to work with people and help them solve problems. Average middle- to upper-middle class people (my client base) don't need a full-blown financial plan. First, it's overwhelming, and second, all they'll really do is file it away with all of their other important papers. Snapshots, as I call them, of a particular set of facts are far more useful to average folks.

"I still use ACT! and have customized it for my practice, and it works very well for me. My website, which seems is constantly under development, is a tremendous marketing tool and I continually improve the content. As the years have passed, it contains more and more information about how I work, how I charge, etc., simply so I don't have to be answering questions on the phone. Many planners underutilize this terrific marketing tool.

"I'm lucky because I love what I do, love my clients, and hope to be able to continue working with them for many years to come."

2007 Update:

"It's interesting to re-read my comments for Nancy's book. In the fall of 2006 I took a position with a large credit union that was launching a trust department, as I felt I was in a 'funk' working independently. Wow is all I can say after five years of working independently. After you've worked for yourself, it's very difficult to work for an organization. At least for me! Corporate culture shock doesn't even adequately portray the total change in my work environment, but it's close. Needless to say, after only nine months, I'm going to return to independent work, because it suits me. The lesson I've learned is—make a plan (business plan) and revisit it—repeatedly. It's funny, because when I read the words I wrote about marketing and getting my practice going, those words are true today.

"Another thing that if I had to do it all over again—I would only operate under my own name and not a business name. When you're first starting out and ongoing really, people

185

remember you, not the business, and then they can't find you if they can't remember the business name. As a result, I'm no longer operating under the Center For Financial Wellness, just promoting financial wellness as Robin Vaccai-Yess!

"The other big lesson that I've learned is don't stick with the status quo of what everyone else is doing. In other words, before I opened my practice, other financial planners told me that I needed to manage assets—hence, most financial planners are really investment managers and provide financial planning as an ancillary service. It was my thinking that I just wanted to do the consulting work, and rather than do just that, I followed what others said and set up a master account at Schwab. Interestingly, the asset management component is what caused me the most stress, the most paperwork, and I found I liked it less than just working with clients and acting as a consultant.

"The end result, when I relaunch my private practice later this month (under my own name this time, not using a business name), I will not be providing asset management services. Consulting, yes. Helping people to properly allocate their investments at discount brokerage firms or through large mutual fund companies like Vanguard and Fidelity, absolutely. So, the moral of my story is to follow your instincts and set up your practice the way you want."

2009 Update:

"It is always a pleasure to hear from Nancy about the update for her book because re-reading my previous comments is a learning experience for me, too. Yes, I have been back in private practice for almost two years now after my nine-month stint in the corporate world. I did as I said and went to straight financial consulting – no asset management – and I help people with many planning issues including developing an asset allocation plan. I help people get started with or transfer assets to Fidelity, Schwab (retail) or Vanguard without ongoing AUM fees. I work only hourly and charge no retainer, percentage based or referral fees. It's clean, easy and I don't need a bookkeeper.

"I operate strictly under my own name, which seems to make it easier for people to find me. I also work from home and no longer have a separate phone line or even a yellow page listing. It does not seem to impact my business, which comes largely from referrals. For those starting out, I would suggest using your own name and if you expand your practice or grow into a real firm with other employees, you can always add 'and Associates' or something similar to the name. It always seemed funny to me that so many "one man shows" always have websites that make it appear that they're part of some big conglomerate when the fact that they are small is what makes them appealing to many people.

"I still work from home and love it, but it does take discipline to go into 'the office' and work rather than head outside for yard work or chores or whatever. It has worked well for me though and does not seem to impact my clients. In the first five and a half years of my practice, I spent a huge amount on rent and related expenses just to have an outside space. When you have those additional expenses, it takes you a lot longer to breakeven and then make a profit.

"I am preparing to launch a divorce-related website, which will be a new line of business for me. It's been a niche area of planning for me since I obtained the CDFA designation way back in 2001 (it was CDP back then) and this will create a separate revenue stream as well as serve as a referral source to my own consulting practice.

"For marketing, get a website. It's more important than brochures or other print materials. My business card now says only my name, phone/fax number, website, email, the CFP logo, and the language: Independent – Fee-Only – Hourly Rates – No Products Sold. On the technology front, I've switched to Outlook because I use a Blackberry now and synchronize my contacts and appointments with my computer so I no longer use ACT. It turns out Outlook works just fine for my needs. Back in 2001 and even through 2004, I used to send and receive a lot of faxes and now I don't even have a separate fax line because faxes are so infrequent and most everything is sent and received via email. Here's something well worth the cost to purchase – full version of Adobe Acrobat – so you can work with and convert files to PDF and not give away your critical files.

"I still say the most important thing anyone interested in financial planning as a profession can do is obtain the CFP designation. Without it, I know I wouldn't be as successful in my practice."

2011 Update:

"Well, it's more than a year now that my office is back out of the house after I began renting space from a law firm in the City of Kingston. I love being out of the house again and believe that the exposure from simple things like going out for lunch and picking up mail at the Post Office are good for business. I guess I didn't realize how much I missed being in the 'normal' working world. Working from home has its advantages, but it also has its disadvantages. With both of my daughters now in high school, the necessity of a flexible schedule isn't so important.

"I still focus on financial consulting for divorce, but continue to do general financial planning as well. I continue to get referrals from clients for that work and so I don't turn it away. I do not manage assets, but rather assist clients with self-managing (i.e., Fidelity, Vanguard, Schwab, etc.) or I refer them to asset managers for that component. I found a long time ago that the paperwork ended up being more of a nightmare than I was willing to take on, but clearly in this business the steady stream of income is generated from asset management fees. The way I operate – fee-only, hourly – requires constant marketing and client recruitment, but I do this myself with a blackberry, a laptop and no administrative staff.

"I have three websites now – robinyess.com, hvdivorce.com and hudsonvalleydivorce.com. They all serve their own purpose and help with referrals and revenue generation. I have had a website since I first opened my practice in 2001 and while the content and domain names have changed dramatically over the years, I can't imagine being in business without one or three!"

Jim Skrydlak, CFP®
Independent Contractor
Pella, Iowa
jim.skrydlak@stanfordalumni.org

Jim's claim to fame is that he was the first man ever to play the banjo in Bishop Auditorium at Stanford Graduate School of Business. That and the fact he wrote his first software program in 1968 while he was a high school senior, when most of us didn't even know what software was.

After earning his MBA from Stanford in 1975, he went to work as a financial analyst for the data processing department of a Chicago bank during a bad job market and record cold weather. Having enough of that, he returned to California and worked as a pricing analyst with various high-tech hardware and software vendors for the next twenty-three years.

In 1989, he met financial planner Curt Weil while watching the fourth (and, as it turned out, final) World Series game between the Giants and the Athletics on television at the apartment of a mutual friend. They learned they had something in common. Each had donated gallons of blood to the blood bank. Later, Curt would pique Jim's interest in financial planning.

Jim's aptitude for the industry can be seen in his own dealings with money, which has allowed him to enter a new career with no income worries. He was in the habit of saving 35% of his pay every year.

Jim started maintaining financial planning software for Carolyn Bell and the Stanford Investment Group in Mountain View early in 2001, and contracted to develop software for financial plans with his second client, Weil Capital in Palo Alto, the Monday after I interviewed him.

Did you have a business plan?

"No. I've spent my life preparing business plans for new products. In spite of the fact I hate working for big corporations, I always felt I would be an employee, not an entrepreneur, and wouldn't need a business plan for myself."

What were the biggest obstacles you faced?

"I have no resilience. I could never be in sales. If a client were to tell me, 'no', I'd just go away. It seemed to me, the financial planning firms were all looking for sales people, not planners. And my own fear, that I wouldn't be able to live my current lifestyle without dipping into my savings."

What did you do right?

"Developed a broad and deep set of skills: math, finance, and programming. And I can talk to people! The fact that I can talk to financial planners and translate their need into a computerized tool places me in high demand now in my area. I set out to get the CFP® as soon as I realized I was going to enter the industry. I completed the program while I was working full time and received the designation in 1996."

How did you get training? Did you have a mentor?

"Curt Weil. We're sort of 'blood' brothers."

How long did it take to start making money?

"I'm astonished at the demand for people like me—more and better geeks! I'm not doing this for the money, but firms are willing to pay for what I have to offer. My savings are a safety net."

If you had it to do over again, what would you do differently?

"Maybe I should have jumped in a little earlier. But I didn't realize at first how to position myself. When it dawned on me that I should be using my computer and quantitative skills rather than more generalized financial planning skills, it became clear that I could go out on my own."

Where do you see yourself in five years?

"Semi-retired, somewhere in Iowa. I'll be doing financial planning and teaching accounting part-time."

What's the best advice you could give someone just starting out?

"Know what you do well. Remember, it's increasingly important to bring computers in to do things that haven't been done before. Be computer-savvy and know how to develop your own tools."

2002 Update:

"No big changes. Curt Weil has sort of re-organized his business to be, as far as I can tell, more of a money-management business, so he didn't have any more work for me. I'm now positioning myself as a software developer with financial skills, rather than a financial planner with software skills, but that's just a matter of which skills I emphasize. I continue on track for retirement in rural Iowa in the second half of 2004."

2005 Update:

"I'm doing considerably more work for people who aren't directly in the personal financial planning field—hard-money lenders needing automation of their interest accrual calculation and reporting, for example, and my work for personal financial planners has extended to include development of databases, and of Excel-based software that generates statements of investment policy as Microsoft Word documents. I'm having enough fun doing this that I'm still in Silicon Valley."

2007 Update:

"I'm now employed four days per week at Brownson, Rehmus & Foxworth, a wealth-management (they seem to prefer that term to financial planning) firm for very high net-worth clients with offices in New York, Chicago, and Menlo Park, California; I'm in the Menlo Park office.

"I've probably moved further down the path of being a software developer with financial knowledge, rather than a financial planner who's good with software.

"It's very clear at this point that my corporate financial experience and CFP® certification provide credibility and open doors, but what people are really paying for is my ability to develop software quickly. The financial credentials give new clients confidence that what I'll develop is what they need."

2009 Update:

"I'm back to working as a free-lance consultant, for people in the financial services business ranging from venture capitalists to personal financial planners. Most of my work uses my Excel, VBA, and Access skills, rather than my financial skills; the fact that I have financial skills gives me credibility with my clients, but it isn't what they're buying. I'm now trying to build a business teaching advanced Excel skills to members of the finance organizations of the big corporations around here. I think that there can be a big pay-off in efficiency when a financial analyst understands things like array formulae, lookups, pivot tables, and data tables."

2011 Update:

"I'm continuing to work as a software developer. My work in the past year, in addition to developing a Roth IRA conversion calculator for personal financial planners, has included a comprehensive financial model for a start-up manufacturer of intelligent energy-efficient windows and a performance dashboard for a human resources consulting firm, so I'm branching out beyond personal finance."

Joseph J Ponzio, President and CEO
Meridian Financial Management

Did you have a business plan?

"Yes. This was, without a doubt, one of the most difficult and crucial steps in the creation of my firm. It helped me, and continues to help me, identify my 'ideal' client, my surrounding competition, my professional and financial goals, and my strengths and weaknesses as a business owner."

190

What were the biggest obstacles you faced?

"The absolute biggest obstacle was an internal one. Namely, 'Am I ready to venture on my own and be an advisor, a CEO, a CFO, a marketer, a portfolio manager, a compliance officer, etc., and still be a good husband, son, and friend to those I care about?' Once I had decided that the answer to this question was an emphatic 'yes,' I came across my second greatest obstacle—convincing my family that I was ready. The third greatest obstacle was, and still is, managing my time to allow for all of this responsibility and work, and still find clients and service clients the way that they need to be serviced."

What did you do right?

"For lack of a better description, I lined my ducks up before I knocked them down. I made sure that I did intense research on my market, my competition, and the required rules and regulations. I created a business plan, and I stick to it. I consulted with at least eight other advisors across the country, as well as clients of fee-only advisors, to get a clear understanding of the business and expectations on both sides of the fence. I relied heavily, but not solely, on the FPi Web boards for information and advice. I ensured that my family and friends were supportive. I have read, and continue to read, everything and anything remotely related to the industry and my practice."

How did you get training? Did you have a mentor?

"After college, I went to work for a well-known insurance agency. I had no knowledge of insurance and felt I needed the training before I could ever advise on the subject. Also, I felt it was important to know what insurance agents would be telling my future clients. When I felt comfortable, I left the agency and became a stockbroker at a large national firm. Because of my passion for investments and portfolio management, I learned very little from my firm in comparison to my self-study. I did have a mentor at both firms, but learned the most through my professional associations with attorneys, CPA's, and CFP®s, and through my own research. It was probably a longer process than most people can afford, but it was the method with which I felt most comfortable."

How long did it take to start making money?

"Because of my home office and low overhead, and the fact that I am an aggressive cost-cutter, I was able to turn a profit in five weeks. So as not to inflate others expectations, this is extremely rare. However, I am not, by any means, drawing a large salary at this point. The profits that the firm has made up to now have been rolled into set-up and training for the two CFP®s that I have on staff to date. As of today, we have been accepting clients for just over three months, and I expect to be drawing a comfortable salary, according to my needs, at the six-month anniversary."

If you had it to do over again, what would you do differently?

"The only thing that I would change would be to go back to day-one and set a time at which I stop working. Though there are days that I finish by 3:30 P.M. and relax the rest of the evening, I find myself more often than not working until 10 P.M. or 11 P.M., breaking only for dinner and coffee with my wife. Also, I work every Saturday and many Sundays. Because I had not set a 'quitting time,' I have created a workaholic routine. Luckily, it is one that I can, and plan to, change in the near future."

Where do you see yourself in five years?

"I see a physical office apart from my home office that houses me, four to five CFP®s, two secretaries, a paraplanner/intern, and a part-time technology/compliance consultant. I expect one or two of these on staff to have earned ownership in the firm. I will no longer be accepting clients, as I will balance my limited number of clients and the business itself. The firm will have large community presence, through both active involvement and charitable gifting. What I foresee are great things for my firm, my employees, and the clients. When I have achieved this, I will be a success. As a side note, my business plan extends well beyond five years, looking forward to my retirement and exit strategy, which is decades away."

What's the best advice you could give someone just starting out?

"Decide, and be honest about, what it is that you hope to achieve throughout your career as a financial planner. Many people try, and fail, because they are focused on the "unlimited income potential" and the successful planners they meet. Create a business plan and stick to it. Identify a target client and work your business around him or her—the money will come regardless of whether they are high net-worth or not. Whatever you do, do it in your client's best interest, even in the beginning when you are struggling. Every person you help, even if you are not compensated monetarily, will repay you ten-fold in referrals and advertising. Determine what it is that you love to do and become a specialist. Finally, talk to other planners. I have found that they are extremely receptive to strangers calling and asking questions. I did it and still do it. If you would like additional information, feel free to contact me as well."

2005 Update:

"Three and a half years have passed since I began Meridian Financial Management, and we have had, in my opinion, tremendous success.

"The first two years were very difficult. The markets were horrible and prospective clients were tired of losing money. We saw two planners come and go. Still, we managed to do well by our existing clients, and that lead to referrals and more business.

"Today, Meridian Financial Management is a mature investment advisory firm. We manage two private funds for clients across seven states. I have assumed the role of lead portfolio manager and, in addition to handling our long-term public and private equity investments, I oversee a team of real estate and short-term equity investors. Our two financial planners are the key contacts for clients, helping ensure that our investment strategies meet clients' goals.

"Three-and-a-half years ago, I envisioned a firm where middle-income Americans would receive high net-worth advice. I believe that, at Meridian Financial Management, this dream is being realized every day."

2007 Update:

"You blink, and five-and-a-half years have passed. Clients have come and gone. Investments grew and fell. And while certain aspects of our business and vision have changed somewhat, including our name (from Meridian Financial Management to The Meridian Business Group), our core business remains the same.

"In the beginning I focused on how we could help people. The business itself came second. We were in our "seed" stage and needed to develop our views and philosophies to handle the concerns of a wide array or clients. Today things have changed. We still keep the client first, but our systems and experience are in place. We are comfortable in our abilities and can now focus on growing the firm (without, of course, sacrificing the needs of our clients).

"As I write this, I admire and laugh at my early optimism. I had no idea what it meant to run a business and believed that I would incorporate, print off business cards, and watch the money roll in. Today, I realize that the business is just as important as the vision. And I also realize that, in five years, I will most likely look back to today and laugh at myself again.

"The truth is that we tell our clients to keep a long-term view but expect something different for ourselves. We tell them about the power of compounding growth but relax a bit too much today at the expense of tomorrow's growth. We tell them to set realistic expectations and then hold ourselves to a different standard. At least, that is how it happened for me.

"I am extremely happy with our firm and am proud of our people. I see what we have done in the past five-and-a-half years and can't wait to see what we can achieve in the next thirty."

2009 Update:

"I am exactly where I want to be. One of the greatest lessons that I've learned over the past seven years in business is that The Meridian Business Group is *my* business. When we began the firm in 2002, we were headed in a certain direction: comprehensive financial planning. In time, we realized that our passions and expertise were in portfolio management, investing, and helping people with their daily finances. So...we changed directions.

"In fact, throughout the past seven years, we've changed directions a number of times. Though we've always focused on helping 'regular' people -- middle-income American families, we grew to realize that we could only help people in those areas in which we were highly passionate experts. We went from 'do everything so that we can do some of what we love' to 'do what we love.' Only by doing what you love can you possibly become the best at what you do.

"Part of that enlightenment caused us to realize that our passion is for working with clients, *not* managing people. Today, our firm is back to its roots -- me, my partner, and some part-time help. It's not for want of revenue or a tough economy. In fact, our business expanded dramatically in 2008 as our 'no nonsense' approach to investing and service continued to bring in new clients. Still, we decided that our time was best spent doing only that which we absolutely love.

"We have a very large presence in the investment community. More than four million people a year read my articles both on- and offline, and I am periodically conducting radio and television interviews. In addition, I have also done a number of speaking engagements, both locally as well as at venues and universities across the country. And in reflecting on those experiences, I can say one thing for certain: None of this would have been possible if we weren't doing what we love.

"Walking into The Meridian Business Group every day is like walking into a dream. That's not to say that it isn't tough. On the contrary, it is extremely difficult to run a business and there are times that I hate the tasks in front of me. (Who likes to pay bills?) Still, the fun times more than make up for the menial tasks, and I look forward to each new day with passion and excitement.

"The best advice I could give an aspiring planner, advisor, or portfolio manager is this: Become a specialist, and do it in the area you love most. Too many people try to be all things to all people. It is impossible to be the best estate planner *and* portfolio manager *and* insurance expert. Though there is a lot of money being a broad generalist, you'll be much happier -- and likely wealthier -- if you specialize in what you love. Only then can you be the best at what you do.

"In the midst of a global credit crisis and stock market crash, our future has never been brighter or better. I can't wait to see what is in store for the next thirty years."

2011 Update

Joe Ponzio, President
Ponzio Capital Inc.
joe@ponziocapital.com
www.ponziocapital.com
(800) 520-2124

"In my 2009 update, I extolled the benefits of doing exactly what you *love* to do, not what you think you *need* to do to be competitive. FINRA oversees some 650,000 registered representatives, which means that you have a ton of competition out there. To attract the business, you have to be the best. To be the best, you must do what you love.

"I also extol the benefits of focusing solely on what you love in my book *F Wall Street: Joe Ponzio's No-Nonsense Guide to Value Investing for the Rest of Us.*[168] Why do people and advisors suffer such miserable investment performance? I believe it's because too many people invest outside their sphere of confidence and competence. And that translates to every aspect of our lives and businesses too. If you try to run a practice and offer services that are well outside your sphere of confidence, competence, and expertise, you may not fail but you will also never realize your full potential for happiness and success.

"Late in 2009, my business partner and I split up as I prepared to move my family to another state. I founded Ponzio Capital to continue doing what I love – concentrated value investing

---

[168] http://www.amazon.com/Wall-Street-No-Nonsense-Approach-Investing/dp/1605500003

194

for long-term growth – while he continued Meridian with a focus on comprehensive planning.

"With Ponzio Capital, I keep it a small, intimate group of long-term clients. Two years ago, I said that walking into my old firm every day was like walking into a dream. That continues to be the case today. I am doing exactly what I love every day.

"I also said that the best advice I could give to an aspiring planner, advisor, or portfolio manager is to become a specialist and do what you love. That continues to hold true today. Too many advisors try to be all things to all people, but all the studies show that clients, in general, are unhappy with their advisors. If you stick to what you know well and love, you'll be the best and your clients will be happy."

Angie Herbers®
Angela Herbers and Associates Inc. (formerly Financial Advisor Resource, Inc.)
AngelaHerbers.com
Manhattan, Kansas

Did you have a business plan?

"In college, my most dreaded class assignment was writing a Business/Career Plan. At the time, I felt that I had no direction, and I was more comfortable just taking it day-by-day and waiting to see where the wind blew me. As it turns out, once I began to write my Career Plan, I knew exactly where I wanted to go. In addition, I found out that some of the things that I was doing were NOT taking me there."

What were the biggest obstacles you faced?

"I am what the industry calls a 'newbie' planner as opposed to a 'career-changer'. The only obstacles were getting through school and finding the job I wanted."

What did you do right?

"My first interest in financial planning was inspired by a nationwide, collegiate competition hosted by American Express Financial Advisors. In April of 2000, I was one of a team of three selected to participate in the First Annual Collegiate Financial Planning Invitational, which required me to be enrolled in a CFP®-Registered program. An accounting major at the time, I enrolled in the CFP® program, and our team went to New York City and won the national title. As a result, our team, Kansas State University's CFP® program, and other participates were featured in major industry publications. After that, I dropped my accounting degree and dove head-first into financial planning."

How did you get training? Did you have a mentor?

"I had both an internship and a mentor. Following the American Express competition, I received a student scholarship to attend the National Association of Personal Financial Advisors (NAPFA) annual conference. Networking at this conference turned out to pave my career path in financial planning. This is where I meet Wayne Cassaday of Covenant Financial, a fee-only financial planning firm in Charleston, South Carolina, who provided me with an incredible internship experience. This is also where I met my mentor and current employer, Sheryl Garrett."

How long did it take to start making money?

"In May of 2001, I earned my Bachelor of Science degree in Personal Financial Planning from Kansas State University and joined Sheryl as a salaried employee, dividing my time between being a staff planner in her small, independent financial planning firm, Garrett Financial Planning, Inc., and providing member support in The Garrett Planning Network, Inc."

If you it to do over again, what would you do differently?

"Without a doubt, I would have taken the CFP® comprehensive exam the first available date after graduation! The greatest benefit to graduating from a CFP®-registered program is fulfilling the educational requirement to take the CFP® exam. Now that I am deep into my career, I have a hard time dedicating myself to study."

What's the best advice you could give someone just starting out?

"There are three pieces of advice that I would give to someone who is just staring out in the financial planning industry—whether you are starting your own business or seeking a job in a planning firm:

1. Learn to market yourself effectively.
2. Develop a Long-Term Business Plan or Career Plan.
3. Accept the TRUTH: Develop a realistic inventory of your strengths and weaknesses."

Where do you see yourself in five years?

"I plan to just keep learning and gaining experience in the financial planning industry. I believe that my youth is my most valuable asset because I have the time to grow with a dynamic industry. As consumers become more aware of the benefits of financial planning, I believe career opportunities in financial planning will expand. All this leaves the doors completely opened for exploration, and *that* is really exciting!"

2007 Update:

"It is exactly five years from the time that I first wrote this insert. It is an interesting experience to go back and read where you were then and how far you've gone in that period of time. I have changed directions, experienced new paths, and opened new doors, so here's the update.

"One the best pieces of advice I received from one of my mentors was 'be careful what career you choose early in life, because there will be a time when it's too late to change.' I took this advice with a grain of salt, but over the past five years, I have come to realize it's very true. I made a hard decision to leave The Garrett Planning Network, Inc. and my mentor Sheryl Garrett in the spring of 2003. I took a couple months off and focused on what I really wanted to do in my career. The two choices I had were, be a financial planner or help financial planners. Consequently, I decided that my unique abilities were in business building, and helping advisors build their businesses was more of my desire than to actually be a financial planner.

"I grew up in a family of a long line of entrepreneurs, so launching my own business was not a surprise to many of my friends and family. At first, launching my company, Financial Advisor Resource, Inc., was simply for the purpose of producing supplemental income while I obtained my Masters degree. However, with a lucky break and a cover article in *Investment Advisor* magazine, my business got bigger than I expected, faster than I expected.

"Today, I help financial planning professionals hire, recruit and retain next generation talent. I work with a group of clients that in total represent over $1 billion in consumer assets. In addition, I write a monthly column in *Investment Advisor* magazine on human capital issues. Of all the things I do, I love them all. But I like the writing the best. I say, in your career, be careful what you wish for…you might just get it!"

2009 Update:

"It seems so long ago that I made this first insert for this book. Things change and they often change so rapidly. As mentioned in my 2007 update, I currently have my own practice management consulting business. The name, however, was changed this year to Angela Herbers and Associates, Inc. www.AngelaHerbers.com. We currently work with financial planning companies who desire to grow their firms by better managing their operations, human capital, client value and financial status.

"In the past two years we have helped build over 100 firms in the industry and we continue to work with and support those firms and their employees. We have worked with firms that produce less than $1M in revenue and we have also built firms that produce over $5M in revenue. Although our range of firm size differs from client to client all our proven systems, apply to any size firm. Our business, Angela Herbers and Associates Inc., now employs four people. Going forward we will continue to build our business and work with advisors."

2011 Update:

"Well, unlike years past with my previous inserts not a whole lot has changed this time. So I will take this opportunity to tell you about some cool things we have done in the past two years. My consulting firm Angela Herbers and Associates Inc. www.AngelaHerbers.com is still operating and thriving. To date, we have worked with over 500 financial advisory firms who employ well over a total of 3000 employees. Over the years, we have learned through our work and research all the ways to build a productive and profitable advisory firm and we continue to share that knowledge with our clients and other financial advisory firms who contract us to help them.

"One big thing we are excited to announce in 2011, is the outcome of a ten year research project. Under the radar, for the past ten years I have been doing research on what really motivates and drives performance of Next Generation talent and employees of the financial planning profession. We have been calling this research project P4, for the four areas of motivation and satisfaction that help drive employees to perform at their highest level. We are very excited to roll out this research in 2011, and much of the results have been amazing and astounding to us. Much of the work we have done in the area of human capital management has been clinical research where we have studied, tracked and followed thousands of employees in the financial profession. We are very excited to share the results to the industry in 2011. We will be doing other cool things at Angela Herbers and Associates Inc., but I am not ready to tell you what they are at this moment (wink.) So watch for us in 2011-2012.

"For me personally, I am still writing my monthly column in Investment Advisor magazine. It's hard to believe that I have been writing my column for about nine years now! You can find my column and blog at www.AdvisorOne.com.

"Finally, I was awarded an Adjunct Faculty position at Kansas State University (KSU) in 2010, where I graduated college and is located in my hometown of Manhattan, Kansas. This was a great honor given to me by the university. My goal at KSU is to work with and train the next generation of talent and begin giving back to the university through fund raising efforts. KSU and its financial planning department have grown rapidly over the past five years and they are out of space! We will be working to build them a new building and also continue to train the next generation of financial advisors, like you."

Mike Curtiss, CFP®
Envisioning Financial, Inc.
Brownsburg, Indiana
www.envisioningfinancial.com
mikec@envisioningfinancial.com

"I was manager of employee benefits for a large corporation for several years and decided, at age 49, to take an early buyout offer and make a career transition into financial planning. After four years I'm still here. I'm president of my own firm and loving every day."

Did you have a business plan?

"Yes, I worked with a small-business consultant to develop and write a business plan. It was a worthwhile exercise and I would encourage anyone starting out to do so. However, I've learned that as the business evolves, the plan must be revised to reflect new realities and circumstances. I believe that having a plan is important, but it must be flexible."

What were the biggest obstacles you faced?

"Reflecting back, two obstacles emerged that I had to learn to deal with. Interestingly, however, I was unaware of the existence of either one as I began this journey.

"The first involved developing confidence when making recommendations to clients. Starting out, I thought that acquiring the necessary securities and insurance licenses would be my biggest obstacle. I had little awareness of the complexities within the financial services industry. The span of available products and services, the multitude of providers for each product and service, the different 'cultures' of the various organizations offering financial planning services, the various methods of compensation and, perhaps, most importantly, the differentiation between client-centered and sales-driven recommendations all were variables that created uncertainty as to what was the "right" recommendation.

"The second involved operating my practice as a business. Starting out, I was not aware of the term 'practice management' but am keenly aware of what it means now. Marketing, internal operations, customer service, and financial management are key elements of any service-oriented business, including a small financial planning practice. Having systems and procedures in place to monitor each of these activities is an ongoing challenge.

"I was able to address these obstacles through a combination of approaches: direct experience (sometimes painful and costly), extensive research and reading, networking, and membership in professional organizations. I subscribe to the Bob Veres' newsletter that informs me of emerging industry trends. Perhaps most significantly, I earned my CFP® in 2004. CFP® is presently the industry-recognized standard for professionalism, and earning it greatly enhanced my confidence."

What did you do right?

"In the spring of 2000, at age 49, I decided to leave a 25-plus year corporate career to enter the financial services business. My last corporate position was manager of employee benefits for a large firm. In this role, I acquired extensive experience with pension, 401(k), medical, life, disability, and executive non-qualified plans and found that I enjoyed the nature of the work.

"Additionally, prior to making the change, I retained a career-consulting firm to help identify my job-related strengths and weaknesses and predict careers I was likely to excel in. Financial services clearly emerged as the top area of interest. Having a deep-rooted belief that I was pursuing a career track that I both enjoyed and was suited for, and was entering an industry poised for substantial growth, helped sustain me during times of doubt."

How did you get training? Did you have a mentor?

"The first position in my new career was as a financial services representative with a large insurance company Broker/Dealer. From there, I joined a local employee benefit consulting firm. I left that position to work as an independent contractor at a small financial planning firm. Two years ago, I decided to start my own firm and am now working every day developing that business.

"Prior to starting my business I never identified someone I truly considered a mentor. I was associated with various trainers along the way, but much of what was provided was more sales-oriented than planning related. All the people I encountered were in the business themselves, and were generally more focused on their own activities rather than my development. This is not a criticism, but a reality of how the independent advisor system works. Anyone going the independent route should understand that learning the business is ultimately his or her responsibility. I continue to work at this by reading, networking, attending conferences, professional memberships, etc., etc."

How long did it take to start making money?

"My departure from the corporate job was part of company-sponsored voluntary separation program, so I received severance pay for several months after I began my new career. When the severance stopped, I was making some money as an advisor, although significantly less than my previous salary. Moreover, as an independent business operator, I had to cover expenses from the reduced income. The first year after the severance stopped was a difficult time and required changes in family budgeting. My income has increased with each passing year, and I should surpass my previous corporate salary this (the fourth) year."

If you had to do it over again, what would you do differently?

"I have learned the importance of identifying a segment or niche in which to concentrate as opposed to trying to cover the entire financial services spectrum. I now "outsource" medical insurance and group 401(k) plans to individuals I've met and trust sending clients to. I have also chosen to work with age 55 and up retirees and pre-retirees, meaning I generally do not work with young families, business owners, professionals, etc. While I've not yet established a minimum account limit, I have begun referring clients away who do not fit clearly into my business model.

"While the reality may be that no one is likely to turn away any business in the tough, early years, I believe that identifying and pursuing an area of concentration as soon as possible will minimize distractions and get the business off the ground sooner."

Where do you see yourself in five years?

"I see myself continuing to grow my financial planning practice over the next five years (and well beyond). I intend to focus on the fee-based element of my practice and expect to increase assets under management several times the current level. Also, because of the rapid rate of land development in the area where I live, I intend to become a source of 1031-exchange expertise. I also intend to address succession planning/business continuation by hiring or partnering up with a younger planner to manage the business when I'm absent and perhaps acquire it when I decide to step aside."

What's the best advice you can give someone just starting out?

"To be aware that success or failure in this business will be determined not so much by how smart you are but by decisions on how you organize your business, who you choose to work with or for, how and to whom you market yourself, the affiliations you make with other professionals and organizations (i.e. broker dealers) and your reputation.

"It is important to remember that this is a business oriented to serving others. It is a mentally challenging business that requires you to keep current with trends and new developments. It is also a business where you must be continually mindful of the need to be client, not advisor focused.

"And for someone starting out, it is business that occasionally results in self-doubt and difficulty sleeping. For me, having a conviction that I was led to this career by something more than coincidence, and having a spiritual peace amid the uncertainty of difficult times, was key to staying the course. And thank God I did."

2007 Update

"In the fall of 2005, I undertook a twelve-month business coaching engagement with Max Bolka that proved very beneficial. We jointly created a customized Envisioning Financial marketing program that expresses what I want clients to know about me as they search for an advisor to work with. I have also become more disciplined in setting and reviewing annual business goals. I feel that working with a professional coach greatly enhanced my practice management skills.

"I continue to search for the right succession planning solution. My son and I have discussed the pros and cons of having him join the business. While not a critically pressing issue, it is one I am continually mindful of. I've also strengthened my relationships with area attorneys and accountants and view those affiliations as sources of future referrals. I've joined the Tenant-in-Common Association (TICA) in preparation to assist prospective clients manage the sale of appreciated real estate. Lastly, I have enrolled in the Accredited Estate Planner (AEP) designation courses with the American College. Increasingly I find myself working with higher net-worth individuals who need more focus on estate planning activities.

"My wife has also joined the business as office manager. The demands of my practice do not require a full-time employee at this time, so Penny is able to handle many of the administrative activities and still have a lot of freedom and flexibility in her schedule. So far, it is working pretty well.

"My revenue and income have both continued to increase at double-digit rates. I am making significantly more than I was before entering this industry, plus am experiencing much more job satisfaction. Most importantly, I truly believe I can have a positive impact on the lives of those I have the privilege to work with."

2009 Update:

"Last fall I brought a younger associate into the business and am serving in a mentoring role as he builds his practice. I consider this an initial step in developing a long range succession plan. We co-located into a larger, more professional office suite with potential for future expansion. I continue to grow my network of professional affiliates and recently contracted with a small public relations firm. Through that effort I've appeared in area print media several times and have been featured on television twice.

"In the fall of 2007 I switched my securities and advisory relationships to a firm with broad experience in the alternative investment arena. This has allowed me to differentiate my practice, especially among higher net worth individuals. I've even set up a subsidiary business that targets the 1031 Tenant in Common marketplace.

"The market turmoil of the past 18 months was my first exposure to a prolonged bear market and was emotionally very draining. The experience challenged me to question some widely accepted investment maxims. My investment recommendations have become more focused on absolute return and active management strategies that offer more predictable returns with less volatility.

"Despite the ongoing challenges, I am still grateful for the sequence of events that lead me to this industry and believe the best days for financial planners lie ahead."

2011 Update:

"Since the 2009 update my most significant accomplishment was hiring an administrative assistant (Alicia). With several years of industry experience and the Registered Paraplanner designation, she quickly picked up much of the service-related workload allowing me to spend my time more productively. She has also increased the systematization of office procedures through heavier reliance on our CRM (a customized version of ACT) and paperless forms handling. With her background as a wedding planner, she has greatly enhanced our marketing activities. We hosted our first large-scale client appreciation event last Christmas and have held two other prospective client events featuring a local economist and a workshop on Social Security/Medicare.

"My practice has evolved almost solely into a fee-based financial planning and asset management business. My transaction business is limited to selling company-issued stock for advisory clients. I utilize the Envestnet Asset Management platform for my advisory business and recently began using the Unified Managed Account feature available through Envestnet.

"My professional education goal for the year is to acquire the Accredited Investment Fiduciary (AIF) designation. I view this as an important step if the present suitability and fiduciary standards are combined into one.

"I am focused on developing and executing a 10-year succession strategy that benefits the successor, me, and most importantly my clients. Who knows – ten years from now I may decide to stick around, but want a viable plan in place to cover any contingency."

Bob Adams, CFP®
Armstrong Retirement Planning, LLC
Cupertino, California

When I met Bob at his second FPA Retreat, he'd been a financial planner for less than a year-and-a-half, and knew he'd made the right choice. After twenty-four years in management with Hewlett Packard, he wanted to make a career change. In 2001, he enrolled in an MS in Financial Planning degree program while still at HP. When HP offered a severance package as part of a company-wide downsizing operation in 2002, the timing was right to turn a lifelong interest in investments into a new career.

Fortunately, that 'long time interest,' coupled with prudent lifestyle decisions and management skills, gave him the ability to go back to school, earn his Masters in Financial Planning, and open the door to his own business.

Bob and his wife Pat live in the Bay Area of Northern California with their teen-aged son, Robert.

Did you have a business plan?

"I wrote my business plan before I opened my practice, and I believe it is a basic business fundamental. You need to treat your practice as a business. A good business plan serves as a roadmap during your start-up phase, but it shouldn't stop there. It should be a "living" and evolving written document. I can't imagine not having one, and I understand that most businesses fail because of a lack of planning and a lack of clear understanding of their value proposition. Clearly, a business plan doesn't guarantee success, but it does focus you on the larger strategic decisions such as a business model, marketing plans, and income/expense models. You can't try to be everything to everyone, so it is important to understand what services you are going to provide, what target market you choose to serve and how you will deliver and price your services. In creating a business plan, I also wanted to create almost a checklist of the many items I needed to complete prior to opening my practice. Nancy's book has a very comprehensive list of these items. I also created a list of other items for year one and year two. As an example, I decided a website wasn't initially critical, but it would be helpful as I began to use other lead generation strategies in my second year.

"*Beginning with the end in mind*, one of Steven Covey's tenets, was the driving force for me to initially create the type of business model that I wanted in the future. In creating your business model, it is important to create a model that will generate a recurring revenue stream that will realistically support your expenses and your income needs. The old adage that a new planner starves for the first three years can be a self-fulfilling prophecy if you don't answer the question, 'How am I going to attract potential clients?' There is no lack of supply of clients needing your help, but you need to connect with them, win them as clients, and earn their ongoing business. Client acquisition is a time-consuming and costly proposition, so it is important to have a client referral strategy, as well as a client retention strategy, as part of your business plan.

"I looked at a number of canned business plan packages, and I found that most of them were focused towards someone who was putting together a glossy financially–oriented, future-projections type plan to show potential investors. This is neither strategically or tactically useful in identifying what you need to do to put together your business. I ended up creating my own outline in Microsoft Word by drawing categories from both Nancy's book and from some of the packages on the market."

What were the biggest obstacles you faced?

"Two big obstacles were the sheer number of things to put in place and also facing the, 'So how long have you been in practice?' question. I have a solo practice, and even though I outsourced all non-critical core activities, I found the set-up and first-year tasks to be large. The experience question I was able to partially deflect with my qualifications (MS in Financial Planning) and several designations I acquired, but this issue will only go away with time and with my earning of the CFP® designation once I have completed three years of experience in early 2006. It is a minor issue with those I have known for many years, but it can be a huge issue with those that are just meeting me.

"There is nothing scarier for a potential client than to open up their kimono to someone else and discuss their family and financial history. It requires an enormous amount of trust. We are in a high-trust relationship with our clients, and trust is built over time and with the comfort provided by knowing that the professional is experienced."

What did you do right?

"Creating and executing a detailed business plan helped me, both because it helped focus me, and because it forced me early on to make some key decisions about my services and my business plan. During the first two years, I attended five FPA regional and national events per year. This has helped me greatly. I would especially recommend the FPA Residency Program and the FPA Retreat. Two months after I opened my practice, I attended my first FPA retreat. I literally went with a list of twenty questions, mostly around practice management, and I got all of them answered as well as learning so much more. Each time you connect with fellow FPA professionals you have the opportunity to learn, share your experiences, and create an ongoing sharing relationship for the future.

"On the marketing side, I contacted 250 acquaintances before I opened my practice and from that created my initial list of potential clients. On the outbound marketing side, I became an active member of my local Chamber of Commerce, a local service club, and I participated in many community projects and charity activities. Potential clients need to meet you in a non-finance setting to get to know you personally, and from that will flow business and referrals."

How did you get your training? Did you have a mentor?

"I chose to get my MS in Financial Planning from Golden Gate University because I wanted a background that extended past the traditional CFP® exam prep classes. I also hope to teach CFP® classes some day. I've found that the MS has given me extra credibility with my potential clients. I don't have a formal mentor, but I've received a great deal of much appreciated help from the many FPA colleagues I've meet through the FPA Residency program and other FPA conferences. I see a great deal of value in a formal mentor or a "coaching" type of situation, and I may pursue this in the future."

How long did it take you to make money?

"I made a small amount of money my first full year of practice. I have a home office, and I use an "hourly" type office at a local executive office center for client meetings. Keeping your overhead low is very important. My single largest expense is the travel and related expenses for my FPA conferences. I consider those a very good use of my budget, and they've helped me immensely. Ongoing professional development needs to be a high priority."

If you had to do it all over again, what would you do differently?

"I would look at the Garrett System and also Cambridge, because I know there were time-consuming tasks that I performed or research I did that I could have probably outsourced more effectively by working with them or someone else like them. The forms, business process and coaching help would have saved me time."

Where do you see yourself in five years?

"It takes time to build a practice, and I hope within three to five years to have a fairly mature practice in terms of meeting my target goals. I also expect at about that time to need to make a decision about whether to grow beyond a solo practice in terms of both personnel and scope of services."

What is the best advice you could give someone just starting out?

"Decide first what you want to do in five years, and then think about how you can start on that road today. If you want a solo practice, think about how you can start now. Become active in your community. Seek out your local chamber and also community groups that embrace passions you share. Before you get a chance to talk to a potential client about their financial challenges and dreams, you have to earn their trust. Earning trust is best done over time face-to-face and is occasionally begun through the referral process.

"Continue to update your business plan and evolve your services and your tools by participating in FPA and by continuing to read and learn. Serving our clients requires continual learning and commitment. Education, integrity and commitment to your clients will pay dividends and will help you build a very rewarding career. There is no shortage of potential clients. It is up to you to find creative ways to connect with them."

2007 Update

"My practice continues to grow, and at this point, I'm about a year ahead of my business plan. About fifteen months ago, I achieved an inflection point where I started receiving one to two good quality referrals a month. My growth can be tied back to the outbound marketing plan within my business plan and the generous clients who recommended me to family and business colleagues.

"I am constantly struck by how many clients are out there wanting our help, and also the wide diversity of clients and client circumstances I've seen in the last four years. We can make a real difference, and I've found Financial Planning to be a very satisfying career that I expect to be engaged in for many years to come."

2009 Update:

"This year I have the privilege of serving as the VP of Career Development on the Silicon Valley's chapter of the FPA. I'm really enjoying working with the students and others in the Chapter. Last year I served as President of our local Chamber of Commerce and I also serve in leadership positions on two other Boards. Civic and professional community service is very enjoyable and is also a great way for your local community to see your ethics and professionalism in action. When you have a solo practice, you are the brand.

"Most of my original clients are still with me and I am still having a lot of fun. The last year has been challenging because of the economy, but on the other hand this is the time where we can be of most help to our clients. The key is as always to maintain good communication with your clients. Most of my original clients are still with me and I am still having a lot of fun. These days I encounter new clients who already understand the value and the credibility of the CFP® marks and I rarely have clients even asking me how long I have been in practice.

"I recently received an inquiry about merging or selling the business, but I enjoy being a solo practice and I especially enjoy the ability to decide how I wish to spend my time and what clients I wish to help. I also really enjoy working with my clients as well as the pro-bono work, student mentoring and educational work I do with my local FPA chapter so I think in 5 years I will be happily helping my clients and continuing to help mentor students."

2011 Update:

"I recently started my 5th year as a CFP® and I will be shortly starting my 8th year in practice. Starting my own solo-practice in 2003 was the right way for me to enter the profession and it has been both satisfying and fun to assist clients. Financial planning professionals really can and do help change lives and it is indeed gratifying when you help illuminate clients to options or alternatives that can enhance their financial future and without sounding too melodramatic, sometimes the quality of their lives and that of their family. It is both a great responsibility and a great deal of fun and reward.

"I've always been very involved with both my professional community as well as my local business and civic community. In 2011, I am serving as the Chapter President of the Silicon Valley Chapter of the Financial Planning Association and I served in 2008 as the President of the Cupertino Chamber of Commerce. I also serve as the Vice-President of the Cupertino Library Foundation and I am very involved with the Cupertino Rotary Club.

"Choosing to become a financial planner has been a great and rewarding journey. It is challenging work and it is never boring because the knowledge base continues to evolve. As a practitioner, you need to continually learn and grow."

Michael A. Dubis, CFP®
Madison, Wisconsin
www.michaeldubis.com

"I knew I wanted to be a financial planner when I read a quote in *Investor's Business Daily* by Harold Evensky that said, when asked about financial planning, 'It's not just your finances we are planning, it's the quality of the rest of your life.' I was 19 years old.

"The next four years, while finishing college, led me down a path of tremendous confusion. Within a year of that discovery, I interned at a big insurance company who still calls themselves financial planners, and I thought to myself, 'If this is financial planning, I want nothing to do with it.' It was all sales and full of people that really were not interested in planning, because the company essentially forced them to meet sales quotas. I quit, not knowing what to do next. I returned to focusing my college efforts on real estate and ignored the idea of financial planning for two years. It wasn't until I got into real estate, and, at the same time, met some real financial planners outside my work, that my energy refocused on my true life calling.

"Briefly, as my website describes me: I am a CERTIFIED FINANCIAL PLANNER™ and President of Touchstone Financial, LLC, a Fee-Only Financial Consulting & Investment Management Firm here in Madison, Wisconsin. Some highlights of my brief career include frequent interviews and quotes by many national and local media venues, such as *Money*, the *Wall Street Journal, Milwaukee Journal Sentinel, Smart Money Magazine, Bloomberg*, and many others. Invited guest speaker for numerous national and local planning engagements. Selected as one of the Madison Area's top 40 Executives Under the Age of 40. Current President of the Southern Wisconsin Financial Planning Association (FPA). Active member with the National Association of Personal Financial Advisors (NAPFA). Board Member & Treasurer of the Natural Heritage Land Trust and head of the investment committee. In my previous life, I was a Development Analyst and Manager responsible for financing and developing premier senior retirement communities throughout Wisconsin and Iowa. I complete my life with my wife Shelley and dogs Amber and Sadie. I am an avid reader, health nut, enjoy photography and outdoors, and devote many hours to my pursuit of perfecting my fly-fishing skills."

Did you have a business plan?

"Yes, I started my business plan the day I decided I wanted to become a financial planner. Although at that time, I really didn't know whether I would go on my own or work for others; in fact, I didn't know what financial planning really was. I just knew that constantly building a business plan allowed me to journal my way into the profession and made me a better advisor and business person.

"Two key resources helped me develop and eventually launch my business: NAPFA Foster Program (which I believe is open to anyone) and the book *The E-Myth Revisited* by Michael Gerber.

"Today, though, I find the business plan has less importance for goal setting as it does as a placeholder for affirmations of who I am, who I want to be, and what I'm going to do to get there. The business plan I use today is more of a life plan, it's an integrated journal of the path I wish to take."

What were the biggest obstacles you faced?

"I look like I'm 12 years old. It took a while for me get over some prospective clients' and colleagues' age bias, which, in actuality, I came to realize, centered on my own age-bias and lack of confidence in myself. After I got over my own concerns, it stopped being a problem.

"I also was not clear on what it was I thought I was offering to my clients. I spent and still spend a significant amount of time honing my value proposition. Today, that confidence and clarity of value is there; charging appropriately for it, though, continues to be an obstacle.

"When I first started, I did not have a CFP®, so that hurt my ability to bring in clients. Fortunately, I picked up the designation within five months of opening. I think getting the CFP® right away is very important not just for yourself, but for the profession as a whole."

What did you do right?

"I believe. I pray a lot. I try to serve God as I feel is His Will. I constantly ask for and thank God for His blessings and guidance.

"I married well. Love is not 50/50, and my wife is an expert on knowing and enduring a very misaligned ratio at times.

"My wife and I try to practice what we preach. We practice with our finances as much as we practice what we preach in life, by living healthy, communicating with each other, traveling, embracing simplicity, being charitable, and supporting one another.

"I maintain outside interests, such as fly-fishing, triathlon training, and community volunteering. This broadens your scope in life, which broadens the value you bring to clients.

"I think about what it must be like to be a client of mine. I hired a money coach for my wife and me, originally, to see what it was like to be a client, but it turned out to be much more than that. She helped me see what colored-lenses I view the world of finance through, and in the process, gave me new insight to become a better husband and advisor. We all have our own biases, and quite frankly, we'll probably never alter them much, but the active awareness of them allows you to be more open in how you provide service to your clients.

"I had adequate start-up funds, emergency reserves, and a wife who earned enough that we could live off of one income for awhile. This created a tremendous amount of complacency because no one owned me or my business. I was and still am, allowed to think clearly about how to serve others.

"I took lessons from and listened well to effective marketers. I am constantly in the media and do speaking engagements at least quarterly. These are big credibility enhancers.

"I said 'no' to prospective clients more than 'yes.'

"I started a systems and procedure manual with detailed steps of everything I do right away.

"I worked for three other firms first—an accounting firm, an insurance sales person, and a true fiduciary comprehensive planning firm.

"I read a lot. But more importantly, I do a lot.

"I built a group of mentors, who I define as people who have done what you want to do and have done so successfully. I still have a group of mentors that evolves over time.

"I hire smart consultants. When I have a question about whatever it is that's troubling me in the business and I know that I need expert or broad-based advice, I try to go right to the top of the who's who pile and pay them for their value.

"I started a peer group that spans nationally. These are all my buddies now, and at the drop of a hat, I can call on any of them to help me with something, or just hear me complain. I think we all need that bond.

"I keep fixed expenses low. I work from home still, although now I rent office space downtown at an hourly rate, originally through a group called HQ Global. The image is there, the costs are not."

How did you get training? Did you have a mentor?

"I grew up in service businesses all my life and have always been an entrepreneur. I paid for college with my own small business and scholarship. I graduated with a degree in Real Estate and Urban Land Economics at one of the top Business Schools and Real Estate programs in the country. I then went to work in corporate real estate development for two years in charge of site acquisitions and financing. The technical skills, the people skills, and the education I had built at a young age made transitioning into the technical side of financial planning relatively easy.

"I then worked for three other financial service firms for two years. At the same time, I spent fifteen months getting my CFP®. I was appointed a position at the last financial planning firm I worked at to build systems in place for the financial planning firm and to first assist the partner in all financial planning work. That led to a significant opportunity to see how to run a firm. The partner of that firm was a wonderful and nurturing person who offered me a tremendous amount of opportunity.

"Yes, I had and still have a number of mentors, who are also good friends and colleagues today. The 'scienc' part of financial planning is not that difficult; the 'art' of financial planning is where mentors are invaluable and where a lifelong commitment to personal and community development yields the greatest rewards. I have a group of mentors: business-focused, spirit-focused, and family-focused. I also have my peer group who are equally important to me. All people I admire and respect."

How long did it take to start making money?

"Less than two years, depending on how you define 'making money.'

"I started in June/July 2002. The first six months, all I did was spend money, about $30,000 up front and about $1000/month fixed thereafter. My first client paid me a total of $2500. That was all I really earned in 2002. I used most of that time to get my CFP® and build systems and procedures.

"The next full calendar year, 2003, I earned an after-expense income of $12,000, although that's not profit. Profit is what you earn after you pay yourself a reasonable salary, I did not pay myself a salary that year.

"The next calendar year, 2004, I earned an after-expense income equal to what I earned when I left the last financial planning firm two-and-a-half years earlier as a salary, but without benefits. To me, this was a big psychological success, because I no longer felt I needed another firm to provide for me.

"This year, calendar year 2005, I expect revenue to increase 50%. I expect take home pay to increase 120%. My income and profit this year is in line with all major studies for solo practitioner firms.

"Going forward, I am looking to increase revenue 30% in 2006, from 2005 estimates, then stabilize 15 to 20% per year for about three more years."

If you had it to do over again, what would you do differently?

"Not to say I've done things perfectly, but I would not do anything differently. I perceive every step that's brought me to where I am today to be Grace. All the mistakes I've made have allowed me to be who I am today, and I feel there's a tremendous amount of value in faith and learning from what's gone wrong.

"Now, what I really think you're asking here is, are there things others could do to make their transition into the industry go smoother? The answer, of course, is yes.

"I did not listen to my gut when taking on a few of my first clients. When I failed to listen to my gut, without fail, the clients turned out bad for me, sometimes, very bad. Fortunately, none of those clients are with me today.

"I did a poor job of hiring an assistant, who I've subsequently had to let go. We had two very different personalities, and I do not have a strong management skill set. I also did not conduct an adequate level of due diligence in hiring her. It led to a tremendous amount of personal stress and guilt.

"I am actively involved in professional organizations like NAPFA and FPA. NAPFA has been wonderful all across the board. FPA has been a mixed blessing. FPA has allowed me to meet wonderful people, many of whom were or are mentors today. I would not change anything I've done with the FPA for the world because of the people I've met and things I've learned. But my leadership role in FPA has often been a time and energy vacuum because it requires so much of you, which you may not have the capacity to do if you are someone who is still building their business.

"I originally spent too much money on things that clients find little value in, such as advanced planning software, complex contact management software, and other time wasters. Clients want simplicity as much as we do. I try to spend as much time on the client's value chain as I can. Anything that's not on the value-chain gets removed from the production."

Where do you see yourself in five years?

"Who knows? Ideally, I feel at this stage of my business career, I want to just build a core group, about thirty retainer clients with room to revolve five to ten clients per year, allowing me to spend twenty to fifty hours per client per year, and an additional thousand hours on business vision, business growth, and other professional contributions. I hope to build that part of the business within the next three years, at which point, I will have to sit down and reflect on whether I grow in or out. Growth, in my assessment, can go two ways at this point: either growing internally by graduating less financially and psychologically profitable clients or growing by bringing on new advisors or partners. At this point, though, I won't know until I get there.

"What I've learned in the past few years, the past few months for that matter, is that setting too specific long-term goals is a way to set yourself up for disaster and possibly miss some great opportunities. I came into this business to 'serve.' Over that time, while my success has escalated, I got dangerously out of focus and started to concentrate on absolute 'goals,' such as how much money I'll make, how many clients I need, what are my margins, etc. The emptiness of setting absolute goals led me to a point of three months of depression until I was reminded why I came into this business in the first place: to serve others.

"My primary objective is to be service-oriented, rather than goal-oriented. Goals are important, though they should just be based on values. A broad approach to service orientation (not just clients, but family, community, self, etc), in my opinion, will open a lot more doors to you, while still making you profitable and successful."

What's the best advice you could give someone just starting out?

1. You are what you think. Your only obstacle to success is yourself.
2. Work for someone else first (and maybe forever).
3. Build a mentor group.
4. Build a peer group.

5. Build up enough cash in both start-up money and personal reserves so you can have a feeling of complacency.

6. Begin with a foundation. One of the first financial planners I ever interviewed with (Paula Hogan) said to me (I'm paraphrasing): "Whenever you're about to make a suggestion or recommendation to a client, you must always ask yourself, 'by making this recommendation, who do I serve?' If it's not 'the client,' then you're making the wrong recommendation." I've never forgotten that, and it has been a foundational component of how I serve my clients and build my business ever since.

7. Finally, grow your life and business with Faith and Spirit.

2007 Update:

"I recently chaired the 2007 NAPFA National Conference in Chicago. The conference was one of the largest ever attended, and many people came up to me saying it was one of the best they've ever attended. I am just truly blessed to have been a part of such a great event and to have met such wonderful people (NAPFA staff, speakers, colleagues) over the course of the twenty months we all worked on it.

"I am a Faculty Lecturer for Real Estate in the Capital Markets at the University of Wisconsin Madison Business School.

"I've aged slightly, including a ridiculous amount of gray hair for so early in my life (genetics). Some folks tell me why it adds to credibility. I don't understand statements like that. If someone hires another based on the amount of gray hair on their head, rather than the talents, process of thinking, and contributions they've offered to the profession and their clients, the planning industry is in big trouble.

"Finally, I feel I am now charging appropriately for my services. Revenue increased 50% in 2006. Going forward, I am looking to increase revenue 30% in 2007, then stabilize at 20% per year for about three more years. My income for 2006 exceeded major studies for solo practitioner firms.

"Looking back, I probably would have reallocated how much time and energy I spent with the local FPA.

"I've built a core group of about thirty family clients and expect to add at least ten to twenty more clients on full retainer and management basis. After that, I will either shut the faucet or hire an advisor. I just don't know. All I know is, my clients come first, and maintaining the integrity of those existing relationships is my number one business goal."

2009 Update:

"Life is still good, even though we're in the midst of recovering from the market crisis of 2008. Income will be down due to the economy, but not due to losing clients because of investment advice. That's because good financial planning works. My mission has always been to educate and involve the client proactively. That has paid huge dividends for clients through all of this. It can sometimes take a lifetime for clients to realize the fruits of the financial planning labor. The crisis has accelerated that awareness. I have seen not only how good financial planning has exponentially helped my clients in this environment, but we have all grown stronger as a community because of it: clients and advisors alike. It's an exciting place to be even though the stress level can reach epic proportions. We grow, though, in crisis.

"Remarkably, I've had a number of folks contact me in the past year interested in becoming a financial planner and my advuce has changed because of the crisis. Before I get into my opinion of the future, let me start by saying: don't listen to me or anyone who might discourage you. If you really want to do this, you should follow your dream if it is a dream. If I had listened to everyone, I would have never gotten into this because so many people discouraged it. Take their advice, but plug away and you'll do it. That's the only way I see someone who has no experience or education getting into the profession at this time: they need a burning desire to succeed.

"Now to the hard reality I see today: At a minimum, you absolutely have to have some level of financial understanding in advance and you should have practical work experience. Anyone can be a financial 'advisor' – that's why 'advisor' has become a commodity and loses its value daily and why the public is losing faith in advisors. Few can be a 'financial planner', though. Clients stay with financial planners. Clients value financial planners. Financial planning is of value and not a commodity. Financial planning is a profession that requires more than just an apprenticeship. It requires what all professions require: strong education; post education; multiple years of experience.

"You need to have a high level of financial planning experience before getting in front of clients. It's dangerous to go out on your own without working for someone for a long time and you run the risk of hurting any client that hires you due to your inexperience.

"The timing for trying to get into this business, unfortunately, is not good. There will be mass layoffs in financial services coming or are already here. There are thousands of qualified CFP®'s and CFA's that will be on the market soon due to layoffs, Wall Street, banking fall out, and those graduating from solid college programs and they will either be starting up new businesses or filling any of the few openings out there. They will work for less too because they're hungry. There are thousands of very qualified sales people that are going to leave the brokerage industry, too, and will want to be doing the same thing as the others. Unless you come armed with those credentials in advance, it will be difficult to compete for any level of reasonable income. Again, financial advising is a commodity, so compensation is low. Financial planning is a profession, but requires the time and education and extreme commitment to get there.

"All in, though, the demand for financial planning appears very good, especially when people stop reeling from the crisis and start realizing they need to take responsibility for their future. Good financial planning works. Good financial planners will succeed."

2011 Update:

"I write this two years after the worst extended bear market since the early 1970's. Not only have we survived through it; we've strived through it. It was very tough going, but a commitment to constant communication with clients and colleagues were the keys to growing during that period. Over the past year, things have picked up. I'm grateful to everyone who has been in my life.

"My family has grown and so my priorities have changed. I am totally obsessed with my kid! Now that I'm a dad, I reflect on how fortunate I was to have started my business when I was so young because I would not have the energy or focus I had in the start-up stages ten years ago. If I started it today, I would have to give up extra time with my daughter which at this point in my life is totally unacceptable. My family gets center stage and I'm so grateful and fortunate I designed and timed the business the way I did so that not only can my clients continue to get top notch service, but I have a fair amount of time and flexibility to be focused on my family as well.

"I have also been very fortunate to grow my business with a foundation of absolutely excellent clients. I have that flexibility to focus on my family now. In my business, my clients have always come first and over the past few years, we've grown closer. I've narrowed down my client focus as well. I have a very defined client graphic at this point.

"So I've decided as well that while my daughter and, God-willing, future kids are young, I'm going to continue to take the business slow and methodical. I have the rest of my life to grow it further if I want and right now I have no need to. I've also seen some colleagues give up personal time for business development and either the family suffers or the health suffers, or unfortunately sometimes both.

"I still have no plans on growing into an ensemble firm. I love my life right now and I have systems in place along with an excellent support team (all resource partners) to provide top-notch level service to my clients in line with almost any larger firm. I may add an administrative or client-support staff within a year, but technology and outsourcing resources are such that it remains under investigation.

"My peer group continues to be an integral part of my business support and development. To have immediate access to eight other industry leaders in their respective markets along with their unique expertise and talents is more than most multi-staffed firms could ever offer their clients. We've also grown as friends.

"I also hired a coach, finally, or I should say, I finally found a coach that I like. Between my family, my peer group, and my coach, I have an incredible source of influence and support.

"Overall, to me, this is a great business. You have to have the passion and love for it though. Real love, not lust. To marry into this profession means dealing with ups and downs. There are very difficult issues we face and the ability to do this job well requires incredible level of personality, diversity, intelligence, discipline, and focus. Ethics must always guide you as well. You are then able to have a tremendous impact on folks' lives; meet other excellent service-oriented colleagues; and you may even have built something that you could do forever."

Ken Weingarten, MBA, CFP®
NAPFA-Registered Financial Advisor

Weingarten Associates, L.L.C.
Lawrenceville, New Jersey
www.weingartenassociates.com

Ken registered for a workshop I planned but was unable to complete. When I learned he was attending the FPA Success Forum in New Orleans, we made arrangements to meet. It was the fall of 2002. Ken and his wife, Trina, a CPA, were just starting their family with Sofia, who was three. It was rare to spend time with a young man so focused. His priorities were clear, and his family was at the top of the list.

I'm glad to see the business is thriving, along with the family, which now includes Elena, who made her appearance in the spring of 2005. Ken's realistic goals and dedicated value system has served him well.

Did you have a business plan?

"Yes, but a very informal one. Some of it did make it to paper!"

What were the biggest obstacles you faced?

"Getting through the first year with very few clients and very little earned income."

What did you do right?

"Prepared myself emotionally to live off of savings. I always felt the need to earn more than I was spending."

How did you get training? Did you have a mentor?

"FPA Residency, NAPFA Basic Training and lots of reading! I consumed many books. I also spoke with many veteran planners that certainly offered words of advice and encouragement."

How long did it take to start making money?

"About a year to see the light at the end of the tunnel. 2005 is my second complete calendar year, and I expect next year to be the year where I earn enough money to start saving again."

If you had it to do over again, what would you do differently?

"Value/Price my services properly right from the start. It is quite common to start with low fees in the beginning. Fortunately I learned how to price my services pretty quickly. I imagine this comes with confidence. Also, I decided to add non-discretionary asset management earlier this year. I should have done this right from the start. It has enabled me to price my services accordingly."

Where do you see yourself in five years?

"Doing the same thing, but with more clients. I expect the business to be mature enough that I will be highly selective regarding how many new clients I accept each year."

What's the best advice you could give someone just starting out?

"Read a lot, talk to a lot of different planners, and know yourself best. Most importantly, do your OWN plan."

2007 Update

"2007 marks our fourth full year in business, and things are going accordingly to plan as we continue to meet our revenue goals each year. At this point of the year, we can already see a clear path towards achieving this year's goals and likely exceeding them. We have decided to stop taking any new tax-only business, which means if someone wants their taxes done, they need to become a financial planning client first. We intentionally raised minimums to certain tax clients to continue to 'focus' this side of the business. Eventually, we want to get to a point where we have *only* financial planning clients.

"On the financial planning side, we have decided to raise the minimum for our annual retainer service to $5000. Again, it is a matter of focusing our business and limiting our growth to 'ideal' clients for our business. We will still do comprehensive plans for clients who do not meet this minimum as we realize how important it is to do planning for everyone, regardless of their current situation.

"We made a big change on the technology side: we are now using Redtail CRM, in addition to Redtail Imaging. We also have all e-mails archived through this one system. We feel it has made a big difference in how we do business and will be even more important in the years ahead, as it will allow us to stay in touch from anywhere in the world as this system is completely Web-based.

"Also, in 2006, we hired another financial planner to do our own plan! There were two motivations for us: first, to ensure we were truly on track and had not missed any big assumptions in our own planning (good news: we had not); and second, to learn how another planning firm does financial planning. It was a great experience and strongly recommended that all financial planners get their own plan done. (How can you advise others to hire you as an objective, third-party adviser, if you have not done so already yourself?)

"On the personal side, our focus on family is just as important. Sofia is now 5 years old and Elena is 2 years old. While at times challenging to raise a family and run your own business, we feel fortunate to have the flexibility to make our own hours and do things on 'our terms.' We would not trade it for anything!"

2009 Update

"2008 was our 5th full year in business and we continued to move ahead with our plan; we significantly downsized the tax side of the business while the financial planning side continued to grow nicely. Our overall net income was up 8% last year from 2007. (Early 2009 is booming so this year looks really good; I expect our net income should be up by at least 8% this year.) Our goal by now was to continue adding financial planning clients and reducing our tax-only clients and that process continues.

"Our retainer model has certainly helped us through this tough market; our fees have not gone down under our model since we lock clients' fees for two years. Considering the increased work load, I think our model is working just fine. We'll see some impact when we re-evaluate client fees at the end of this year and this will have some limitation on our growth in 2010-2011. As long as the economy recovers and clients continue adding to their portfolios, and we continue to attract new clients, growth should continue to be near 10% year-over-year until 2012. That is when I expect we could have a very strong year (15%+ growth) as we are hopeful that the market puts forward strong gains in the next few years after the recent meltdown.

"On the technology side we added AssetBook's portfolio accounting system in 2008; this allows us to download client portfolio information into our Redtail CRM system and from there into MoneyGuidePro; outsourcing this has been a tremendous productivity boost. AssetBook allows clients to log into their own portal to view performance information whenever they want.

"As we get busier and busier there are certainly times when we feel the strain of running your own business and raising a family, but I think compared to most, we have it pretty good; the flexibility of setting our own schedule cannot be beat. Our girls will be 7 and 4 respectively this summer and traveling with them is getting much easier! We are even planning a trip to Europe for next summer."

2011 Update

"It was interesting to look back over the past two years to see how our growth stacked up to expectations. We have continued to progress at a very steady rate over the past two years with net income up nearly 11% in 2009 and nearly 13% in 2010. I suspect we will continue with this double digit growth rate in 2011 and as mentioned in the prior update I do think that 2012 will see a fairly large increase of 15-20%.

"Our technology systems are working great and providing tremendous efficiencies in how we do business. We have improved how we handle rebalancing by utilizing the rebalancing reporting features within Asset Book. While part of the process is still manual, the amount of time we spend on portfolio reviews is much lower than it was two years ago.

"We continue to maintain a healthy life-work balance. Working from home is still a great advantage for maintaining this balance. Our girls are now 8 and 5. While we did not make the trip to Europe as expected, we are planning our first trip outside the USA this summer. (We will be going to Canada!)"

"I had researched the Alliance of Cambridge Advisors (www.acaplanners.org) for quite some time and realized that I was really trying to reinvent what had already been done. I decided to go through their training program and that is when my practice really started coming together. ACA is dedicated to helping fee-only financial advisors build profitable practices using holistic planning strategies.

"Also, when advisors partner with ACA they receive access to proven practice management systems and tools; a comprehensive training program, and the ongoing support of like-minded colleagues. This has saved me an enormous amount of time and money and I did not end up having to solve a lot of issues by trial and error. Even though I'm a sole practitioner, I'm never really alone. I can call on any or all of these planners, giving me hundreds of years of their collective experience. This gives me a lot of confidence when I'm meeting with clients.

"The education and training never ends and I continue to attend national conferences and local FPA and NAPFA study groups. I still have lunch once a week with Ken and he continues to help me solve more complex issues when they come up. More importantly, he has become a good friend.

"I pay all my bills and draw a salary but I'm not where I want/need to be yet. This is really more by my design than anything else. I am trying to work only with clients I really enjoy and I don't do a lot of marketing. I have consciously chosen to grow slowly so I can spend more time with my young children. I'm fortunate to be in a position to do that. I still think that 3-5 years is sufficient to grow a great and profitable practice but you should not go off on your own unless you have other financial resources for at least the first three years.

"If I had it to do over again, I would have joined and gone through the ACA training program immediately. I also would have worked on finding and building professional relationships more quickly. You need to think about building a strong relationship with a local estate planning attorney to refer your clients. If you are a Fee-Only planner then you also need to partner with good insurance agents that are comfortable working with Fee-Only planners. I refer a lot of my clients to Low Load Insurance Services (www.LLIS.com)."

Renée E. Cabourne, CFP®, CSA
Cabourne & Associates
La Verne, California
www.cabourneandassoc.com

Did you have a business plan?

"Yes …but it no longer resembles what I started out with."

What were the biggest obstacles you faced?

"Getting it all done was the hardest obstacle. I entered financial planning through the insurance door without any brokerage experience. It was difficult to learn the ropes without any guidance from people who didn't have a stake in my next action."

What did you do right?

"I found three mentors who I trusted to guide me through the unknown. They suggested getting my CFP®, which I'm near finishing the coursework for and will sit for the exam at the end of 2007. In addition, I've always collaborated with attorneys and CPAs which enhanced my knowledge in those disciplines, and enabled me to speak intelligently to the advisors and elevated my client's perception of me."

How did you get training? Did you have a mentor?

"Initially, my training was on-the-job. However, over the years, my CFP® classes and testing, continuing education of my choosing, and conversations with my mentors trained me. Taking CFP® courses affirms my acquired knowledge; I know much more than I thought. My mentors gave depth to my academic studies and were able to expound on the real life case studies helping convert knowledge to application."

How long did it take to start making money?

"My first two years were mostly insurance-related and very little planning, so I won't count those. But when I switched to financial planning after getting my 7 and 65, it took four years to make some decent money."

If you had it to do over again, what would you do differently?

"I'd get my CFP® first. Taking these courses has fortified my confidence. That fear of not knowing enough has subsided. It's also very difficult trying to develop an independent practice and study ten to twelve hours a week. And knowing what I know now, I'd probably bypass the 7 and work only with the 65."

Where do you see yourself in five years?

"After acquiring my CFP® certificate, I look forward to registering my own RIA and dropping my 7. Fee-only is where I am headed. In five years, I see myself much more relaxed and enjoying the practice more. Initially my goal was to make money, and then it became to manage the practice better. Now, I'm on the course to develop the business in a virtual sense, while advising the clients I enjoy working with and living a balance life…the latter is my current goal."

What's the best advice you could give someone just starting out?

"Find a mentor or two or three as soon as possible, someone you can trust and ask your most embarrassing questions. I was always amazed at how my fear of the unknown magnified specs into landmines. I have three, two men and a woman. Sometimes I'd get three different answers to the same question, but all the answers were valuable. The guidance enabled me to shape my best talents into a practice that has meaning in its deliverables, as well as fill in the blanks when I really didn't know what advice to give in certain situations. Good luck and don't give up!"

2009 Update:

"The past two years have been wonderful while challenging for me and my company, Cabourne & Associates. Starting in the fall of 2006, I began teaching two classes: 'Introduction to Personal Finance' and 'Investment Fundamentals' at a local college. My intent was to build my résumé and reputation in my local region; what I didn't expect was how much I enjoyed the classroom. In November 2007, I passed the CFP® certificate exam and on January 1, 2009, received the Investment Advisor Certificate with the State of California. With the change of registration, I updated my image with a new logo and a corporate look. My 'new' practice focuses on fee-only family wealth planning for those with estate and income tax challenges. I've maintained my life agent license and accept commissions for life, disability, and long-term-care insurance product placements. Most of my new work comes by way of referral from attorneys and CPAs. These were my goals at the last printing of this book and I'm proud to say I've accomplished them.

"I have to admit that dropping the broker-dealer during an extended down market and challenging economy wasn't the best timing. Many of my existing clients didn't fit my new client profile and a fair percentage of the ones that did were reluctant to do planning in such an uncertain and turbulent time. Many felt they could no longer afford to keep their assets under management. Thankfully, the few clients that did fit my profile moved with me and they have kept me afloat. Now in 2Q 2009, business is beginning to pick back up. Cash flow has been extremely tight, but it's getting better.

"My long-term goal has always been to have a 'virtual' practice, and I haven't let go of that vision. Much of what I do with my high-net worth clients is done over the internet; however, another revenue stream was beginning to reveal itself. With the classroom as my incubator and many of my students asking for second opinions on their financial plans, 401(k) allocations, and other information long after class had ended, I began to counsel them over the internet. They were willing to pay me and refer me. It also fed my passion to educate them. My role is split between financial coach and advisor. I teach them how to do it themselves, a DIY approach.

"Start Smart Advisor™ will address the financial needs of 20-50 year olds seeking independent, objective advice from someone willing to educate them over the internet. Start Smart AdvisorTM marketing is done through social networking, including webinars, podcasts, and eVideos utilizing FINRA-approved content. Online meetings are held via Skype, face-to-face, and go-to-meeting. I admit, it's not as glamorous as working with high-net worth clients, but the work feeds my passion for financial literacy.

"I'm looking forward to the launch of Start Smart Advisor™ in the summer of 2009 and have no intentions of abandoning Cabourne and Associates. I'll continue to provide strategic family wealth planning through Cabourne & Associates and coaching and advice through Start Smart Advisor™. I'll let you know how it goes."

2011 Update:

"What a wild ride the last two years have been. I'm very proud to say that I am still here providing financial management and advice to my very small practice. Currently I am recovering from a serious car accident the summer of 2009; I had no idea recovery would take such a long time. It has caused me to question my purpose, motives, and values (including my personal values and my value to my clients). Thankfully, my boutique practice remains intact and stable. I've increased my focus on existing clients creating closer relationships with them. I haven't lost any; in fact, I've gained two through referral.

"As a result of the accident, succession planning became a very important issue. I still don't have a plan I feel totally comfortable with, but I do have an emergency plan in place. Finding the best fit is ongoing.

"Where am I going? Well, I've taken a step or two back to reassess what is really important to me and then to pick a path. My productivity has been curtailed, so my involvement in professional associations has nearly disappeared. Having earned my CERTIFIED FINANCIAL PLANNER™ Certificate, the ability to put those letters behind my name gives me the confidence to pursue whatever path I feel best suited for, and I'm very grateful for that.
"I'm grateful to my husband, friends, and associates who have stood by me when I wasn't sure what the future held. Their value in my life is more than their weight in gold. My clients are also very important to me, more so now than ever. It's funny how tragedy can shape a new reality by forcing a detour that ultimately could surpass previous expectations or possibilities.

"We'll have to see how things turn out in the next edition."

Barrett Porter, CFP ®
Abacus Wealth Partners
Pacific Palisades, California

"In 2000, just as my interest in 'the film biz' (what I wanted to do until I actually did it) was waning, opportunity literally came a knockin' through a new friend. If I could pass three NASD securities exams, I would be hired as a business development specialist for his independent Broker/Dealer, and work in a 'salary plus commission' arrangement, essentially recruiting financial advisors from other firms to this one.

"Soon into the recruiting adventure, it dawned on me that I could take on clients while I was recruiting as long as I hit my quotas. Why should the brokers have all the fun? When asked what funds I should buy for my soon-to-be clients, a colleague replied 'stick with American Funds and you won't get sued.' Seemed simple enough…but then I learned about variable annuities and the 7% commissions one could earn. Wow! Then it was oil and gas partnership deals and private REITs. Three annual firm conferences later, it hit me. I was receiving all of my real-world investment education by product sponsors (wholesalers), and I was considering their products based on the attention they paid me. All of the data entering my brain was tainted with conflicts of interest!

"It was time for two changes. First, I was ready to wear my 'financial advisor' cap full-time. And it was time to say goodbye to the revenue-centered Broker/Dealer world and hello to the client-centered world of a 'Registered Investment Advisor'."

Did you have a business plan?

"A business what? I've heard of those. Actually, I did finally get around to creating one in 2004 and am thankful for it, as it helped me to focus on who I really wanted to serve and how I would go about serving them."

What were the biggest obstacles you faced?

"Money, or a lack thereof. Building a commission-based business allows brokers to sell a couple of front-loaded annuities, and they've got bread and water for a year. Not so easy for an advisor with more fingers than clients and a commitment to being fee-only. Everything I was reading was about referrals, referrals, referrals—how to ask clients for them and how that is the key to a successful firm. But no one was showing me the best way to get those first thirty clients, and I was stubbornly refusing to do any cold calling or go door-to-door. That was a broker thing…or at least I wanted to believe that, so I wouldn't have to do any of it.

"Another obstacle was not having a mentor in the early years with whom I could shadow during client and prospect meetings. I had to learn by asking hundreds of questions to colleagues and various departments at my firm, and pay close attention at conferences. Still, that was no match for the real world experience of being in the middle of an advisor/prospect meeting. I learned more in one year with a senior advisor overseeing my activities than in the five years of going it alone."

What did you do right?

"While recruiting, I paid close attention to what brokers and advisors didn't like about their current firm or practice, and I learned all about the financial services landscape. I think this saved me from chasing the elusive carrot that so many large financial services firms dangle in front of newly-licensed and hungry advisors. So many advisors feel trapped when a new vision for how to serve their clients is on the other side of a big hurdle called a non-solicitation clause."

How did you get training? Did you have a mentor?

"My teachers were trade association magazines, books, colleagues, and the many brokers who shared their experiences with me during my recruiting days. The closest thing I had to a mentor was a colleague with twenty years of experience, who lived on the other side of the country."

How long did it take to start making money?

"I was able to subsidize my modest advisory fee income stream with other duties for my first couple of years as an independent fee-only advisor (helping with compliance, website design, contact management, e-marketing, writing newsletters, etc.). These duties helped me in understanding how to actually run an RIA. It was in year four that my client base really kicked into the next gear and allowed me to focus almost entirely on being an advisor."

If you had it to do over again, what would you do differently?

"The year in which I made my commitment to a fee-based model, I followed the lead of a colleague/friend by leaving my Broker/Dealer for his Broker/Dealer of choice. I was essentially working from home with no office environment and no face-to-face mentor. I thought I knew more than I did, and I flew solo for a year. Thank goodness for credit cards and for passing my CFP® exam that year. If I did it again, I would have searched for a local firm that could put a little fire under my feet while paying me a small salary to handle whatever needed to be handled. I later learned that there are plenty of Investment Advisory firms that really operate as a team and pay newly licensed CFP®s to handle the smaller accounts and client retention duties. If you can find that arrangement, grab it!"

Where do you see yourself in five years?

"My search for 'the perfect firm' was thorough and time-consuming, so I have every intention of building my business with Kubera Portfolio for the long haul. Their dedication to passive investment strategies, being fee-only, and investing in a way that doesn't harm the planet, is my perfect match. They also were very supportive of my client base, which consists of many members from the gay and lesbian community. In five years, I envision doing exactly what I am doing today, but with a client base that will allow me for some greater freedom to focus on my other goals in life. I also envision elevating my responsibilities to include mentoring another advisor."

What's the best advice you could give someone just starting out?

"As Abraham Lincoln said, '*Give me six hours to chop down a tree and I will spend the first four sharpening the axe.*' First, get clear about your intentions, your strategy, and your 'niche.' If you intend to be a 'comprehensive financial planner,' it probably makes sense to use an hourly/retainer model such as the one used by the Garrett Planning Network. These planners seem to rate highest on the 'scale-o-happiness' because they really know why they're in this game and it ain't the money. If investment management is your passion or area of expertise, how will you charge, and will you build 'planning' services into the practice as well? Or do you want to enter the realm of 'financial life-planning' where advisors really go beneath the surface to help clients realize their deepest life passions before addressing any 'financial' goals? You get the idea."

2009 Update:

"Two major lessons have been learned. First, there's no schooling like the real world and second, it really is all about referrals! While I give full credit to the market downturn for the gray hairs turning up on my head at the age of 35 (watch out Anderson Cooper), it's been one heck of a learning experience. Within a year of affiliating with Abacus Portfolios (previously known as Kubera Portfolios), I reached the agreement I had been pursuing. In 2007 Abacus handed me a significant book of clients where I would serve as "senior financial advisor." My primary role is to work with clients on their risk tolerance and general financial planning issues, and the investment committee does the research and builds the portfolio models. At last, I was about to have a real income stream and I didn't have to spend the next five years going door to door (just not in my wiring). Three months later, the recession began. Doh!

"The good news: With the incredible rainmaking of our two principals, along with referrals from existing clients (and some tenacious follow-thru with anyone who blinked in our direction), I was bringing in almost enough in new assets (about 1 new client per week) to offset the market's downward spiral (while also reaching out regularly to existing clients; there's no quicker way to lose a client than to leave them hanging during scary times, or so I hear). So I was essentially filling a leaky bucket. But now the stage is set for a prosperous future, assuming the market get back to its old habit of going up more often than down. The best part of this job is that I wake up every day knowing exactly what my purpose is, and I know that our clients' lives are better because they hired us."

2011 Update:

"I've learned that gray hair doesn't go back to being brown during market recoveries, but it's been an incredible two years with Abacus. The challenge every advisor yearns to face landed in front of me in 2010 – having too many clients. I credit this to being with a firm that has an incredible ability to attract clients through two great rainmakers, and all that I have learned about how to connect with prospective client. Abacus hired a new advisor whom I have been introducing to many of my clients, with the goal of establishing her as full-time client relationship manager within 1 year. This has allowed me to be a teacher and mentor (which I love), and to be more selective in the clients I serve. The latter is helping me to reach personal goal of having less clients, deeper relationships with each client, and income growth every year.

"When it comes to sales, advisors often want to fool themselves into thinking that's not in their job description, because we spend years getting degrees and certifications, only to realize that clients don't retain us simply for our integrity and skills. Once I realized that sales is about connecting and not convincing, and that the process is about determining if there's a mutual fit, not just a good fit for the client, the sales process became enjoyable. I thank our weekly advisor "sales" calls for my personal growth in this department. Each advisor is asked to be vulnerable, talk about a situation they are facing, and do role-plays for the other advisors. The more vulnerable and open the advisor is to trying new things and accepting criticism, the better. I have learned that vulnerability, confidence, leadership, good listening skills, and a structured format (script) for prospecting meetings/calls, are everything when it comes to building trust and establishing new client relationships."

Judy Haselton, CFP®, RLP®

Harmony Financial Advisors, LLC
New York, New York
JSH@HarmonyFinancial.com

"I started my business in 2006 after a life journey that took me from Wall Street, to motherhood, to becoming a CFP* professional. I studied anthropology in college and I earned an MBA in finance shortly thereafter. I spent twelve years on Wall Street working with the owners or managers of corporations looking to raise money or buy or sell businesses. I left investment banking after my second child was about a year old. The hours were long and the environment was not 'family friendly,' especially for women with children. In the late 90s, I managed several private equity ventures, which were all sold by the end of 2002.

"It was then that I decided that I wanted to work in a financial field where I could help people, have flexible hours and utilize the skills I had developed in previous careers. I wanted to have balance in my life and continue to be available for my children when needed. I didn't know much about financial planning but I knew that there were many people, particularly women, who needed financial guidance. I thought that I could provide financial advice on an hourly basis and I start taking financial planning courses at a local university.

"I was a 'stay at home' mom while I took the coursework and CFP® exam. After passing the exam, I interviewed with a financial services company that indicated that they were receptive to providing financial planning services but found the work environment to be product oriented and sales incentive driven. Not finding an ideal situation with another financial planning or financial services company, I decided to start my own business, Harmony Financial Advisors, LLC. My first clients were family members."

Did you have a business plan?

"I didn't put together a written plan until almost one year after starting my firm. I wanted the freedom to try out different approaches to the business until I had a clear idea of what I wanted the firm to look like. I now have a one-page plan that focuses on business goals and financial objectives, helping me to stay on track."

What were the biggest obstacles you faced?

"The biggest obstacle that I faced was lack of experience in this field because I was a 'career-changer'. I was just over 50 years old when I began my career as a financial planner, and at that age, and with my experience in other financial arenas, I didn't want to start at the bottom. I had business skills which I was able to apply to my new line of work, but I didn't have years of experience analyzing the financial planning needs of clients. There was so much to learn, even after passing the CFP* exam!

"Other obstacles included lacking the computer skills necessary to work with software programs. I found it very challenging to assess which software programs to purchase for my practice. It was also tough to deal with the filing and compliance issues of being a Registered Investment Advisor."

What did you do right?

"What I did right was to not let go of my dream to do my own thing! I didn't find a firm to work with doing what I wanted to do, in the way I wanted to do it. So I started my own business. I am glad that I didn't compromise my vision of providing holistic, fee-only financial planning and investment advisory services to women and their families, with an emphasis on creating a sense of well-being and harmony around financial matters. It will take some time to make money as an independent planner and investment advisor, but I am doing what I love, and I have balance in my own life.

"I would not have been able to get this far without talking to many experienced planners who also work independently on a fee-only basis. I was not afraid to ask for guidance from the planners I met early on. Many people were extremely helpful in providing me with information on how they set up a successful financial planning and investment advisory business. While I was taking the financial planning courses, I read an earlier version of this book, which was also enormously helpful!"

How did you get training? Did you have a mentor?

"After passing the CFP® exam, which gave me the credentials and a basic knowledge of financial planning issues, I took the five-day FPA Residency Course, which was a wonderful way to develop client relationship skills and meet experienced, successful planners. I attended a NAPFA regional conference 'Boot Camp,' another great learning and networking experience. I joined Nazrudin and became interested in life planning. I took the two-day and five-day Kinder Institute Life Planning training, and I am currently in the Kinder mentoring program.

"I went to the monthly meetings of the local FPA, to learn more about practice management issues for clients in my area, and I joined their membership committee. I interviewed several New York based planners about their background and business efforts, going back to a couple of them repeatedly for advice as my practice evolved.

"I had many people help me along the way—the instructors at the FPA Residency program, fellow members of Nazrudin and the Kinder Institute, and local New York City planners who shared their experiences with me. I now have one primary 'mentor,' an experienced planner who has successfully developed a business similar to the model that I am pursuing. We have recently decided to "affiliate" our firms in order to service new client referrals jointly and to provide back-up support when needed."

How long did it take to start making money?

"I am close to breakeven about a year after taking on my first client. Many planners have told me it takes three to five years to make money especially as a career-changer. I started from scratch to develop my own client base, which has mostly been done through word-of-mouth.

"It has taken some time to get the word out about the services that I provide, but I am currently seeing a significant increase in referrals. Since I work out of my home, the bulk of my expenses are for technology, marketing materials, seminars, and training sessions. I also hired a part time administrative assistant six months ago. I was aware that I would need financial resources to live on during the early "lean" years, and had set aside funds to cover my own financial needs."

If you had it to do over again, what would you do differently?

"If I had the opportunity to do it differently, I would have become a planner fifteen years ago, right after leaving Wall Street. I would have worked for another planner for a period of time before starting my own firm. I also would have liked to partner with another experienced planner from the beginning to move up the learning curve faster."

Where do you see yourself in five years?

"In five years, I hope to be spreading financial harmony throughout the New York City area, serving clients with their financial planning and investment management needs. I plan to promote and provide financial life planning to New Yorkers so they can focus on more than just making money. I want to help women feel empowered and educated around financial matters through my financial advisory services, workshops, websites and networking. I will be living a life that balances serving my clients needs and spending time with family and friends."

What's the best advice you could give someone just starting out?

"First of all, get the educational credentials and become a CFP® professional. I would recommend attending local and national FPA and NAPFA events to get to know the community. This field is full of smart, caring and supportive planners who are generous with their time and experience. Take advantage of that!

"If you need to earn money right away, work with a firm that reflects your values and standards. I believe that it is helpful to become involved with nonprofit organizations that you believe in and offer opportunities to meet new clients.

"Begin to give back to the community right away by volunteering with the local FPA chapter or providing pro bono services to those who can't afford financial planning but still need it! This is a great way to develop your new planning skills. Make sure to have your own financial plan in place so that you can be an authentic model for your new clients."

2009 Update:

"Harmony has grown in many ways over the last two years. I have quite a few new financial planning and investment clients and tripled the amount of money under management. I have expanded my professional qualifications to become a Registered Life Planner® with the

Kinder Institute and I joined the Sudden Money Institute as an adviser member. I am a NAPFA member and continue to participate in the annual Nazrudin Project conference. I moved my office to Greenwich Village, a more central location for clients in New York City. My affiliation with another experienced CFP® has expanded and we collaborate on an increasing number of new client relationships each year. The opportunity to work along side a 'seasoned' professional has facilitated my professional development tremendously. I now have two part time assistants, one of which works from a virtual office. Almost two years ago, I joined Schwab Institutional which has been great; especially during 2008 when several New York-based financial institutions ceased to exist.

"I have raised my fees and provide two distinct services. Comprehensive planning services are offered on an hourly basis with a minimum fee of $3,000 to prepare a financial plan. I also provide investment management services for a fee based upon a percentage of assets under management. Nearly all of my investment management clients have undergone the financial life planning process. I have found that the in-depth knowledge that I have about my clients' lives as a result of life planning is extremely helpful in managing client portfolios and relationships. This was particularly useful during the recent decline of the financial markets.

"Now that I have a clearly defined business model in place, a great staff, the right hardware and software systems, and a fantastic office location, I am focusing my efforts on being a superb adviser to my existing clients and growing the business to spread financial peace of mind to more New Yorkers. I am working on a number of marketing projects and developing my contacts among allied professionals. I believe that now, more than ever, there is a tremendous need for financial life planning and goal oriented, fee-only investment management services. After several years in business, Harmony Financial Advisors is well positioned to meet those needs in New York City."

2011 Update:

"Harmony Financial continues to grow by providing holistic fee-only financial planning and investment management to clients in New York and California. After five years, I am making a good living from the firm but would like to double in size (in terms of assets under management) in the next three years. I have a variety of types of clients but I am now focusing my marketing efforts on individuals and couples in need of transitional planning services.

"Major life transitions such as a career change, marriage, children, divorce, or an inheritance can be both positive and negative, and all of these events put money in movement. I use techniques developed by the Sudden Money Institute and my own proprietary tools to guide clients through a customized approach to providing integrated financial options. I believe that comprehensive and careful planning, especially during a major life transition insures a more desirable and beneficial long-term result for clients, including saving money, managing financial realities, preserving net worth, and protecting resources.

"This focus on transitional financial planning has provided me with a distinct service offering in the crowded financial planning and investment management arena in New York City. It also allows me to make a difference in people's lives, which is the mission of

Harmony Financial and has been from the beginning."

Peggy Doviak, Ph.D., CFP®
D.M. Wealth Management, Inc.
Norman, Oklahoma
peggy@dmwealth.com

Did you have a business plan?

"At first, I really had nothing concrete—just basic ideas of minimizing expenses while maximizing client service and, ultimately, revenue. This caused me to spend more money on research and data tools than items like desks. Now that the practice is a little more than three years old, I have a more formalized business plan and growth goals. I think if you are beginning a practice "from scratch" the idea of a business plan can be overwhelming, and all those zeroes get depressing. I tried to complete a couple of templates, but when revenue is low and expenses are high, it's very difficult."

What were the biggest obstacles you faced?

"Before I entered financial planning, I had been a corporate trainer with little business and finance background. Although I served as an intern in another financial services firm for a year, when I opened my practice, it was truly a "ground-up" process. Family members and some friends provided both support and some early accounts. I was fortunate that some non-family members read my ad in the paper, liked my practice model, and took a chance with me. I also wanted to provide fee-only asset management and financial planning, so cash flow was steady, but at the beginning, it was steadily very small!"

How did you get training? Did you have a mentor?

"I have been so blessed to have had help from different people throughout my process. I mentored with a wonderful person in Norman who gave me encouragement at the beginning. Then, I met members of our local Financial Planning Association chapter, one of whom was a member of the national board. This planner even today gives me encouragement, offers advice when asked, and has helped me meet many of the incredibly talented practitioners in our field. I believe that developing a professional friendship with an experienced planner is one of the greatest gifts a new planner can receive. I completed online courses for the CFP® certificant curriculum requirements, and then attended a live review to prepare for the exam."

What did you do right?

"I set very high standards and goals from the beginning, and I always worked to create protocols and systems. Since I was the only one in the office, I knew I had to stay absolutely organized, or I wouldn't make it. I also focused more on providing financial literacy training to people, rather than the traditional sales-oriented seminars, and my clients love it."

How long did it take to start making money?

"After I quit the corporate training position and entered financial planning and asset management full-time, it took about two years. I held both positions concurrently for sixteen months."

If you had it to do over again, what would you do differently?

"I would focus on the financial planning process with the same intensity as the asset management process from the beginning. I have had to retrain some of my first clients to understand the scope of comprehensive financial planning."

Where do you see yourself in five years?

"I am very happy with the direction of the practice at this time. I am working with my clients, teaching for the College for Financial Planning, and working with a friend in his practice. I hope my life is similar to this model in five years."

What's the best advice you could give someone just starting out?

"Get your CFP® certification as early as possible; your practice will just grow and grow, and the process requires almost your full attention. Cut no corners and make very few compromises. Don't give away too much time. Many people need financial literacy training, but if you are in the business of financial planning, help match people with the great not-for-profit organizations already in existence."

2009 Update:

"I'm happy to report that two years later, all is going extremely well in my practice, in spite of the horrific occurrences in the economy. As the company has matured, so have my ideas and understanding of how I can assist clients best. I practice comprehensive financial planning with specialties in tax planning and asset management.

"To assist in asset management, I am completing a master's in financial analysis program, which would provide the coursework to sit for the CFA exams. I am not taking the exams, having decided that it's the knowledge I need, not another certification. I have one year to go, and I will be thrilled when I'm finished. I believe that one reason I survived last year in tact was the ability to really explain to clients what happened and why it occurred. The curriculum in the financial analysis program has provided me with the background to be able to have that discussion. If any planners provide active asset management for their clients, I think it would be a worthwhile endeavor.

"I also passed my insurance license exam this spring, deciding it was more important to be able to serve clients directly in that area rather than having to refer them to someone else. Although D.M. Wealth Management, Inc. is an RIA fee-only firm, I run the insurance through my own name and disclose all compensation schedules to both D.M. Wealth clients and insurance clients. I've come to the conclusion that poor products are poor products, however they charge, and that being a fiduciary to your clients is a higher standard than the fee versus commission fight. I avoided the insurance area for six years because of the commission issue, and I finally have decided that it's not in my clients' best interest.

"In all, I am very pleased with my career choice; I've never regretted changing fields or learning new material. I look forward to the future."

2011 Update:

"In 2010, I earned my Master's of Finance, with a major in Financial Analysis. As my practice has grown, I have developed a strong focus on portfolio management. Although I highly value my CERTIFIED FINANCIAL PLANNER™ designation, I believe I needed more rigorous training in asset valuation, quantitative analysis, and risk reduction techniques. I am comfortable now with my background and feel that as long as I continue an ongoing learning process, I have the skill set necessary to grow my practice in the ways I want.

"A second major milestone in 2010 was the addition of a full-time assistant who serves as my Client Management Specialist. She saves me time in completing the administrative, paperwork, and filing tasks that I have never really enjoyed! She also helps ensure that clients receive prompt attention, and I have found it easier to grow the practice, as my time is not occupied with so many activities.

"A third milestone is that in 2011, I will be moving to a new office in downtown Norman. I am currently located in an executive suites building with a shared conference room and front desk support. With my own assistant, I no longer need the suite services and look forward to having my own space. The location is fabulous and will allow me to participate in monthly 'art walks', where downtown businesses invite local artists for showings attended by Norman residents. I believe that a strong community presence is a good way to help people understand the financial planning process. At the time of this update, they are just about to add my interior walls!

"I feel as though my business has matured greatly during the last two years. I am very comfortable in what my practice offers, and I look forward to an exciting future!"

Jeremy E. Portnoff, CFP®, AIF®, CRPS^SM
Portnoff Financial LLC
Union, New Jersey
jeremy@portnofffinancial.com

While working on a Bachelor's Degree in Marketing, Jeremy discovered that he was better suited for a career in finance. After the switch, he decided to take a "Personal Financial Planning" course. At the time, he didn't realize the class was about financial planning for others, however he found financial planning to be exactly what he was looking for in a career. Upon graduating, Jeremy was eligible to sit for the Certified Financial Planner exam; however, he wanted to get some real-world experience before taking the exam.

Jeremy took an associate position with a small financial planning and investment management firm affiliated with an indpendent Broker/Dealer. At first, he was very eager to help people plan for their financial futures. However, it wasn't long until he realized that the company he worked for was more interested in selling financial products than actually providing financial planning and investment management. He was often pressured by his superiors to sell products that were suitable but not in the best interests of his clients. He did not like this environment and often disagreed with the philosophy of the firm. Jeremy quickly discovered how difficult it was to offer comprehensive financial planning on a fee-only basis in a primarily commission-based enviornment. He wanted to utilize his education in financial planning without having to sell financial products for commission.

In 2004 Jeremy decided to move from California to New Jersey. Shortly thereafter, his firm was transitioning to a new Broker/Dealer, so he felt this would be the best time to leave and took the opportunity to go off on his own and establish an independent fee-only practice. He Registered as an Investment Advisor with New Jersey, New York, and California, and soon after passed the CERTIFIED FINANCIAL PLANNER™ exam.

Did you have a business plan?

"No, I didn't and this was a big mistake. I knew what I wanted to do and what I wanted to accomplish; however, without articulating it on paper, I felt that I was running in circles for a long time. I should have developed a business plan long before I went on my own, so that when I had to make the decision to jump, I would have been ready and I would likely have saved myself tremendous headaches."

What were the biggest obstacles you faced?

"Learning how to work efficiently from home. In the beginning, it was very difficult to get enough work done. There were simply too many distractions. It took a long time to be able to avoid the distractions that took away from work and get done what I needed to get done."

"Since I had moved across the country, I found it very difficult to get started on my own. I knew very few people, and those people really did not understand what I did for people. No matter how I would explain my role as a financial planner, I seemed to get pigeon-holed as a broker. This made getting referrals very challenging."

What did you do right?

"I believed in myself. This wasn't something I was willing to give up on. Failure simply wasn't an option. I struggled quite a bit in the first few years, but I finally learned not to sell myself short and believe in myself. I didn't listen to the naysayer's, who said there was too much competition, and that no one would want to work with me because I was young and not with a brand name firm. Becoming a member of NAPFA was a huge help. They provided the tools and the knowledge required to establish a fee-only practice."

How did you get training? Did you have a mentor?

"I received some sales training and basic product knowledge from the firm I started at. I also read as many books about financial planning, practice management, and sales as I could. I did not have a formal mentor; however, when I became a member of NAPFA, members such as Bernard Kiely, provided invaluable advice and guidance."

How long did it take to start making money?

"It took me a little over three years to really start making a decent living. I would not have been able to get where I am today without the support of my wife, my family, and a few breaks that came along the way."

If you had it to do over again, what would you do differently?

"I would not have gone to a Broker/Dealer firm right out of college. Had I understood that it was really about selling products, I would have looked for a fee-only firm that I could work for and gain experience. I may have even discovered that I didn't need to go out on my own. Also I would have taken the CFP® exam as soon as I could."

Where do you see yourself in five years?

"In five years, I plan to be a full-fledged qualified plan expert. The dramatic changes that have come with the Pension Protection Act of 2006 will likely create a shift from a sales-driven market to an advisory one. This will require greater specialized education in order to properly serve this market. I also want to grow to the point where I need one or two assistants and/or junior planners. After my wife and I have children, I plan to bring her into the business."

What's the best advice you could give someone just starting out?

"Consider all options before making a decision who to go to work for. One must decide if they are content selling financial products or if they want to provide financial advice for a fee. The enormous pressure to sell products pushes many potentially great financial planners out of the business. It usually takes several years to build a book of business and referral base, so patience is a must."

"It is very challenging to build a fee-only practice from scratch; however, if you stick it out and believe in yourself, you will be in position to take advantage of those lucky breaks that come along."

2009 Update:

"Over the past two years much has changed. I transitioned from working exclusively from home to having a shared office outside the home. In November 2008 I moved to a new and bigger office that I did not have to share.

"My practice has been growing at a substantial rate over the last two years. I attribute this growth to the following:

- I stopped doing 'one-time' financial plans for a fee and began offering ongoing financial planning services on a monthly retainer. I found the monthly retainer to be more affordable for the middle income clients I was looking to work with. Instead of doing a formal financial plan that required a large upfront cost to the client, I broke the work down and spread out the fee. This made the financial planning process much more flexible.

- I switched to web-based planning software what made data gathering much more efficient. With the use of web meeting software, I was able to work with my clients online and show them how to enter and update their financial fact finder. In addition, the web meetings have allowed me to have most meetings online saving time and travel costs for both my clients and myself; a value clients appreciated when fuel costs became very high.

"I decided to become a retirement plan specialist. I have focused my studies on IRA and retirement plan rules as they relate to estate planning. The knowledge I have gained is immeasurable. I am convinced that several prospects that became clients did so because of discussions we had about relatively unknown tax rules for retirement accounts."

2011 Update:

"My business has continued to grow at a rapid pace. The specialization with retirement plan distribution rules has helped me gain new clients looking for an expert in this area. I continue to work as a solo practitioner however I am considering adding a support person in the next year.

"Given how my practice has grown I have been able to charge higher fees and be more selective in who I choose to work with. I continue to work on expanding my education and hope to complete a Master's Degree in Financial Services this year. As I expand my education, I find that higher net worth individuals have been inquiring about my services."

Jeremy J. Hudson, CFP®
Howard Financial Services, Ltd.
Dallas, Texas
www.howardfinancialservices.com

Did you have a business plan?

"No, my situation has warranted more of a career plan instead of a business plan."

What were the biggest obstacles you faced?

"One of the biggest obstacles I faced early on was my age. I was 22 when I graduated from college and was lucky enough to work with a firm who allowed me to develop client relationships from day one. At times, I could tell clients were skeptical when they first met me. Although, the skepticism was always short-lived."

What did you do right?

"I was lucky and had an opportunity to obtain a college degree in financial planning from Texas Tech. I was eligible to sit for the CFP® exam upon graduation, but decided to wait for a while and gain some experience in the industry before taking the exam.

"Also, my first job out of college was a salaried position, and I didn't have the pressure of building my own book of business. I was able to gain valuable experience without worrying about my next paycheck."

How did you get training? Did you have a mentor?

"I received incredible training from the principals of Wealth Builders, Inc. They provided me with an extremely comprehensive training program which started with my internship and continued for the better part of three years. The training focused on the core areas of financial planning and sales."

How long did it take to start making money?

"I guess you can say I've made money from day one, since I've always been an employee and do not own my own firm. More importantly, I have a passion for my job and the financial planning industry."

If you had it do over again, what would you do differently?

"I would have made the transition to the fee-only financial planning environment sooner."

Where do you see yourself in five years?

"It's hard to imagine anything different than where I am now. I work for a great firm, have wonderful client relationships, and am married to my soul mate and best friend. Professionally and personally I am in a great place. I've truly been blessed."

What's the best advice you could give someone just starting out?

"I would strongly recommend looking into a collegiate program, such as Texas Tech, for educational training. I would also recommend joining the local FPA chapter and/or NAPFA study group for the educational and networking opportunities."

2009 Update:

"I am venturing into my ninth year in the financial planning industry and the last couple of years have been filled with challenges and tremendous opportunities alike. The tough economic times have undoubtedly left a lasting impression on us all. Luckily our firm has weathered the storm so far.

"We have continued to exhibit strong growth despite the downturn in the economy. We hired another financial planner (Shaun Dowling) from Texas Tech's financial planning program in January of 2008. Shaun did a great job as our intern the year prior and we decided to make him a full-time offer prior to his graduation. It's been very rewarding teaching Shaun the intricacies of the financial planning industry. At the same time Shaun has taught me several things and it's refreshing to share ideas with the next generation of financial planners.

"On a personal level the past couple of years have been very rewarding. Jacqueline and I purchased our first home. Now I can totally relate to clients when I see housing repairs and maintenance comprising such as large portion of their budget!"

2011 Update:

"The last couple of years have been great. Where to start? Our firm continues to grow in multiple facets. Finding and attracting top talent is always a challenge, yet extremely rewarding. I feel strongly that the key to any successful organization starts with their team members. The last couple of years we've placed an emphasis on adding top notch talent to our firm. We've continued to have success with Texas Tech's financial planning program. We've hired two interns within the financial planning division since 2009 and both joined our team as full-time members upon their graduation. We've also expanded our operations team by hiring somebody who brings valuable experience and fresh ideas to the table. We've also added a Managing Director who joined our team a few years ago after a very successful 25 year career in private banking. We feel like we are positioned very well for years to come.

"It's a constant challenge to find balance between allocating time personally and professionally. I finally gave up and synced my work email with my iPhone after a few years of holding out. Jacqueline was not too happy at first, but it is working great now. I love being plugged in at all times."

Eric Mote, CFP® and Jean Mote, CFP®
Mote Wealth Management, LLC
Cedar Rapids, IA

"MWM is a fee-only, comprehensive financial planning firm with two employees, Eric and Jean Mote, husband and wife. He is 59 years old and I am 60. While we offer hourly, project and asset management services, our focus is on long-term asset management and comprehensive planning clients. Hourly and project work is available on a very limited basis. Our office is in our house, and our business model is to meet with clients at their convenience at their home or place of business. We meet evenings or weekends as necessary.

"We have $23 million under management, though that number is lower right now with the economic downturn, and we have approximately 30 clients. We are very much relationship advisors, assisting our clients on many aspects of their lives beyond the standard investing, retirement, taxes, risk management and estate planning. We have helped clients buy and/or sell houses, cars, and pets; set electronic thermostats; research hearing aids and insurance for them, etc., etc. etc. Our clients are predominantly retirement and pre-retirement age, but at least 25% are young professionals.

"Eric handles the investment, technology and billing part of the business, and Jean is responsible for dealing with custodians and the administrative issues. We are both involved in the planning work and always meet with clients together. Eric usually takes the lead in client meetings except in cases where clients seem to relate better with Jean.

"We are career changers, having met, worked together and then married while we were working in telecommunications. We interned (worked for free) with a fee-only, sole practitioner in another town for a few months. While our original intent was to work with him for a while and then buy his business, our working styles were too different to make it work. We began writing our ADV and establishing our own RIA in October 2000 and started in business 01/01/2001."

Did you have a business plan?

"As embarrassing as it is to admit, we started our business without a written plan. We talked through as many of the key issues as we were capable of discussing, and even made some attempt to put it in writing, but the time was short and it was an area in which we had too little background and the project was abandoned. A year or so into the business, we were invited to participate in the beta test of the NAPFA FOSTER (Fee-Only Support, Training, Education and Resources) program. Again, although a part of the course included writing a business plan, we were unable to complete one. We are currently at work on our plan, though we are probably going to have to involve a business coach to help us coordinate our plans."

What were the biggest obstacles you faced?

"Our biggest obstacles were our fear and our lack of experience and training. Although we had been immersing ourselves in learning about financial planning for a few years before we considered going into the profession, we had huge gaps in our education and in the basics of how the industry works, such as with custodians. Despite that, we had a backlog of people who wanted us to be their financial advisors because we had become zealots about financial matters and talked about it to everyone we knew at every opportunity. We were not intentionally building a client base, rather we were shocked at what our broker had done and determined to let others know they needed to be better informed. The result was that people we knew wanted us to help them with their finances. However, once we began actually dealing with client issues, we recognized our very limited skill sets and were constantly concerned whether we were offering appropriate and accurate services to them. At times, we were nearly paralyzed with fear, delaying working on projects because of the scope of what we didn't know. Somehow, we managed to research and "gut through" issues, though our progress was slower than it should have been. Our clients never questioned our abilities."

What did you do right?

"One thing we did right was talk to people about what we believed and what we were doing. As far as running the business, we both have operations and management backgrounds, and we were able to lay out a workable plan for creating the business.

"The most important thing was that we recognized the resources available to us and used them extensively but judiciously so they continued to be willing to help. We had been introduced to NAPFA, and the NAPFA planners generously gave us copies of the forms and processes they used and talked through their business models. We also paid for value, hiring the best known business attorney in the area to ensure our agreements and methods of doing business were all appropriate. We are both willing to ask questions of others and to really listen, take notes and ask for enlightenment as necessary."

How did you get training? Did you have a mentor?

"We were originally looking for a fee-only planner to take care of our financial issues for us. Through our research, we had discovered fee-only and NAPFA. There were no fee-only planners in Cedar Rapids; the nearest were in Des Moines, about two hours from us. The more we learned about fee-only planning, the more we thought this could be a career path for Eric. He was running his own telecommunications consulting business at that time, and was tired of the travel required. I was working at a telecommunications company. One of the Des Moines firms was a husband and wife team, Phil and Barb Svanoe. Eric called and asked if he could pay for an hour of their time just to learn about their business. Phil said Eric could not pay for the time but that he would gladly meet for an hour to talk through what they do.

"In the course of their meeting, Phil told Eric the NAPFA national conference was being held in Minneapolis within a couple of weeks and encouraged him to attend to learn more about fee-only. We both had other commitments that would make it impossible to attend, but at the last minute, our other plans fell through.

"What a welcoming, open, sharing group the NAPFA organization is! Our early training and mentors came almost exclusively through NAPFA. We had thought the first planner we worked with would be our mentor, but that didn't pan out. Although he was not a NAPFA member, we met him at that first NAPFA conference. He, in turn, introduced us to the NAPFA Chicago Study Group which is a four and a half hour drive from CR. At those meetings, we not only developed more mentoring relationships, but also planners who were willing to nag and cajole us about earning our Certified Financial Planner™ certification. Pat Doland was always chief nag. We also gained incredible support from Chris Long, Gloria Smith, David Walz, Leisa Aiken, Sid Blum and Nancy Hradsky, as well as others.

"In February 2004, we finally began our CFP® course work from the College for Financial Planning. A telecommunications co-worker, Tom Garner, asked if he could join us for study, not because he wanted to become a planner necessarily, but because he wanted to learn more about finances. We had made a couple of false starts, always finding client issues that prevented study. With our study partner, we made commitments we had to keep. We would not have completed the course work when we did, if ever, had it not been for Tom. We sat for and passed the exam November 2005."

How long did it take to start making money?

"Because of our very low overhead, we were showing a profit at the beginning of the second year. We were not fully supporting ourselves, though, until midway through our 3rd year in business."

If you had it to do over again, what would you do differently?

"First, we would find a way to intern with a fee-only firm for at least a year and perhaps more. We would attain a CFP® designation prior to starting the business, and we would not start the firm without a written business plan and a written marketing plan."

Where do you see yourself in five years?

"We are currently struggling with this issue, and are in the process of finding a business coach to help us work through our thoughts. Eric and I have very different approaches to our business, and it is keeping us at a standstill.

"My vision (not necessarily fully shared by my partner) is to have office space outside our house, and to adapt our business model to meeting with some clients at their homes but having most clients come to the office. I envision two or three additional planners and probably one administrative person plus possibly a half-time admin or an intern. Because these are huge changes for us, the next five years will possibly be the most demanding since we started the company. But in order for us to reach the level of satisfaction we want from the business, these kinds of changes will be necessary."

What's the best advice you could give someone just starting out?

1. "Be sure you have enough money to live on for at least four or five years
2. Join organizations and network with other financial planners – they know what you need to know and they are great support
3. Complete your education (such as a CFP®) before you start your company
4. Work with an experienced planner or company for a time if at all possible"

2011 Update:

"The last two years have increased our satisfaction with our business, which is saying a lot, because we already loved our work with clients. Certainly, the economic downturn was difficult for everyone, but it helped reinforce the concepts of short-term versus long-term assets. Maintaining an adequate cash cushion is a crucial part of the success of a financial plan. We increased communication with clients to ensure our voice of calm and assurance was available to offset the fear and hype from many in the media, and we feel relationships with our clients have been strengthened by withstanding the turbulent times.

"We engaged a business coach in July 2009. After researching the wide range of coaches available, we decided to work with Diane MacPhee of DMac Consulting Services, a former NAPFA-Registered fee-only financial advisor and a coach highly recommended by fellow NAPFA members. Although we had seen Diane at numerous NAPFA conferences and were impressed by her positive attitude and high energy, we did not know her personally. Our hesitation in working with a coach was uncertainty over how much impact an "outsider" could have on our business, but we hoped a different perspective would help us clarify our thinking. It did that and more. During the time we worked with Diane, we implemented a new CRM system, created a systematic marketing plan, and developed a critical eye toward examination of both existing clients and future client selection. She also exhorted us to take the steps necessary to change our NAPFA memberships from Affiliate level to full-fledged NAPFA-Registered Financial Advisors. Her most important role, though, was helping us establish better communication and a renewed passion for our business.

"As difficult as it was to do, we severed our relationship with a few clients, we turned down the opportunity to accept some work we would previously have accepted, and we became NAPFA-Registered Financial Advisors. Although our assets under management have only increased by about a million dollars in the last two years, we believe we are poised to grow the firm efficiently in ways that will enhance rather than diminish the levels of service we offer to our existing clients. We look forward to the next two years with enthusiasm."

Illa Amerson, Ph.D., CFP®
Pinnacle Advisory Group, Inc.
Columbia, Maryland
www.pinnacleadvisory.com

"I currently practice as the lead advisor for one of seven teams under my firm's umbrella. At this time, I have approximately 70 clients and close to $100 million under management. Some of my clients came from one of our founding partners, while others have been added as clients referred their friends and family members to me. My clients range in age from early 20s to mid 80s and have a wide variety of planning needs. Several of my clients are small business owners and medical or dental practitioners. I am paid a percentage of gross revenues, and there are no additional charges for financial planning or client service work. Our company has a dedicated investment team that does all of our research, makes investment decisions for our five investment strategies, and executes trades for all clients. My daily life involves financial planning for my clients, portfolio reviews, client education, client service, leading my support team, coordination with other professionals (CPAs, etc.), and business development through new and existing networks. Occasionally, I am involved in internal firm projects such as participating on a financial planning policy team or, currently, developing a technology strategy plan for the company."

Did you have a business plan?

"Up to this point in my career, I have not had a business plan. Because I joined an existing firm as soon as I decided to pursue financial planning, I was initially focused on doing what was necessary to move through the ranks from intern to full-time planner to junior advisor to senior advisor. My career path was relatively clear, and I hadn't yet begun to view myself as a practitioner with a business to run. I did, however, do a tremendous amount of research about the financial services industry and what role I wanted to play in it. I knew I wanted to start at an independent firm with excellent planners from whom I could learn. I recognized early on that my ideal position was going to be difficult to find, and I *did* have a focused plan for getting into that position."

What were the biggest obstacles you faced?

"My biggest obstacle from the beginning was that there nothing in my background that related to a financial planning practice. I had no financial planning, sales, marketing, or related professional experience. I was an environmental engineer with a Ph.D. making a drastic career change. This was not an easy sell to an independent wealth management firm that wasn't planning on hiring. In fact, in my interview for my internship, I was told 'There's nothing here for you after 6 months.' Fortunately, my only goal for the internship was to leave with references from well-known practitioners in my area. More fortunately, after 4 months of working longer hours than expected and taking on any challenging planning project, I got the full-time planning associate job as well as the references.

"The second significant obstacle occurred during the evolution of my practice. When I was initially promoted to an advisor position in January 2007, I served as the junior advisor for one of our founding partners as part of his succession plan. Eventually, I was to become the senior advisor for those clients, allowing him to invest his time and energy in running the firm. This is much easier said than done. Transitioning clients is an extraordinarily difficult process. The primary concern, of course, is the continued comfort and trust of the clients. The whole process fails if clients feel that they are being abandoned or passed off to a less capable advisor. That was the obvious obstacle. What was less obvious at the beginning was the strain the process can place on a working relationship. The partner had to give up control and accept that I was going to work with those clients differently than he did. I was developing my own style and relationships with those clients and felt constrained by the approach that had been successful for him. Anyone considering being part of a succession plan needs to be aware of the time, energy, and patience required to negotiate the process successfully."

What did you do right?

"Looking back now, I feel like I had a charmed entry into this field, and without question, there was some luck involved. Nonetheless, I think I did a few things that put me in a position to take advantage of lucky circumstances. First, before I ever contacted anyone in the financial planning profession, I developed a crystal clear vision of why I wanted to be in this field, what I could bring to the table, what kind of firm I wanted to join, and what role I ultimately wanted to play with clients. Not only did that keep me from wasting time in a scattered job search, but it helped the planners I met along the way point me in the right direction.

"My involvement in the Financial Planning Association has also been instrumental. As soon as I was sure that I wanted to be a planner, I paid my own way to FPA's national conference in Denver in 2004. Attending that conference and networking with a group of Next Gen planners ultimately paved the way to my current practice. More recently, I attended the FPA Retreat in April 2009, which has opened up opportunities and practice ideas that I had never previously considered. FPA may not be the right organization for everyone considering this field, but the key is really to keep finding new ways to learn and challenge my current thinking.

"Perhaps most important for a career changer like myself, I made a decision and threw myself into it. The initial decision was not to become a financial planner but to leave my science and engineering career behind. The decision to become a financial planner came after a year of soul searching, career counseling, and research. To provide some context, the year that I made the first decision, I had just finished a year as a Science Fellow in the US Senate, the Senator I had worked for was willing to make a personal phone call to recommend me for my job of choice, and I was at the top of my earning potential to date. Leaving that behind to rebuild from scratch was not easy, but once I committed to it, I never looked back. From that point this new career had to work. Failing simply ceased to be an option for me."

How did you get training? Did you have a mentor?

"My training as a financial planner came in two forms. First, I had determined that I would pursue the Certified Financial Planner™ designation so I was working my way through CFP® curriculum. Second, I learned an amazing amount about planning on the job. This turned out to be one of those lucky breaks. My firm had 7 experienced planners to help me on my way, including one who is nationally recognized for being on the cutting edge of financial planning. To their credit, they handed me challenging work to do from the beginning and invited me into their client meetings so I could see the connection between the written plan and people's lives. Today, there are 12 of us who are experienced planners and the culture of mutual teaching and learning continues.

"One thing that I did not have was a true mentor. I had hoped when I was chosen to work alongside a founding partner that he would serve as a mentor, but that was the not nature of our working relationship. I know that finding a mentor is a frequent recommendation to new planners, but finding a good mentor can be tough. I think I had something better, a wealth of teachers. I think I've learned just as much, and perhaps more, from a cadre of teachers who were all readily available. Among them are my fellow planners, my administrative and operations support staff, my early supervisors, other professionals, and my clients (especially my clients). Some of those teachers are people I strive to emulate, while others are people with whom I disagree. Nonetheless, I reach the end of every day having learned something that will make me a better planner, advisor, and practitioner."

How long did it take to start making money?

"Technically, since I started as a salaried employee, I was making money from the beginning, but not much. My income is now tied entirely to revenue generated from the assets I have under management, which means market returns, client retention, and business development are the keys to my current and future income. I reached an income level that is comfortable (meaning necessities and entertainment are not mutually exclusive) last year, but I am still not quite where I would like to be. I will need to generate another $50,000/year of income to reach a point that I find acceptable and another $75,000/year beyond that to consider myself financially successful in this career."

If you had it to do over again, what would you do differently?

"There's very little that I would have changed about my career path thus far, but there is one thing that I wish I had done a bit differently. I would have stayed in my staff planner role longer. This may sound a bit odd, but as a practitioner, your technical knowledge is just the beginning of what you need to know to be successful. I was on a very steep, very rapid learning curve from fall 2005 forward. I had to learn complex planning topics, a difficult investment strategy, how to conduct client meetings, how to juggle the competing demands of working with clients, business development, and what it means to run a practice within a 3 year period. That learning curve was largely self-imposed. I've enjoyed the rapid development of my career, but I probably should have taken more time to be a technician while I had that option."

Where do you see yourself in five years?

"It admittedly seems odd to me to contemplate where I will be five years from now considering that five years ago I was still trying to figure out what to do with the rest of my life. Within five years, my practice will have grown to 100 clients with a minimum 30% growth in revenue. At that point I will need to make a decision about if or when I will need additional planning support for myself in order to continue growing the practice. I expect to have developed new, currently untapped networks that will have begun to generate prospective clients consistently. Recently, I have decided to specialize in working with grieving clients and will be focusing on developing my expertise and reputation in that area. Five years from now I hope to be known for that expertise. Finally, I've just begun to participate in programs that bring financial planning assistance into the community. I look forward to that becoming a significant part of my broader career over the next five years."

What's the best advice you could give someone just starting out?

"There are four things I would say to someone starting out. First, commit to this field. It is too tough and requires too much from you to dip your toes in and expect to be successful. Will it be easy? No. Will you have to make sacrifices and possibly spend down savings? Absolutely. If you are committed, do it anyway. Find the path that works for you and move forward as if your life depends on it.

"Second, trust your instincts. You will, no doubt, have situations that feel like a natural fit and others that just seem wrong in some way. To complicate things, the 'not quite right' situations may very well be the ones that present the best-looking immediate package to you.

It's incredibly easy to get stuck in the mindset of doing what you think *should* do instead of doing what is best for you. In the long run you will be more productive and more successful if you aren't fighting yourself (even subconsciously). I learned this lesson the hard way. After trying to make a frustrating situation work, I just let it go. My practice and my life have been much more enjoyable since that point, and I feel like I'm getting paid to do something I love again.

"Third, if you've read various discussion boards, you have no doubt noticed that there are ongoing arguments about which education program is best. You should pick the one that supports what you want to do. For me, the CFP® was a natural fit. If you really like insurance and that will be the basis of your work, focus on your insurance license and the CLU®. If you are already a CPA, the PFS designation may be a good entry point. Maybe you need to start with securities licenses. The point is to not let the noise distract you. Choose your path and proceed. Somewhere down the road, you will find that you need or want more education, but you can deal with that when it happens.

"Lastly, write the business plan before you think you need it. It's easy to get absorbed in the daily details of this career. There is always something urgent pulling on you. At the beginning, you are just trying to get going and stay afloat financially. You may not feel like you can write a business plan when you are just starting. That will work for a while, but not indefinitely. If you find yourself thinking you don't have time, aren't sure where you really want to land, or that everything is going just fine, start writing."

2011 Update:

"I can't believe it has been 2 years already! My practice is continuing to grow slowly, and I'm enjoying the way it is developing. I have started to bring on the 30-45 year old children of some of my older clients. It feels great to see family relationships developing and to see the next generation of financial planning clients taking steps toward a secure financial future. I have become more selective about what types of clients I want to pursue. In part that resulted from evaluating who my favorite and best clients are and what characteristics they have in common. It has also come from a realization that I work best with clients with whom I share common experiences. I am starting to focus my work on clients who are dealing with a recent death in the family, a divorce, or a significant career change.

"A relatively new development that I am very excited about is the addition of coaching to my repertoire. All of the work we do as financial planners means nothing if the recommendations never get implemented. I remember working with a coach when I was changing careers and how valuable he was when I ran up against roadblocks (or at least they looked like roadblocks to me). I enrolled in a coaching curriculum last summer mainly to learn techniques that would help me support my clients better. In the process, I really started to enjoy the whole coaching process. I'm not sure where this will ultimately fit in my financial planning practice, but I'm looking forward to the journey of figuring it out."

Erik C. Milam, CFP*, RLP*

TrustCore Financial, Inc.
Brentwood, TN

"Growing up I always wanted to be in a career that helps people accomplish meaningful goals and reach their full potentials. My choice to be a financial planner was significantly influenced by my own life experiences. I was born with cerebral palsy and a severe speech impediment. Multiple surgeries, years of speech therapy, and hard work allowed me to achieve a better quality of life than anyone imagined for me. I went from a child who could barely walk to playing on a state championship football team; from being hardly able to answer the phone to making frequent motivational talks to schools, church groups, businesses, and sports teams.

"The physical difficulties in my life have taught me some valuable lessons that can apply to personal finances. The most important lesson I have learned from cerebral palsy is that we all face adversity; it is part of the human experience. Adversity can challenge our aspirations but financial planning can be a transformational force that allows dreams to become reality. My speech therapists and orthopedic surgeon did not only help me talk and walk, but they changed my life. I hope my clients feel that our work together not only increases their financial abilities, but also changes their lives for the better.

"My current practice is with TrustCore Financial, an independent financial planning firm in Brentwood, Tennessee. TrustCore now has over 30 financial planners who run their own practices. We share ideas, resources, staff support, investment research, etc. I have been with TrustCore for over 7 years and started in the firm's Planning Department where I supported the established financial planners and gained valuable knowledge and experience. I worked as a full time staff member and then transitioned to part-time as I grew my own practice. In October of 2008, I left my staff duties and devoted all my time to my financial planning clients. I focus on helping small business owners, retirees, and heirs to wealth. I believe in a life-centered approach to financial planning that deals with financial health and overall well-being.

"My interest in Financial Planning started the summer before my Senior year at Baylor University. I was majoring in Entrepreneurship and wanted sales experience so I interned for the summer at a large insurance company selling life insurance. The internship served as my first exposure to financial services and compelled me to add the Financial Services and Planning major. I wanted to learn more about financial planning and complete the prerequisite courses for the CFP® exam. I not only learned more, but also found my life's passion."

Did you have a business plan?

"Yes, but I did not need to create the infrastructure of a business since TrustCore already had that in place. I have client service and revenue goals that I update every year and have steadily improved all areas of my business."

What were the biggest obstacles you faced?

"I listened to people telling me that my age was a limiting factor. I do not think that is correct. Maturity, wisdom, and expertise are important.

"I had to learn to delegate to my support staff. Financial planning and servicing client needs requires organization, processes, and systems to allow for effective delegation. I am constantly improving my own process and ability to delegate to others."

What did you do right?

"My passion is helping people improve their lives in the present and future through financial planning and strategies. I could not be happier in my career choice.

"When I started in my career, I knew I wanted to be a fiduciary and focus on financial planning as a service, not just sell financial products. I was interested in working for a fee not a commission and that has been a good fit for me.

"I surrounded myself with great people. TrustCore has been a great building block for my success because I have the independence of my own practice, and yet have support and resources comparable to a large financial institution. My colleagues are amazing planners and individuals. The support staff has enabled me to focus on my clients.

"In addition, I am quick to ask for help and guidance from other professionals and have learned a lot about financial planning in a relatively short amount of time. I learn from others and then do what makes sense for my practice.

"On a personal note, in 2006 I met a wonderful woman who became my wife in 2009. My wife Michelle's unwavering support and encouragement is an incredible gift I receive each day."

How did you get training? Did you have a mentor?

"Studying Financial Planning at Baylor University was a good start. I received the CFP® designation in 2006 and enjoyed that learning process. My financial planning skills have improved through personal experience working with clients, my 3+ years supporting other planners at TrustCore, and doing joint work with several other planners in the office. I also have many planners around the country who I consider my mentors who I have met through various organizations and conferences I have attended. Most notably were my mentors Ed Jacobson and Debbie Wiggin in the Kinder Institute's Mentorship program. Ed hosts Open Mic conference calls, which offer a chance for Financial Planners around the country to talk about matters that matter. Ed has made immense contributions to financial planning community and has been a beacon of light in my career and personal life.

"I believe in continuing education and life-long learning. Many of the books and articles I read allow me to know what other planners are doing. I find most individuals are receptive if I contact them with a question about their work. George Kinder's books on Life Planning resonated with me so I attended his workshops and became a Registered Life Planner® through the Kinder Institute. I am a member of the Financial Planning Association and attend local chapter meetings and a monthly study group. I am a member of the Middle

Tennessee Estate Planning Council to improve my knowledge of estate planning. Recently I joined the Financial Therapy Association to learn more about the emotional and mental aspects of money in life."

How long did it take to start making money?

"Because I work for an independent firm and started on staff while growing my practice, my overhead was minimal. I was profitable my first year in business and I started working with clients on a part-time basis in 2006 and 2007. Fortunately, income from my practice doubled in 2008, 2009, and 2010. My practice has grown from referrals and from my professional development classes at Sandler Training in Nashville. Working with colleagues at TrustCore and many conversations with Mike Wiley, TrustCore's Marketing Director, has significantly increased my confidence."

If you had it to do over again, what would you do differently?

"Using a line from a recent Brad Paisley song, I would write a letter to me and tell myself to have more confidence and that I do not need to know everything about financial planning to be a good professional and help my clients. I never want to be someone who thinks he knows everything about a particular subject, but rather someone who knows where to get information when I need it."

Where do you see yourself in five years?

"I expect to continue my work as a financial planner. About 10% of my current revenue comes from commissions on insurance and investments. While this is a convenience for my clients, I see myself dropping the securities and insurance licenses and doing fee-only financial planning work. This would allow me to work only in an investment advisor capacity and not also as a registered representative. At that time, I might write a column on personal finance in a local publication or a financial planning blog."

What is the best advice you could give someone just starting out?

"Financial Planning is just as much an art as it is a science. It is as much about people as it is their money. I might be so bold to say it is more about peoples' lives and less about their money. In addition, sometimes getting a 'no' from a prospective client is a blessing in disguise."

Summary

How should the novice financial planner approach the business? According to those I interviewed, there is a definite pattern. Below is a summary of the advice they impart:

Did you have a business plan?

Most planners who didn't have a business plan wish they had!

What were the biggest obstacles you faced?

Misconceptions about what the financial planning career encompasses and fears about the unknown, especially of not being able to support oneself in the transition.

What did you do right?

Patience, preparation, commitment. Knowing what it is you want to do as well as who your initial market is!

How did you get training? Did you have a mentor?

Self-confidence, discipline and early attainment of the CFP® coursework, coupled with strong industry relationships. Join the FPA and network.

How long did it take to start making money?

Three to five years. Having an income source in the meantime helps!

If you had it to do over again, what would you do differently?

Research the industry. Set aside capital. Get started while current income is available.

Where do you see yourself in five years?

Most planners want to continue on their chosen path, with established relationships and more definition.

What's the best advice you could give someone just starting out?

Get the CFP® designation. Prepare a business plan.[169] Be confident with goals. Read! Begin marketing with resources you know and use well.

One Person's Path to the FP Holy Grail

What follows is a bonus from someone currently in transition, who has asked to remain anonymous:

I am in my middle years and have a successful career now, but I find myself strongly drawn to the field of Financial Planning; and I believe after I come up to speed, I can really help people and make a contribution to society in this field. Like many others, I plan to start on a part time basis.

---

[169] MS Office has a business plan template. Business Plan Pro software by Palo Alto is an easy-to-use program. View a demo plan at http://www.paloalto.com/ps/bp/

First Step: I enrolled in the CFP® course offered by the College for Financial Planning[170]. I have completed the first of five modules successfully (General Financial Planning, Risk Management and Insurance), and am part-way through the second (Investing and Asset Management). The other three modules are Income Tax Planning, Estate Planning, and Retirement Planning. Each module takes up to four months to complete, although you could easily do it quicker if you were willing/able to put in the time. Excellent program—I highly recommend it. I may also take their Chartered Mutual Fund Counselor course, partly to be able to use their CMFC designation, but also because I will be doing a lot with mutual funds in my planning work.

Second Step: Took the Series 65 Exam because it is required to be registered with the State of Maryland. Anyone who holds himself out as a financial planner in Maryland must be registered with either the SEC or the state. But the SEC won't let you register without having at least $25M of assets under management. I want to register now, so that I can legitimately set up a financial planning business and start gaining hours toward my CFP® experience requirement. Also, there is the psychological aspect that I will take the whole program more seriously and get more out of it if I begin to practice while I am studying.

My current Financial Planning Career Goal: I want to be independent, not work for a Broker/Dealer or a large company. I want to be a fee-only planner, at least to begin with. I want to work first primarily with young singles and families, and eventually with middle-class older families and those close to, or in, retirement. I'm not currently interested in working with "high net-worth clients" (nor do I expect they would be interested in working with me).

Problem: Who would hire a rank beginner like me?

Solution: I'll begin working with friends and family. I have several adult children for whom I will be doing a financial plan, and a couple of close friends. All this meshes with my career goals. I will charge very modest fees—not primarily for the money, but for the experience. (Added benefit: Hopefully my kids won't sue me when I foul up.)

As I gain more confidence and knowledge, I will gradually begin to market myself to others. Many planners don't seem to be interested in the middle-class, since they aren't willing/able to pay very much. So there is a need I think I can satisfy. (Needless to say, I'm not getting into this primarily for the money).

Once I complete the CFP® course, in about eighteen months or so, I will consider leaving my current job if I can afford to. I will be eligible for early retirement, and have a growing 401(k), which may be enough. Otherwise, I will keep on doing the financial planning work part time. I will also consider, however, going to work for a planning firm for a couple of years at that time, to get jump-started and get the CFP® experience requirement out of the way more quickly than I could do it part-time. I will make the decision on which route to take after I complete the CFP® course.

---

[170] College for Financial Planning offers the courses leading to the CFP® Certification Exam at http://www.cffp.edu.

I have also subscribed to *Financial Planning Magazine* [171], and I plan to join the FPA[172] this year. I find *Financial Planning Magazine* to be an excellent publication, and I think this publication, plus membership in the FPA, will be invaluable in learning first-hand how experienced planners think and what they do. I bought—and highly recommend—Katherine Vessenes' book *Protecting Your Practice* [173], along with her diskette of forms, letters, contracts, etc. Katherine's book is an excellent introduction to many of the legal/compliance issues, as well as having many helpful tips on keeping clients happy. Two other books that I have found very helpful in getting oriented and learning how to think like a planner are *The Excellent Investment Advisor* [174] by Nick Murray, and *Best Practices for Financial Advisors* [175] by Mary Rowland.

Next step: File Form ADV with the Office of the Attorney General, Securities Division, State of Maryland, to register with the state[176].

Next step, plus one: Set-up shop—probably as a sole proprietorship; figure out how to set-up record-keeping and accounting, etc., all on a shoestring budget. I will freely admit, the thought of registering is a mite scary—once I register, I am then bound to comply with all of the record-keeping and other compliance requirements, even if my clients ARE friends and family. Being a born do-it-yourselfer and an engineer, I'll probably try to do this with a minimum of legal and accounting assistance— just enough to keep myself out of trouble.

Warning: All of this costs money (not to mention time). $3245 for the CFP® course in digital format, including print curriculum; $750 for the comprehensive review exam course; $595 for the Certification Exam (plus transportation, food and lodging, if required); $140 for the Series 65 Study Guide; $120 for the Series 65 exam; $300/year to register with the state of Maryland, $100 for Katherine's book and diskette; $385 to join the FPA (student rate, for full time students enrolled in the CFP® course, $35, other discounts available); $$ for computer; $$ for home accounting software; $$ for home office setup; etc., etc. And they continue to increase!!!

Bottom line: All this is a big investment in both time and money. If you're serious, I think it is well worth it. If you're not willing to make these kinds of investments, in my opinion you're not serious enough to succeed.[177]

Digression on financial planning software search: After evaluating six or seven software packages, I have decided to start without one. I think it's best to develop my own style first. So, I'm going to create my own questionnaire and use spreadsheets for the calculations. Eventually, I may revert to a commercial financial planning software package if I find one that fits my style (and that I can afford).

---

[171] Request a free subscription to *Financial Planning Magazine* through http://www.financial-planning.com/subscribe
[172] Information about the Financial Planning Association can be found at http://www.fpanet.org.
[173] Vessenes, Katherine, *Protecting Your Practice*, Bloomberg Press, 1997.
[174] *The Excellent Investment Advisor* by Nick Murray, The Nick Murray Company, Inc., 1996.
[175] *Best Practices for Financial Advisors* by Mary Rowland, Bloomberg Press, 1997.
[176] See http://www.nasaa.org/QuickLinks/ContactYourRegulator.cfm?state=md#contactinfo. Most states have registration forms and instructions available for downloading.
[177] Prices as of 08/2005

Well, that's my plan, for what it's worth. I don't recommend it for everyone. Perhaps you young'uns out there may want to take a different path—get yourself hired by a small firm that operates in a style you're comfortable with, get them to pay for some of the training, courses, etc., and get the experience requirement out of the way quickly. But I hope some of my thoughts will be useful to some of you.

Chapter Eight

Get a Life!

Financial planning may well be the world's most rewarding career. Where else can helping others realize their hopes and dreams bring not only personal satisfaction, but also your own financial freedom? Most planners tell me they will never retire. They love their profession and intend to keep on doing it for the rest of their lives.

Colin Benjamin Coombs was an inspiration to me when I was starting out. Ben built an incredibly successful practice and his clients adore him. At a time when other people his age consider retirement, Ben simply moved his office to Three Rivers, California, got out his fishing pole, and began conducting review meetings with clients out on beautiful Klamath Lake. The guest room is always ready and the food's great. After a day or two, everyone is up to speed and the next client arrives to kick back and talk with Ben.

I'll be the first to admit experiencing serious problems in my life when it comes to balance. Quite literally, because I love doing what I do so much, nearly everything is wrapped up in my business. My hope, with this chapter, is to remind people entering the profession to do some planning with their own lives right from the beginning, so they're not consumed by their work as I, and countless other planners, tend to be. Don't wait until it's too late to remember that you have a family, a hobby, and a life after five o'clock.

The Roger Reaction

This was brought home to me in spades during the FPA Master's Retreat in 2001. Early in my career as a financial planner, I attended a conference session on asset allocation given by Roger Gibson. His ideas seemed, to me, pretty esoteric. Observing Mr. Gibson in his suit and tie, academic to the core, showing hieroglyphics on an overhead, I somehow knew this was an important presentation, but frankly, I was bored. My perception of the man was that of someone so wrapped up in numbers and scientific research that I wondered how on earth he could ever have any fun.

Fast-forward fifteen years or so, and perched on a stool before me sat a highly regarded author, whose work explained one of the most valuable analytic concepts in the financial planning world. That day in 2001, he was just a relaxed guy, in an open sport shirt and Levi's, casually telling an intimate audience about a turning point for him and giving us each a powerful lesson in life.

In the mid-1980s, Roger Gibson had finally achieved a modicum of success in an independent financial planning firm that was proud of his concentrated effort in developing an asset allocation model. The talk I heard so long ago was his first foray into the speaker's arena, and he was feeling pretty good about it. So good, in fact, that he planned a holiday after the conference to spend time with his wife in celebration of their achievements—two children, a respected position with his firm, a decent income at last, a little savings. He actually purchased a ring for his wife, unaffordable before, to commemorate the occasion. Her response: "I want a divorce."

Suddenly everything was gone. Focus on his career was instantly changed to a desperate struggle for custody of his son and daughter. Eventually, he was granted 50% custody. He joked about being, "half dad and half bachelor, not such a bad thing!" But the battle he won had been an enormous setback, and the life he had anticipated and planned for was permanently shattered.

Shaking himself loose from the remnants of his previous existence, Gibson took the lemons he'd been handed, and made the proverbial lemonade for his kids and himself. In an effort to establish a healthy environment for his children, he reduced his client load from sixty-five to six, left the firm he was working for, created a home office and, simply as a way to stay home with his children and keep food on the table, began writing what was to become a cornerstone for every serious financial planner's repertoire.

Now there was time. Time to consider stuff there'd never been time for in the past. Gibson picked up a clarinet for the first time in years and joined a local band. Never mistaken for Charles Atlas in his prior life, he took his son for Tae Kwon Do lessons, and today, he and his son each hold a black belt. Fireworks are fun, so Gibson pursued a childhood dream, and now he's a licensed pyrotechnics expert, or whoever it is that lights the match setting off those spectacular Fourth of July shows. That quiet academic I saw giving his first public seminar is flying high. Really! He even earned his pilot's license, another forgotten childhood dream brought to life, in his spare time.

It may have been an unexpected and unwanted turn of events that prompted it, but today, Roger Gibson has a life! You need one too. Don't wait until you get kicked in the ass by an unfortunate event. Take a holistic approach with your future, just as you'd do with a client. Build in the fun times, right from the get go!

Many of your clients, particularly during the first few years, are likely to come from friends you meet with socially, during family get-togethers, or while engaging in your favorite hobby or pastime—if not the exact people you're associating with, then often from their referrals. Be careful not to neglect current activities and relationships because they're not obvious sources of business for you. I belonged to the American Business Women's Association for more than a year before getting my first referral from a member. After the first one, referrals came frequently. Early on, at least 50% of my business was from ABWA referrals, yet not one single ABWA member was a client.

On the other end of the spectrum, however, far too many planners are caught up in the lives of their clients and what's going on in the industry, to the detriment of their own family and future. Precisely because it is so personally rewarding (and often, fun), financial planning work has a tendency to become addictive. There is certainly nothing wrong with having passion for the work you do, but it's important not to let your work become an addiction. Here are some suggestions to help keep your life on an even keel.

Get a Calendar

One sure-fire way to schedule time for yourself is to simply put it on your calendar. For the past twenty years, I've spent the first Tuesday of every month in absolute ecstasy. It began when I won a free session with a massage therapist. Thinking a massage was a sort of kinky thing to do, I initially ignored the prize.

Eventually, I was coerced into making an appointment. I still remember lying half naked and stiff as a board while Debbie spread oil over me and tried to get me to relax. Once she was finished, I couldn't wait for my next appointment! Everyone who knows me, including clients, friends and associates, is aware I never, ever see anyone but Debbie on the month's first Tuesday. I'm such a fanatic about it, if you looked on my calendar you'd see Debbie already scheduled on the first Tuesday for the next ten years!

Franklin Covey Co. has built an empire, combining time management with the Seven Habits concept. Stephen Covey's seventh habit is taking time to "sharpen the saw." In *The Seven Habits of Highly Effective People* [178] he tells the story of the woodsman who appeared exhausted after spending five hours sawing. When asked why he didn't take a break and sharpen his saw so things would go faster, he emphatically answered that he was too busy sawing!

I suggest programming regular saw-sharpening times into your calendar. With the terrific assortment of smartphones, electronic schedulers, personal data management devices, websites that coordinate with personal organizers and paper planners, there is no excuse for not making the time for fun and balance in your life!

Local chapters of the Financial Planning Association meet monthly for breakfast or lunch in most areas. Schedule the meetings on your calendar for the next year or two. Block out the times you'll be on vacation, well in advance, even if it's just a couple days away from the office. Make plans to attend national conferences and conventions where you can share ideas with your colleagues. Combine vacation time with your family around out-of-state industry events by adding a week or two for leisure. Put the kids' recitals and sports events down, and the PTA meetings.

After pre-arranged meetings, massages, vacations and conferences, I blocked out afternoons or even whole days every week without appointments to play catch up or just to reflect. One evening a week and one Saturday a month, I saved for clients who couldn't make it into the office during normal business hours. This alleviated the guilt from taking a day off during the week! If someone asked to see me on the first Tuesday, I simply whipped out my planner and said, "Sorry! I'm booked!" No need to explain that I'm booked on a table where Debbie will pour warm oil over my poor aching shoulders and work her magic.

---

[178]Stephen R. Covey, *The Seven Habits of Highly Effective People,* (Simon & Schuster, 1989).

Get a Financial Planner

Yes, I know. You **are** a financial planner. Have you heard of the cobbler's family who ran around barefoot? A surprising number of financial planners are living examples of that analogy and forget to take time to set goals and objectives for themselves and their families. In their zeal to improve the lives of their clients, planners often neglect their own investment portfolio, become too emotionally involved to make prudent financial decisions, or forget to update their own wills and trusts. As you begin your new career, walk carefully around this career trap. Interview some planners. See what it feels like to sit on the other side of the desk, and talk about how you spend money and what your plans are for the rest of your life. You will be glad you did!

Mike Ling, my portfolio designer and owner of Berkeley, Inc., an investment advisory and financial planning firm in Boise, Idaho, only works with clients he likes. I guess he likes me, because when I asked him to be my financial planner he agreed. Even after he told me he wants his clients to be comfortable and excited about coming to see him, I was anything but comfortable during our first few meetings. That's how I discovered how incredibly difficult it is to bare your financial soul to someone, even if he likes you! This awareness is as important, in my opinion, as knowledge of the technical aspects of estate planning.

To get my own financial plan, I had to fill out a lengthy questionnaire and face some tough questions. Believe me when I tell you, the questions are easier to ask than answer. Of course, I zeroed in on retirement, and it didn't take Mike long to learn things about me that I didn't even know myself. I realized that my idea of retirement is pretty much doing the fun part of what I'm already doing. It would be nice, I told him, if I could spend more time meeting with my clients and traveling. I mentioned what fun I had working with the financial planning discussion boards on the Internet, helping would-be planners get started, and how one day I'd like to write a book, something I'd never really thought about until he got me focused.

For some reason, it seems to me I'm spending a lot of time traveling recently. You're reading the book. Occasionally, I wonder if I wouldn't still be caught up in the rat race if Mike hadn't insisted on getting me to focus on what my successful future would look like. I hope my clients were half as pleased with what I did for them as I am with the way Mike has freed me so I can stop worrying and start thinking about what really matters. I guess they did, because when Mike purchased my practice in 2004, we had a 97% transition to Berkeley, Inc.

Get a Grip

I'm very fortunate to know personally, and in many cases intimately, some of the most successful members of one of America's top-rated careers. Let me share with you a few of their words of balancing advice.

"For the past four or five years, I've been sneaking off to a little three bedroom house called the Lindley Institute for Conflict Resolution on the ocean front at Rincon Point," confesses J. Michael Fay, CFP® of the Claremont Financial Group in Claremont, California. Mike's daughter discovered the retreat while studying at the University of California at Santa Barbara and working part-time for her father. She suggested the office staff spend a weekend there, doing some strategic planning.

These days Mike won't allow himself to take work with him on visits to the Institute. Sometimes he goes alone, other times with his wife and daughter. But when he's there, he's reading spiritual books, cooking vegetarian meals or just lazily wandering the deserted beach. "I try to break away for two or three days every quarter. It's a stress reducer…a centering experience," he says.

One of the busiest planners I know is former Co-Chair of the Financial Planning Association, Elissa Buie, CFP®, from Falls Church, Virginia. "I don't go to the office on Fridays but, rather, sit on my deck or take a drive or do something else," she explains. "It gives me the space to think big thoughts, dream big dreams, think about my clients and my staff in terms of what is important in their lives, and to just be. I am much more productive on the days I am in the office for having had this time and space to focus on the spirit of life."

"I go off to a wildlife refuge in the Oregon high desert with five or six women friends for a week each spring," says Laurie McClain with Socially Responsive Investing in Eugene, Oregon. "We stay in an old double-wide trailer, cook lots of good food, and get up early each morning to go birding. Sometimes we're organized enough to use the local park naturalist as a tour guide. We also sleep, gossip, hike, meditate and do yoga. I get nice womanly energy, good exercise, Zen practice in sitting still and watching birds, mammals and scenery, and a very spiritual connection to the universe."

"I ~ laugh!" admits Gayle Coleman, with Coleman Knight Advisory Group in Carlisle, Massachusetts. "I am most relaxed and full of Aloha when I am laughing, happy and smiling.

"I consciously and intentionally think about my happiness (and those around me) and how to maintain it in this sometimes chaotic/frenetic world," she continues. "I relieve stress by simple practices of breathing, finding clarity in the situation and trying to find the humor. If I can laugh, I know I have succeeded in processing 'the stress'. Life is just not as serious as most of us make it out to be. Though these words may seem rather feeble, my father used to say: 'Gayle, you're not going to fall off the face of the earth.' And, I haven't.

"Laughter is part of who I am, and luckily, it takes me to a less stressful place. Knowing my clients need help finding ease and peace of mind, if I can't walk my talk as I practice financial planning, it is pretty hard for me to be counseling and advising others."

Once a month, Patti and I get together. She's not a social acquaintance or a professional colleague. I only see her once a month, when we have breakfast together. I wouldn't miss that breakfast any more than I'd miss my appointment with Debbie, or Christmas! I hand-picked Patti, from a number of candidates, to be the person to whom I'm accountable.

256

She's the sort of person I can count on to tell me I look like the dickens in that dress I paid too much for.

When we first decided upon this alliance, we agreed to be ruthless. We promised to listen to each other, and that we wouldn't hold back when we felt too depressed, or ashamed, or embarrassed, to tell anyone else. I can tell Patti how excited I am that I made a difference in someone's life…and how frustrated I am that a favorite client decided to move her account to a different planner. She pats me on the back, reprimands me like a Dutch uncle, and patiently lets me get it all out. Of course, I don't tell her names or specifics, but it's terribly important that she's there for me, and it's rewarding for me to be there for her. Everyone needs a Patti. She is intelligent, nonjudgmental, and trustworthy—and she demands those qualities in me.

Get a Hobby

"What puts me back together is writing. I write fiction," says Bev Chapman, CFP®, who's been a planner since 1994 and has a fee-only practice, Values: Financial Counseling and Education, in Newton, Massachusetts. "Just give me a little time alone to write fiction, and the nectar of the gods' flows in my veins. That and being in nature, in one way or another. I love to walk, bike, kayak, canoe and hike. As long as it's in pristine beauty or rugged beauty or pastoral beauty, I'm one happy woman. Bubbling over, actually!"

"My passion is photography," insists my new friend Naguib Kerba, CFP®, who hails from Mississauga, Ontario, Canada. "It seems that my camera is always the first item packed if I'm going anywhere. No subject is too boring, but I do have my favourites—I love exploring anywhere I go at sunrise. Maybe I'm looking at life as—'*You wake up and the rest of the day is a bonus.*' There is a certain sense of renewal and being at one with the world. There's nothing like the peace of being out on a northern lake in a canoe when the only sounds you hear are the droplets of water falling from your paddle as they hit the glass-like surface of the lake. My heart's core is to capture that on film and share it, maybe even publish a book someday."

"Eating is my hobby, my passion," admits Rick Kahler, CFP®, who has the distinction of being South Dakota's first CERTIFIED FINANCIAL PLANNER™ practitioner.[179] "Dining is an event, something that has long been celebrated by the European culture and never embraced by us Americans. I can think of nothing nicer than enjoying an excellent meal with great friends that lasts for hours.

"It was my passion for food that caused me to start a restaurant guide, which rates our local eateries," he continues. "Because of my high profile in the community, I published the guide anonymously. Following our first two publications, we moved the guide to the Web. After a hard day's work helping my clients plan their financial futures, there is nothing more rewarding than retreating to one of our finer restaurants…and then writing it up in the guide!

---

[179] Rick is a skinny guy, and co-author of *Conscious Finance* http://www.consciousfinance.com and a slew of other publications.

"I also enjoy wine collecting." Rick claims he was a teetotaler, "until I met my wife, who introduced me to the finer things in life. Since then, I have become a compulsive wine investor. I began the day I discovered that some of the 1990 and 1991 Silver Oaks that I had purchased had tripled in value. Being a value investor, there is no way I could drink a bottle of wine that had a Parker rating of 91 and was selling for $95! Instead, I sold them at an Internet auction, and purchased some French wine rated 92 by Parker for $15 a bottle. I have traveled that road ever since, investing in the cult wines, selling them when they triple in value, and buying equivalent wine for a fraction of the price!"

Get Exercise

Twice a week, I work out with Traison, my Personal Trainer[180]. When I embarked upon a fitness program in 1998, I decided to do it right and hire someone to show me the ropes. I've been through some good trainers, but Tra's the best. A real slave driver. I don't dare not work out the rest of the week, because he has a way of knowing if I've sloughed off! The result is a level of energy much higher than I had years ago! The real advantage is feeling good about me! Taking good physical care of yourself is vitally important when it comes to serving your clients. Don't think for a moment you don't have time to stay healthy!

Mark P. Tolan, CFP®, a 35-year veteran with Ameriprise, keeps in shape by coaching year-round. Whether it's basketball, baseball or his twelve-year-old daughter Caitlin's softball league, he's at practice two or three days every week. Active in sports since his youth, and coaching since 1984, Mark uses the sports world to impart business principles to his kids. "It's important to keep in touch with them," he says, taking great pride in the fact son Kevin is now working beside him as an advisor.

Get Away

"Getting away to me means not thinking about matters financial, says William K. Dix, creator of Fortune Management Group in Raleigh, North Carolina. "So I ride a motorcycle (across country if possible) with my bride." Bill says his bride of more than forty years has "been on the back of the bike from the moment I first began riding. Our Honda Goldwing is a large six cylinder touring bike.

"Motorcycling is an acquired skill that can be done well," he continues. "It is also an activity that rewards concentration and punishes inattention. It is absolutely the best way to see, hear and smell the countryside—especially with Bach playing through the helmet speakers from the cassette player. Maybe one day we'll do the Alps!

"I bought my first bike in the spring of '81, after a several-week riding course at a community college in California. All the riding tests in the California Department of Motor Vehicle's arsenal was our final exam. I have sought recurring training so that I don't have to learn everything by painful experience. You see kids today riding in shorts and tee shirts,

---

[180] http://www.bodybytra.com

which just tells you they have never fallen. Once they do, and find out how uncharitably asphalt treats skin, they will wear long pants and a jacket every time they ride...if they continue riding. It's risky and fun. Paying attention and building skills helps manage the former and enhance the latter."

It's easy to get away and encounter new and wonderful experiences at professional events. Just by attending industry conferences, retreats and educational sessions, I've heard terrific presentations by Colin Powell, John Wooden, Michael Gerber, John Glenn and Stephen Covey, just to name a few. I've attended classes at Yale, spent a week in my very own apartment just off Times Square, tasted antelope at a winter Olympics resort, had my picture taken with Willy Mays, helped pull an Amish family's wagon from a ditch, ridden a tiny capsule to the top of the arch in St. Louis, cruised the Caribbean, seen the Terracotta Warriors in Xian and wandered New Orleans' French Quarter...before Katrina.

Most of this was beyond my wildest dreams until I became a financial planner. Opportunities abound to learn from the best minds, in the most exciting cities, under advanced technological systems. And much of it's tax deductible!

Get a Back-up

"It seems workaholism is especially prevalent among people in the financial services industry," wrote Leslie Rosenberg for *Ticker Magazine*. She goes on to quote financial planners who are "shifting their priorities to make room for their personal lives—and their businesses are thriving as a result."

Whether your office is the corner of the dining room table or a suite atop the Sears Tower, you're going to need help. There are forms to fill out, phones to answer, records to keep, things to file, appointments to schedule and letters to write. You may think you have superhuman powers and know you can do these things better than anyone else, and maybe you can. But you're crazy if you don't bring in someone to free you from these tasks and put you before clients, which is where you should spend your valuable time!

Some of the more popular excuses include:
1. I can't afford to hire any help.
2. I can do this faster and better myself.
3. I need to handle all the details if I'm going to build my practice.
4. I love this business and want to do it all myself!

Whoa! It's terrific to have such enthusiasm, but stop and think why you wanted to be a financial planner in the first place. Did you picture yourself filing statements at 2 A.M.? Were you anxious to spend hours at the computer researching airfare to your next conference? Perhaps you wanted to show off your writing skills composing appointment letters. My guess is it had nothing to do with any of these things. Prevent burnout by making it a top priority to get help.

I had amazing luck! My best friend, Ronnie, a chief cost analyst for General Dynamics, took early retirement when the company was sold to Hughes in 1993. Since I was beginning to feel a time crunch, I asked if she would consider coming in to help me out one day a week and was thrilled when she accepted. Ronnie went to the College for Financial Planning and earned her Paraplanner certification. She put in about thirty hours a week, right up to the day I sold my practice.

Someone asked me once what Ronnie does. I went on and on about how she knows all my clients, keeps the books, makes travel arrangements and a million other things. When I took a breath, he said, "You have no idea what she does, do you?" I had to stop and think, but the fact was, I didn't. I just knew that when a client came for an appointment, the completed report was always on my desk. If I told her I had a conference in Baltimore, I know that when it was time to go, she'd hand me my ticket, hotel reservation and itinerary. If the securities auditor came calling, she'd produce the file he asked for.

It makes me laugh to think there was a time when I felt I couldn't afford help. Now I wonder how I ever managed, even during the early days, without her! Aside from the obvious, knowing that someone was there when I wasn't took a huge load off my mind. Whether I was across the country on vacation, in the next office with a client, or home in bed with the flu, I was confidant things were taken care of in my office.

Get a Perspective

"My personal 'respite' is found in the air," explains Beverly Fogle, CFP®, with Cambridge Financial Management Corp. in Vancouver, Washington. "I'm a pilot, and flying requires me to actually leave my ground-bound concerns behind and seriously concentrate on the task at hand. When I was active as a primary flight instructor, I sometimes had to tell certain students that they'd better give up the idea of flying, because they couldn't shift psychological gears, so to speak. This can literally be a matter of life and death."

"Since I do fly in serious weather, and sometimes to remote and foreign destinations, it is imperative that I train regularly," she continues. "I have a training partner with whom I've had a great relationship for about fifteen years now. We work each other over aggressively, doing the difficult stuff in the airplane, including the things you hope to never actually need. When we get through, I know that I've definitely been concentrating and working very hard. It does keep one sharp. Plus, it's a great change of pace.

"The really beneficial part," adds Bev, "is that when I haven't been flying much, for whatever reason, I find myself getting tired, cranky, impatient, and entirely too intense. Then someone will say, 'You need to go flying.' They're right. Amazing how just an hour or even less in the air can change my whole mental state. The airplane is truly a necessity in my life, my tranquilizer, so to speak."

Get a New Interest

Ever tried belly dancing? Lena Mandelis, CFP®, from Wellesley, Massachusetts, does it every chance she gets. When something exciting happens in her office, it's not unusual to see Lena doing the shimmy for her associate! In fact, taking belly-dancing lessons is practically a requirement for her staff at Mandelis & Associates. "I find it gets me out of my head and back into the rest of my body. It allows me to connect with my spiritual self. Every woman should experience it!" she claims.

"My business partner started playing the piano," relates Dennis Means, CFP®, with Financial Services Network, Inc. in Denver, Colorado. "One night, we were at his house for a dinner party, and he sat down and began to play. I had taken lessons as a child way back in the dark ages, and had remembered that I actually liked it as a kid and had quit when it wasn't 'cool' to play the piano. That night at my partner's house brought back the desire to play again. I ended up buying a used piano, just to see if I would like it. I started taking lessons. It is one of the most relaxing things that I do. I can sit down and play for two hours, and it doesn't even seem like a moment. I get totally engrossed in it. It causes me to forget everything except the focus on playing a particular piece. It is really fun and enjoyable. I am far from concert quality yet, but I expect in about thirty days, you will be able to schedule to hear me play as I begin to tour the country. Yeah, right," He laughs. (Knowing Dennis, it wouldn't surprise me in the least!)

"Five years before our twenty-fifth wedding anniversary, my husband and I started planning for a trip to Italy," enthuses Cynthia S. Myers, in Sacramento, California, who writes a column entitled "Myers on Money" for her local newspaper. "We researched the Renaissance and took Italian lessons. We thoroughly enmeshed ourselves in Italian culture and had an incredible time doing it. It's how I do everything! I make it all a part of my life."

A shy young woman, Cynthia took voice lessons in the early 80s to help build her confidence. She ran from her first audition, petrified. But performing at Senior Citizen Centers helped her gain self-assurance and led to participation in community theatre.

"One day," she recalls, "a client in her late 60s came into the office really soured on life. We started talking and she let slip that she had always wanted to sing. I invited her to come with me to a community musical theatre audition, and she won the part. It changed her life! She's still acting," Cynthia laughs, "but I'm not. I'm too busy with my Italian lessons!"

Get Outside of Yourself

"I boss people around with a hammer in my hand," jokes Kathleen Parks, CFP®, with Greenbrier Capital Management. "Working with Habitat for Humanity has taught me new skills. I can build a house!

"In 1995, when we moved to Tennessee, my husband and I wanted to do something together for the community," she says. "We knew no one in Knoxville. I had just left my job as treasurer for a medical consulting firm and hadn't started my financial planning practice yet." Kathy picked up the phone book and looked for volunteer organizations. "It's consumed us," she said, of their work building homes for those in need. "We're together two Saturdays a month, managing crews on construction sites!"

When she first contacted Habitat for Humanity, they asked her to teach a budgeting class. That led to development of an entire curriculum for the other teachers on simple skills such as balancing a checkbook and making a spending plan. Kathy's involvement has extended from teaching budgeting classes to serving as president of the Knoxville Habitat Board.

"What we do for a client is so cerebral," she says. "It's mentally and emotionally draining. Habitat construction is physical. When Im directing a crew of eight or ten volunteers to raise a 28' gable that weighs a few hundred pounds, I'm really concerned about setting it on the wall safely and not dropping it on somebody! This kind of focused activity gives me a mental rest from the hundreds of details swirling around in my head. I come away from the experience physically exhausted, mentally refreshed, and spiritually exhilarated!"

Get Your Priorities Straight[181]

"I sat down one day and did a little arithmetic. The average person lives about seventy-five years. I know, some live more and some live less, but on average, folks live about seventy-five years.

"Now then, I multiplied 75 times 52 and I came up with 3900, which is the number of Saturdays that the average person has in their entire lifetime. It took me until I was 55 years old to think about all this in any detail, and by that time I had lived through over 2800 Saturdays. I got to thinking that if I lived to be 75, I only had about a thousand of them left to enjoy. So I went to a toy store and bought every single marble they had. I ended up having to visit three toy stores to round up 1000 marbles. I took them home and put them inside of a large, clear plastic container right here in my workshop next to the radio. Every Saturday since then, I have taken one marble out and thrown it away.

"I found that by watching the marbles diminish, I focused more on the really important things in life. There is nothing like watching your time here on this earth run out to help get your priorities straight.

"Now let me tell you one last thing before I sign-off with you and take my lovely wife out for breakfast. This morning, I took the very last marble out of the container. I figure if I make it until next Saturday, then I have been given a little extra time. And the one thing we can all use is a little more time."

---

[181] From a story passed around from time to time on the Internet. Author Unknown

Appendices

Who would have thought this was the hard part? I began with the desire to put everything there is to know about financial planning into the Appendix but finally came to my senses and realized everything is already out there. Throughout this book, there are links to much of what you need to know about entering the financial planning profession.

If you're going to be a Financial Planner, you'd better know how to navigate the Internet and research on your own. The Financial Planning Association[182] or the CFP Board of Standards[183] website will get you started.

In lieu of a normal appendix, which I initially thought should include samples of Form ADV, the CFP Board's Annual Report, extensive data gathering forms, and completed financial plans, I've come up with a very short list. I suggest a few books and a couple of other things you won't easily find without asking.

If you're looking for more stuff, like copies of engagement agreements and business plans, post a note on the Financial Planning Discussion Boards at http://www.financial-planning.com/forums/. Simply ask.

Appendix A: "Sensitive Financial Services" by Frank Sisco, CPA, PFS

Appendix B: Recommended Reading

Appendix C: Complimentary Interview Form for Prospective Clients

Appendix D: Cambridge E&O Insurance Application and Checklist

Appendix E: Setting Up Shop Shopping List

Appendix F: NexGen

Appendix G: Your Entry Level into the Financial Planning Profession

---

[182] http://www.fpanet.org
[183] http://www.cfp.net/

Sensitive Financial Services

By Frank Sisco, CPA, PFS

An article about the new "sensitive" approach to personal financial services.

Can my financial planner and advisor truly help me get what I really want? Is "sensitive" financial services the next big thing or just another sales gimmick in different clothing?

It seems like it came out of the blue, but the "sensitive" approach to personal financial services has been boiling under the surface for several years. It now has exploded on the scene to be perhaps the most radical change in financial services since personal financial planning became a legitimate profession two decades ago.

A. What is it and why does it seem like the next big thing?

1. "Sensitive Financial Services" defined

Sensitive Financial Services (also called "SFS") are personal financial advisory and planning services which are provided to clients in a manner that is openly very sensitive to the client's feelings, needs, goals, temperament, past experiences, emotional and family issues, values, philosophies about life and financial context. Compared to traditional services, sensitive financial services have a greater likelihood of satisfying the client's innermost desires, including goals, which are not apparently money-related. Clients often attain a higher level of peace, security, balance and self-expression. In brief, they get happier. Providers of sensitive financial services (also called "sensitive advisors") usually have a never-ending supply of qualified clients. Such advisors recognize that a client's feelings are not necessarily right or wrong, and that these feelings often run a person more than their intellect. The heart often rules the head. Often, the advisor and the client reach an understanding of the feelings-based thinking and behavior, and then progress to either surmount it or work within its context. SFS is not for every client. Also, it takes special temperament, skills and experience to be a sensitive advisor.

2. How are "SFS" different from traditional services

Sensitive financial services ("SFS") have many practices similar to more traditional services including comprehensive financial planning, estate planning, retirement planning, and investment and insurance services, but there are certain key differences. For SFS, unlike predecessors:
- The consumer usually initiates the request for help. Rarely does the provider solicit clients, primarily due to a very high demand.
- All facets of personal finance are considered, not just a narrow band.
- Family relationships are center stage, instead of mere context.
- Time-efficiency and simplification have veto power..
- Money is quantified in order to measure its influence
- Fees and other costs to the consumer are often based on "extra money" realized by the consumer as a result of implementing certain strategies.
- The performance of investments is a factor but plays a minor role.
- Consumers sometimes experience an emotional and psychological breakthrough as a result of the process. Emotion-based obstacles often get overcome.

Art vs. science

Traditional services look more like science. The recommendations from the advisor often are universal and applied in a wholesale fashion. Input from other advisors is rare. The advisor usually pushes strategies on the client. The process is businesslike and detached; something necessary which appeals to the mind.

Sensitive services look more like art. The recommendations from the sensitive advisor often are very personalized and applied to one unique client. Recommended strategies vary greatly from client to client, even those with what appear to be similar characteristics. Other advisors are often consulted. The advisor and client work together in a joint effort. The process is enjoyed by the clients, lifts the spirits, feels good, and appeals to the heart and soul, as well as the mind.

3. Here are some examples of why Sensitive Financial Services eliminates problems often associated with traditional services.

1. A sensitive advisor probes deeply when a client has significant concerns about safety and security, and will develop an investment allocation, which is truly more stable and contains a larger amount of principal-assured investments, like bonds or principal-protected equity investments.

2. When the advisor is very sensitive to a client's desire to remain in control, the advisor will often suggest an estate plan whereby a smaller amount of their estate is given away during their lifetime, even though the future estate taxes might be quite substantial.

3. In cases when the client is not easily trusting, the sensitive advisor builds trust gradually, implementing strategies in stages with a high level of disclosure so that the client always feels in control and understood.

4. For a client who feels a great weight of responsibility for their elderly parents, a sensitive advisor could empower the client to get siblings motivated to all share the expenses of long-term care policies, which ordinarily might be shunned due to limited resources of the parents.

5. A sensitive advisor recognizes when a client has limited financial knowledge and then creates simpler strategies even if they result in less financial gain, and the advisor spends more time explaining in order to gradually enhance the client's knowledge. Then the advisor builds more complicated strategies as the client's knowledge and comfort level increases, and reviews progress with the client more frequently to help the client understand cause and effect relationships of financial transactions.

6. A client who is obsessive about details and organization is handled by a sensitive advisor much differently than a client who is more laid back. The sensitive advisor will provide more information to support or corroborate strategies, often including very detailed projections of cash flow and investment growth. In many cases, several what-if scenarios are developed. Additionally, the ongoing relationship with the client is usually more hands-on. Sometimes, the high level of client involvement in the details necessitates that the framework be established at a simpler level at the outset to keep advisory time and fees to a minimum.

7. A sensitive advisor recognizes when a client is driven to be efficient with time and with money. The advisor should continually check with the client on ways to streamline financial affairs and to streamline the advisor's services. Sometimes, a client will forsake many thousands of dollars in potential extra money from a complicated strategy because it will take too much time or fees to implement, even if a significant net benefit. The sensitive advisor must recognize these situations and handle them with the client, either overcoming concerns through open discussions or not proceeding at the client's request.

B. What caused Sensitive Services to come into vogue?

The most significant developments and the related trends leading to the emergence of Sensitive Services are the following:

1. Stultifying information

Computerization and the Internet have bestowed wondrous gifts on us. We can be more efficient with mundane tasks and spend the saved time on more humanistic and spiritual endeavors. However, too often we fill our time with other mundane tasks and leisure activities, which leave us unsatisfied. But for sure, the easy access to so much information, through a search engine on the Web or by clicking away at the TV remote device, or the scan button on our car radio, we do not get more secure but less so. In fact, we get frazzled and fried. It is tougher to make a decision because we feel guilty if we do not check at least five sources where one was fine in the good old days. And to save $20, we will go to extremes often spending hours. Our trust of specialists is reduced because we trivialize the importance of the knowledge they have, since a search engine like Google gives us hundred times as much for free, and at three in the morning if we want.

The information revolution has brought great benefits, but for us individuals seeking financial well-being, it has only confused matters. Financial advisors have gotten carried away with the info explosion too. If you have stock options to sell, the typical advisor will recommend running the numbers with tax impacts 10 ways to Sunday. If you are thinking about evaluating your investments' performance and voice it to a caring financial advisor, then before you know it you are knee deep in Morningstar mutual funds and stock reports, prospectuses, mounds of data on alternative investments such as 17 different money managers, news articles from far-out mags, etc. We've all got caught up in the info bubble, which is now bursting.

2. Stressed-out baby-boomers

For an 18-year- old in the Summer of '67, like me, the summer of love was exhilarating and the future was rich with promise. Let's face it boomers, most of us still haven't found what we're looking for. Those of us who had kids later, now have teenagers who are driving us crazy with their rebellious attitudes and blatant contempt for authority, namely us, with no let up in sight. Do the 2 million kids on prescription antidepressants like Ritalin really have Attention Deficit Disorder or do parents and children find drugs the only path to cope. Those baby boomers with children in college are up to their eyeballs in education expenses, often paying with home-equity funds. Those boomers with children out of college are sometimes supplementing their children's income or still providing them with a place to sleep. Making matters worse for many baby-boomers, also called the Sandwich Generation, is that there are parents and sometimes grandparents needing help in their retirement years. Who cares if you can afford a pleasure craft because there just is not an hour to spare to even take it out into the harbor! And the 3-day get-away weekends just do not do enough to expunge the stress.

3. Prolonged lives and their meaning

There is a growing trend of people seeking more meaning and spirituality in their lives. One causative factor is a greater awareness of the preciousness of life and to live it as fully as possible now. We have been seeing people around us live into their 90s and 100s. Some age gracefully, some with major medical problems, and some kept alive artificially. Also, thanks to the shrinking world and globalization of media, we are reminded of lives cut short around the world due to disease, poverty, war, and natural catastrophe. Barraged continually by these images and messages, we cannot help but believe it is important to treat life as quite precious, and to live it fully, and live it now. We are driven to live it fully because we may live to 120, God willing, and who wants to be stuck in a dead-end job for the next 70 years. Also, we want to live fully because we may die next year and what a shame to have wasted so much time not doing what had always been our passion.

Another reason for the additional emphasis on life's meaning and importance is that the idealistic generation of the 1960s, the baby boomers, are now in middle age and have the resources, sheer numbers, and influence that can shape the world. With this power comes a feeling of responsibility to do meaningful things. The men's weekend retreat I attended last January was emblematic of this trend. Forty men, most in their forties and fifties, in a mutual quest for truth, shared life stories with each other, openly, and often quite emotionally.

4. Feminization of money

Women have become, if they were not already, the main financial decision maker. It is true that the man might open the discount brokerage online trading account, but it is often the woman who calls the shots on major purchases like cars, homes, home improvements, retirement plan investments, which college for the child, etc. In the last 30 years, women have taken a much greater role in family financial planning. In addition, women on average live much longer than men, and women head up more single-parent families and thus are forced into being the decision makers. This may account for the fact that many financial advisors, myself included, serve more women than men. In divorced or separated situations, women have had to retool, become better income earners, and be more diligent in getting the estranged husband to pay his share. Watch 50 television commercials and skim through 10 general interest magazines and newspapers and you will see who are being appealed to - it's the women. In my financial planning sessions with couples over the years, I find women participate much more actively and often contribute the greatest insights.

5. The individual is better than the group

Hurray for the entrepreneur! So many deca-millionaires and billionaires have been created by the entrepreneurial boom and by the internet revolution, giving more ammunition to the argument that true innovation comes from small packages not big. As the individual start-up man or woman takes their risks and are successful, more people join the crowd and shun the status quo, and then big emulates small and the related benefits for flexibility and growth. However this sometimes leads to an unfortunate bubble but for now seems to lead to greater prosperity for all. This focus on the individual has been brewing for decades and not just in the business arena. Positive developments in the movements for more equal rights for races, religions, genders and nationalities have fostered a greater appreciation for the individual, no matter how different from the group. In fact, many firms now seek out unique individuals because of the greater insights, which a diverse group often brings to the mix. Many years ago the slogan was to "Adapt or perish" and now more and more it is "Viva la difference!"

C. Who are the Sensitive Advisors?

1. Personal

You cannot find Sensitive Advisors in planning departments of the leading wirehouse brokerage firms, nor in separate kiosks at the neighborhood bank. You will not find ads for seminars in the papers nor will you get an invitation in the mail. The mutual fund companies will not be mailing you a Sensitive Financial Services Compact disk or tout the best website to do Sensitive Financial Services online. Why not? Because SFS cannot be done efficiently by large organizations. It takes an individual who has at least most of the 12 traits listed below, and those individuals are usually not working for such large organizations. They usually work on their own or in very small groups, sometimes partnerships and sometimes associations.

2. Caring vs. knowing

You've heard the expression "People don't really care how much you know, but they really know how much you care." For us in the financial services industry, if we are to maintain the trust of clients we already have, and gain the trust of new clients, we must pay more attention to how much we care versus how much we know. If we do not genuinely care, we should find other work, and quickly before we do damage. If we do genuinely care, we need to continually demonstrate it by providing great service tailored to the particular client. We must see the financial planning and advisory function as a process of distilling the enormous array of products and services into a manageable set which relates to the client's unique situation and then keep shaping it as the client changes in the ever-changing world around them. Wherever we lack skills, we must get them or network with others who do have them. We are more than change agents, helping clients cope with change. We are also change portals - channels through which the clients can see their future and step into it.

3. Profile of the sensitive advisor
The people getting the most recognition as Sensitive Advisors seem to fit the following profile:
1. Caring.
1. Experienced in several facets of financial services (e.g. was a stock broker and insurance agent, was a full-time CPA or attorney or start-up incubator manager with a yen for personal financial services) and experienced in several facets of other industries, providing sharp financial acumen, learned in the trenches where the knowledge sticks.
2. Passionate about serving people as individuals.
3. Female or male with a keen awareness of female aspirations and attitudes and comfortable in female company as well as in male company.
4. Seasoned with life experiences to draw from. Age-wise, this often means 45 or older.
5. Successful financially in the overall, but with several failures, which led to greater appreciation for risk and understanding of complexities.
6. Very creative and innovative, often bringing new perspectives to the issues.
7. Networked well, knowing many people she can call on to get their knowledge and opinions.
8. Impatient with bureaucracy but tolerant of it until changed.
9. Glass half-full vs. half-empty.
10. Excellent at communication and spurring discussions of important issues.
11. Solid citizen with good character and community-minded.
12. Leadership strengths to be a quarterback, marshaling the services of other professionals.

D. What are the attributes of sensitivity?

Research shows that decision-making about financial services has many aspects in common with decision-making about other endeavors and activities in life. Thus, if the provider of financial services is sensitive to these attributes, and tailors financial services and products accordingly, then there is a much greater likelihood that they will indeed meet with success and that the client will benefit.

These are the 11 key attributes of sensitivity of clients, which impact significantly on SFS:
1. Secure and safe
2. Free and not burdened or controlled
3. Not left out and in-the-know
4. Not taken advantage of
5. Understood
6. Respected as an individual
7. Efficient
8. Responsible and not too risky
9. Young at heart, fresh, innovative
10. Successful financially and successful life-wise
11. Loving, harmonious, spiritual, and not controversial

All clients have these attributes, but the prioritization greatly differs with each individual and is impacted very differently by the scores of aspects of financial services. For example, one client might feel she is being responsible by saving 20% of her salary for her 12-year-old daughter's future college education by investing in a mutual fund of large capitalization stocks, whereas another client would feel responsible only if the money was invested in bank certificates deposit. Because empirical evidence about market volatility could be interpreted to support either view, it is important for the advisor to appreciate the client perceptions and help shape them into an actionable plan in line with client feelings. Another example is that one client might feel he is more loving and considerate about his children by setting aside money into irrevocable trusts for their benefit so that future estate taxes could be reduced and that more money will be available for them. Another client might see the situation completely differently and believe the children should not get large inheritances, which might spoil them and cause them to be less high-achieving and entrepreneurial in their lives.

The Sensitive Advisor not only must be mindful of these attributes as they show up in their clients but also be mindful of how the advisor's attributes show up for the client, affecting the process. Often the greater the alignment of attributes, the greater the success of the relationship.

E. The process of Sensitive Financial Services

1. The main phases are simple:
1. First contact is through a referral from the prospect to the sensitive advisor
2. Setting the context
3. Building rapport and developing understanding
4. Identifying real needs and goals
5. Creation of financial strategies, holistically and sensitively
6. Implementation of key strategies
7. Follow-up, empowerment, referral

For each phase, the sensitive advisor gathers information about the client's 11 sensitivity attributes, and what influences them most. Completing specially-designed questionnaires is one way to get information about the attributes and their ranking of importance for the client. Throughout the process, another important way for the advisor and the client to communicate is through the telling of stories and of their views about matters of the day, always protecting the confidentiality and anonymity of the parties involved. The advisor should tell stories of cases where the client's lives were impacted significantly and how it happened. The client should tell stories about their own lives, successes and failures, and stories about the lives of others they respect and emulate and of those who they do not.

2. Details about each phase

1. The first contact is through a referral from the prospect to the provider
Providers of Sensitive Financial Services make it a practice not to actively solicit new business through conventional means of seminars, mailings, radio, internet, letter-writing or calling. Instead, such providers rely on satisfied clients to spread the word of their satisfaction with SFS to their family, friends, business associates etc. who will then call or write to the providers if interested. In this way, the providers can focus on doing their work rather than marketing which is really unnecessary due to the very high success rate of converting an interested prospect to a paying client, due to the referral basis.

2. Setting the context

At the outset, there must be frank discussions between clients and providers about the expectations, steps in the process, time and cost considerations, reasonable short-term and long-term goals. Here are examples of the detailed steps:

a. Family tree - Clients and advisors complete this chart together, discussing relationships, the financial resources of family members, the expectations of responsibilities, the quirks as well as successes of family members, etc. As the chart is built, the uniqueness of the client's situation becomes apparent. Many financial strategies are identified during this step. Often the conversations cross into the other areas mentioned below. The advisor is mainly a listener, asking open-ended questions to trigger deeper discussions. (e.g. Tell me about how your father with a limited income was able to provide for you and your siblings and pay for all your education through college. How did your mother or your father approach big money decisions?)

b. Explore past - Many clients have strong views about certain money issues as a result of past experiences (e.g. lost money in a business, gambling problem of a relative, cousin who hit it rich with an IPO, etc.). Discussing the past helps everyone see what is driving the present and helps distinguish what is real and what is drama, and what is steadfast and what is changeable.

c. Map future - Discussions of the future need to be as visual and specific as possible. For a vibrant 40-year-old successful English professor, writing and publishing short stories during retirement is a more realistic goal than just playing golf. If so, perhaps a small income can be assumed during retirement that augments investment income and social security.

d. Focus on key strategies - Establish what is most important. Develop a list of the 4 or 5 essential issues to resolve, and discuss tentatively sample strategies to deal with these issues, evaluating sensitivity attributes.

e. Discuss key elements of the process - There must be a clear discussion of fees (and the type of fee structure such as value-based fees), the steps to gather information (including completion of various forms and questionnaires, schedules of expenses, assets and cash flow), the methods of reporting results, the use of computers and the internet, the advisor's network of associates and clients and the client's network of other advisors such as attorney, insurance agent, investment broker and accountant.

3. Building rapport and developing understanding

If there is not chemistry, mutual respect and a clear appreciation and trust of each other after the first meeting, it is strongly suggested that the advisor and client should openly discuss this matter, and if there is not resolution immediately, then the process should not go forward, and the advisor should not accept the engagement. If the process does move forward, it is important for both the advisor and the client to take steps to bolster the rapport and understanding, such as additional meetings, phone calls and e-mails, clarifying discussions, sharing of stories, and attending certain dinners or events together. For example, the way a client reacts to a waitress serving her during a dinner can speak volumes about the client's consideration of others, expectations, self-centeredness, etc. Likewise, the client should note that an advisor who knows no one at a professional gathering is probably not well networked, and this can spell limitations of financial strategies. The process is helped when the advisor and the client take part in conferences (e.g. conference phone calls) with other advisors such as CPAs, attorneys, insurance agents, etc. and with other family members. Of course, attending events such as plays, movies, sports, etc. can further the relationship; however these events should not be too frequent which could cause a blurring of the client/advisor relationship and a fostering of a relationship that is too cozy and comfortable, making it difficult for either party to stand ground when needed.

Because sensitive advisors usually get more involved with more emotional and psychological aspects of a client's life, there are often more matters for which a client requests the sensitive advisor's help. Sensitive advisors must be careful not to get so involved as to taint the advisor's objectivity or render the client over-reliant.

4. Identifying real needs and goals

It is one thing for a client to express a goal like retiring at age 60. It is another thing to delve deeper to find out why at age 60, what is there planned after age 60, will there be sufficient resources to make it happen, what will the spouse be doing, does the client have hobbies or other interests to occupy time, etc. Often it is important to prepare a detailed projection of cash flows and investment growth (e.g. using electronic spreadsheets going out many years) in order to test and refine the goals. Looking ahead to identify other events that might impact the goals is an important step in the process. For example, children may be getting married, parents might die or get ill in advanced years, possibly leading to more or less money, income might not grow as quickly, a mortgage might get paid off, etc. Once the needs and goals are discussed, evaluate them in terms of the 11 sensitivity attributes, and refine them again. For example, a client who wants to be in control might not really be able to handle emotionally the downsizing of a house and move into a retirement community.

5. Creation of financial strategies, holistically and sensitively

The sensitive advisor must have the skills and experience to survey the information obtained in a holistic manner and then create the best few financial strategies which can help the client achieve their goals and satisfy their needs. The advisor must be sensitive to the client's attributes in developing the strategies. For example if the client is not very analytical and prefers broad concepts, the advisor should not inundate the client with detailed analysis but rather summarize it clearly for the client, perhaps not even sharing the analytical methods used, whereas for another client who might like analysis, the advisor might walk through all the analytical steps, sharpening the strategy with the client's input. If the client is loath to spending current cash flow on insurance like long-term care insurance, the advisor might propose that the client pay premiums by using the build-up within tax-deferred annuities, which are in excess of future needs. This could save future estate taxes and also future income taxes, by paying taxes at the present income tax bracket rather than the beneficiary such as a high-earning adult child paying taxes at a much higher rate.

As part of the creation process, the advisor should review all typical strategies, decide which ones are the most worthwhile and then determine ways to creatively combine them or enhance them. The advisor should refer to manuals and checklists for traditional strategies, supplemented by strategies discussed in publications and the media. The advisor should also use financial websites and search engines to explore potential strategies.

The advisor should look for opportunities to simplify the client's life, and sometimes zero-basing in this regard helps. For example, let's suppose that stagnant low salary income is interfering with the client's ability to save for retirement. Instead of recommending that she drastically cut personal expenses which could be disempowering, the sensitive advisor might suggest that the client should seriously consider her own business, using some of her invested money for start-up capital, assuming the risks when reviewed are not significant (e.g. the client has very good skills, great network of potential customers, solid business plan, etc.).

The advisor should request colleagues to review the basic information and findings to see if additional strategies can be created. Each strategy should be evaluated in terms of the client's sensitivity attributes, and if helpful ranked from 1 to 5 on a grid.

6. Implementation of key strategies

The advisor's role in the implementation should depend not only on the advisor's skills, licenses and powers, but also should depend on the client's sensitivity attributes. For example, an advisor who can easily implement investment allocation recommendations by purchasing and selling securities should not do so if the client is the type of person to question the advisor's objectivity even if the advisor is very objective in reality. Also, the advisor must be sensitive that some clients want to have a very involved role in implementing strategies and using their existing network as much as possible, while other clients may want one person, the advisor, to be responsible for everything. Of course, other key areas of sensitivity involve the matter of time (e.g. implement all strategies right away, or do gradually) and money (e.g. each client will view the advisor's compensation, the amount and type, differently). In some cases, the advisor might be able to reshape the client's views and feelings, but usually not. Thus, the advisor is often better off identifying the sensitivities and adjusting her ways of doing business, or else run the risk of a client being dissatisfied over one point, spoiling the entire batch.

7. Follow-up, empowerment, referral

Client relationships can be lifelong with the right follow-up, which can keep the client empowered to continue the improvement of their financial health and attainment of goals and objectives. Look again at the 11 attributes of sensitivity. Efficient cost-conscious self-starting clients will probably want an expeditious schedule of follow-up, perhaps quick reports and discussions on a semi-annual basis. Other clients who want to be more in control of the information and perhaps are less trusting of the overall plan will want more frequent follow-up, and perhaps in greater depth. Those clients who closely intertwine life and money may desire the advisor's involvement in many endeavors and events throughout the year, planning often to make the life event as rich and meaningful as possible. For example, a client evaluating the purchase of a new house may involve the advisor not only to advise on lending and tax implications but also on the other implications on one's life (e.g. on family, on cash flow, on school selection, on future needs) of buying an expensive home requiring high maintenance situated far from one's employment.

Finally, some clients will easily refer friends, associates and relatives to the advisor, and other clients will shun such referrals, often having little to do with the degree of excellence of the advisor's services and more to do with the client's feelings and attributes. Yet, there will usually be many more referrals when an advisor uses the sensitive approach to financial services. It is more likely that the feelings that might have been obstacles to a referral get a chance to be seen by both the client and advisor, addressed by them in an ever-growing mutually-respectful relationship that is often seen as emblematic of each other's life mission, which is to grow as a good person, serving others to the benefit of all. The client gets an opportunity to serve the advisor by making a referral, and the referred person becomes an eager open new client for the advisor to continue his or her mission to serve, and to serve in a sensitive manner.

F. Conclusion

Sensitive personal financial services represents a quickly-growing trend, which often results in services which are better suited to the client, and lead to greater fulfillment for the advisor. The trend is in harmony with societal trends of individualism, diversity appreciation, and emphasis on life's more important issues including self-actualization, love and inner peace.

For more information, contact Frank Sisco at 914.740.4422

Appendix B: Suggested Reading

Getting Started:

Financial Planning - The Next Step: A Practical Approach to Merging Your Clients' Money with Their Lives by Roy T. Diliberto, CFP®, FPA Press, 2006, Paperback 198 pages ($35.00)

Fee-Only Financial Planning by John E. Sestina, CFP®, ChFC, John Wiley & Sons, Inc., 2001, Hardcover 235 pages ($49.95)

Getting Started as a Financial Planner by Jeffrey H. Rattiner, Bloomberg Press, July 2000, Hardcover 304 pages ($34.95)

Getting Started in Financial Consulting by Edward J. Stone, John Wiley & Sons, March 2000, Paperback 304 pages ($18.95)

How to Become A Successful Financial Consultant by Jim H. Ainsworth, John Wiley & Sons, January, 1997, Hardcover 221 pages ($29.95)

Practice Management:

Run It like a Business: Top Financial Planners Weigh in on Practice Management by Richard J. Koreto, Dearborn Trade Publishing, 2004, Hardcover 236 pages ($35)

In Search of the Perfect Model: the Distinctive Business Strategies of Leading Financial Planners by Mary Rowland, Bloomberg Press, January 2004, Hardcover 233 pages ($50)

The Cutting Edge in Financial Services by Bob Veres, The National Underwriter Company, 2003, Paperback 320 pages ($39.99)

Virtual-Office Tools for a High-Margin Practice: How Client-Centered Financial Advisers Can Cut Paperwork, Overhead, and Wasted Hours by David J. Drucker and Joel P. Bruckenstein, Bloomberg Press, October 2002, Paperback 249 pages ($50)

Rattiner's Financial Planning Bible: The Advisor's Advisor by Jeffrey H. Rattiner, John Wiley & Sons, August 2002, Hardcover 304 pages ($34.95)

Your Clients for Life: The Definitive Guide to Becoming a Successful Financial Life Planner by Mitch Anthony, Barry LeValley, Carol Anderson, Dearborn Trade Publishing, April 2002, Hardcover 272 pages ($35)

Tools and Templates for Your Practice by Deena B. Katz, Bloomberg Press, 2001, Softcover + CD-ROM 296 pages ($50)

Keeping Clients for Life by Karen Caplin Altfest, John Wiley & Sons, April 2001, Hardcover 240 pages ($49.95)

Getting Clients Keeping Clients: he Essential Guide for Tomorrow's Financial Advisor by Dan Richards, John Wiley & Sons, April 2000, Hardcover 400 pages, ($59.95)

Deena Katz on Practice Management for Financial Advisers, Planners, and Wealth Managers by Deena B. Katz and Ross Levin, Bloomberg Press, September, 1999, Hardcover 308 pages ($50)

Protecting Your Practice by Katherine Vessenes, Bloomberg Press, October 1997, Hardcover 491 pages ($50)

Marketing:

Garrett's Guide to Financial Planning: How to Capture the Middle Market and Increase your Profits! By Sheryl Garrett, National Underwriter, October 2002, Softcover + CD-ROM ($39.99)

Building a World-Class Financial Services Business: How to Transform Your Sales Practice into a Company Worth Millions by Don Schreiber, Jr., Dearborn Trade Publishing, July 2001, Hardcover 304 pages ($40)

The Personal Branding Phenomenon by Peter Montoya, Tim Vandehey, Paul Viti, Peter Montoya & Tim Vandehey, April 2002, Hardcover 235 pages ($24.95)

Storyselling for Financial Advisors: How Top Producers Sell by Scott West and Mitch Anthony, Dearborn Trade Publishing, June 2000, Hardcover 246 pages ($30)

High Probability Selling by Jacques Werth and Nicholas E. Ruben, ABBA Publishing Company, http://www.highprobsell.com, 2000, Paperback 178 pages ($19.95)

Effort-Less Marketing for Financial Advisors by Steve Moeller, American Business Visions, October 1999, Paperback 395 pages ($44.95)

Get Media Smart! By Lisbeth Wiley Chapman, Ink & Air, http://www.inkair.com, 1998, Paperback 67 pages + 50-minute Tape ($49.95)

Selling the Invisible: A Field Guide to Modern Marketing by Harry Beckwith, Warner Books, 1997, Hardcover 252 pages ($19.95)

The Excellent Investment Advisor by Nick Murray, The Nick Murray Company, Inc., November 1996, ($42.50)

Values Based Selling: The Art of Building High-Trust Client Relationships by Bill Bachrach, Bachrach & Associates, May 1996, Hardcover 368 pages ($34.95)

Business and Personal Development:

The One Thing…You Need to Do by "D" Shannon and David Drucker, The Financial Advisor Literary Guild LLC, 2005, Hardcover 230 pages ($39.95)

Successful Business Planning in 30 Days by Peter J. Patsula, Patsula Media www.businessplan30days.com, 2002, Paperback 212 pages ($19.95)

The One Page Business Plan[SM] by Jim Horan, The One Page Business Plan Company, 1998, Paperback 97 pages ($19.95)

The E-Myth Revisited: Why Most Small Businesses Don't Work and What to Do About It by Michael E. Gerber, Harperbusiness, Updated Edition April 1995, Paperback 288 pages ($16.00)

The 7 Habits of Highly Effective People: Powerful Lessons in Personal Change by Stephen R. Covey, Fireside, Reprint Edition August 1990, Paperback 360 pages ($14.00)

What Consumers are Reading:

Conscious Finance: Uncover Your Hidden Money Beliefs and Transform the Role of Money in Your Life by Rick Kahler, CFP[®] and Kathleen Fox, FoxCraft, Inc., 2005, Paperback 272 pages ($22.95)

Facing Financial Dysfunction: Why Smart People Do Stupid Things with Money! by Bert Whitehead, MBA, JD, Infinity Publishing.com, August 2002, Paperback 167 pages ($24.95)

Spiritual Finance: The Relationship between Spirituality and Your Financial Planning by Sheldon Zeiger, JD, CFP[®], Cypress Publishing Group, 2002, Paperback, 241 pages ($21.95)

The New Retirementality: Planning Your Life and Living Your Dreams…at Any Age You Want by Mitch Anthony, Dearborn Trade Publishing, April 2001, Paperback, 241 pages ($16.95)

The Right Way to Hire Financial Help by Charles A. Jaffe, The MIT Press, 2nd Edition February 2001, Paperback 352 pages ($19.95)

Get A Life: You Don't Need a Million to Retire Well by Ralph Warner, Nolo, Third Edition August 2000, Paperback 336 pages ($24.95)

Seven Stages of Money Maturity: Understanding the Spirit and Value of Money in Your Life by George Kinder, Dell Publishing, April 2000, Paperback 369 pages ($12.95); also in Hardcover.

Appendix C: Complementary Interview Form for Prospective Clients

> ## *Your Company*

Your Address
Your Phone and Fax
You@youremail.com
visit our website: www.You.com

Complimentary Interview Form

***Appointment Date:*_____ *Time:*_____ *Referred by:*_____**

Your Name:_____ Date of Birth:____/___/____
Employer/Profession:_____ Bus.#:_____

Spouse/Partner's Name:_____ Date of Birth:____/___/____
Employer/Profession: _____ Bus.#:_____

Home Address:_____
Home #: (_____)____-_____ Fax #: (_____)____-_____ Pgr/Mbl: (_____)____-_____
E-mail: _____ What is the best way to contact you:_____

Child: 1._____ Date of Birth: _____/_____/_____
      2._____ Date of Birth: _____/_____/_____
      3._____ Date of Birth: _____/_____/_____

1. How did you hear about Your Company?_____

2. What is your primary motivation for contacting a financial planner at this time?
_____
_____

3. What are your most important financial concerns?
A)_____
B)_____
C)_____

4. What are your most important *non*-financial concerns & objectives right now?
A)_____
B)_____
C)_____

5. Do you or your spouse/partner have any of the following?

Wills_____   Trusts_____   Life Insurance_____   Disability Insurance_____

Family Owned Business_____   Investment Real Estate_____

6. Who makes important investment decisions in your family?_____

7. Have you ever worked with a financial advisor before?   Yes_____   No_____

What was good about that experience?_____
_____

Unsatisfactory?_____
_____

8.What changes do you expect in the future that you wish to plan for?

FamilyObligations: _____
_____

Inheritances:_____

Other: _____

9.What would you like to accomplish through this engagement?_____
_____
_____

10. Is there anything else we need to talk about? _____
_____
_____

Please bring this completed questionnaire along with copies of the following with you for your appointment:

    Cash Flow Statement (list of income and expenses)
    Net Worth Statement (list of assets and liabilities)
    Most recent Income Tax Return

**Summary of
Concerns:**_____

_____

_____

_____

**Summary of benefits we can
provide:**_____

_____

_____

_____

Next step:_____

_____

_____

Appendix D: Markel Cambridge E&O Insurance Application and Checklist

o Essex Insurance Company
o Evanston Insurance Company
P.O. Box 64998
Burlington, VT 05406
(800) 691-1515 Fax (802) 864-9369

APPLICATION FOR FINANCIAL ADVISORS PROFESSIONAL LIABILITY INSURANCE

☐ NEW ☐ RENEWAL

Please return this page and the following items with your application materials:

☐ Completed, dated and signed application.

☐ Form ADV Part I, unless the Applicant has filed electronically with IARD.
NOTE Part I must be a current and accurate disclosure of the Applicant.

☐ Form ADV Part II and all Schedules, unless the Applicant has filed electronically with IARD.
NOTE Part II must be a current and accurate disclosure of the Applicant.

☐ Sample client contract(s) for each professional service rendered.

☐ A copy of any regulatory audits performed in the last three (3) years and the Applicant's response. Renewal policyholders do not need to include audits previously submitted.

☐ Balance Sheet and Income Statement (unaudited is acceptable).

ATTACHED DETAILS ON A SEPARATE SHEET IF:

☐   Yes answer on Question 6., 7. and 8. Claim(s), Complaint or Proceedings

☐   Yes answer on Question 9. Conflicts of Interest

☐   Yes answer on Question 17.

☐   Yes answer on Question 18. Disclosure Events

☐   Yes answer on Question 22. Public Clients

NEW BUSINESS APPLICANTS ONLY:

☐   If the Applicant wants prior acts coverage and has maintained continuous claims made coverage, attach a Certificate of Insurance for current coverage and a coverage synopsis or a copy of the current declarations, policy and endorsements.

☐   Attachment for Questions 24 (a) and (b).

RETURN THIS PAGE WITH THE APPLICATION TO YOUR INSURANCE BROKER

FP3003-01 12/07

APPLICATION FOR FINANCIAL ADVISORS PROFESSIONAL LIABILITY INSURANCE

Notice: The policy for which application is made applies only to "Claims" first made against the Insured during the "Policy Period" or within sixty days after the expiration of the "Policy Period", unless the Extended Reporting Period is exercised. The limits of liability shall be reduced by "Claims Expenses" and "Claims Expenses" are subject to the deductible.

Full Legal Name of Applicant	
Principal Business Address	

Telephone		Fax	
Email		Web Site	

1. List all employed (W-2) financial advisors. CPA firms should list only those that provide financial planning/investment advisory services. Independent Contractors (1099) are not covered under policy and require separate applications or, if requested, can be added as additional insureds.

Name of All Employed Financial Advisors	Professional Designations	FINRA Number	FPA	NAPFA	Garrett Network	BAM	FI360	Other Associations

2. List the names of any independent contractors (non-employees) giving investment advice on behalf of the Applicant:

   _____

   If None, check here ☐
   Does the Applicant want coverage for the listed independent contractors? .... ☐ Yes ☐ No

3. FORM ADV DISCLOSURES

(a) Is the Applicant's Form ADV Part I as filed and dated on the SEC IARD a current and accurate disclosure of Applicant as of the date of this application? If not SEC IARD filed, provide complete Form ADV Part I in paper format.	☐ Yes ☐ No ☐ Not IARD filed
(b) Is the Applicant's Form ADV Part II including schedules as filed and dated on the SEC IARD a current and accurate disclosure of Applicant as of the date of this application? If not SEC IARD filed, provide complete Form ADV Part II in paper format.	☐ Yes ☐ No ☐ Not IARD filed
(c) Does the Applicant agree to notify the Company of any change to facts presented in the Application between the date of Application and the effective date of coverage?	☐ Yes ☐ No

4. List all Professional Liability Insurance currently carried (e.g. accountants, tax preparation, group broker-dealer, life agent).

Insurer	Limits of Liability	Deductible	Type of Insurance	Policy Period	Retroactive Date

5. REQUESTED LIMITS AND DEDUCTIBLES

PER CLAIM/AGGREGATE LIMITS REQUESTED

☐ $ 100,000/$ 200,000   ☐ $ 1,000,000/$2,000,000
☐ $ 250,000/$500,000   ☐ $ 2,000,000/$2,000,000
☐ $ 500,000/$1,000,000   ☐ Higher Limits: _____
☐ $ 1,000,000/$1,000,000

DEDUCTIBLE REQUESTED

☐ $1,000   ☐ $15,000
☐ $2,500   ☐ $20,000
☐ $5,000   ☐ $25,000
☐ $10,000   ☐ $50,000

THE COMPANY DOES NOT GUARANTEE TO OFFER ANY OF THE ABOVE LIMITS AND/OR DEDUCTIBLES.

6. Has any Professional Liability claim(s), complaint or proceeding been made against the Applicant or any person or organization proposed for this insurance or any predecessor organization? .... ☐ Yes ☐ No
   If Yes, provide details on a separate sheet.

7. Is (are) any person(s) or organization(s) proposed for this insurance aware of any fact, error, omission, circumstance or situation that might provide grounds for any claim under the proposed insurance? .... ☐ Yes ☐ No
   If Yes, provide details on a separate sheet.

FP3003-01 12/07   Page 1 of 5

8. Has the Applicant and/or any of its directors, officers and/or employees, its predecessors, subsidiaries, affiliates, employees and/or any other person or organization proposed for this insurance been involved in or have knowledge of any pending or completed governmental regulatory, investigative or administrative proceedings? ...... ☐ Yes ☐ No
If Yes, provide details on a separate sheet.

9. CONFLICTS OF INTEREST
By attachment provide explanation of any Yes response.

(a) Does the Applicant or any or its partners, officers, directors, employees or associated professionals:

(i) Act as both trustee and advisor to any client?	☐ Yes ☐ No
(ii) Advise clients to invest in any enterprise in which any firm member has more than a 5% ownership interest?	☐ Yes ☐ No
(iii) Advise clients to invest in any enterprise in which another client has more than a 5% ownership interest?	☐ Yes ☐ No
(iv) Act as advisor to an organization in which the Applicant its members or associated persons has more than a 5% ownership interest?	☐ Yes ☐ No

(b) Do any of the Applicant's partners, officers, directors, employees or associated professionals have more than a 5% ownership or act as a director, officer, an employee or act in any position of control for any organization in which clients are solicited to invest? .... ☐ Yes ☐ No

(c) Is any person proposed for insurance under this application a director, an officer, an employee, or in a position of control for any organization or enterprise including all subsidiaries and affiliates which is also an advisory client?
.... ☐ Yes ☐ No

(d) Is the Applicant or any or its partners, officers, directors, employees or associated professionals a CPA?
.... ☐ Yes ☐ No

If, Yes, do any such persons perform attest work/consulting services for any accounting client who is an advisory client? .... ☐ Yes ☐ No

10. Does the Applicant use a Compliance Attorney or Consultant? .... ☐ Yes ☐ No
If Yes, provide the name of such attorney and/or consultant:_____

11. Provide gross annual revenues derived from financial planning, advisory activities, commissions and/or product sales. Do not include professional accounting services revenues unless the Applicant wants coverage for tax preparation.

Year	Annual Total Gross Revenues (100%)	% Fee Only Revenues	% Commission Revenues	No. of Financial Advisors
Last Year _____	$	%	%	
Present Year _____	$	%	%	
Projected for Next Year _____	$	%	%	

12. Provide professional services by approximate percentage. Must equal 100%. Indicate all services provided by the Applicant regardless of whether the revenues are included in Question No. 11.

%	NATURE OF PRACTICE	%	NATURE OF PRACTICE
	Modular/Comprehensive Financial Plan Preparation/Advice		Timing Services
	Divorce Financial Consulting		Tax Preparation
	Discretionary Asset Management (LPOA)		Accounting Services Other Than Tax Preparation
	Non-Discretionary Asset Management (LPOA with Prior Consent)		Third Party Pension Administration
	Asset Monitoring (No Limited Power of Attorney to Direct Trades)		Hourly Advice
	Investment Management Consulting (No LPOA)		Wrap Accounts
	Product Sales Based On Financial Plan		Referral To Third Party Managers
	Product Sales Not Based On Financial Plan		Other:

281

13. As an advisor, does the Applicant provide advice on, recommend or use alternative investments? .... ☐ Yes ☐ No
If Yes, provide the percentage of the Applicant's total practice advice and/or portfolio use that the following alternative investments represent to the total advice and/or assets managed. Do not include investments that are used within a mutual fund.

%	Type Of Investment		%	Type Of Investment
	Private Placements			General or Limited Partnerships
	Hedge Funds/Fund of Hedge Funds			Foreign Securities Excluding ADR's
	Mortgages, mortgage pools, mortgage backed securities			REITS Privately Traded
	Commodity Futures			Promissory Notes
	Unrated Bonds			Tangibles (gold, silver, collectibles, coins, etc.)
	Investment Related Real Estate			Derivative Instruments
	Options Contracts			Other:
	Unregistered Securities			

14. Does the Applicant receive commissions? .... ☐ Yes ☐ No
If Yes, provide a breakdown of total commission income by percent. Must equal 100%

%	Type Of Product		%	Type Of Product
	Mutual Funds			Promissory Notes/Leases/Receivables
	Variable Annuities			Private Placements
	Life/Health/Disability/Accident Sales/Long Term Care			REITS other than REIT Mutual Funds
	Viatical Agreements/Senior Settlements/Life Settlements			General or Limited Partnerships
	Listed Stocks			Unregistered Securities
	Unlisted Stocks			Foreign Securities/ADR'S
	Investment Grade Bonds			Hedge Funds or Fund of Hedge Funds
	Junk Bonds			Options/Futures/Tangibles/CMO's/Derivatives

15. What percentage of the Applicant's revenue is derived from professional entertainers, celebrities, athletes and musicians?_____% If None, check here ☐

16. Does the Applicant provide personal management services (e.g. sports management or bill paying, etc.) to any client?.. ☐ Yes ☐ No

17. (a) Is any advisory client an investment company (mutual fund), REIT, limited partnership or private placement?
.... ☐ Yes ☐ No
(b) If Yes, provide details._____
(c) If No, does the Applicant agree to notify the insurance company within thirty (30) days if the Applicant starts to render advisory services to such a client? .... ☐ Yes ☐ No

18. Has the Applicant or any associated professional ever: Provide details to any question that is answered Yes.

(a) Had a professional license or registration denied, suspended, revoked, nonrenewed or restricted?	☐ Yes ☐ No
(b) Been formally reprimanded by any court, administrative or regulatory agency?	☐ Yes ☐ No
(c) Had a complaint filed with any consumer agency, state securities department, insurance department or the Applicant's broker-dealer, SEC, NASD, or other regulatory agency?	☐ Yes ☐ No
(d) Been audited by the SEC, NASD, any state securities department, or other licensing or regulatory agency? If Yes, provide a copy of the audit letter and the Applicant's response.	☐ Yes ☐ No
(e) Been formally accused of violating any professional association's code of ethics?	☐ Yes ☐ No
(f) Been convicted of a felony?	☐ Yes ☐ No
(g) Been involved in or is aware of any fee disputes including suits?	☐ Yes ☐ No
(h) Ever had a trading error loss in excess of $5,000? If Yes, provide details including dates, amounts and by whom the loss was paid.	☐ Yes ☐ No

19. During the last three (3) years has the Applicant or any affiliate been involved in, or presently considering or contemplating any merger, acquisition, divestiture or significant change in principals?..... ☐ Yes ☐ No
If Yes, provide details._____

20. Does the Applicant direct trades in client's custodial accounts?..................................... ☐ Yes ☐ No
If Yes, complete the following:

(a) Use a written Investment Policy Statement for other than ERISA accounts?	☐ Yes ☐ No	
(b) Have Limited Power of Attorney to direct trades in the client's account? If Yes: please answer:	☐ Yes ☐ No	
☐ The Applicant uses full discretion to trade without prior consent of the client.		
☐ The Applicant uses discretion to trade within an Investment Policy Statement or written parameters.		
☐ The Applicant declines to exercise discretion and obtains prior consent for each and every trade.		
(c) Excluding advisory fees and authorized disbursement to an account with the same registration or the client, does the Applicant have power to withdraw/disburse funds in the account?	☐ Yes ☐ No	
(d) Custodians: ☐ Fidelity ☐ TD Ameritrade ☐ Schwab ☐ Pershing ☐ FISERV ☐ Assetmark ☐ NATC ☐ SSG ☐ Other._____		
(e) Are any assets under management invested in Exchange Trade Funds?	☐ Yes ☐ No	
If Yes, what percentage of: (i) total assets under management are invested in Exchange Traded Funds?_____ % (ii) Exchange Traded Funds are leveraged? _____ %		

ALL APPLICANTS – COMPLETE THE FOLLOWING:

21. Types of Accounts:

TYPES OF ACCOUNTS	Number of Accounts	Market Asset Value	Largest Account Asset Value
Discretionary ERISA Pension/Employee Benefit Plans		$	$
Discretionary All Other Accounts		$	$
Non-Discretionary ERISA Pension/Employee Benefit Plans		$	$
Non-Discretionary All Other Accounts		$	$
Investment Management Consulting Accounts (No Direct Management)		$	$
Referral to Third Party Money Manager Accounts (No Direct Management)		$	$
Total All Accounts		$	$

22. Does the Applicant act as advisor or consultant for any Taft-Hartley, union, or governmental employee benefit plan? .... ☐ Yes ☐ No
If Yes, attach a list of accounts and assets.

23. (a) Number of accounts lost in the last twelve (12) months: _____

(b) Total assets under management for accounts lost in the last twelve (12) months: $_____

(c) Reasons for loss of accounts: _____

NEW BUSINESS APPLICANTS ONLY:

24. (a) Attach a separate sheet briefly describe the Applicant's investment philosophy.

(b) Attach a separate sheet listing the types and percentages of investments used in portfolios.

25. Has any insurer declined, cancelled or nonrenewed any Investment Advisor Professional Liability Insurance or any similar insurance on behalf of any person(s) or organization(s) proposed for this insurance? .... ☐ Yes ☐ No
If Yes, provide details. _____

_____

_____

NOTICE TO THE APPLICANT - PLEASE READ CAREFULLY

No fact, circumstance or situation indicating the probability of a Claim or action for which coverage may be afforded by the proposed insurance is now known by any person(s) or organization(s) proposed for this insurance other than that which is disclosed in this application. It is agreed by all concerned that if there is knowledge of any such fact, circumstance or situation, any Claim subsequently emanating therefrom shall be excluded from coverage under the proposed insurance.

For the purpose of this application, the undersigned authorized agent of the person(s) and organization(s) proposed for this insurance declares that to the best of his/her knowledge and belief, after reasonable inquiry, the statements in this application, the form ADV Parts I and II and in any attachments, are true and complete. Markel Cambridge Alliance or the Company is authorized to make any inquiry in connection with this application. Signing this application does not bind the Company to provide or the Applicant to purchase the insurance.

This application, information submitted with this application and all previous applications and material changes thereto of which Markel Cambridge Alliance receives notice is on file with Markel Cambridge Alliance and the form ADV Parts I and II and is considered physically attached to and part of the policy if issued. Markel Cambridge Alliance and the Company will have relied upon this application, all such attachments and the form ADV Parts I and II in issuing the policy.

If the information in this application, any attachment and the ADV for Part I and II materially changes between the date this application is signed and the effective date of the policy, the applicant will promptly notify Markel Cambridge Alliance, who may modify or withdraw any outstanding quotation or agreement to bind coverage.

The undersigned declares that the person(s) and organization(s) proposed for this insurance understand that:

(i)   the policy for which this application is made applies only to "Claims" first made during the "Policy Period" and reported to the company during the "Policy Period" or within sixty days after the expiration date of the "Policy Period" unless the Extended Reporting Period is exercised. If the Extended Reporting Period is exercised, the policy shall also apply to "Claims" first made during the Extended Reporting Period and reported to the company during the Extended Reporting Period or within sixty days after the expiration of the Extended Reporting Period;

(ii) the limits of liability contained in the policy shall be reduced, and may be completely exhausted by "Claims Expenses" and, in such event, the Company will not be liable for "Claims Expenses" or the amount of any judgment or settlement to the extent that such costs exceed the limits of liability in the policy; and

(iii) "Claims Expenses" shall be applied against the "Deductible".

WARRANTY

I/We warrant to the Company, that I/We understand and accept the notice stated above and that the information contained herein is true and that it shall be the basis of the policy and deemed incorporated therein, should the Company evidence its acceptance of this application by issuance of a policy. I/We authorize the release of claim information from any prior insurer to Markel Cambridge Alliance or the Company, P.O. Box 64998, Burlington, Vermont 05406.

Note: This application is signed by undersigned authorized agent of the Applicant(s) on behalf of the Applicant(s) and its, owners, partners, directors, officers and employees.

Must be signed by the owner, principal, partner, executive officer or equivalent (within 60 days of the proposed effective date).

NOTICE TO APPLICANT: Any person who knowingly files an application for insurance or statement of claim containing any false information, or conceals for the purpose of misleading, information concerning any fact material thereto, commits a fraudulent insurance act, which is a crime and also punishable by civil penalties in certain jurisdictions.

Print Name: _____   Title: _____

Signature: _____   Date: _____

Signing this application does not bind the Company or the Applicant or the underwriter to complete the insurance.

Appendix E: Setting Up Shop Shopping List

	Item	Expected Cost	Actual Cost	Notes
Real Estate				
	Executive Suite			
	Home Office			
	Rent			
	Shared Space			
Registrations				
	ADV Registration			
	Business License			
	Permits			
Education				
	CFP® Course			
	Series Exam Course			
	Testing Fees			
Insurance				
	Casualty			
	Errors & Omissions			
	Service Agreements			
Staff				
	Bookkeeper			
	Clerk			
	Coach			
	Computer Consultant			
	Office Assistant			
	Paraplanner			
Furniture				
	Bookcase			
	Computer Station			
	Conference Table & Chairs			
	Desk			
	Desk Accessories			
	Executive Chair			
	Filing Cabinets			
	Lighting			
	Office Chairs			
	Wall Décor			
	Waste Basket			

	Item	Expected Cost	Actual Cost	Notes
Hardware				
	Computer			
	Desktop			
	Laptop			
	Copier			
	Monitor			
	Overhead Projector			
	PDA			
	Printer			
	Laser			
	Ink Jet			
	Safe			
	Scanner			
	Shredder			
Supplies				
	Binding Machine & Supplies			
	Brief Case			
	Brochure			
	Business Bank Account			
	Business Cards			
	Calculator			
	Card File			
	Computer Disks			
	Copy Paper			
	Desk Organizer			
	File Folders			
	Labels			
	Logo			
	Message Pads			
	Paper Clips			
	Paper Products			
	Paper Trimmer			
	Pens, Markers			
	Postage Scale			
	Printer/Fax Cartridges			
	Reference Books			
	Scissors			
	Staplers			
	Stationary			

	Item	Expected Cost	Actual Cost	Notes
Software				
	Accounting			
	Allocation			
	Analysis			
	Asset Tracking			
	Contact Management			
	Education			
	Financial Planning			
	Office Suite			
	Presentation			
	Regulatory			
	Word Processing			
Telecom				
	Answer Machine/Service			
	Domain Name			
	E-Mail			
	Internet Service Provider			
	Telephone			
	Desktop			
	Extensions			
	Cellular			
	Headset			
	Web Site Design			

Appendix F: NexGen

NexGen Group Information

Vision Statement

"To ensure the transference of wisdom, tradition, and integrity, from the

pioneers of financial planning to the next generation of our profession"

Mission Statement

NexGen is intended to be a community of the next generation of financial planners.
Our main purposes are to:

➢ Support, advise, and encourage one another in our professional advancement.
➢ Promote, foster, and direct programs that aid in passing the baton.
➢ Explore issues common to younger planners and seek means of accentuating the positives and finding resolutions for the negatives.

Full Member Agreement*

I am currently 36 years old or younger, when joining
I will commit at least 5 acts of honoring an industry predecessor each year
I am a CFP® certificant or enrolled in a program
I am a member of FPA

I am employed or seeking employment in a financial planning capacity
I desire to be actively involved in advancing the financial planning profession
I will keep all conversations confidential to this group unless otherwise agreed
I will participate, support, and encourage
I will share my experiences that others may learn from them
I will aid in promoting agreed messages through various outlets

Activities/Resources

Message Board: E-mail acoates@compasswa.com to begin the
enrollment process.
Annual Conferences
Meetings at FPA Conferences and Retreats
Activities with Rat Pack

*Affiliate Membership is available to those not meeting all above qualification criteria on approval of leadership from submission of membership form.

Appendix G:

Your Entry Level into the Financial Planning Profession

by Frank M. Gleberman, CLU, CFP®

Building a successful financial planning practice can take you on differing journeys. They say there are many roads to the top of the mountain, but the view's just the same once you get there. That old bromide may have some veracity, but in our profession, the road you take can actually determine just how far you progress up the pinnacle of success.

You face a number of challenges as you contemplate a career in financial planning:

- How will I be educated?

- How will I be trained?

- Will my supervisor(s) work in the field with me, or do they simply pass along theory in their offices?

- Where will I obtain my prospective clients?

- How will I persuade my prospective clients that I am the one to help them accomplish their financial planning objectives?

- How will I be paid?

- What type of professional image do I wish to project?

- Do I want to be a specialist or a general practitioner?

- Should I be the boss or a member of a firm? Can I be satisfied being a one-person practitioner, be simply a salesperson with a big company, or will I have the opportunity to build a BUSINESS (essentially my own firm) within the framework of whichever company I join?

- Can I afford (and do I have the technical knowledge) to build my own practice right out of the gate?

- Will I be pressured to use my primary company's products, or will I have the flexibility to use products available in the marketplace that may better meet my clients' needs?

. . . and these are only a *few* of the questions buzzing in the heads of those looking at the profession.

Having spent many years on several sides of this subject, I can assure you that a comprehensive set of answers to just the above questions would take up the space of several books. Some years ago, I faced these same challenges. I was an advertising manager who wanted to carve out more independence for myself, earn a more lucrative income, and be able to associate with the type of people who had the same sets of values I possessed. By interviewing a number of financial services companies, I waded through many interviews and was fortunate to ferret out many answers. But as it turned out, not 100% of the correct ones. These notes may help you reach closer to 100%!

As a life insurance agent, I built my beginning clientele from people I knew from advertising and from my sports activities, plus some from my years wandering across campus at the University of Southern California. Referrals, direct mail, cold calls on businesses, and personal observation gained me additional prospects, who turned into clients.

In my second year, referred leads were my main source of new clients, plus people I met in community activities.[184] Some still came from direct mail (one of the "automatics" that talented trainers can get new agents using) and I would still pick office parks, office buildings and retail establishments for cold calls a day or two weekly, for an hour or however long it would take me to give out 20 business cards and get names and phone numbers of some "suspects."

(Let me note that I used most prospecting methods to determine which would produce the best results for ME. I had instilled in my mind the old saying that, "Successful people make a habit of consistently doing the things unsuccessful people are unwilling to do." Another was, "Pleasant results do not always come from pleasant methods." What both old bromides are saying is that one must put some effort into building a business and get in the habit of prospecting until you get to the point of having enough clients that referrals and repeat sales [or in the case of financial planning, recurring fees] provide the cash flow to support you and your business).

"Advancing" to management positions, I took on the responsibility to recruit and train new colleagues, so gained a view of the delivery of financial products and services from a different perspective. My particular life company did not allow those in management to also continue in personal production . . . to me now, that was a mistake. For that company's objectives, of course, a good way to go. But with loyal clients providing income from personal production, one can walk away with a nice security blanket in the event a management opportunity does not work out.

---

[184] A note on belonging to organizations for the purpose of developing a marketplace of future clients: be certain of two cardinal philosophies, (1) Select an organization in which you believe, one that represents values and attracts people for whom you have respect. You may think that you can "operate" in an organization that espouses values different than yours, but that won't be a satisfying experience in the long run. (2) Be certain you're not just a "joiner." Obviously, you need to plan your time in that organization wisely so you don't go broke by spending too many hours working in that organization. But use the hours you have to work hard. Get to be known as a quality individual who does an organization job or two well. The other members of the organization will recognize you as a quality person and that image will burnish your financial planning persona positively. If you get to be known as an opportunist or someone who slips by with a minimum of effort, that will carry over to your professional image, too.

While I enjoyed management and promotions, the time came when some hard decisions had to be made. Not wishing to relocate from a very desirable climate, marvelous set of friends, and a host of avocational interests for other parts of the country caused me to turn down several attractive management positions in other states and return to building my own practice. I kiss the sun-drenched beaches of Southern California, the decks of my Marina del Rey home, the comfort of my country club and my yacht club, the varnish on my sailboat and the amiable oceanfront communities "where everybody knows my name" whenever I think back on making that decision!

Reaching the point where I work because I enjoy it so much and continue to practice even when I no longer need the money has taken me to the level where I spend time giving back to the profession. This has been accomplished through professional organizations (such as the International Association for Financial Planning and The Financial Planning Association, serving both groups as President in Los Angeles County), and also through one of my consulting companies as I coach others in our profession by retainer. A great feeling, indeed.

You know, money is a whole lot like air. If you don't have enough, you panic. If you have enough money, other things in life become more important, such as the personal freedom that has allowed me to travel and sail all over the world for 10 – 15 weeks a year, plus attend a number of financial industry meetings in many countries.

I've also enjoyed participating in community organizations to a substantial degree. Great for giving back to the community for treating me well, in addition to providing a continual new source of prospective clients.

Let me take you through several approaches you may take in evaluating the best entry level for yourself. You may also hear some well-intended advice, as you search and seek advice, to "Find a big life insurance company or wirehouse (stock brokerage) who will give you a lot of training and a beginning salary or draw against commissions. After a year or two (before the forfeiture of any renewal commissions becomes too onerous), head for the exit and set up your own independent practice."

That attitude may have some foundation in fact, but dictates you begin a career built on false premises. If you are going to be above reproach and practice ethics to the highest level as an adviser, why not do it right and above board from the beginning?

Life Insurance Companies

While life insurance is viewed as a hard sell proposition, many life insurance companies have also embraced the planning process for some years. But sales create income, so compensation for most life agents is commission based and requires pretty much the entire first year's premium from the policyholder be used to pay the agent commission and override compensation to that agent's manager or general agent.

The agent earns around 50% in most companies, a bit higher in others. When the policyholder pays the second year renewal premium, 2 to 5% will often be paid to the agent and another percent or so to the manager or the general agent. This process will continue for the balance of the first ten years of the policy being in force with premiums being paid. A good life insurance agent can create 25 to 40% of his or her income coming from renewal commissions, assuming that clients keep those policies in force. Some companies will pay renewal commissions or "service fees" beyond the ten years, so long as you provide ongoing service to those policyholders. Many companies also require a minimum ongoing level of first-year premium production (new sales) to qualify for those payments . . . a fact that is important for you to know.

Many insurance companies will start new agents on a salary for six months or a year, or a draw against future commissions that may last for one, two or even three years . . . so long as the agent is selling enough insurance to create commissions sufficient to validate the salary arrangement.

Getting off to a fast start is obviously important. As they evaluate you for the career, insurance companies are interested in who you know and even more interested in how your friends, family, current business contacts and acquaintances view you. Do they hold you in high regard? Would they be likely to follow advice you provide them if that advice helped them accomplish financial goals and objectives?

Most insurance companies will give you tests to determine your social mobility, your willingness to offer advice even to those who have resistance to that advice, and your likelihood of sticking to a marketing and prospecting schedule on a daily basis. They need to know that you not only have a reasonable number of contacts who will give you the opportunity of presenting a sales talk or doing a fact-finding interview, but that you will continue the process even when two-thirds or more of those folks will not buy anything from you. They also need to know that you will not hesitate to ask for referrals to others.

Some insurance companies have developed investment sales divisions (known as broker dealers) that venture beyond the traditional "guarantees" that have been the hallmark of insurance marketing for generations. Life companies such as MassMutual, New York Life, Prudential, Guardian, Northwestern Mutual, The New England, Metropolitan, AXA, and others are known as career agent companies. Their training programs are recognized as good to excellent but are only as good as the local general agent or manager, who delivers them to new and more seasoned agents.

Other life companies that are geared more to recruiting agents with some prior experience also have broker dealers. Jefferson Pilot, ING and others fit this mold. They rarely offer salaries or draws, but usually pay higher commissions from what they save by not supporting expensive training departments and new agent financing contracts. They are sometimes known as "PPGA" (personal producing general agent) companies.

My view is that The Financial Planning Process[185] is more likely to be part of the overall training process or marketing process of a life insurance company that also maintains an *active* broker dealer. Most life companies will maintain a Broker/Dealer simply to be able to market variable life and annuity products but are limited in providing much beyond a few

---

[185] For a comprehensive look at the steps in The Financial Planning Process, refer to the CFP® Board of Standards at: http://www.cfp.net. Click on "Learn About Financial Planning."

mutual funds in addition to the insurance products. A few life companies grow their Broker/Dealers to include several thousand mutual funds, direct participation products, wrap accounts, more sophisticated forms of investment products, software for comprehensive financial planning activities, and more.

There are always exceptions, of course. A creative local general agent of a career or non-career company may be very talented in building a financial planning organization. If financial planning is your career objective, you will want to interview with two or three career companies and one or two local general agents from non-career companies who include securities in their overall operations.

Do your due diligence. Be sure the Broker/Dealer is for real. Talk to the more experienced agents and ask them penetrating questions. Confirm with them the promises made to you by the recruiter with whom you are interviewing. If you're not allowed to do that, run – don't walk – out the exit.

Wirehouses

Over the years, the big Wall Street brokerage houses have been known as "transaction-oriented" institutions, though many are now moving inexorably into gathering assets under management and charging fees as well as commissions. Some are championing financial planning as a public face, but you'll still want to talk with veterans to see just how far that direction is actually being taken in a particular wirehouse or branch of that wirehouse.

Payouts for a wirehouse will run from 30 to 60% for newer to reasonably experienced associates, with the superstars gaining a larger slice of the dealer concession or commissions earned. While the payout is smaller than in a regional Broker/Dealer, independent Broker/Dealer or some life companies, the services provided *may* be greater. An office or cubicle, phone, percentage of an assistant, research and other services are usually provided by wirehouses for top notch prospective brokers, and that's worth something.

Financial Planning Practices

If your interest is to immediately immerse yourself in The Financial Planning Process, you may well find that associating with a bona fide financial planning firm is a better alternative than a wirehouse or insurance company.

Some writing this section would be inclined to separate this section into "Regional Broker/Dealers" and "Small Financial Planning Practices." With the strong growth of The Financial Planning Process now coursing through the ranks of regional broker dealers, I have combined the two. In fact, there are some individual financial planning practices that have a half billion, a billion dollars or two or more under management, placing them shoulder to shoulder with many regional BDs.

You are more likely to find an entry level opportunity with a regional broker dealer. You would probably not spend as many hours sitting in their training programs as you would at a wirehouse or insurance company. However, the hours in training in most cases should be more concentrated on The Financial Planning Process.

Which ones should you investigate? My recommendation is to contact your local Financial Planning Association chapter to find the Broker/Dealers most active in your community. Contact the FPA at: www.fpanet.org. Some – but not all of the – excellent broker dealers are ING and Jefferson Pilot, noted above, AIG, Mutual Service, LPL and Associated Securities (the latter two require high previous production to consider affiliation). There is a list of Broker/Dealers included on the Financial Planning interactive (FPi) website at www.financial-planning.com.

It is rare for a regional BD to offer salary or draw arrangements. You produce commissions by making a sale or fees by charging hourly rates to your clients or asset-based percentage fees. Sometimes, you may charge a project-based fee. Commissions and fees are paid to the Broker/Dealer and usually labeled as dealer concession. Depending upon the amount of dealer concession you generate, you are generally paid a percentage of that concession ranging from 50 to over 90%. Some Broker/Dealers pay high producers near 100%, those firms making their income by fees from product providers.

If you have the opportunity to interview with a boutique financial planning practice, you may be able to hire on as an apprentice. You won't start out in the mail room like many top entertainment talent agents have done, but you will more likely find yourself as a "processor" than a "creator."

If you have completed the Personal Financial Planner curriculum (PFP) or CERTIFIED FINANCIAL PLANNER™ course of study (CFP®), you may actually begin your employment helping create comprehensive financial plans for review by one of the principals of the firm. If not, you may find yourself involved in a training program ranging from eclectic (examining mutual fund performance, filing, contacting insurance companies for determining cash values and beneficiary designations, helping prepare documents, testing software, etc.) to focused (examining alternative tax treatments of portfolio planning decisions, considering legal alternatives for preparation by legal counsel, meeting with family members of clients to help coordinate their goals and objectives, and more).

Smaller financial planning firm principal(s) may have developed a very well-defined training program for new recruits, or may foster a more relaxed approach and rely on the new colleague gaining education through CFP® studies and similar courses. They may also be in a position to pay a modest salary to new associates in return for carrying out administrative and basic planning functions until they begin generating clients on their own.

Now What?

After a year or two or three with the company with which you begin your career, you may well say, "I am where I will spend the balance of my career. My colleagues are good people. The management of my company is helping me grow my practice. They are worth the percentage of dealer concession I am paying them. The philosophy of this firm is congruent with mine. I like the identity."

Make no mistake, however. The reason you may be successful at this time with your clients is YOU. Certainly, you may find a well-known company name helps you market your services or gives your clients confidence that <u>someone</u> will be in business to help them. Well-funded back room services, technology support, and research capabilities more than make up for a smaller percentage of dealer concession that goes into your pocket.

You may be happy that your firm provides you an attractive office and maybe even the services of an assistant.

On the other hand, you may find that you are earning a substantial amount of fees for your firm, but not receiving a commensurate amount of support. Let's take a look at an actual scenario, a planner generating $260,000 of fee and commission income. Her firm provided an office for her, an assistant and a cubicle for that assistant. She had obtained her CFP® designation, was gaining in her marketing skills, and did not feel she needed the well-known name of her firm to help her gain clients. Most of her business was in managed accounts, so back room services were not critical.

Her payout was 50%, and she would have to rise to $500,000 to qualify for a 60% payout, a larger office, and better company convention.

Her decision was to establish her own office in the same complex where an estate planning attorney with whom she worked was a partner in a law firm. Office space would be $18,000 per year, an assistant/office manager $60,000 per year, and benefits and miscellaneous expenses would cost another $12,000 per year. She would receive a 90% payout from a well-respected regional Broker/Dealer.

Net result: with the change, she would pay $90,000 more annually in expenses, but has $104,000 more under the new arrangement to pay those expenses. She drives five minutes from home rather than thirty-five minutes to her old office. She has calculated that her gross income should rise to at least $400,000 annually within two to three years, which would provide her more than sufficient additional income to hire a junior partner and still take home more money.

She made the move, and she reached $347,000 of gross income after thirteen months, even after taking three weeks of negotiating the move and nearly a full month of vacation four months later. Nicely enough, her original employer (a wirehouse) still receives business from her, as three of their mutual funds are on her regional Broker/Dealer's managed account calendar. She is now negotiating a trial partnership with another established planner who plans to retire in five years. If the process works, the projected gross income in five years will be $1,200,000 <u>after</u> including a three-year buyout of the retiring planner's practice, then jumping to $1,600,000 per year. Not bad!

In Retrospect

I do not represent that the scenario described is always rule of thumb, but it does lay out an exciting opportunity that awaits an energetic practitioner in our profession.

So many men and women settle for the first appealing recruiter's story because they must cement a relationship and get their cash flow started in their new profession. They shortchange themselves by not interviewing with a sufficient number of prospective companies to obtain a more informed perspective.

A good interviewing model should include three or four insurance companies, a like number of wirehouses, two or three regional Broker/Dealers, and at least two boutique financial planning practices. This is a career decision to last for a lifetime. It is well worth taking a few extra weeks to help ensure a more informed evaluation.

Which are the best companies to select for the interview process? As mentioned above, a visit or two to the local Financial Planning Association chapter is a great start. Who better to solicit for suggestions than successful financial planning practitioners?

One thought to keep in mind is that you're not likely to be able to look down the road and determine EXACTLY where you'll want to end up in this profession. Many dream of building independence and simply tending to the financial planning needs of clients on a one-on-one basis. Following that model, you can make a very nice living. I think that in most cases, a sole planning practitioner will be limited to a net income in the low six figures at best. Not working through a staff puts you face-to-face with the reality that there are only so many hours in the day. And, you'll be more of a TECHNICIAN than you will be a business owner, since YOU are the chief cook and bottle washer of your practice.

If you build a firm that includes others who take on aspects of your business (some interviews with your clients, doing service work, perhaps working up financial plans for your review before implementation, etc.), you can leverage your income to higher levels and find more personal time for yourself away from your BUSINESS while others are tending to the needs of your clients. Note that I said "business," rather than a practice. The differences between the two will fill several books.

And, if the sale of products is your holy grail, the highest-paid folks in the financial world other than the ones who head up the largest public finance companies are those who SELL. Very few sole practitioners earn seven figures. A greater percentage of those who build a financial services BUSINESS make it to the seven figure level. A still greater percentage of those who sell life insurance, sell stocks and bonds and sell other products make it to that higher level. Some do this as a solo act, and others do build a business, but they are still the star of the organization.

Just remember not to fall in love with the first company or two with whom you interview, or you'll always be looking over your shoulder wondering if you made the best choice. Take several months to make your final decision, and be prepared to do some testing, research, projects, and deep thinking before making the leap. You'll be thankful you did!

Frank M. Gleberman, CLU, CFP®
(1938 - 2005)

Thanks for the Help From

MY FRIENDS

INDEX

ABOUT THE AUTHOR

In the early eighties, Nancy was a dissatisfied Realtor, having serious concerns with the proliferation of "creative financing" among lenders. When the College for Financial Planning presented a program for Realtors about a new profession called "financial planning," she was intrigued and enrolled in the CERTIFIED FINANCIAL PLANNER™ (CFP®) course in September of 1983.

Six months into the CFP® program, she left real estate to begin her full time career in financial planning. Her instructors agreed that the only way to thrive as a financial planner was to sell commissioned products. For several years she was affiliated with a Broker/Dealer and prepared tax returns on her own. When she learned that she could actually write financial plans for a fee, she established an independent practice to prove that selling on commissions was not a prerequisite to success.

She applied for a position as **adjunct faculty with the College for Financial Planning (1986-1994)** and taught every course in the CFP® program while earning her **Masters in Financial Planning** and the designation **Accredited Tax Advisor** from the same institution.

Writing financial plans on retainer for other planners and preparing income tax returns for clients helped cash flow as she struggled to build her sole proprietorship. Naively, she entered into a partnership in 1994, which became the **December, 1995 cover story for the** *Dow Jones Investment Advisor Magazine*, entitled "Can This Partnership Survive?" It didn't.

Starting over for the fourth time, she began working with a turnkey investment management firm, placing assets under management. She volunteered for the **CFP Board Item Writing Committee (1994-1998)** and wrote multiple-choice questions for the series exams. That led to participation writing Case Study questions, questions for the CFP® Comprehensive Exam, and, in 1999, appointment to the **North American Securities Administrators Association Investment Advisor Competency Exam Advisor Council**.

From 1997 through 1999, she wrote a **monthly consumer column on Financial Planning for the publication** *Debt-Free and Prosperous Living*™

In 1995, she began posting on **Financial Planning Interactive** and shortly thereafter was asked to help moderate their **"Getting Started" discussion boards**. Today, she spends hours every month corresponding with individuals, asking for guidance in making a career move to financial planning. After answering the same questions repeatedly, she realized the need for a comprehensive publication on the topic of how an individual can get started as a financial planner.

Today, she continues as **Moderator on Financial Planning Interactive**. In 1999, and again in 2000, she was a **panelist for the** *Los Angeles Times'* **Investment Strategies Conference**, and was the **Industry Speaker for the North American Securities Administrators Association's 1999 National Conference**. In 2002, Nancy was named one of the **Most Influential People in the Profession** by readers of *Financial Planning*, and is an **American Business Women's Association 2003 Top Ten**. In 2005, she received the Pioneer Award from the Inland Empire Chapter of the **National Association of Women Business Owners**.

She is listed in Marquis' **Who's Who of Finance in Industry, Who's Who of American Women, Who's Who in America,** and **Who's Who in the World** and is widely quoted in the financial press.

In 2004, after twenty years in practice, she sold her comprehensive financial planning and asset management business to devote more time to her book and volunteer effort on career development for the **Financial Planning Association**.

Nancy and her husband, professional actor/director Claude Earl Jones, live in Claremont, California.

CPSIA information can be obtained at www.ICGtesting.com
Printed in the USA
BVOW051750271112

306593BV00001B/2/P

9 781603 530156